Taking
SIDES

Clashing Views
on Controversial
Social Issues

Eighth Edition

Edited, Selected, and with Introductions by

Kurt Finsterbusch
University of Maryland
and
George McKenna
City College, City University of New York

The Dushkin Publishing Group, Inc.

To John, Jane, Alec, Ned, Lori, Lisa, Laura, Maria, and Christopher, who must live these issues now and in the years ahead.

Photo Acknowledgments

Part 1   The Dushkin Publishing Group, Inc.
Part 2   Courtesy of PSE&G
Part 3   UN PHOTO 154606/P. Sudhakaran
Part 4   Maine State Development Office
Part 5   EPA Documerica
Part 6   UN PHOTO 152627/Kata Bader

Cover Art Acknowledgment

Charles Vitelli

Manufactured in the United States of America

Eighth Edition, First Printing

Library of Congress Cataloging-in-Publication Data

Main entry under title:
Taking sides: clashing views on controversial social issues/edited, selected, and with
introductions by Kurt Finsterbusch and George McKenna.—8th ed.
Includes bibliographical references and index.
1. United States—Social conditions—1980–. 2. United States—Social policy—1980–1993.
3. Social conflict—United States. 4. Social problems. I. Finsterbusch, Kurt, *comp.* II.
McKenna, George, *comp.*
HN59.2.T35   306'.0973—dc20
ISBN: 1–56134–295–5   94–2129

Printed on Recycled Paper

DPG

The Dushkin Publishing Group, Inc.

PREFACE

The English word *fanatic* is derived from the Latin *fanum*, meaning temple. It refers to the kind of madmen often seen in the precincts of temples in ancient times, the kind presumed to be possessed by deities or demons. The term first came into English usage during the seventeenth century, when it was used to describe religious zealots. Soon after, its meaning was broadened to include a political and social context. We have come to associate the term *fanatic* with a person who acts as if his or her views were inspired, a person utterly incapable of appreciating opposing points of view. The nineteenth-century English novelist George Eliot put it precisely: "I call a man fanatical when... he... becomes unjust and unsympathetic to men who are out of his own track." A fanatic may hear but is unable to listen. Confronted with those who disagree, a fanatic immediately vilifies opponents.

Most of us would avoid the company of fanatics, but who among us is not tempted to caricature opponents instead of listening to them? Who does not put certain topics off limits for discussion? Who does not grasp at euphemisms to avoid facing inconvenient facts? Who has not, in George Eliot's language, sometimes been "unjust and unsympathetic" to those on a different track? Who is not, at least in certain very sensitive areas, a *little* fanatical? The counterweight to fanaticism is open discussion. The difficult issues that trouble us as a society have at least two sides, and we lose as a society if we hear only one side. At the individual level, the answer to fanaticism is listening. And that is the underlying purpose of this book: to encourage its readers to listen to opposing points of view.

This book contains 40 selections presented in a pro and con format. A total of 20 different controversial social issues are debated. The sociologists, political scientists, economists, and social critics whose views are debated here make their cases vigorously. In order to effectively read each selection, analyze the points raised, and debate the basic assumptions and values of each position, or, in other words, in order to think critically about what you are reading, you will first have to give each side a sympathetic hearing. John Stuart Mill, the nineteenth-century British philosopher, noted that the majority is not doing the minority a favor by listening to its views; it is doing *itself* a favor. By listening to contrasting points of view, we strengthen our own. In some cases we change our viewpoints completely. But in most cases, we either incorporate some elements of the opposing view—thus making our own richer—or else learn how to answer the objections to our viewpoints. Either way, we gain from the experience.

Organization of the book Each issue has an issue *introduction*, which sets the stage for the debate as it is argued in the YES and NO selections. Each issue concludes with a *postscript* that makes some final observations and points the way to other questions related to the issue. In reading the issue and forming your own opinions you should not feel confined to adopt one or the other of the positions presented. There are positions in between the given views or totally outside them, and the *suggestions for further reading* that appear in each issue postscript should help you find resources to continue your study of the subject. At the back of the book is a listing of all the *contributors to this volume*, which will give you information on the social scientists whose views are debated here.

Changes to this edition   This new edition has been significantly updated. There are eight completely new issues: *Does Third World Immigration Threaten America's Cultural Unity?* (Issue 2); *Should Homosexuality Be Accepted by Society?* (Issue 5); *Do Social and Mental Pathologies Largely Account for Homelessness?* (Issue 11); *Is Government Dominated by Big Business?* (Issue 12); *Should Government Intervene in a Capitalist Economy?* (Issue 13); *Are Central Cities Becoming Obsolete?* (Issue 15); *Should Drugs Be Legalized?* (Issue 17); and *Is America Declining?* (Issue 20). In addition, the YES and NO readings in Issue 1 have been updated, and either the YES or the NO readings have been updated in Issues 4, 10, 14, 18, and 19. The issues that were dropped from the previous edition were done so on the recommendation of professors who let us know what worked and what could be improved. In all, there are 23 new readings. Wherever appropriate, new introductions and postscripts have been provided.

A word to the instructor   An *Instructor's Manual With Test Questions* (multiple-choice and essay) is available through the publisher for the instructor using *Taking Sides* in the classroom. A general guidebook, *Using Taking Sides in the Classroom*, which discusses methods and techniques for integrating the pro-con approach into any classroom setting, is also available.

Acknowledgments   We received many helpful comments and suggestions from our friends and readers across the United States and Canada. Their suggestions have markedly enhanced the quality of this edition of *Taking Sides* and are reflected in the new issues and the updated selections.

Our thanks go to those who responded with suggestions for this edition:

Vicki Abt
Pennsylvania State University,
   Ogontz

Donald F. Anspach
University of Southern Maine

Bret L. Billet
Wartburg College

Roy Childs
University of the Pacific

Ken Clark
Kansas City, Kansas, Community
   College

Sharon K. Davis
University of La Verne

Moustapha Diouf
University of Vermont

Lynda Dodgen
North Harris College

Jack L. Franklin
University of Houston

Eric P. Godfrey
Ripon College

Susan F. Greenwood
University of Maine

Thomas D. Hewitt
Pennsylvania State University,
    Du Bois

Colleen H. Hyden
Washington-Jefferson College

Frances Kominkiewicz
Indiana University at South Bend

Kenneth C. Land
Duke University

Ramona Linville
Idaho State University

James Mannon
Depauw University

Jack Niemonen
University of South Dakota

Robert G. Parr
Cedarville College

Bernard S. Phillips
Boston University

Fred L. Pincus
University of Maryland, Baltimore
    County

James Poulos
Community College of Vermont

D. Wayne Root
Lake Michigan College

Robert Sherfield
Florence-Darlington Technical
    College

Harry Silverstein
City College, City University of
    New York

Richard A. Zeller
Bowling Green State University

We also wish to acknowledge the encouragement and support given to this project over the years by Rick Connelly, president of The Dushkin Publishing Group, Inc. We are grateful as well to Mimi Egan, publisher for the Taking Sides series. Finally, we thank our families for their patience and understanding during the period in which we prepared this book.

Kurt Finsterbusch
University of Maryland

George McKenna
City College, City University of New York

CONTENTS IN BRIEF

CONTENTS

Dinesh D'Souza, a research fellow at the American Enterprise Institute, argues that attempts by many colleges to change their curricula by inserting minority and Third World studies have weakened higher education in the United States. Professor of education James A. Banks describes some of the achievements of multicultural education and explains why it is necessary.

Writer Lawrence Auster asserts that the large influx of immigrants threatens to undermine the cultural foundations of American unity. Francis Fukuyama, a former deputy director of the U.S. State Department's policy planning staff, argues that today's immigrants may actually strengthen America's cultural foundations because they share many of America's traditional values.

Professor of philosophy Michael Levin argues that feminism tries to impose an inappropriate equality on men and women that conflicts with basic biological differences between the sexes. Novelist and literary scholar Marilyn French advocates the transformation of existing patriarchal structures to elevate feminine values to the same level as masculine values.

Ellen Bravo, the executive director of 9to5, the National Association of Working Women, and her colleague Ellen Cassedy argue that women are increasingly subjected to sexual harassment in the workplace and that corporations must take steps to curtail the problem. Gretchen Morgenson, senior editor of *Forbes* magazine, argues that the notion of pervasive sexual harassment in the workplace is largely the product of hype by an "anti-harassment industry" and that actual incidents of harassment are dwindling.

Philosophy professor Richard D. Mohr argues that homosexuality is neither immoral nor unnatural and that homosexuals should have the same rights as heterosexuals. Author and publisher Dennis Prager contends that homosexuality is not morally equivalent to heterosexuality and should not be given the same legal status.

Sociologist David Popenoe decries the demise of the traditional nuclear family and asserts that corrective actions need to be taken. Sociologist Judith

Stacey argues that the falsely labeled traditional family is not an option for many families, nor is it the preferred family practice for a majority of women.

Social critic George Gilder argues that the American political economy provides many incentives for people to get ahead and make money and that, as a result, all classes of people benefit. Professor of psychology William Ryan contends that income inequalities in America are immoral because they vastly exceed differences of merit and result in tremendous hardship for the poor.

Sociologist Edward Banfield asserts that it is the tendency of the poor to avoid hard work and to shun middle-class values that keeps them in poverty. Professor of psychology William Ryan argues that it is wrong to blame the poor for the conditions that surround them and that poverty endures because of a lack of decent job opportunities.

Professor of economics Glenn C. Loury contends that government programs aimed at relieving black poverty rarely meet their goals and that self-help has historically been the key to black progress. National Urban League president John E. Jacob argues that the notion of blacks pulling themselves out of poverty by their own bootstraps is a myth.

Associate professor of English Shelby Steele contends that, instead of solving racial inequality problems, affirmative action mandates have generated racial discrimination in reverse. Professor of law Stanley Fish argues that to equate affirmative action with reverse racism is to view a terrifying and punishing racism as comparable to minor efforts to remedy some of the harms of that racism.

Essayist Myron Magnet argues that the vast majority of the permanently homeless consist of pathological individuals taking advantage of public shelters and other state-run charities. Social commentator Jonathan Kozol maintains that homelessness is the result of the lack of affordable housing and an economic downturn that has forced the poor into the streets.

Political reporter Thomas Byrne Edsall argues that big business dominates the policy-making process because of its increasing political sophistication and the breakdown of political parties. Jeffrey M. Berry, a professor of political science, contends that public interest pressure groups have effectively challenged the political power of big business.

Author Ernest Erber argues that capitalism creates serious social problems
that require government intervention to correct. Economists Milton and Rose
Friedman maintain that the market operates effectively when permitted to
work without the interference of government regulations.

Economist Murray Weidenbaum argues that the welfare system discourages
poor people from working, making their condition worse, not better. Social
analysts Theodore R. Marmor, Jerry L. Mashaw, and Philip L. Harvey hail
welfare's achievements and contend that conservative "reforms" will only
increase the misery of the poor.

Associate professor of history Robert Fishman argues that suburban rings are
now taking over the business and residential roles that were, until recently,
the sole province of the central cities. Ruth Messinger, New York City's Manhattan Borough President, and her press secretary, Andrew Breslau, maintain
that edge cities depend entirely on the central city of which they are satellites
and that central cities are still centers for business and culture.

John J. DiIulio, Jr., an associate professor of politics and public affairs, analyzes the enormous harm done to all of society by street criminals and their activities. Professor of philosophy Jeffrey Reiman argues that the dangers posed by negligent corporations and white-collar criminals pose a greater threat to society than do typical street criminals.

Ethan A. Nadelmann, an assistant professor of politics and public affairs, argues that drug prohibition is costly and that it exacerbates the drug problem. He maintains that controlled legalization would reduce the drug problem in the United States. Professor of history David T. Courtwright argues that the government should continue the war against drugs because legalizing drugs would not eliminate drug-related criminal activity and would increase drug use.

Professor of economics Morgan O. Reynolds argues that "crime pays" for most criminals but that catching, convicting, and imprisoning more criminals would greatly reduce the crime rate. Judge David L. Bazelon discusses the high moral and financial costs of the incapacitation approach and argues that this approach would be ineffective in the long run.

Lester R. Brown, president of the Worldwatch Institute, argues that the environment is deteriorating because of economic and population growth. Professor of economics and business administration Julian L. Simon maintains that the environment is actually becoming more benificent for human beings despite a fast-growing population.

Foreign policy strategist Edward N. Luttwak believes that Japan and Europe will soon be richer and more powerful than the United States because of America's failing economic policies and social programs. Robert L. Bartley, the editor and vice president of the *Wall Street Journal*, asserts that America is the wealthiest country in the world and that it will continue to play the role of world leader.

INTRODUCTION

Debating Social Issues

Kurt Finsterbusch
George McKenna

WHAT IS SOCIOLOGY?

"I have become a problem to myself," St. Augustine said. Put into a social and secular framework, St. Augustine's concern marks the starting point of sociology. We have become a problem to ourselves, and it is sociology that seeks to understand the problem and, perhaps, to find some solutions. The subject matter of sociology, then, is ourselves—people interacting with one another in groups.

Although the subject matter of sociology is very familiar, it is often useful to look at it in an unfamiliar light, one that involves a variety of theories and perceptual frameworks. In fact, to properly understand social phenomena, it *should* be looked at from several different points of view. In practice, however, this may lead to more friction than light, especially when each view proponent says, "I am right and you are wrong," rather than, "My view adds considerably to what your view has shown."

Sociology, as a science of society, was developed in the nineteenth century. Auguste Comte (1798–1857), the French mathematician and philosopher who is considered to be the father of sociology, had a vision of a well-run society based on social science knowledge. Sociologists (Comte coined the term) would discover the laws of social life and then determine how society should be structured and run. Society would not become perfect because some problems are intractable, but he believed that a society guided by scientists and other experts was the best possible society.

Unfortunately, Comte's vision was extremely naive. For most matters of state there is no one best way of structuring or doing things that sociologists can discover and recommend. Instead, sociologists debate more social issues than they resolve.

The purpose of sociology is to throw light on social issues and their relationship to the complex, confusing, and dynamic social world around us. It seeks to describe how society is organized and how individuals fit into it. But neither the organization of society nor the fit of individuals is perfect. Social disorganization is a fact of life—at least in modern, complex societies such as the one we live in. Here, perfect harmony continues to elude us, and "social problems" are endemic. The very institutions, laws, and policies that produce benefits also produce what sociologists call "unintended effects"— unintended and undesirable. The changes that please one sector of the society may displease another, or the changes that seem so indisputably healthy at first turn out to have a dark underside to them. The examples are endless. Modern urban life gives people privacy and freedom from snooping neighbors that the small town never afforded; yet, that very privacy seems to breed an uneasy sense of anonymity and loneliness. Or to take another example: Hierarchy is necessary for organizations to function efficiently, but hierarchy leads to the creation of a ruling elite. Flatten out the hierarchy and you may achieve social equality—but at the price of confusion, incompetence, and low productivity.

This is not to say that all efforts to effect social change are ultimately futile and that the only sound view is the tragic one that concludes "nothing works." We can be realistic without falling into despair. In many respects, the human condition has improved over the centuries and has improved as a result of conscious social policies. But improvements are purchased at a price—not only a monetary price but one involving human discomfort and discontent. The job of policymakers is to balance the anticipated benefits against the probable costs.

It can never hurt policymakers to know more about the society in which they work or the social issues they confront. That, broadly speaking, is the purpose of sociology. It is what this book is about. This volume examines issues that are central to the study of sociology.

SOCIALIZATION AND VALUES

A common value system is the major mechanism for integrating a society, so it is essential that young people understand the roots of their society's value system. But it is also important for young people to understand and appreciate other cultures, lest they fall into the kind of narrowness and ethnocentrism that prevents society from adapting to change. These are the concerns that underlie the debates in Issues 1 and 2. In Issue 1, Dinesh D'Souza argues that "multicultural" studies, at least as they are envisaged by their proponents, are trivializing the college curricula, politicizing the campus, and promoting hatred among groups in America. James A. Banks contends, on the contrary, that multiculturalism is a genuine expression of American pluralism that is deeply rooted in the American tradition. In Issue 2, Lawrence Auster argues that the current levels of immigration are too large and that the immigrant cultures are too different from American culture to be assimilated, both of which threaten America's cultural unity. Francis Fukuyama, in opposition, maintains that many of the new immigrants have very strong family values and work ethics, which will strengthen—not weaken—American culture.

SEX ROLES, GENDER, AND FAMILY VALUES

An area that has experienced tremendous value change in the last several decades is sex roles and the family. Women in large numbers have rejected major aspects of their traditional gender roles and family roles while remaining strongly committed to much of the mother role and to many feminine characteristics. In fact, on these issues women are deeply divided. The ones who seek the most change identify themselves as feminists, and they have been in the forefront of the modern women's movement. Now a debate is raging as to whether or not the feminist cause really helps women. In Issue 3, Michael Levin attacks feminism as intellectually unsound and morally bankrupt. Feminist Marilyn French identifies positive changes that feminists have accomplished and many changes that are still needed. Issue 4 highlights an issue that had been smoldering for years before it finally burst into the headlines with the Clarence Thomas–Anita Hill controversy in the fall of 1991: Is sexual harassment a pervasive problem in America? Ellen Bravo and Ellen Cassedy assert that it is, while Gretchen Morgenson contends that the extent of genuine sexual harassment has been greatly exaggerated by self-serving interest groups. Issue 5 deals with the gay rights movement, which also concerns questions of treatment and fairness. Richard D. Mohr argues that homosexuals should be treated the same as heterosexuals with regard to civil and legal rights, while Dennis Prager argues that not all lifestyles are equally valid or functional for society and that society should give preference to heterosexual lifestyles. Issue 6, which is much debated by feminists and their critics, asks, Should traditional families be preserved? David Popenoe is deeply concerned about the decline of the traditional family, while Judith Stacey thinks that such concern amounts to little more than nostalgia for a bygone era.

STRATIFICATION AND INEQUALITY

Issue 7 centers around a perennial sociological debate about whether or not economic inequality is beneficial (functional) to society. George Gilder claims that it is, and William Ryan argues that inequalities should be greatly reduced. Closely related to this debate is the issue of why the poor are poor. The "culture of poverty" thesis maintains that most long-term poverty in America is the result of a culture that is all too common among the poor. The implication is that those who always seek immediate material gratification will not climb out of poverty, even if they are helped by welfare and social programs. Others see most of the poor as victims of adverse conditions; they ridicule the culture of poverty thesis as a way of "blaming the victim." Issue 8 offers a clear-cut exchange on this issue, with Edward Banfield saying yes to the question of whether or not "lower-class" culture perpetuates poverty and William Ryan saying no.

The next two issues deal with lively debates that have divided the African American community in recent years: black self-help and affirmative action. Glenn Loury, who rose from a Chicago ghetto and became a professor at Harvard's prestigious Kennedy School, argues in Issue 9 that blacks must learn to do more for themselves instead of always turning to the government for help, while National Urban League president John Jacob claims that the "bootstrap" approach does not work "when you're talking to people who don't have boots." Then there is the controversy over affirmative action. Is equality promoted or undermined by such policies? Shelby Steele and Stanley Fish take opposing sides on this question in Issue 10. The final issue under the topic of stratification deals with those closest to the bottom of American society: the homeless. Who are the homeless, and why do they live in the streets? This is a divisive issue because people have very different feelings toward and notions about the homeless. In Issue 11, Myron Magnet minimizes their numbers and portrays them as largely socially and mentally pathological. Jonathan Kozol maximizes their numbers and depicts the majority of them as regular people who have been very unfortunate.

POLITICAL ECONOMY

Sociologists study not only the poor, the workers, and the victims of discrimination but also those at the top of society—those who occupy what the late sociologist C. Wright Mills used to call "the command posts." The question is whether the "pluralist" model or the "power elite" model is the one that best fits the facts in America. Does a single power elite rule the United States, or do many groups contend for power and influence so that the political process is accessible to all? In Issue 12, Thomas Byrne Edsall argues that the business elite have a dominating influence in government decisions and that no other group has nearly as much power, while Jeffrey M. Berry argues that liberal citizen groups have successfully opened the policy-making process and made it more participatory. Currently, grassroots groups of all kinds have some power and influence. The question is, how much?

The United States is a capitalist welfare state, and the role of the state in capitalism (more precisely, the market) and in welfare is examined in the next two issues. Issue 13 considers whether or not the government should step in and, through regulations, policies, and programs, attempt to correct for the failures of the market. Ernest Erber argues that an active government is needed to protect consumers, workers, and the environment; to bring about greater equality; and to guide economic and social change. Milton and Rose Friedman argue that even well-intended state interventions in the market usually only make matters worse and that governments cannot serve the public good as effectively as competitive markets can. One way in which the government intervenes in the economy is by providing welfare to people who cannot provide for their own needs in the labor market. Issue 14 debates the wisdom of current welfare policies. In it, Murray Weidenbaum claims that many welfare programs of the "Great Society" have mired people in dependency and should be abandoned, while Theodore Marmor, Jerry Mashaw, and Philip Harvey argue that the conservative case against welfare "dependency" is ill-founded and can only produce greater degradation among America's poor.

Issue 15 examines the role of central cities in the evolving political and economic landscape. Robert Fishman articulates the viewpoint that the suburbs are drawing middle-class residents, offices, stores, jobs, and entertainment away from the central cities. Ruth Messinger and Andrew Breslau maintain that the centers of power and culture remain in the cities and that cities are still alive and well.

CRIME AND SOCIAL CONTROL

Crime is interesting to sociologists because crimes are those activities that society makes illegal and will use force to stop. Why are some acts made illegal and others (even those that may be more harmful) not made illegal? Surveys indicate that concern about crime is extremely high in America. Is the fear of crime, however, rightly placed? Americans fear mainly street crime, but Jeffrey Reiman argues in Issue 16 that corporate crime—also known as "white-collar crime"—causes far more death, harm, and financial loss to Americans than street crime. In contrast, John DiIulio points out the great harm done by street criminals, even to the point of social disintegration in some poor neighborhoods. Much of the harm that he describes is related to the illegal drug trade, which brings about such bad consequences that some people are seriously talking about legalizing drugs in order to kill the illegal drug business. Ethan A. Nadelmann argues this view in Issue 17, while David T. Courtwright argues that legalization would greatly expand the use of dangerous drugs and increase the personal tragedies and social costs resulting therefrom. Finally, we examine the extent to which deterrence or tough sentencing of criminals reduces crime. The debate is whether American society should focus on deterrence by meting out sentencing on a tougher and more uniform basis, or whether the emphasis should be on rehabilitating criminals and eliminating the social conditions that breed crime. These alternatives are explored in the debate between Morgan Reynolds and David Bazelon in Issue 18.

THE WORLD AND THE FUTURE

Many social commentators speculate on "the fate of the earth." The environmentalists have their own vision of apocalypse. They see the possibility that the human race could overshoot the carrying capacity of the globe. The resulting collapse could lead to the extinction of much of the human race and the end of free societies. Population growth and increasing per capita levels of consumption, say some experts, are leading us to this catastrophe. Others believe that these fears are groundless. In Issue 19, Lester Brown and Julian Simon argue over whether or not the world is really threatened by population growth.

The last issue in this book deals with the future of America. In Issue 20, Edward N. Luttwak projects the trends of the past two decades into the future and sees America becoming a Third World country because it is squandering its wealth instead of investing in the future. Robert L. Bartley reorganizes the economic data in a way that shows that America is and will remain the wealthiest nation in the world. He contends that it is experiencing a second industrial revolution, is in better shape than its competitors, and will continue to be the leader of the world.

THE SOCIAL CONSTRUCTION OF REALITY

An important idea in sociology is that people construct social reality in the course of interaction by attaching social meanings to the reality they are experiencing and then responding to those meanings. Two people can walk down a city street and derive very different meanings from what they see around them. Both, for example, may see homeless people—but they may see them in different contexts. One fits them into a picture of once-vibrant cities dragged into decay and ruin because of permissive policies that have encouraged pathological types to harass citizens; the other observer fits them into a picture of an America that can no longer hide the wretchedness of its poor. Both feel that they are seeing something deplorable, but their views of what makes it deplorable are radically opposed. Their differing views of what they have seen will lead to very different prescriptions for what should be done about the problem. And their policy arguments will be based upon the pictures in their heads, or the constructions they have made of reality.

The social construction of reality is an important idea for this book because each author is socially constructing reality and working hard to persuade you to see his or her point of view; that is, to see the definition of the situation and the set of meanings he or she has assigned to the situation. In doing this, each author presents a carefully selected set of facts, arguments, and values. The arguments contain assumptions or theories, some of which are spelled out and some of which are unspoken. The critical reader has to judge the evidence for the facts, the logic and soundness of the arguments, the importance of the values, and whether or not omitted facts, theories, and values invalidate the thesis. This book facilitates this critical thinking process by placing authors in opposition. This puts the reader in the position of critically evaluating two constructions of reality for each issue instead of one.

CONCLUSION

Writing in the 1950s, a period that was in some ways like our own, the sociologist C. Wright Mills said that Americans know a lot about their "troubles"

but that they cannot make the connections between seemingly personal concerns and the concerns of others in the world. If they could only learn to make those connections, they could turn their concerns into *issues*. An issue transcends the realm of the personal. According to Mills, "An issue is a public matter: some value cherished by publics is felt to be threatened. Often there is a debate about what the value really is and what it is that really threatens it."

It is not primarily personal troubles but social issues that we have tried to present in this book. The variety of topics in it can be taken as an invitation to discover what Mills called "the sociological imagination." This imagination, said Mills, "is the capacity to shift from one perspective to another—from the political to the psychological; from examination of a single family to comparative assessment of the national budgets of the world.... It is the capacity to range from the most impersonal and remote transformations to the most intimate features of the human self—and to see the relations between the two." This book, with a range of issues well suited to the sociological imagination, is intended to enlarge that capacity.

PART 1

Culture and Values

Sociologists recognize that a fairly strong consensus on the basic values of a society contributes greatly to the smooth functioning of that society. The functioning of modern complex urban societies, however, often depends on the tolerance of cultural differences and equal rights and protections for all cultural groups. In fact, such societies can be enriched by the contributions of different cultures. But at some point the cultural differences may result in a pulling apart that exceeds the pulling together. Two areas where the issue of cultural consensus or cultural clashes is prominent today are the college liberal arts curriculum and the immigration of peoples from different cultures. Analysis of these issues involves strongly held value differences.

■ Does "Multiculturalism" Debase
the Curriculum?

■ Does Third World Immigration Threaten
America's Cultural Unity?

ISSUE 1

Does "Multiculturalism" Debase the Curriculum?

YES: Dinesh D'Souza, from *Illiberal Education: The Politics of Race and Sex on Campus* (Free Press, 1991)

NO: James A. Banks, from "Multicultural Education: Development, Dimensions, and Challenges," *Phi Delta Kappan* (September 1993)

ISSUE SUMMARY

YES: Dinesh D'Souza, a research fellow at the American Enterprise Institute, argues that poorly conceived attempts by many colleges to change their curricula by inserting minority and Third World studies have weakened and politicized higher education in the United States.

NO: Professor of education James A. Banks answers the criticisms of multicultural education, explains the need for it, and describes some of its achievements.

The issue of multiculturalism—what it means, what its role should be in the educational curriculum, and whether it is good or bad for the nation's youth—is of interest to sociologists because the school is one of the key agents of socialization. The courses that are taught in schools and colleges impart to society's young people the skills and values that society considers important or essential for functioning in that society.

Multiculturalism has sparked a major controversy, especially on America's campuses. To proponents it represents a long-overdue effort to bring greater diversity into a curriculum dominated by Western white male studies. To critics it stands for the dilution and corruption of liberal arts by ideologues. Neither side seems to take much trouble to define terms. Does *multiculturalism* mean simply adding to the traditional liberal arts reading lists some authors and books outside the traditional bounds? Or is it something more involved, such as a deliberate policy of assigning books that attack Western culture, or the requirement that all students take special Third World courses, or the establishment of entire curricula in black studies?

It might help to look at this issue from a historical perspective. In the early 1960s, the usual liberal arts curriculum in the United States included courses on the classics of Western culture, plus European and American history, philosophy, and politics. It was rare for any student to read any classics of

Asian or Indian literature, and there were virtually no courses—certainly no required ones—on the Third World. A few women authors, such as Jane Austen, might be assigned in literature courses, but no women's studies courses were available. Perhaps not so coincidentally, about two-thirds of the students and a much larger majority of the faculty were male, and, at a time when only 3 percent of American blacks completed college, the percentage of racial minorities on campus was almost infinitesimal.

Changes started in the late 1960s and gathered momentum over the next two decades. Increasing numbers of blacks began entering college, as did other racial minorities as changing immigration laws brought more Third World immigrants to U.S. shores. Women, seeing new career opportunities or simply wanting more education, also began entering college in record numbers. Colleges and universities helped to augment these numbers by establishing outreach and affirmative action programs for student populations that were formerly underrepresented. In terms of demographics alone, there was bound to come a time when awkward questions would be asked about the appropriateness of Western Civilization courses for the new student body.

In addition to the civil rights and women's movements, another catalyst was at work in the late 1960s: the Vietnam War. As the decade came to a close, the United States found itself bogged down in a bloody war that to many, particularly on leading campuses in the United States, seemed to be morally atrocious. Serious questions were raised about the legitimacy not only of the war but of the United States and its moral underpinnings. Social critic Susan Sontag wrote in 1969 that American culture was "inorganic, dead, coercive, authoritarian," and full of "dehumanized individuals" and "heartless bureaucrats of death and empty affluence." Indeed, Sontag suggested, the entire culture of the West was sick: the white race "is the cancer of human history." Views such as these, not at all uncommon at the time, struck a chord among many of the younger academics—undergraduates, graduate assistants, and junior professors. Today, many of those former students occupy leadership positions in the universities, so modern faculties are more receptive to demands for a liberal arts curriculum that is less focused on Western culture.

In the following selections, Dinesh D'Souza (himself an immigrant from India) expresses worry about the way Third World studies, feminism, and black nationalism are manifesting themselves on U.S. campuses. D'Souza argues that the curriculum is weakened by replacing many great works with ones of much lower quality and that many of the new works express a rather ignorant ideology that is anti–Western culture. James A. Banks argues that fears about multiculturalism are based upon myths, not facts, and points to the need for and benefits of multicultural education. He denies that multicultural education seeks to supplant Western tradition, and he maintains that by including more minority works in curricula, the nation will become more united, not divided.

3

YES
Dinesh D'Souza

ILLIBERAL EDUCATION

Each fall some 13 million students, 2.5 million of them minorities, enroll in American colleges. Most of these students are living away from home for the first time. Yet their apprehension is mixed with excitement and anticipation. At the university, they hope to shape themselves as whole human beings, both intellectually and morally. Brimming with idealism, they wish to prepare themselves for full and independent lives in the workplace, at home, and as citizens who are shared rulers of a democratic society. In short, what they seek is liberal education.

By the time these students graduate, very few colleges have met their need for all-round development. Instead, by precept and example, universities have taught them that "all rules are unjust" and "all preferences are principled"; that justice is simply the will of the stronger party; that standards and values are arbitrary, and the ideal of the educated person is largely a figment of bourgeois white male ideology, which should be cast aside; that individual rights are a red flag signaling social privilege, and should be subordinated to the claims of group interest; that all knowledge can be reduced to politics and should be pursued not for its own sake but for the political end of power; that convenient myths and benign lies can substitute for truth; that double standards are acceptable as long as they are enforced to the benefit of minority victims; that debates are best conducted not by rational and civil exchange of ideas, but by accusation, intimidation, and official prosecution; that the university stands for nothing in particular and has no claim to be exempt from outside pressures; and that the multiracial society cannot be based on fair rules that apply to every person, but must rather be constructed through a forced rationing of power among separatist racial groups. . . .

DOWN WITH ARISTOTLE

Although minority activists dominate race relations on campus, their original troubles began in the classroom, and it is to the classroom that their political energy ultimately returns. This phase of the struggle begins with a new recognition. Usually within the atmosphere of their separate enclaves, and often under the tutelage of an activist professor, minority students learn that extensive though their experience has been with campus bigotry, the subtlest and yet most pervasive form of racism thrives undiscovered, right in front of their eyes. The curriculum, they are told at Stanford and Duke and other colleges, reflects a "white perspective." Specifically, as Stanford Professor Clayborne Carson said earlier, it reflects a predominant white, male, European, and heterosexual mentality which, by its very nature, is inescapably racist, indisputably sexist, and manifestly homophobic.

This realization comes as something of an epiphany. Many minority students can now explain why they had such a hard time with Milton and Publius and Heisenberg. Those men reflected white aesthetics, white philosophy, white science. Obviously minority students would fare much better if the university assigned black or Latino or Third World thought. Then the roles would be reversed: they would perform well, and other students would have trouble. Thus the current curriculum reveals itself as the hidden core of academic bigotry.

At first minority students may find such allegations hard to credit, since it is unclear how differential equations or the measurement of electron orbits embody racial and gender prejudices. Nevertheless, in humanities and social science disciplines, younger scholar-advocates of the *au courant* [fully informed] stripe are on hand to explain that the cultural framework for literature or history or sociology inevitably reflects a bias in the selection or application of scholarly material. Restive with the traditional curriculum, progressive academics such as Edward Said at Columbia and Stanley Fish and Henry Gates at Duke seek a program which integrates scholarship and political commitment, and they form a tacit partnership with minority activists in order to achieve this goal.

Since all knowledge is political, these scholar-advocates assert, minorities have a right to demand that their distinct perspectives be "represented" in the course readings. Ethnic Studies professor Ronald Takaki of Berkeley unabashedly calls this "intellectual affirmative action."

Tempted by these arguments, many minority leaders make actual headcounts of the authors and authorities in the curriculum, and they find accusations of white male predominance to be proven right. Why are Plato and Locke and Madison assigned in philosophy class but no black thinkers? How come so few Hispanics are credited with great inventions or discoveries? Feminists ask: Why is only a small percentage of the literature readings by women? These protests sometimes extend beyond the humanities and social sciences; at a recent symposium, mathematics professor Marilyn Frankenstein of the University of Massachusetts at Boston accused her field of harboring "Eurocentric bias" and called for "ethno-mathematics" which would analyze numerical models in terms of workforce inequalities and discrimination quotients.

Few minority students believe that democratic principles of "equal representation" should be rigorously applied to curricular content. Feminists make this argument because they want to replace alleged sexists like Aquinas and Milton with Simone de Beauvoir and Gloria Steinem. Blacks, Hispanics, and American Indians generally assent to this proposition because it provides an immediate explanation for the awkward gaps in academic performance. Not only are these differences evident in classroom discussion, grades, and prizes, but also in suspension and dropout statistics. Minority students must face the disquieting fact that many of their peers at places like Berkeley fail to graduate, if indeed they even stay through freshman year. It seems irresistible to adopt the view that if only the curriculum were broadened or revised to reflect black (or female, or Third World) perspectives, these academic gaps would close or possibly reverse themselves....

PROFILES IN COWARDICE

Many university presidents are not intellectual leaders but bureaucrats and managers; their interest therefore is not in meeting the activist argument but in deflecting it, by making the appropriate adjustments in the interest of stability. When a debate over the canon erupts, university heads typically take refuge in silence or incomprehensibility; thus one Ivy League president responded to Allan Bloom's book by saying that the purpose of liberal education was to "address the need for students to develop both a private self and a public self, and to find a way to have those selves converse with each other." Earlier incidents reveal the posture of presidents Heyman of Berkeley, Kennedy of Stanford, Cheek of Howard, Duderstadt of Michigan, Brodie of Duke, and Bok of Harvard to be a curious mixture of pusillanimity, ideology, and opportunism.

As we saw at Stanford, Duke, and Harvard, when minority groups, assisted by activist professors, urge the transformation of the curriculum toward a "race and gender" agenda, they face potential opposition from a large segment of faculty who may be sympathetic to minority causes but at the same time believe that the curriculum should not be ideologically apportioned. These dissenters are branded as bigots, sexists, and homophobes, regardless of their previous political bona fides. If minority faculty and student activists are not a numerical majority, they inevitably are a kind of Moral Majority, and they wield the formidable power to affix scarlet letters to their enemies. Few dare to frontally oppose the alliance between minority groups and faculty activists; like Stanford's Linda Paulson, most wrestle with their conscience and win and even professors with qualms end up supporting curricular transformation with the view that change is inevitable....

Moreover, most university leaders have no answer to the charge that the curriculum reflects a white male culture, and consequently embodies all the hateful prejudices that whites have leveled against other peoples throughout history. Nor can they explain why, if not for discrimination, minority students aren't doing as well as other students. As we saw with Harvard's "Myths and Realities" letter, universities have insisted from the outset that standards have not been lowered, so why do black and Hispanic students fall behind if not for curricular racism? And won't the rationing of books among different ethnic "perspectives" make an indispensable contribution to "diversity"?

Thus begins the process, already far advanced, of downplaying or expelling the core curriculum of Western classics in favor of a non-Western and minority-oriented agenda. Universities like Stanford, Berkeley, and Harvard establish ethnic studies requirements, multicultural offerings, Afro-American Studies and Women's Studies departments. The typical rationale is that white professors cannot effectively communicate with, or provide role models for, minority students. This argument is somewhat transparent, since it relies on the premise that interracial identification is impossible, and no one has ever alleged that minority professors are racially or culturally disabled from teaching white students. College administrators will privately admit that "minority perspectives" is a pretext for meeting affirmative action goals. The so-called "studies" programs also serve the purpose of attracting minority students who are having a difficult time with the "white" curriculum, but who, like Harvard's Tiya Miles, Eva Nelson, and Michelle Duncan, feel psychologically at home in a department like Afro-American Studies.

What transpires in the "race and gender" curriculum is anything but "diverse." As we saw at Harvard, typically these programs promulgate rigid political views about civil rights, feminism, homosexual rights, and other issues pressed by the activists who got these departments set up in the first place. Thomas Short, a professor of philosophy at Kenyon College, observes that "ideological dogmatism is the norm, not the exception, in the 'studies' programs, especially Women's Studies. Intimidation of nonfeminists in the classroom is routine." Short adds that, curiously, ideologues in these programs practice the very exclusion that they claim to have suffered in the past.

Even if some faculty in the "race and gender" curriculum seek to promote authentic debate or intellectual diversity, this is difficult in an atmosphere where activist students profess to be deeply offended by views which fall outside the ideological circumference of their victim's revolution. Once a professor finds himself the object of vilification and abuse for tackling a political taboo—the fate of Farley, Thernstrom, and Macneil—

others absorb the message and ensure that their own classes are appropriately deferential.

Eugene Genovese, a Marxist historian and one of the nation's most distinguished scholars on slavery, admits that "there is just too much dogmatism in the field of race and gender scholarship." Whatever diversity obtains, Genovese argues, is frequently "a diversity of radical positions." As a result, "Good scholars [who] are increasingly at risk are starting to run away, and this is how our programs become ghettoized."

The new awareness of racially and sexually biased perspectives is not confined to the "studies" programs, however; minority activists inevitably bring their challenging political consciousness into other courses as well, although this usually does not happen until junior or senior year. At this point, the students begin to function as sensitivity monitors, vigilant in pointing out instances of racism and sexism in the course readings or among student comments. Other students may inwardly resent such political surveillance, but seldom do professors resist it: indeed they often praise it as precisely the sort of "diversity" that minority students can bring to the classroom.

Minority students are often given latitude to do papers on race or gender victimization, even if only tangentially related to course material: thus some write about latent bigotry in Jane Austen, or tabulate black underrepresentation in the university administration. Minority activists can be offended when they do not receive passing grades on such papers, because they believe that their consciousness of oppression is far more advanced than that of any white professor. Further, they know how reluctant most professors are to get involved in an incident with a black or Hispanic student; hence they can extract virtually any price from faculty anxious to avoid "racial incidents."

University administrations and faculty also permit, and sometimes encourage, minority students to develop myths about their own culture and history, such as the "black Egypt" industry evident at Howard and elsewhere. This cultural distortion is routine in multicultural and Third World studies—the case of Stanford is typical. Bernard Lewis, professor of Near Eastern studies at Princeton, describes what he calls "a new culture of deceit on the campus," and adds, "It is very dangerous to give in to these ideas, or more accurately, to these pressures. It makes a mockery of scholarship to say: my nonsense is as good as your science." But even university officials who agree with Lewis say they aren't sure what they can do to counter these distortions, since the ideological forces behind them are so strong.

Although curricular and extracurricular concessions by the university greatly increase the power of minority activists, it is not clear that they help minority students use knowledge and truth as weapons against ignorance and prejudice, nor that they assuage the problems of low morale and low self-esteem which propelled them in this direction to begin with. Nor does an apparently more even "balance of power" between minority and nonminority students produce greater ethnic harmony. In fact, like Michigan activists Kimberly Smith and Tracye Matthews, many minority students find themselves increasingly embittered and estranged during their college years, so that by the time they graduate they may be virtually isolated in a separatist culture, and espouse openly hostile sentiments against other groups.

At graduation time, it turns out that only a fraction of the minority students enrolled four years earlier are still around, and even among them the academic record is mixed: a good number (most are probably not affirmative action beneficiaries) have performed well, but a majority conspicuously lag behind their colleagues, and a sizable group has only finished by concentrating in congenial fields such as Afro-American or Ethnic Studies, under the direction of tolerant faculty advisers. Relatively few of these students have developed to their full potential over the past four years, or have emerged ready to assume positions of responsibility and leadership in the new multiracial society.

PRINCIPLES OF REFORM

... [T]here is no conflict between equal opportunity for individuals in education, and the pursuit of the highest standards of academic and extracurricular excellence. After all, equal opportunity means opportunity to achieve, and we achieve more when more is expected of us. Test scores and grade point averages are mere measurements of achievement, which are necessary to register how much intellectual progress is being made. They provide a common index for all who seek to improve themselves, regardless of race, sex, or background. High standards do not discriminate against anyone except those who fail to meet them. Such discrimination is entirely just and ought not to be blamed for our individual differences.

... [L]iberal education settles issues in terms of idealism, not interest; in terms of right, not force. There is nothing wrong with universities confronting controversial contemporary issues, especially those involving human difference that are both timely and timeless. Nor is radicalism itself the problem; if radical solutions may not be contemplated in the university, where else should they be considered? Because they are sanctuary institutions, universities can be a philosophical testing ground for programs of revolutionary transformation which, if improperly executed, might lead to lawlessness, violence, or anarchy. "The university sponsors moral combat in an atmosphere where ideas can be tested short of mortal combat," in the words of sociologist Manfred Stanley of Syracuse University.

... [L]iberal education in a multicultural society means global education. Provincialism has always been the enemy of that broad-minded outlook which is the very essence of liberal learning. Today's liberally educated student must be conversant with some of the classic formulations of other cultures, and with the grand political and social currents which bring these cultures into increased interaction with the West. Such education is best pursued when students are taught to search for universal standards of judgment which transcend particularities of race, gender, and culture; this gives them the intellectual and moral criteria to evaluate both their own society and others. There is much in both to affirm and to criticize....

Equality and the Classics

Universities can address their curricular problems by devising a required course or sequence for entering freshmen which exposes them to the basic issues of equality and human difference, through a carefully chosen set of classic texts that deal powerfully with those issues. Needless to say, non-Western classics belong in this list when they address questions relevant to the subject matter. Such a solution would retain what Matthew Arnold termed "the best that has been thought and said," but at the same time engage the contemporary questions of ethnocentrism and prejudice in bold and provocative fashion.

It seems that currently both the teaching of Western classics as well as the desire to study other cultures have encountered serious difficulties in the curriculum. As the case of Stanford illustrates, an uncritical examination of non-Western cultures, in order to favorably contrast them with the West, ends up as a new form of cultural imperialism, in which Western intellectuals project their own domestic prejudices onto faraway countries, distorting them beyond recognition to serve political ends. Even where universities make a serious effort to avoid this trap, it remains questionable whether they have the academic expertise in the general undergraduate program to teach students about the history, religion, and literature of Asia, Africa, and the Arab world.

The study of other cultures can never compensate for a lack of thorough familiarity with the founding principles of one's own culture. Just as it would be embarrassing to encounter an educated Chinese who had never heard of Confucius, however well versed he may be in Jefferson, so also it would be a failure of liberal education to teach Americans about the Far East without immersing them in their own philosophical and literary tradition "from Homer to the present." Universal in scope, these works prepare Westerners to experience both their own, as well as other, ideas and civilizations....

The liberal university is a distinctive and fragile institution. It is not an all-purpose instrument for social change. Its function is indeed to serve the larger society which supports and sustains it, yet it does not best do this when it makes itself indistinguishable from the helter-skelter of pressure politics, what Professor Susan Shell of Boston College terms "the academic equivalent of Tammany Hall." Nothing in this [selection] should be taken to deny the legitimate claim of minorities who have suffered unfairly, nor should reasonable aid and sympathy be withheld from them. But the current revolution of minority victims threatens to destroy the highest ideals of liberal education, and with them that enlightenment and understanding which hold out the only prospects for racial harmony, social justice, and minority advancement.

Many university leaders are supremely confident that nothing can jeopardize their position, and they regard any criticism with disdain. As Professor Alan Kors of the University of Pennsylvania has remarked, "For the first time in the history of American higher education, the barbarians are running the place." Liberal education is too important to entrust to these self-styled revolutionaries. Reform, if it comes, requires the involvement of intelligent voices from both inside and outside the university—students who are willing to take on reigning orthodoxies, professors and administrators with the courage to resist the activist high tide, and parents, alumni, and civic leaders who are committed to applying genuine principles of liberal learning to the challenges of the emerging multicultural society.

NO

James A. Banks

MULTICULTURAL EDUCATION: DEVELOPMENT, DIMENSIONS, AND CHALLENGES

The bitter debate over the literary and historical canon that has been carried on in the popular press and in several widely reviewed books has overshadowed the progress that has been made in multicultural education during the last two decades. The debate has also perpetuated harmful misconceptions about theory and practice in multicultural education. Consequently, it has heightened racial and ethnic tension and trivialized the field's remarkable accomplishments in theory, research, and curriculum development. The truth about the development and attainments of multicultural education needs to be told for the sake of balance, scholarly integrity, and accuracy. But if I am to reveal the truth about multicultural education, I must first identify and debunk some of the widespread myths and misconceptions about it.

Multicultural education is for the others. One misconception about multicultural education is that it is an entitlement program and curriculum movement for African Americans, Hispanics, the poor, women, and other victimized groups. The major theorists and researchers in multicultural education agree that the movement is designed to restructure educational institutions so that all students, including middle-class white males, will acquire the knowledge, skills, and attitudes needed to function effectively in a culturally and ethnically diverse nation and world. Multicultural education, as its major architects have conceived it during the last decade, is not an ethnic- or gender-specific movement. It is a movement designed to empower all students to become knowledgeable, caring, and active citizens in a deeply troubled and ethnically polarized nation and world....

Multicultural education is opposed to the Western tradition. Another harmful misconception about multicultural education has been repeated so often by its critics that many people take it as self-evident. This is the claim that multicultural education is a movement that is opposed to the West and to Western civilization. Multicultural education is not anti-West, because most writers of color—such as Rudolfo Anaya, Paula Gunn Allen, Maxine Hong Kingston, Maya Angelou, and Toni Morrison—are Western writers.

From James A. Banks, "Multicultural Education: Development, Dimensions, and Challenges," *Phi Delta Kappan*, vol. 75, no. 1 (September 1993). Copyright © 1993 by Phi Delta Kappa, Inc. Reprinted by permission. Notes omitted.

Multicultural education itself is a thoroughly Western movement. It grew out of a civil rights movement grounded in such democratic ideals of the West as freedom, justice, and equality. Multicultural education seeks to extend to all people the ideals that were meant only for an elite few at the nation's birth.

Although multicultural education is not opposed to the West, its advocates do demand that the truth about the West be told, that its debt to people of color and women be recognized and included in the curriculum, and that the discrepancies between the ideals of freedom and equality and the realities of racism and sexism be taught to students. Reflective action by citizens is also an integral part of multicultural theory. Multicultural education views citizen action to improve society as an integral part of education in a democracy; it links knowledge, values, empowerment, and action....

Multicultural education will divide the nation. Many of its critics claim that multicultural education will divide the nation and undercut its unity. Schlesinger underscores this view in the title of his book, *The Disuniting of America: Reflections on a Multicultural Society.* This misconception is based partly on questionable assumptions about the nature of U.S. society and partly on a mistaken understanding of multicultural education. The claim that multicultural education will divide the nation assumes that the nation is already united. While we are one nation politically, sociologically our nation is deeply divided along lines of race, gender, and class. The current debate about admitting gays into the military underscores another deep division in our society.

Multicultural education is designed to help unify a deeply divided nation rather than to divide a highly cohesive one. Multicultural education supports the notion of *e pluribus unum*—out of many, one. The multiculturalists and the Western traditionalists, however, often differ about how the *unum* can best be attained. Traditionally, the larger U.S. society and the schools tried to create unity by assimilating students from diverse racial and ethnic groups into a mythical Anglo American culture that required them to experience a process of self-alienation. However, even when students of color became culturally assimilated, they were often structurally excluded from mainstream institutions.

The multiculturalists view *e pluribus unum* as an appropriate national goal, but they believe that the *unum* must be negotiated, discussed, and restructured to reflect the nation's ethnic and cultural diversity. The reformulation of what it means to be united must be a process that involves the participation of diverse groups within the nation, such as people of color, women, straights, gays, the powerful, the powerless, the young, and the old. The reformulation must also involve power sharing and participation by people from many different cultures who must reach beyond their cultural and ethnic borders in order to create a common civic culture that reflects and contributes to the well-being of all. This common civic culture will extend beyond the cultural borders of any single group and constitute a civic "borderland" culture....

MULTICULTURAL EDUCATION HAS MADE PROGRESS

While it is still on the margins rather than in the center of the curriculum in most schools and colleges, multicultural content has made significant inroads into both the school and the college curricula within the last two decades. The truth lies somewhere between the claim that no progress has been made in infusing the school and college curricula with multiethnic content and the claim that such content has replaced the European and American classics.

In the elementary and high schools, much more ethnic content appears in social studies and language arts textbooks today than was the case 20 years ago. In addition, some teachers assign works written by authors of color along with the more standard American classics. In his study of book-length works used in the high schools, Applebee concluded that his most striking finding was how similar present reading lists are to past ones and how little change has occurred. However, he did note that many teachers use anthologies as a mainstay of their literature programs and that 21% of the anthology selections were written by women and 14% by authors of color.

More classroom teachers today have studied the concepts of multicultural education than at any previous point in our history. A significant percentage of today's classroom teachers took a required teacher education course in multicultural education when they were in college....

Some of the nation's leading colleges and universities, such as the University of California at Berkeley, the University of Minnesota, and Stanford University, have either revised their general core curriculum to include ethnic content or have established an ethnic studies course requirement. The list of universities with similar kinds of requirements grows longer each year. However, the transformation of the traditional canon on college and university campuses has of-

ten been bitter and divisive. All changes in curriculum come slowly and painfully to university campuses, but curriculum changes that are linked with issues related to race evoke primordial feelings and reflect the racial crisis in American society. For example, at the University of Washington a bitter struggle ended with the defeat of the ethnic studies requirement.

Changes are also coming to elementary and high school textbooks, as Jesus Garcia points out elsewhere in this special section of the *Kappan*. I believe that the demographic imperative is the major factor driving the changes in school textbooks. The color of the nation's student body is changing rapidly. Nearly half (about 45.5%) of the nation's school-age youths will be young people of color by 2020. Black parents and brown parents are demanding that their leaders, their images, their pain, and their dreams be mirrored in the textbooks that their children study in school....

THE DIMENSIONS OF MULTICULTURAL EDUCATION

One of the problems that continues to plague the multicultural education movement, both from within and without, is the tendency of teachers, administrators, policy makers, and the public to oversimplify the concept. Multicultural education is a complex and multidimensional concept, yet media commentators and educators alike often focus on only one of its many dimensions....

I will use the following five dimensions to describe the field's major components and to highlight important developments within the last two decades: 1) content integration, 2) the knowledge construction process, 3) prejudice reduction, 4) an equity pedagogy, and 5) an empowering school culture and social structure. I will devote most of the rest of this article to the second of these dimensions.

CONTENT INTEGRATION

Content integration deals with the extent to which teachers use examples, data, and information from a variety of cultures and groups to illustrate the key concepts, principles, generalizations, and theories in their subject area or discipline. In many school districts as well as in popular writing, multicultural education is viewed almost solely as content integration. This narrow conception of multicultural education is a major reason why many teachers in such subjects as biology, physics, and mathematics reject multicultural education as irrelevant to them and their students.

In fact, this dimension of multicultural education probably has more relevance to social studies and language arts teachers than it does to physics and math teachers. Physics and math teachers can insert multicultural content into their subjects—e.g., by using biographies of physicists and mathematicians of color and examples from different cultural groups. However, these kinds of activities are probably not the most important multicultural tasks that can be undertaken by science and math teachers. Activities related to the other dimensions of multicultural education, such as the knowledge construction process, prejudice reduction, and an equity pedagogy, are probably the most fruitful areas for the multicultural involvement of science and math teachers.

KNOWLEDGE CONSTRUCTION

The knowledge construction process encompasses the procedures by which social, behavioral, and natural scientists create knowledge in their disciplines. A multicultural focus on knowledge construction includes discussion of the ways in which the implicit cultural assumptions, frames of reference, perspectives, and biases within a discipline influence the construction of knowledge. An examination of the knowledge construction process is an important part of multicultural teaching. Teachers help students to understand how knowledge is created and how it is influenced by factors of race, ethnicity, gender, and social class.

Within the last decade, landmark work related to the construction of knowledge has been done by feminist social scientists and epistemologists, as well as by scholars in ethnic studies. Working in philosophy and sociology, Sandra Harding, Lorraine Code, and Patricia Hill Collins have done some of the most important work related to knowledge construction. This ground-breaking work, although influential among scholars and curriculum developers, has been overshadowed in the popular media by the heated debates about the canon. These writers and researchers have seriously challenged the claims made by the positivists that knowledge can be value-free, and they have described the ways in which knowledge claims are influenced by the gender and ethnic characteristics of the knower. These scholars argue that the human interests and value assumptions of those who create knowledge should be identified, discussed, and examined.

Code states that the sex of the knower is epistemologically significant because knowledge is both subjective and objective. She maintains that both aspects should be recognized and discussed....

Curriculum theorists and developers in multicultural education are applying to the classroom the work being done by the feminist and ethnic studies epistemologists. In *Transforming Knowledge*, Elizabeth Minnich, a professor of philosophy and women's studies, has analyzed the nature of knowledge and described how the dominant tradition, through such logical errors as faulty generalization and circular reasoning, has contributed to the marginalization of women.

I have identified five types of knowledge and described their implications for multicultural teaching. Teachers need to be aware of the various types of knowledge so that they can structure a curriculum that helps students to understand each type. Teachers also need to use their own cultural knowledge and that of their students to enrich teaching and learning. The types of knowledge I have identified and described are: 1) personal/cultural, 2) popular, 3) mainstream academic, 4) transformative, and 5) school. (I will not discuss school knowledge in this article.)

Personal/cultural knowledge consists of the concepts, explanations, and interpretations that students derive from personal experiences in their homes, families, and community cultures. Cultural conflict occurs in the classroom because much of the personal/cultural knowledge that students from diverse cultural groups bring to the classroom is inconsistent with school knowledge and with the teacher's personal and cultural knowledge. For example, research indicates that many African American and Mexican American students are more likely to experience academic success in cooperative rather than in competitive learning environments. Yet the typical school culture is highly competitive, and children of color may experience failure if they do not figure out the implicit rules of the school culture.

The popular knowledge that is institutionalized by the mass media and other forces that shape the popular culture has a strong influence on the values, perceptions, and behavior of children and young people. The messages and images carried by the media, which Carlos Cortés calls the societal curriculum, often reinforce the stereotypes and misconceptions about racial and ethnic groups that are institutionalized within the larger society.

Of course, some films and other popular media forms do make positive contributions to racial understanding. *Dances with Wolves, Glory,* and *Malcolm X* are examples. However, there are many ways to view such films, and both positive and negative examples of popular culture need to become a part of classroom discourse and analysis. Like all human creations, even these positive films are imperfect. The multiculturally informed and sensitive teacher needs to help students view these films, as well as other media productions, from diverse cultural, ethnic, and gender perspectives.

The concepts, theories, and explanations that constitute traditional Western-centric knowledge in history and in the social and behavioral sciences constitute mainstream academic knowledge. Traditional interpretations of U.S. history—embodied in such headings as "The European Discovery of America" and "The Westward Movement"—are central concepts in mainstream academic knowledge....

Transformative academic knowledge challenges the facts, concepts, paradigms, themes, and explanations routinely accepted in mainstream academic knowledge. Those who pursue transformative academic knowledge seek to expand and substantially revise established canons, theories, explanations, and research methods. The transformative research methods and theory that have been developed in women's studies and in ethnic studies since the 1970s constitute, in my view, the most important developments in social science theory and research in the last 20 years.

It is important for teachers and students to realize, however, that transformative academic scholarship has a long history in the United States and that the current ethnic studies movement is directly linked to an earlier ethnic studies movement that emerged in the late 1800s. George Washington Williams published volume 1 of the first history of African Americans in 1882 and the second volume in 1883. Other important works published by African American transformative scholars in times past included works by W. E. B. Du Bois, Carter Woodson, Horace Mann Bond, and Charles Wesley.

The works of these early scholars in African American studies, which formed the academic roots of the current multicultural education movement when it emerged in the 1960s and 1970s, were linked by several important characteristics. Their works were transformative because they created data, interpretations, and perspectives that challenged those that were established by white, mainstream scholarship. The work of the transformative scholars presented positive images of African Americans and refuted stereotypes that were pervasive within the established scholarship of their time.

Although they strove for objectivity in their works and wanted to be considered scientific researchers, these transformative scholars viewed knowledge and action as tightly linked and became involved in social action and administration themselves. Du Bois was active in social protest and for many years was the editor of *Crisis*, an official publication of the National Association for the Advancement of Colored People. Woodson cofounded the Association for the Study of Negro (now Afro-American) Life and History, founded and edited the *Journal of Negro History*, edited the *Negro History Bulletin* for classroom teachers, wrote school and college textbooks on Negro history, and founded Negro History Week (now Afro-American History Month).

Transformative academic knowledge has experienced a renaissance since the 1970s. Only a few of the most important works can be mentioned here because of space. Martin Bernal, in an important two-volume work, *Black Athena*, has created new interpretations about the debt that Greece owes to Egypt and Phoenicia. Before Bernal, Ivan Van Sertima and Cheikh Anta Diop also created novel interpretations of the debt that Europe owes to Africa. In two books, *Indian Givers* and *Native Roots*, Jack Weatherford describes Native American contributions that have enriched the world.

Ronald Takaki, in several influential books, such as *Iron Cages: Race and Culture in 19th-Century America* and *Strangers from a Different Shore: A History of Asian Americans*, has given us new ways to think about the ethnic experience in America. The literary contribution to transformative scholarship has also been rich, as shown by *The Signifying Monkey: A Theory of African-American Literary Criticism*, by Henry Louis Gates, Jr.; *Long Black Song: Essays in Black American Liter-*

ature and Culture, by Houston Baker, Jr.; and *Breaking Ice: An Anthology of Contemporary African-American Fiction,* edited by Terry McMillan.

A number of important works in the transformative tradition that interrelate race and gender have also been published since the 1970s. Important works in this genre include *Unequal Sisters: A Multicultural Reader in U.S. Women's History,* edited by Carol Ellen DuBois and Vicki Ruiz; *Race, Gender, and Work: A Multicultural Economic History of Women in the United States,* by Teresa Amott and Julie Matthaei; *Labor of Love, Labor of Sorrow: Black Women, Work, and the Family from Slavery to the Present,* by Jacqueline Jones; and *The Forbidden Stitch: An Asian American Women's Anthology,* edited by Shirley Geok-lin Lim, Mayumi Tsutakawa, and Margarita Donnelly.

THE OTHER DIMENSIONS

The "prejudice reduction" dimension of multicultural education focuses on the characteristics of children's racial attitudes and on strategies that can be used to help students develop more positive racial and ethnic attitudes. Since the 1960s, social scientists have learned a great deal about how racial attitudes in children develop and about ways in which educators can design interventions to help children acquire more positive feelings toward other racial groups. I have reviewed that research in two recent publications and refer *Kappan* readers to them for a comprehensive discussion of this topic.

This research tells us that by age 4 African American, white, and Mexican American children are aware of racial differences and show racial preferences favoring whites. Students can be helped to develop more positive racial attitudes if realistic images of ethnic and racial groups are included in teaching materials in a consistent, natural, and integrated fashion. Involving students in vicarious experiences and in cooperative learning activities with students of other racial groups will also help them to develop more positive racial attitudes and behaviors.

An *equity pedagogy* exists when teachers use techniques and teaching methods that facilitate the academic achievement of students from diverse racial and ethnic groups and from all social classes. Using teaching techniques that cater to the learning and cultural styles of diverse groups and using the techniques of cooperative learning are some of the ways that teachers have found effective with students from diverse racial, ethnic, and language groups.

An *empowering school culture and social structure* will require the restructuring of the culture and organization of the school so that students from diverse racial, ethnic, and social-class groups will experience educational equality and a sense of empowerment. This dimension of multicultural education involves conceptualizing the school as the unit of change and making structural changes within the school environment. Adopting assessment techniques that are fair to all groups, doing away with tracking, and creating the belief among the staff members that all students can learn are important goals for schools that wish to create a school culture and social structure that are empowering and enhancing for a diverse student body.

MULTICULTURAL EDUCATION AND THE FUTURE

The achievements of multicultural education since the late Sixties and early Seventies are noteworthy and should be acknowledged. Those who have shaped the movement during the intervening decades have been able to obtain wide agreement on the goals of and approaches to multicultural education. Most multiculturalists agree that the major goal of multicultural education is to restructure schools so that all students will acquire the knowledge, attitudes, and skills needed to function in an ethnically and racially diverse nation and world. As is the case with other interdisciplinary areas of study, debates within the field continue. These debates are consistent with the philosophy of a field that values democracy and diversity. They are also a source of strength.

Multicultural education is being implemented widely in the nation's schools, colleges, and universities. The large number of national conferences, school district workshops, and teacher education courses in multicultural education are evidence of its success and perceived importance. Although the process of integration of content is slow and often contentious, multicultural content is increasingly becoming a part of core courses in schools and colleges. Textbook publishers are also integrating ethnic and cultural content into their books, and the pace of such integration is increasing.

Despite its impressive successes, however, multicultural education faces serious challenges as we move toward the next century. One of the most serious of these challenges is the highly organized, well-financed attack by the Western traditionalists who fear that multicultural education will transform America in ways that will result in their own disempowerment. Ironically, the successes that multicultural education has experienced during the last decade have played a major role in provoking the attacks.

The debate over the canon and the well-orchestrated attack on multicultural education reflect an identity crisis in American society. The American identity is being reshaped, as groups on the margins of society begin to participate in the mainstream and to demand that their visions be reflected in a transformed America. In the future, the sharing of power and the transformation of identity required to achieve lasting racial peace in America may be valued rather than feared, for only in this way will we achieve national salvation.

POSTSCRIPT

Does "Multiculturalism" Debase the Curriculum?

D'Souza portrays the universities as being in the control of the multiculturalists, who are teaching that "the ideal of the educated person is largely a figment of bourgeois white male ideology, which should be cast aside." Instead of a liberal education based on reason and open inquiry, he argues, multiculturalist universities are providing an illiberal education based on intimidation and intolerance. Is this true, an exaggeration, or completely false? Evaluate his statements with regard to your campus. Banks portrays multiculturalism in less threatening terms. He begins by trying to correct what he considers to be a number of misconceptions about multiculturalism, especially the charge that it is divisive. On the contrary, Banks says, it is the traditionalist approach that is divisive, for it narrows the field of study; multiculturalism, by its inclusiveness, reaches out to a higher, more comprehensive unity. In Banks's view, the unity sought by D'Souza is narrow and exclusive.

D'Souza's *Illiberal Education* hit a responsive chord with the reading public and was on the *New York Times* best-seller list for several weeks, as was a book written a few years earlier, Allan Bloom's *The Closing of the American Mind* (Simon & Schuster, 1987), in which Bloom laments what he saw as politically inspired tampering with the liberal arts curriculum. Other recent books in the same vein include Roger Kimball, *Tenured Radicals* (HarperCollins, 1990), and Charles Sykes, *The Hollow Men* (Regnery Gateway, 1990). Thomas Sowell presents a pungent attack on multicultural education in "Multicultural Instruction," *The American Spectator* (April 1993). For an exchange of different views on multiculturalism, see "The Idea of the University," *Partisan Review* (Special Issue, 1991). Participants include Brigitte Berger, Wilson Moses, Catharine Stimpson, and Jean Elshtain. For justifications of multicultural education, see Gerald Graff, *Beyond the Cultural Wars* (W. W. Norton, 1992), and Becky W. Thompson and Sangeeta Tyagi, eds., *Beyond a Dream Deferred* (University of Minnesota Press, 1993).

The problems associated with defining multiculturalism are more than just a matter of coming up with the right words. It is a question of defining what kind of a society America will be. For a discussion of several points of view on multicultural education, see the Winter 1991 edition of *American Educator*, which contains a special section on various aspects of this debate and what it means in the schools. Finally, for the Afrocentric perspective on this debate, see Molefi Kete Asante, *The Afrocentric Idea* (Temple University Press, 1988).

ISSUE 2

Does Third World Immigration Threaten America's Cultural Unity?

YES: Lawrence Auster, from *The Path to National Suicide: An Essay on Immigration and Multiculturalism* (American Immigration Control Foundation, 1990)

NO: Francis Fukuyama, from "Immigrants and Family Values," *Commentary* (May 1993)

ISSUE SUMMARY

YES: Writer Lawrence Auster asserts that the large influx of immigrants from non-European countries threatens to undermine the cultural foundations of American unity.

NO: Francis Fukuyama, a former deputy director of the U.S. State Department's policy planning staff, argues that today's immigrants share many of America's traditional values and may actually strengthen America's cultural foundations.

Today the number of legal immigrants to America is close to 1 million per year, and with illegal ("undocumented") immigrants, the total is probably well over that figure. In terms of numbers, immigration is now comparable to the level it reached during the early years of the twentieth century, when millions of immigrants arrived from southern and eastern Europe. A majority of the new immigrants, however, do not come from Europe but from what is loosely called "the Third World." The largest percentages come from Mexico, the Philippines, Korea, and the islands of the Caribbean, while European immigration has shrunk to about 10 percent. Much of the reason for this shift has to do with changes made in U.S. immigration laws during the 1960s. Decades earlier, in the 1920s, America had narrowed its gate to people from certain regions of the world by imposing quotas designed to preserve the balance of races in America. But in 1965 a series of amendments to the Immigration Act put all the world's people on an equal footing in terms of immigration. The result, wrote journalist Theodore H. White, was "a stampede, almost an invasion" of Third World immigrants. Indeed, the 1965 amendments made it even easier for Third World immigrants to enter the country because the new law gave preference to those with a family member already living in the United States. Since most of the European immigrants who had settled in the early part of the century had died off, and since few Europeans had immigrated in more recent years, a greater percentage of family-reuniting immigration came from the Third World.

Immigrants move to the United States for various reasons: to flee tyranny and terrorism, to escape war, or to join relatives who have already settled. Above all, they immigrate because in their eyes America is an island of affluence in a global sea of poverty; here they will earn many times what they could only hope to earn in their native countries. One hotly debated question is, What will these millions of new immigrants do to the United States—or for it?

Part of the debate has to do with bread-and-butter issues: Will new immigrants take jobs away from American workers? Or will they fill jobs that American workers do not want anyway, which will help stimulate the economy? Behind these economic issues is a more profound cultural question: Will these new immigrants add healthy new strains to America's cultural inheritance, broadening and revitalizing it? Or will they cause the country to break up into separate cultural units, destroying America's unity? Of all the questions relating to immigration, this is the one that seems to touch the most sensitive nerves.

In 1992 conservative columnist Patrick Buchanan set off a firestorm of controversy when he raised this question: "If we had to take a million immigrants next year, say Zulus or Englishmen, and put them in Virginia, which group would be easier to assimilate and cause less problems for the people of Virginia?" Although Buchanan later explained that his intention was not to denigrate Zulus or any other racial group but to simply talk about assimilation into Anglo-American culture, his remarks were widely characterized as racist and xenophobic (related to a fear of foreigners). Whether or not that characterization is justified, Buchanan's rhetorical question goes to the heart of the cultural debate over immigration, which is the tension between unity and diversity.

In the selections that follow, Lawrence Auster contends that earlier immigrants may have brought new ingredients into America, but they did not overwhelm it because the immigration laws of the 1920s limited their numbers. But today, he argues, the sheer number of immigrants from other cultures threatens to overwhelm traditional safeguards against cultural disintegration. This foreign influx is turning America from a nation into a collection of separate nationalities. Francis Fukuyama insists that, in some respects, the values and customs of new immigrants to the United States are more traditionally "American" than those of many native-born Americans. Whereas American families are falling apart, he asserts, immigrant families tend to be more tightly knit. And although illegitimacy, drug addiction, and other social problems are on the rise in America, many immigrants lead clean, sober, exemplary lives.

YES
Lawrence Auster

THE PATH TO NATIONAL SUICIDE

THE PROBLEM OF CULTURAL IDENTITY

The history of assimilation has not been, as our mythology now tells us, a simple, glorious progress. Each wave of immigrants, especially the "new" immigrants from southern and eastern Europe, brought dislocation and conflict as well as new vitality; loss as well as gain. But the important thing was that the "new" immigrants still had much in common with the earlier Americans; the fact that they were of European descent and came from related cultures within Western civilization made it relatively easy for them to assimilate into the common sphere of civic habits and cultural identity.... Americans thus remained a *people*—though obviously not (because of persisting ethnic distinctions) in the same sense that the Japanese, the English or even the French are a people. The relative degree of similarity helped make it possible to stretch America's cultural fabric without ripping it. For example, it was eastern and southern European immigrants—men like Irving Berlin, George Gershwin, Frederick Loewe, Samuel Goldwyn, Louis B. Mayer, Frank Capra, Ernst Lubitsch, Billy Wilder, Michael Curtiz, Ben Hecht—who gave us many of the songs, plays and movies that are our twentieth century popular classics; who, in fact, created Hollywood. There was no insurmountable obstacle preventing these individuals from identifying with, and giving artistic expression to, the Anglo-American archetypes of our common culture; they so deeply identified with the American ideal that they created new and powerful aesthetic forms to convey that ideal.

But it is not immediately apparent that people from radically diverse backgrounds and cultural identities—a Central American *indio*, a Cambodian peasant, a Shi'ite Muslim—can feel the same sort of ready identification with American myths and ideal figures. David M. Hwang, author of the racial morality play "M. Butterfly," pinpoints the psychological dimension of this problem: "Growing up as a person of color, you're always ambivalent to a certain degree about your own ethnicity. You think it's great, but there is necessarily a certain amount of self-hatred or confusion at least, which results from the fact that there's a role model in this society which is basically a

Caucasian man, and you don't measure up to that."

To the extent that David Hwang's views on the wounded self-image of racial minorities in predominantly white America are representative (and such views have indeed become commonplace), he may have pointed out a human dilemma that the ideal of cultural assimilation can no longer fully obscure. Generally speaking, human beings most readily identify and feel comfortable with people (and cultural figures) similar to themselves, a fact that explains the successful assimilation of European immigrants into Anglo-American culture. It follows that if the new Americans from Asia and the Third World are to feel truly comfortable as Americans (and if white Americans are to be cured of their own race-consciousness and not experience the massively increasing numbers of Asians and other minorities as a disturbingly alien presence in this society), then America's role model, its ideal figures and unifying myths, must change, diversify, embrace all the races, ethnic types and cultures on earth. This implies a metamorphosis in our art, our drama, our popular entertainment, our literature, our teaching of history—a mutation of our very identity as a people. And the force that creates the irresistible demand for this cultural change is—it must be emphasized again—the sea-change in America's ethnic and racial character. In David Hwang's words: "Sophisticated American whites realize their group is in the process of changing from an outright majority to just a plurality in the U.S., and are beginning to be ready to hear what the rest of us thing"—i.e., admit Asian values, images and cultural idiom into the heart of American culture. Paradoxically, while he admits that "M.

Butterfly" is anti-Western, Hwang insists: "But it's very pro-American, too." Translation: Kwang is "pro" a future, *multicultural* America—an America that has become "good" by surrendering its historic identity....

Even if there were no immigration at all, America would still be experiencing what can only be called a terrifying social and moral decline. Concerns over mediocrity are hardly a new thing in this country, but surely the attack on the intellect, the decay of family and individual character that have occurred over the past 25 years are phenomena of an entirely different order, posing a very real threat to the freedoms and the high level of civilization this country has enjoyed. The combination of both factors—progressive degeneracy and divisiveness of the existing society on one hand and perpetual mass immigration on the other—must be fatal.... [I]f America continues "the slide into apathy, hedonism and moral chaos," as Christopher Lasch has called it, and at the same time its present population is replaced by a chaotic mix of peoples from radically diverse, non-European cultures, then there will be no basis for continuation or renewal. Like ancient Greece after the classical Helenes had dwindled away and the land was repopulated by Slavonic and Turkic peoples, America will have become literally a different country. There will be no American Renaissance—except perhaps as some faceless subdivision of the global shopping mall.

The decisive factor, ignored by almost everyone in our sentimental land, is the sheer force of numbers. The United States has shown that it has the capacity to absorb a certain number of ethnic minorities into its existing cultural forms. The minorities, so long as there remains a majority culture that believes in itself, have powerful incentives to accept the legitimacy of the prevailing culture even as they add their own variety to it. But as they continue to grow in numbers relative to the whole population, a point of critical mass is reached. The new groups begin to assert an independent peoplehood, and the existing society comes to be seen as illegitimate and oppressive; what was once (granting its flaws) applauded as the most beneficent society in the history of the world, is suddenly, as though by a magician's curse, transformed into an evil racist power. That this point has already been reached can be seen from the following comment which appeared, not in some organ of the far left, but in the *New York Times:*

> How can teachers blindly continue to preach the virtues of "our" cultural tradition in classrooms where, in regions such as California, most students are now African-Americans, Latinos, Asians and native Americans, whose families' main experience of Western civilization has been victimization?

If it is the sheer *number* of non-Europeans in places like California that obligates us to abandon "our" cultural tradition, is it not an inescapable conclusion that the white majority in this country, if it wishes to preserve that tradition, must place a rational limit on the number of immigrants? ...

* * *

The argument presented [here] is that the combined forces of open immigration and multiculturalism constitute a mortal threat to American civilization. At a time when unprecedented ethnic diversity makes the affirmation of a common American culture more important than ever, we are, under the pressure of that diversity, abandoning the very idea of a common culture. "We are asking America to open its linguistic frontiers," one multiculturalist spokesman has said, "and to accept an expanded idea of what it means to be an American"—a standard that, in terms of immigration and language policies, seems to include everyone in the universe. Whether we consider America's porous borders; or the disappearing standards for naturalization; or the growth of official multilingualism; or the new "diversity" curricula aimed at destroying the basis of common citizenship; or the extension of virtually all the rights and protections of citizenship to legal *and* illegal aliens; or the automatic granting of citizenship to children of illegals; the tendency is clear: we have in effect redefined the nation to the point where there is no remaining criterion of American identity other than the physical fact of one's being here. It is, to quote Alexander Hamilton, "an attempt to break down every pale which has been erected for the preservation of a national spirit and a national character."

The irony is that most Americans support immigration as a "liberal" policy. That is, they want America to remain open and to help people, and they also expect that the new immigrants will assimilate into our existing society. It was on this basis that the opening of America's doors to every country on earth was approved in 1965 and continues to enjoy unassailable political support. But we are beginning to see, simply as a practical, human matter, that the successful assimilation of such huge numbers of widely diverse peoples into a single people and viable polity is a pipe dream. It is at this point that multiculturalism comes along and says: "That's not a problem. We don't want to assimilate into this oppressive, Eurocentered mold. We want to reconstruct America as a multicultural society." And this radical pluralist view gains acceptance by retaining the moral legitimacy, the patina of humanitarianism, that properly belonged to the older liberalism which it has supplanted. We have thus observed the progress, largely unperceived by the American people, from the liberal assimilationist view, which endorses open immigration because it naively believes that our civilization can survive unlimited diversity, to radical multiculturalism, which endorses open immigration because it wants our civilization to end....

THE POLITICAL CONSEQUENCES

... Of course, it is commonly believed today that the anti-immigration sentiment in the past, particularly in the post-World War I years, discredits similar concerns in the present; that is, just as the earlier fears of an unassimilable mass of immigrants proved to be unwarranted, so will the present fears. But this argument ignores the fact that the great wave of the "new" immigration was brought to a halt in 1922. This reduction in immigration vastly eased the assimilation process in the following decades and led to a dramatic decrease in the nativist fears that had been the prime motive for the 1920s legislation. "Somewhere, in the mid-1930's," writes immigration historian Oscar Handlin, "there was a turn. Americans ceased to believe in race, the hate movements [against the European immigrants] began to disintegrate, and discrimination increasingly took on the

aspect of an anachronistic survival from the past, rather than a pattern valid for the future.... In the face of those changes, it might well have been asked: 'What happened to race?' " It is revealing that, among the explanations Handlin offers for this sudden and welcome drop in the nativist fever, he says nothing about the most obvious cause: the fact that immigration had been drastically lowered by the 1920s legislation (and later completely stopped by the Depression); such acknowledgement would undercut Handlin's own moralistic criticism of the restrictive 1920s laws. Whatever we may think of those restrictions from a humanitarian point of view, their importance in advancing the assimilation of white ethnics in the mid-twentieth century cannot be denied. Certainly, the United States would not have been nearly so strong and united a society as it was from the beginning of the Second World War until the 1960s if the country had received, as had been feared, two million immigrants per year during the 1920s and beyond.

It ought also to be mentioned, in light of the present habit of blaming everything on racism, that the Founders were concerned about the divisive effect of white Europeans from monarchical societies, who they feared would resist American republican principles. Similarly, the anti-Irish feeling in the mid-nineteenth century had nothing to do with race. It was only with the rise of the new immigration from southern and eastern Europe in the 1880s, along with the Chinese and Japanese immigrations, that the fear of unassimilability began to focus on race. The concern common to all the historical stages of anti-immigrant sentiment was not race as such but the need for a harmonious citizenry holding to the same values and political principles and having something of the same spirit. Now, certainly, our experience with cultural assimilation in the twentieth century has widened our sense of the ethnic parameters of a viable polity far beyond what either the Founding Fathers or the 20th century nativists thought possible; but the question we forget at our peril is, how far can those parameters be expanded while still maintaining a viable cultural and political homogeneity? The importance of harmony, of a "radius of identification and trust," is still paramount for a free society.

Unlimited Diversity—A Threat to Equality

As diversity continues to expand beyond the point where genuine assimilation is possible, the ideal of equality will also recede. "Iceland's population of 240,000 is a notably homogeneous society," writes the *New York Times*. "Like these other well-off homogeneous nations [i.e., Scandinavia and Japan] Iceland's wealth is evenly distributed and its society is remarkably egalitarian." Even liberals seem to recognize the correlation between homogeneity and equality—for every country, that is, except the United States, where we have conceived the fantastic notion that we can achieve equality *and* unlimited diversity at the same time. A far more likely result is a devolution of society into permanent class divisions based on ethnicity, a weakening of the sense of common citizenship, and a growing disparity between islands of private wealth and oceans of public squalor. America's effort to create a society that is both multicultural and equal may end by destroying forever the age-old hope of equality.

Unlimited Diversity—A Threat to Liberty

Finally, unlimited diversity threatens liberty itself. The inequality, the absence of common norms and loyalties, and the social conflict stemming from increased diversity require a growing state apparatus to mediate the conflict. The disappearance of voluntary social harmony requires that harmony be imposed by force. As historian Robert Nisbet has argued, the demand in this century for ever more innovative forms of equality has already resulted in a vast enlargement of the state. Radical pluralism raises to a new level this threat to our liberty, since now the state will be called upon to overcome, not just the inequality of individuals, but the inequality of *cultures*. The inherent vastness and endlessness of such an enterprise matches the intrusiveness of the state power that must be exercised to achieve it. The signs of this new despotism are all around us:

• the de jure and de facto repression of speech dealing with racially sensitive subjects;

• the official classification and extension of privileges to people according to ethnic affiliation;

• the expansion of judicial and bureaucratic power to enforce racial quotas in more and more areas of society;

• the subjection of the American people to an unceasing barrage of propaganda telling us we are all brothers, that we must "respect all cultures," etc., even while government policies are unleashing a wave of cultural diversity and ethnic chauvinism that is making spontaneous brotherly feeling a receding dream. In other words, the "family" that Governor Mario Cuomo keeps telling us we all belong to is really—the *state*.

THE END OF AMERICAN CIVILIZATION

I have been attempting... to suggest a few of the myriad potential effects of mass immigration and multicultural-ism on this country's future. There are darker scenarios I have not explored—the spread of Third-World conditions in parts of our country; the collapse of civic order (nightmarishly portrayed in Tom Wolfe's *Bonfire of the Vanities*), or the disintegration of the United States along regional and ethnic lines. What-ever the future America may look like, it will not be a country that we—or our forebears whose legacy we are so care-lessly throwing away—would be able to recognize.

In the years and decades to come, as the present American people and their descendants begin to understand what is happening to their country; as they see their civilization disappearing piece by piece, city by city, state by state, from before their eyes, and that nothing can be done to stop it, they will suffer the same collapse of spirit that occurs to any people when its way of life, its historical identity, is taken away from it. Beneath all the hopeful names they will try to find for these changes—diversity, world-nation, global oneness—there will be the repressed knowledge that America is be-coming an utterly different country from what it has been, and that this means the end of their world. But the pain will not last for long. As the clerics of diversity indoctrinate new generations into the Or-wellian official history, even the memory of what America once was will be lost.

Finally, if we want to consider "cul-tural equity," there seems to be an ex-traordinary kind of *inequity* in the propo-sition that the United States must lose its identity... while the countries that the new immigrants are coming from are free to preserve *their* identities. In a hundred years, the United States will have become in large part an Hispanic nation, while Latin America will still be what it has always been; Mexico has strict immigra-tion laws even against other Latin Amer-icans. China, Korea, the Philippines and India will still have their historic cultures intact after having exported millions of their people to America, while America's historic culture will have vanished. If the situation were reversed and North Amer-icans were colonizing Latin America and Asia, it would be denounced as racist im-perialism. Why, then, does every other country in the world have the right to preserve its identity but the United States has not? The answer, as I've tried to show, is that the end of multiculturalism is not some utopian, "equal" society, but simply the end of American civilization.

So much for America; if other Western nations continue *their* openness to Third World immigration, we may be witness-ing the beginning of the end of Western civilization as a whole. And this defeat of the West will have been accomplished, not by the superior strength or civiliza-tion of the newcomers, not by the "forces of history," but simply by the feckless generosity and moral cowardice of the West itself. In the prophetic words of so-cial psychologist William McDougall:

As I watch the American nation speeding gaily, with invincible optimism down the road to destruction, I seem to be contem-plating the greatest tragedy in the history of mankind.

NO
Francis Fukuyama

IMMIGRANTS AND FAMILY VALUES

At the Republican convention in Houston last August, Patrick J. Buchanan announced the coming of a block-by-block war to "take back our culture." Buchanan is right that a cultural war is upon us, and that this fight will be a central American preoccupation now that the cold war is over. What he understands less well, however, is that the vast majority of the non-European immigrants who have come into this country in the past couple of decades are not the enemy. Indeed, many of them are potentially on his side....

II

The most articulate and reasoned recent conservative attack on immigration came last summer in an article in *National Review* by Peter Brimelow. Brimelow, a senior editor at *Forbes* and himself a naturalized American of British and Canadian background, argues that immigration worked in the past in America only because earlier waves of nativist backlash succeeded in limiting it to a level that could be successfully assimilated into the dominant Anglo-Saxon American culture. Brimelow criticizes pro-immigration free-marketeers like Julian Simon for ignoring the issue of the skill levels of the immigrant labor force, and their likely impact on blacks and others at the bottom end of the economic ladder. But his basic complaint is a cultural one. Attacking the *Wall Street Journal*'s Paul Gigot for remarking that a million Zulus would probably work harder than a million Englishmen today, Brimelow notes:

> This comment reveals an utter innocence about the reality of ethnic and cultural differences, let alone little things like tradition and history—in short, the greater part of the conservative vision. Even in its own purblind terms, it is totally false. All the empirical evidence is that immigrants from developed countries assimilate better than those from underdeveloped countries. It is developed countries that teach the skills required for success in the United States... it should not be necessary to explain that the legacy of [the Zulu kings] Shaka and Cetewayo—overthrown just over a century ago—is not that of Alfred the Great, let alone Elizabeth II or any civilized society.

Elsewhere, Brimelow suggests that culture is a key determinant of economic performance, and that people from certain cultures are therefore likely to do less well economically than others. He implies, furthermore, that some immigrants are more prone to random street crime because of their "impulsiveness and present-orientation," while others are responsible for organized crime which is, by his account, ethnically based. Finally, Brimelow argues that the arrival of diverse non-European cultures fosters the present atmosphere of multiculturalism, and is, to boot, bad for the electoral prospects of the Republican party.

A similar line of thought runs through Buchanan's writings and speeches, and leads to a similar anti-immigrant posture. Buchanan has explicitly attacked the notion that democracy represents a particularly positive form of government, and hence would deny that belief in universal democratic principles ought to be at the core of the American national identity.[1] But if one subtracts democracy from American nationality, what is left? Apparently, though Buchanan is somewhat less explicit on this point, a concept of America as a Christian, ethnically European nation with certain core cultural values that are threatened by those coming from other cultures and civilizations.

* * *

There is an easy, Civics 101-type answer to the Brimelow-Buchanan argument. In contrast to other West European democracies, or Japan, the American national identity has never been directly linked to ethnicity or religion. Nationality has been based instead on universal concepts like freedom and equality that are in theory open to all people. Our Constitu-tion forbids the establishment of religion, and the legal system has traditionally held ethnicity at arm's length. To be an American has meant to be committed to a certain set of ideas, and not to be descended from an original tribe of *ur*-Americans. Those elements of a common American culture visible today—belief in the Constitution and the individualist-egalitarian principles underlying it, plus modern American pop and consumer culture—are universally accessible and appealing, making the United States, in Ben Wattenberg's phrase, the first "universal nation."

This argument is correct as far as it goes, but there is a serious counterargument that reaches to the core of last year's debate over "family values." It runs as follows:

America began living up to its universalist principles only in the last half of this century. For most of the period from its revolutionary founding to its rise as a great, modern, industrial power, the nation's elites conceived of the country not just as a democracy based on universal principles, but also as a Christian, Anglo-Saxon nation.

American democracy—the counter-argument continues—is, of course, embodied in the laws and institutions of the country, and will be imbibed by anyone who learns to play by its rules. But virtually every serious theorist of American democracy has noted that its success depended heavily on the presence of certain pre-democratic values or cultural characteristics that were neither officially sanctioned nor embodied in law. If the Declaration of Independence and the Constitution were the basis of America's *Gesellschaft* (society), Christian Anglo-Saxon culture constituted its *Gemeinschaft* (community).

Indeed—the counterargument goes on—the civic institutions that Tocqueville observed in the 1830's, whose strength and vitality he saw as a critical manifestation of the Americans' "art of associating," were more often than not of a religious (i.e., Christian) nature, devoted to temperance, moral education of the young, or the abolition of slavery. There is nothing in the Constitution which states that parents should make large sacrifices for their children, that workers should rise early in the morning and labor long hours in order to get ahead, that people should emulate rather than undermine their neighbors' success, that they should be innovative, entrepreneurial, or open to technological change. Yet Americans, formed by a Christian culture, possessed these traits in abundance for much of their history, and the country's economic prosperity and social cohesion arguably rested on them.

It is this sort of consideration that underlay the family-values controversy during last year's election. Basic to this line of thought is that, all other things being equal, children are better off when raised in stable, two-parent, heterosexual families. Such family structures and the web of moral obligations they entail are the foundation of educational achievement, economic success, good citizenship, personal character, and a host of other social virtues.

... [W]hile many Americans did not sign on to last year's family-values theme, few would deny that the family and community are in deep crisis today. The breakdown of the black family in inner-city neighborhoods around America in the past couple of generations shows in particularly stark form the societal consequences of a loss of certain cultural values. And what has happened among blacks is only an extreme extension of a process that has been proceeding apace among whites as well.

The issue, then, is not whether the questions of culture and cultural values are important, or whether it is legitimate to raise them, but whether immigration really threatens those values. For while the values one might deem central either to economic success or to social cohesion may have arisen out of a Christian, Anglo-Saxon culture, it is clear that they are not bound to that particular social group: some groups, like Jews and Asians, might come to possess those values in abundance, while Wasps themselves might lose them and decay. The question thus becomes: which ethnic groups in today's America are threatening, and which groups are promoting, these core cultural values?

III

The notion that non-European immigrants are a threat to family values and other core American cultural characteristics is, in a way, quite puzzling. After all, the breakdown of traditional family structures, from extended to nuclear, has long been understood to be a disease of advanced industrial countries and not of nations just emerging from their agricultural pasts.

Some conservatives tend to see the third world as a vast, global underclass, teeming with the same social pathologies as Compton in Los Angeles or Bedford-Stuyvesant in Brooklyn. But the sad fact is that the decay of basic social relationships evident in American inner cities, stretching to the most intimate moral bonds linking parents and children, may well be something with few precedents in human history. Economic conditions in most third-world countries simply would not permit a social group suffering so total a collapse of family structure to survive: with absent fathers and no source of income, or mothers addicted to drugs, children would not live to adulthood.

But it would also seem *a priori* likely that third-world immigrants should have stronger family values than white, middle-class, suburban Americans, while their work ethic and willingness to defer to traditional sources of authority should be greater as well. Few of the factors that have led to family breakdown in the American middle class over the past couple of generations—rapidly changing economic conditions, with their attendant social disruptions; the rise of feminism and the refusal of women to play traditional social roles; or the legitimization of alternative life-styles and consequent proliferation of rights and entitlements on a retail level—apply in third-world situations. Immigrants coming from traditional developing societies are likely to be poorer, less educated, and in possession of fewer skills than those from Europe, but they are also likely to have stronger family structures and moral inhibitions. Moreover, despite the greater ease of moving to America today than in the last century, immigrants are likely to be a self-selecting group with a much greater than average degree of energy, ambition, toughness, and adaptability.

These intuitions are largely borne out by the available empirical data, particularly if one disaggregates the different parts of the immigrant community.

The strength of traditional family values is most evident among immigrants from East and South Asia, where mutu-ally supportive family structures have long been credited as the basis for their economic success. According to Census Bureau statistics, 78 percent of Asian and Pacific Islander households in the United States were family households, as opposed to 70 percent for white Americans. The size of these family households is likely to be larger: 74 percent consist of three or more persons, compared to 57 percent for white families. While Asians are equally likely to be married as whites, they are only half as likely to be divorced.[2] Though dropping off substantially in the second and third generations, concern for elderly parents is high in Chinese, Japanese, and Vietnamese households; for many, the thought of sticking a mother or father out of sight and out of mind in a nursing home continues to be anathema. More importantly, most of the major Asian immigrant groups are intent on rapid assimilation into the American mainstream, and have not been particularly vocal in pressing for particularistic cultural entitlements.

* * *

While most white Americans are ready to recognize and celebrate the social strengths of Asians, the real fears of cultural invasion surround Latinos. Despite their fast growth, Asians still constitute less than 3 percent of the U.S. population, while the number of Hispanics increased from 14.6 to over 22 million between 1980 and 1990, or 9 percent of the population. But here as well, the evidence suggests that most Latin American immigrants may be a source of strength with regard to family values, and not a liability.

Latinos today constitute an extremely diverse group. It is certainly the case that a segment of the Latino community has experienced many of the same social problems as blacks. This is particularly true of the first large Latino community in the U.S.: Puerto Ricans who came to the mainland in the early postwar period and settled predominantly in New York and other cities of the Northeast. Forty percent of Puerto Rican families are headed by women, compared to 16 percent for the non-Hispanic population; only 57 percent of Puerto Rican households consist of families, while their rate of out-of-wedlock births is almost double the rate for non-Hispanics. In New York, Puerto Ricans have re-exported social pathologies like crack-cocaine use to Puerto Rico over the past generation.

Other Latino groups have also brought social problems with them: the Mariel boat lift from Cuba, during which Castro emptied his country's jails and insane asylums, had a measurable impact on crime in the U.S. Many war-hardened immigrants from El Salvador and other unstable Central American countries have contributed to crime in the U.S., and Chicano gangs in Los Angeles and other Southwestern cities have achieved their own notoriety beside the black Bloods and Crips. Half of those arrested in the Los Angeles riot last year were Latinos.

Such facts are highly visible and contribute to the impression among white Americans that Latinos as a whole have joined inner-city blacks to form one vast, threatening underclass. But there are very significant differences among Latino groups. Latinos of Cuban and Mexican origin, for example, who together constitute 65 percent of the Hispanic community, have a 50-percent lower rate of female-headed households than do Puerto Ricans—18.9 and 19.6 percent versus 38.9 percent. While the rate of Puerto Rican out-of-wedlock births approaches that of blacks (53.0 vs. 63.1 percent of live births), the rates for Cuban and Mexican-origin Latinos are much lower, 16.1 and 28.9 percent, respectively, though they are still above the white rate of 13.9 percent.[3]

When looked at in the aggregate, Latino family structure stands somewhere between that of whites and blacks. For example, the rates of female-headed families with no husband present as a proportion of total families is 13.5 percent for whites, 46.4 percent for blacks, and 24.4 percent for Hispanics. If we adjust these figures for income level, however, Hispanics turn out to be much closer to the white norm.

Poverty is hard on families regardless of race; part of the reason for the higher percentage of Latino female-headed households is simply that there are more poor Latino families. If we compare families below the poverty level, the Hispanic rate of female-headed families is very close to that of whites (45.7 vs. 43.6 percent), while the comparable rate for blacks is much higher than either (78.3 percent). Considering the substantially higher rate of family breakdown within the sizable Puerto Rican community, this suggests that the rate of single-parent families for Cuban- and Mexican-origin Latinos is actually lower than that for whites at a comparable income level.

Moreover, Latinos as a group are somewhat more likely to be members of families than either whites or blacks.[4] Another study indicates that Mexican-Americans have better family demographics than do whites, with higher birth-weight babies even among low-income mothers due to taboos on smoking, drinking, and drug use during pregnancy. Many Latinos remain devout Catholics, and the rate of church attendance is higher in the Mexican community than for the U.S. as a whole as well. But even if one does not believe that the United States is a "Christian country," the fact that so many immigrants are from Catholic Latin America should make them far easier to assimilate than, say, Muslims in Europe.

These statistics are broadly in accord with the observations of anyone who has lived in Los Angeles, San Diego, or any other community in the American Southwest. Virtually every early-morning commuter in Los Angeles knows the street-corners on which Chicano day-laborers gather at 7:00 A.M., looking for work as gardeners, busboys, or on construction sites. Many of them are illegal immigrants with families back in Mexico to whom they send their earnings. While they are poor and unskilled, they have a work ethic and devotion to family comparable to those of the South and East European immigrants who came to the U.S. at the turn of the century. It is much less common to see African-Americans doing this sort of thing.

* * *

Those who fear third-world immigration as a threat to Anglo-American cultural values do not seem to have noticed what the real sources of cultural breakdown have been. To some extent, they can be traced to broad socioeconomic factors over which none of us has control: the fluid, socially disruptive nature of capitalism; technological change; economic pressures of the contemporary workplace and urban life; and so on. But the ideological assault on traditional family values—the sexual revolution; feminism and the delegitimization of the male-dominated household; the celebration of alternative life-styles; attempts ruthlessly to secularize all aspects of American public life; the acceptance of no-fault divorce and the consequent rise of single-parent households—was not the creation of recently-arrived Chicano agricultural workers or Haitian boat people, much less of Chinese or Korean immigrants. They originated right in the heart of America's well-established white, Anglo-Saxon community. The "Hollywood elite" that created the now celebrated Murphy Brown, much like the establishment "media elite" that Republicans enjoy attacking, does not represent either the values or the interests of most recent third-world immigrants.

In short, though the old, traditional culture continues to exist in the United States, it is overlaid today with an elite culture that espouses very different values. The real danger is not that these elites will become corrupted by the habits and practices of third-world immigrants, but rather that the immigrants will become corrupted by them. And that is in fact what tends to happen.

While the first generation of immigrants to the United States tends to be deferential to established authority and preoccupied with the economic problems of "making it," their children and grandchildren become aware of their own entitlements and rights, more politicized, and able to exploit the political system to defend and expand those entitlements. While the first generation is willing to work quietly at minimum- or subminimum-wage jobs, the second and third generations have higher expectations as to what their labor is worth. The extension of welfare and other social benefits to noncitizens through a series of court decisions has had the perverse effect of hastening the spread of welfare dependency. Part of the reason that

Puerto Ricans do less well than other Latino groups may be that they were never really immigrants at all, but U.S. citizens, and therefore eligible for social benefits at a very early stage.

As Julian Simon has shown, neither the absolute nor the relative levels of immigration over the past decade have been inordinately high by historical standards. What *is* different and very troubling about immigration in the present period is that the ideology that existed at the turn of the century and promoted assimilation into the dominant Anglo-Saxon culture has been replaced by a multicultural one that legitimates and even promotes continuing cultural differentness.

* * *

The intellectual and social origins of multiculturalism are complex, but one thing is clear: it is both a Western and an American invention. The American Founding was based on certain Enlightenment notions of the universality of human equality and freedom, but such ideas have been under attack within the Western tradition itself for much of the past two centuries. The second half of the late Allan Bloom's *The Closing of the American Mind* (the part that most buyers of the book skipped over) chronicles the way in which the relativist ideas of Nietzsche and Heidegger were transported to American shores at mid-century. Combined with an easygoing American egalitarianism, they led not just to a belief in the need for cultural tolerance, but to a positive assertion of the equal moral validity of all cultures. Today the writings of Michel Foucault, a French epigone of Nietzsche, have become the highbrow source of academic multiculturalism.

France may have produced Foucault, but France has not implemented a multicultural educational curriculum to anything like the degree the U.S. has. The origins of multiculturalism here must therefore be traced to the specific circumstances of American social life. Contrary to the arguments of multiculturalism's promoters, it was not a necessary adjustment to the reality of our pluralistic society. The New York City public-school system in the year 1910 was as diverse as it is today, and yet it never occurred to anyone to celebrate and preserve the native cultures of the city's Italians, Greeks, Poles, Jews, or Chinese.

The shift in attitudes toward cultural diversity can be traced to the aftermath of the civil-rights movement, when it became clear that integration was not working for blacks. The failure to assimilate was interpreted as an indictment of the old, traditional mainstream Anglo-Saxon culture: "Wasp" took on a pejorative connotation, and African-Americans began to take pride in the separateness of their own traditions. Ironically, the experience of African-Americans became the model for subsequent immigrant groups like Latinos who could have integrated themselves into mainstream society as easily as the Italians or Poles before them.

It is true that Hispanic organizations now constitute part of the multiculturalist coalition and have been very vocal in pushing for bilingual/bicultural education. There is increasing evidence, however, that rank-and-file immigrants are much more traditionally assimilationist than some of their more vocal leaders. For example, most Chinese and Russian immigrant parents in New York City deliberately avoid sending their children to the bilingual-education classes offered to them by the public-school system, believing that a cold plunge into English will be a much more effective means of learning to function in American society.

Hispanics generally show more support for bilingual education, but even here a revealing recent study indicates that an overwhelming number of Hispanic parents see bilingualism primarily as a means of learning English, and not of preserving Hispanic culture.[5] This same study indicates that most Hispanics identify strongly with the United States, and show a relatively low level of Spanish maintenance in the home. By contrast, multiculturalism is more strongly supported by many other groups—blacks, feminists, gays, Native Americans, etc.—whose ancestors have been in the country from the start.

* * *

Brimelow's *National Review* piece suggests that even if immigrants are not responsible for our anti-assimilationist multiculturalism, we need not pour oil on burning waters by letting in more immigrants from non-Western cultures. But this argument can be reversed: even if the rate of new immigration fell to zero tomorrow, and the most recent five million immigrants were sent home, we would still have an enormous problem in this country with the breakdown of a core culture and the infatuation of the school system with trendy multiculturalist educational policies.

The real fight, the central fight, then, should not be over keeping newcomers out: this will be a waste of time and energy. The real fight ought to be over the question of assimilation itself: whether we believe that there is enough to our Western, rational, egalitarian, democratic civilization to force those coming to the country to absorb its language and rules, or whether we carry respect for other cultures to the point that Americans no longer have a common voice with which to speak to one another.

Apart from the humble habits of work and family values, opponents of immigration ought to consider culture at the high end of the scale. As anyone who has walked around an elite American university recently would know, immigration from Asia is transforming the nature of American education. For a country that has long prided itself on technological superiority, and whose economic future rests in large part on a continuing technical edge, a depressingly small number of white Americans from long-established families choose to go into engineering and science programs in preference to business and, above all, law school. (This is particularly true of the most dynamic and vocal part of the white population, upwardly mobile middle-class women.) The one bright spot in an otherwise uniform horizon of decline in educational test scores has been in math, where large numbers of new Asian test-takers have bumped up the numbers.[6] In Silicon Valley alone, there are some 12,000 engineers of Chinese descent, while Chinese account for two out of every five engineering and science graduates in the University of California system.

Indeed, if one were to opt for "designer immigration" that would open the gates to peoples with the best cultural values, it is not at all clear that certain European countries would end up on top.

In the past decade, England's percapita GNP [Gross National Product] has fallen behind Italy's, and threatens to displace Portugal and Greece at the bottom of the European Community heap by the end of the decade. Only a fifth of English young people receive any form of higher education, and despite Margaret Thatcher's best efforts, little progress has been made over the past generation in breaking down the stifling social rigidities of the British class system. The English working class is among the least well-educated, most state- and welfare-dependent and immobile of any in the developed world. While the British intelligentsia and upper classes continue to intimidate middle-class Americans, they can do so only on the basis of snobbery and inherited but rapidly dwindling intellectual capital. Paul Gigot may or may not be right that a million Zulus would work harder than a million English, but a million Taiwanese certainly would, and would bring with them much stronger family structures and entrepreneurship to boot.

IV

This is not to say that immigration will not be the source of major economic and social problems for the United States in the future. There are at least three areas of particular concern.

The first has to do with the effects of immigration on income distribution, particularly at the low end of the scale. The growing inequality of American income distribution over the past decade is not, as the Democrats asserted during the election campaign, the result of Reagan-Bush tax policies or the failure of "trickle-down" economics. Rather, it proceeds from the globalization of the American economy: low-skill labor increasingly has to compete with low-skill labor in Malaysia, Brazil, Mexico, and elsewhere. But it has also had to compete with low-skill immigrant labor coming

into the country from the third world, which explains why Hispanics themselves tend to oppose further Hispanic immigration. The country as a whole may be better off economically as a result of this immigration, but those against whom immigrants directly compete have been hurt, just as they will be hurt by the North American Free Trade Agreement (NAFTA), the General Agreement on Tariffs and Trade (GATT), and other trade-liberalizing measures that are good for the country as a whole. In a city like Los Angeles, Hispanics with their stronger social ties have displaced blacks out of a variety of menial jobs, adding to the woes of an already troubled black community.

The second problem area has to do with the regional concentration of recent Hispanic immigration. As everyone knows, the 25 million Hispanics in the United States are not evenly distributed throughout the country, but are concentrated in the Southwest portion of it, where the problems normally accompanying the assimilation of immigrant communities tend to be magnified. The L.A. public-school system is currently in a state of breakdown, as it tries to educate burgeoning numbers of recent immigrants on a recession-starved budget.

The third problem concerns bilingualism and the elite Hispanic groups which promote and exist off of it. As noted earlier, the rank-and-file of the Hispanic community seems reasonably committed to assimilation; the same cannot be said for its leadership. Bilingualism, which initially began as a well-intentioned if misguided bridge toward learning English, has become in the eyes of many of its proponents a means of keeping alive a separate Spanish language and culture.

Numerous studies have indicated that students in bilingual programs learn English less well than those without access to them, and that their enrollments are swelled by a large number of Hispanics who can already speak English perfectly well.[7] In cities with large Hispanic populations like New York and Los Angeles, the bilingual bureaucracy has become something of a monster, rigidly tracking students despite the wishes of parents and students. The *New York Times* recently reported the case of a Hispanic-surnamed child, born in the United States and speaking only English, who was forced by New York City officials to enroll in an English as a Second Language Class. Bilingualism is but one symptom of a much broader crisis in American public education, and admittedly makes the problems of assimilation much greater.

These problems can be tackled with specific changes in public policy. But the central issue raised by the immigration question is indeed a cultural one, and as such less susceptible of policy manipulation. The problem here is not the foreign culture that immigrants bring with them from the third world, but the contemporary elite culture of Americans—Americans like Kevin Costner, who believes that America began going downhill when the white man set foot here, or another American, Ice-T, whose family has probably been in the country longer than Costner's and who believes that women are bitches and that the chief enemy of his generation is the police. In the upcoming block-by-block cultural war, the enemy will not speak Spanish or have a brown skin. In Pogo's words, "He is us."

NOTES

1. See, for example, his article, "America First—and Second, and Third," the *National Interest*, Spring 1990.

2. Census Bureau Press Release CB92–89, "Profile of Asians and Pacific Islanders."

3. Data taken from Linda Chavez, *Out of the Barrio* (Basic Books, 1991), p. 103.

4. Figures taken from *Poverty in the United States: 1991*, Bureau of the Census, Series P-60, no. 181, pp. 7–9; the percentage of people in families for whites, blacks, and Hispanics is 84.5, 84.8, and 89.0, respectively (pp. 2–3).

5. See Rodolfo O. de la Garza, Louis DeSipio, *et al.*, *Latino Voices: Mexican, Puerto Rican, and Cuban Perspectives on American Politics* (Westview Press, 1992).

6. This same group of Asians appears also to have lowered verbal scores, though this is something that will presumably be corrected over time.

7. On this point, see Linda Chavez's *Out of the Barrio*, pp. 9–38.

POSTSCRIPT

Does Third World Immigration Threaten America's Cultural Unity?

Both Auster and Fukuyama oppose "multicultural" education, which they think neglects and even denigrates America's unifying traditions. Where the two clearly differ is in the way they frame the issue and their attitudes toward today's immigrant peoples. In Fukuyama's view, many of the cultural traits that Asian and Latino immigrants commonly have resemble those that Americans once had but are now losing. In some respects, Fukuyama seems to say, the new immigrants are more American than the Americans! Auster maintains that the similarity is only superficial and that the new immigrants lack the truly "civic" culture that once defined America. He also worries that, although the new immigrants may want to assimilate, they have now reached such a critical mass that the United States has lost the ability to absorb everyone into its own, slowly dissipating culture. The result is that immigrants are encouraged to maintain and promote the cultures that they arrive with, which further dilutes the original culture of America.

For a fascinating study of the roots of American traditional culture, see David Hackett Fisher, *Albion's Seed: Four British Folkways in America* (Oxford University Press, 1989). Herbert G. Gutman's *Work, Culture, and Society in Industrializing America* (Random House, 1977) contains a number of articles that explore the "work ethic" and how it affected immigrant groups in nineteenth-century America. Ronald Takaki, *Strangers from a Different Shore: A History of Asian Americans* (Little, Brown, 1989), is a noted history of Asian immigrants that describes the racism that they faced. Stanley Lieberson and Mary C. Waters, in *From Many Strands* (Russell Sage Foundation, 1988), argue that ethnic groups with European origins are assimilating, marrying outside their groups, and losing their ethnic identities. Two major works debate whether or not immigrants, on average, economically benefit America: George Borjas, in *Friends or Strangers* (Basic Books, 1990), says that they do not, and Julian L. Simon, in *The Economic Consequences of Immigration* (Basil Blackwell, 1989), maintains that they do. Wilton S. Dillon, *The Cultural Drama: Modern Identities and Social Ferment* (Smithsonian Institution, 1974), is a collection of essays exploring the tension between cultural diversity and American identity. Lawrence E. Harrison, in "America and Its Immigrants," *National Interest* (Summer 1992), argues in favor of selective immigration, which would allow only those people with "correct" skills and values to immigrate to the United States. Fukuyama makes reference to Peter Brimelow's anti-immigration essay, "Time to Rethink Immigration," *National Review* (June 22, 1992). For an opposing viewpoint, see Ben Wattenberg and Karl Zinmeister, "The Case for More Immigration," *Commentary* (April 1990). For additional information on how immigration is affecting America, see the special issue of *Time* magazine entitled "The New Face of America: How Immigrants Are Shaping the World's First Multicultural Society" (Fall 1993).

PART 2

Sex Roles, Gender, and the Family

*The modern feminist movement has advanced the causes
of women to the point where there are now more women
in the workforce in the United States than ever before.
Professions and trades that were traditionally regarded as
the provinces of men have opened up to women, and
women now have easier access to the education and
training necessary to excel in these new areas. But is
feminism as a universal philosophy harmful in any way?
What is happening to sex roles, and what are the effects
of changing sex roles? How have related problems such
as sexual harassment and the deterioration of the
traditional family structure affected work, men and
women, and children? And how should a heterosexual
society accommodate the gay rights movement? The
issues in this part address these sorts of questions.*

- Is Feminism a Harmful Ideology?

- Is Sexual Harassment a Pervasive Problem in
  America?

- Should Homosexuality Be
  Accepted by Society?

- Should Traditional Families
  Be Preserved?

ISSUE 3

Is Feminism a Harmful Ideology?

YES: Michael Levin, from *Feminism and Freedom* (Transaction Books, 1987)

NO: Marilyn French, from *Beyond Power* (Summit Books, 1985)

ISSUE SUMMARY

YES: Professor of philosophy Michael Levin faults feminism for trying to impose an inappropriate equality on men and women that conflicts with basic biological differences between the sexes.

NO: Novelist and literary scholar Marilyn French advocates both equality between the sexes and the transformation of existing patriarchal structures to elevate feminine values to the same level as masculine values.

The publication of Betty Friedan's *The Feminine Mystique* in 1963 is generally thought of as the beginning of the modern women's movement, and since that time significant changes have occurred in American society: Occupations and professions, schools, clubs, associations, and governmental positions that were by tradition or law previously reserved for men only are now open to women. Women are found in increasing numbers among lawyers, judges, physicians, and elected officials. In 1981, then-president Ronald Reagan appointed the first woman, Sandra Day O'Connor, to the Supreme Court. In 1983, the first American woman astronaut (Sally Ride) was included in the crew of a space shuttle, and women have been on more recent space shuttle missions as well. The service academies have accepted women since 1976, and women in the military participated in the U.S. invasion of Panama in December 1989 and the Persian Gulf War in 1990–1991. There are ongoing debates in Congress and among the armed services themselves about whether or not to lift restrictions on women serving in combat. And Elizabeth Watson became the first woman to head a big-city police department when the mayor of Houston appointed her chief of police in January 1990.

These sorts of changes—quantifiable and highly publicized—may signal a change in women's roles, at least to this extent: women now engage in occupations that were previously exclusive to men, and women can pursue the necessary training and education required to do so. But three decades after Friedan's book, to what extent do females and males have equal standing? Are femininity and femaleness prized or valued the same as maleness and masculinity? What is happening to society's concepts of both? Even as changes are occurring in the public world, what is happening on a personal level to the roles of men and women? How do we value the domestic sphere? What is happening to child care? To our concept of the family?

Feminism—an ideology that, in its most basic form, directly opposes sexism by supporting gender equality and portraying women and men as equals—has been a driving force in shaping the modern women's movement. The final legal victory of the women's movement was supposed to be the passage of the Equal Rights Amendment to the Constitution (ERA), which would have made a person's sex an irrelevant distinction under the law, and which passed both houses of Congress by overwhelming margins in 1972, but it failed to win ratification from the required three-fourths of the state legislatures. The amendment was not ratified in part due to the efforts of a coalition of groups, composed overwhelmingly of women, who went to battle against it. Thus, the women's movement did not represent the views of all women; many continued to believe in the traditional gender roles.

In the readings that follow, Michael Levin argues that feminists falsely assume that women are the same as men, so their agenda of eliminating all observable social differences between men and women is doomed to fail and will inflict more pain than gain in the process. He contends that the income inequalities of men and women result largely from women's choices, not discrimination, and he objects to the citing of gender inequalities as proof of discrimination. In contrast, Marilyn French argues that the feminist agenda is a sound one that needs to be pushed further. She maintains that the innate differences between men and women cannot justify unequal treatment at the workplace and that the workplace itself must be transformed by placing women's values on a par with men's values.

YES

Michael Levin

FEMINISM AND FREEDOM

When the eighty-eight women who took the New York City Fire Department's entrance examination in 1977 failed its physical strength component, they filed a class-action sex discrimination lawsuit in federal court. The court found for the plaintiffs, agreeing in *Berkman v. NYFD* that the strength test was not job-related and therefore in violation of Title VII of the Civil Rights Act. The court thereupon ordered the city to hire forty-five female firefighters and to construct a special, less demanding physical examination for female candidates, with males still to be held to the extant, more difficult—and ostensibly inappropriate—standard. In addition, the court ordered the city to provide special training to the eighty-eight female plaintiffs—but none for the 54 percent of the males who also failed the test—on the grounds that certain "tricks of the trade" available to all male candidates were not available to them.

New York declined to appeal *Berkman* and instructed its regular firemen to maintain public silence. Since *Berkman*, 38 of the original group of 145 women given special training by the NYFD have entered service as firefighters, and almost all personnel actions taken by the NYFD have required the approval of the presiding judge, Charles Sifton. Continuing litigation has resulted in further easing of the physical standards applied to female firefighting applicants.

The use of statistics in *Berkman* is particularly instructive. According to the guidelines of the Equal Employment Opportunity Commission, which are controlling in cases like *Berkman*, a test for a job is presumed to be discriminatory if the passing rate for women is less than 80 percent of that rate for men. The wider the gap, the less defeasible is the presumption. The court accordingly asked how likely it would be, in the absence of discrimination, that none of the eighty-eight women passed while 46 percent of the men did. As the court correctly noted, "the pass rates were separated by more than eight standard deviations" (1982 at 205), and the probability that this could happen is so small—less than one in 10 trillion—as to amount to virtual impossibility. The court's conclusion that discrimination must have occurred is entirely cogent, *if strength is assumed to be uncorrelated with sex*. A difference in failure rates on a strength test is consistent with the absence of bias if it is allowed that men are on average stronger than women. The court found an outcome of fewer than thirty-seven passes unacceptably improbable because it adopted the hypothesis that gender and strength are independent variables. Rejecting the hypothesis that gender and strength are in any way connected, the court construed an observed correlation between gender and strength as an artifact to be eliminated by special treatment for one sex. Since women are the same as men, the EEOC and the court reasoned, special steps must be taken to compensate for their manifest differences....

Berkman illustrates as well the extent to which feminism has achieved its effects through the state, particularly unelected officials of the courts and the regulatory agencies, and those elected officials most remote from their constituencies. Gender quotas, limitations on free speech to combat "psychological damage to women" (to cite EEOC guidelines once again), among many other feminist innovations, are all state actions. What is more, the vagueness of such feminist-inspired initiatives as have been passed by elected officials—chiefly civil rights legislation governing gender, and the Equal Rights Amendments of various states—require that they be constantly interpreted, usually by unelected officials.

This, in short, is the thesis of the present book: It is not by accident that feminism has had its major impact through the necessarily coercive machinery of the state rather than through the private decisions of individuals. Although feminism speaks the language of liberation, self-fulfillment, options, and the removal of barriers, these phrases invariably mean their opposites and disguise an agenda at variance with the ideals of a free society.

Feminism has been presented and widely received as a liberating force, a new view of the relations between the sexes emphasizing openness and freedom from oppressive stereotypes. The burden of the present book is to show in broad theoretical perspective and factual detail that this conventional wisdom is mistaken. Feminism is an antidemocratic, if not totalitarian, ideology.

Feminism is a program for making different beings—men and women—turn out alike, and like that other egalitarian, Procrustes, it must do a good deal of chopping to fit the real world into its ideal. More precisely, feminism is the thesis that males and females are already innately alike, with the current order of things—in which males and females appear to differ and occupy quite different social roles—being a harmful distortion of this fundamental similarity. Recognizing no innate gender differences that might explain observed gender differences and the broad structure of society, feminists are compelled to interpret these manifest differences as artifacts, judged by feminists to benefit men unfairly. Believing that overtly uncoerced behavior is the product of oppression, feminists must devise ever subtler theories about the social pressures "keeping women in their place"—pressures to be detected and cancelled.

The reader may feel an impulse to object that I am talking about radical feminism while ignoring moderate feminism, a more responsible position which concedes innate sex differences and wishes only to correct wrongs undeniably done to women.... [But] I believe... that complete environmentalism—the denial that innate sex differences have anything to do with the broad structure of society—is central to feminism, and that moderate feminism is a chimera. But even the reader wishing to distinguish moderate from radical feminism must concede that *Berkman* is radical by any standards, and that if radical feminism is sufficiently influential to sway the federal judiciary, its credentials and implications deserve close scrutiny.

The second major contention of this book complements the first. If, as I argue,... those broad features of society attributed by feminism to discriminatory socialization are in fact produced by innate gender differences, efforts to eradicate those features must be futile and never-ending. Reforms designed to end when sexism disappears will have to be retained indefinitely, imposing increasingly heavy costs on their nonmalleable subjects. Since innate gender differences express themselves as differences in the typical preferences of men and women, so that people will never freely act in ways which produce a world devoid of sexism, the equalization of the sexes in personal behavior and in the work world demands implacable surveillance and interference. In the end it is impossible to overcome the biological inevitability of sex roles, but it is possible to try—and to violate liberal values in the process. A good summary of my main thesis might run: equality of outcome entails inequality of opportunity....

Despite the propensity of feminists and their commentators to frame issues in terms of the "politics" of women's status, legal reform is of interest to most feminists mainly as an instrument for working wholesale changes on society. Indifference to legal reform is in any case forced on feminists by the absence of anything to reform. Private discrimination against women has been illegal since 1964, and public discrimination at the state and municipal levels has been illegal since 1972. When at the behest of President Ronald Reagan the State of Georgia reviewed its statutes for possible discrimination, it reported that the most serious inequity in the state code was the occurrence of 10,000 "he's" as against 150 "she's." Popular discourse continues to allude to "much outright sex discrimination," but the examples of discrimination cited invariably concern the use of criteria in various activities that men are more likely to meet. Without some showing that these criteria are deployed *for the purpose* of excluding women, or that the discrepant effects of these criteria are *caused by* arbitrary socialization, these effects are not "discriminatory." The actual state of affairs is well illustrated by *Berkman*: extensive institutionalized preference favoring women over men. Feminists who explain their grievance in terms of laws against women driving buses may have a legitimate case, but it is one against Edwardian England, not a society in which female bus drivers are promoted over males with greater seniority.

To be sure, the claim that women do not yet enjoy equal opportunity is most frequently made not in connection with legal barriers but in terms of the tendency of people to think sex-stereotypically and to communicate sex-typed norms to the young. This claim will be considered in due course, but it suffices for now to reflect that, if the formation of stereotypic beliefs is a spontaneous response to perceptions of the world, altering these possibly oppressive beliefs will require manipulation of both the average person's spontaneous tendency to form beliefs and the social environment which prompts them. If the social environment is itself a spontaneous expression of innate sex differences, attempting (and inevitably failing) to alter this environment will require yet further intrusion.

Shifting the locus of unfairness from the realm of law to that of sex role stereotyping involves a shift from what can reasonably be called "political" to the entire range of extra-political institutions and behavior. Most of society's institutions emerge from the myriad uncoordinated decisions of individuals; to call these practices and institutions "political" suggests a disregard for the distinction between public and private and disdain for the private realm itself. It is not surprising that feminists who use the word "political" so expansively also speak as if they believe in an actual worldwide conspiracy against women. Once this usage is adopted, everything from office flirtation to children's horseplay becomes assessable for its tendency to abet the political decision about women's condition. Erstwhile private matters become questions of socially determined rights, and are pulled within the authority of the state.

To deny that women are victims of systematic discrimination is not to assert that contemporary Western civilization is perfect....

The reader may be anxious to inform me of cases known to him of a competent woman being denied a desirable position just because she is a woman. I do not deny that such cases exist, but I ask the reader to remember three points. First, no accumulation of anecdotes can demonstrate an intrinsic societal bias against women. Second, a social arrangement can do no more than treat people better than other possible arrangements; perfect justice is unattainable. Third, the wrongs with which the reader is acquainted must be kept in perspective.

Can being denied a merited promotion honestly be compared to being beaten for drinking from a Whites-only fountain, the sort of treatment Blacks experienced two generations ago?...

As groundless as the idea that feminism is a movement of liberal reform is the idea that it is passé. The immoderate language of twenty years ago is encountered less frequently today, but no doctrine is more influential in shaping institutional and public life than feminism. Under current federal law, a prospective employer is forbidden to ask a female job applicant if she plans to have children. The Supreme Court has outlawed pension plans that use the greater longevity of women as a factor in computing premiums....

Political leaders of every persuasion reflexively employ gender quotas. The liberal governor of New York State reprimanded a selection committee for not including a female among its candidates for the state's Supreme Court while simultaneously praising all the candidates as "first-rate." A conservative president highly critical of quotas as a private citizen decided that his first Supreme Court appointment had to be a woman.... [T]he quota mentality now dominates all phases of employment....

The popular press continues to suggest that wanting to marry and raise children is a curious goal for a woman. It is becoming somewhat more acceptable for a woman to find parenting important, but it is still unacceptable to assert that it is more important for a woman than for a man....

Gender differences will emerge in any human social organization. Since every human activity is either the province of one sex or a joint endeavor of both in which these differences manifest themselves, it is possible to find sexism everywhere. While in that sense feminism conflicts with every human activity, the present book concentrates on the conflict between feminism and those institutions central to a free society. Among the most important are the free market and education. The only way to stifle, or try to stifle, the manifestation of gender differences in people's working lives is through a rigid program of job quotas and pay scales.... The only way to stifle, or try to stifle, the manifestation of gender differences in children's perceptions of each other is through a rigid program of exhorting them to disregard their senses....

THE UNIVERSALITY OF MALE DOMINANCE AND SEX-ROLE DIFFERENTIATION

No student of human behavior denies the male advantage in dominance-aggression and its universal correlate, preparedness to use force. After a determinedly skeptical review of the literature, [Eleanor E.] Maccoby and [Carol N.] Jacklin conclude that "the male's greater aggression has a biological component," as evidenced by boys' greater indulgence in mock fighting and "aggressive fantasies," and the greater aggressiveness of male primates....

Every society that has ever existed has associated familial authority with the male and conferred the overwhelming majority of positions of power on males. Efforts to eliminate these features in Israel, Sweden, and the Soviet Union have failed. Male dominance and the sexual division of labor are observed among such reputedly uncorrupted people as the !Kung. !Kung juvenile playgroups are single-sex; boys spend far more time than girls in exploring technology (e.g.

digging up termite mounds with arrows) and play rough-and-tumble play. !Kung men hunt and !Kung women gather; although what the women gather accounts for most of the tribe's calories and protein, hunting enjoys greater prestige. Margaret Mead remarked in *Male and Female:* "In every known society, the male's need for achievement can be recognized."...

The male advantage in dominance-aggression makes patriarchy inevitable because men will always strive harder than women to reach the top of hierarchies they encounter, and create hierarchies to reach the top of if none exist. Just as the social structure of a gorilla band does not exist apart from the tendencies of individual gorillas to react to each other in various ways, hierarchies exist because of the relational dispositions of individual human beings. That men monopolize leadership positions because they try harder to get them does not mean that men deserve these positions or that men do a better job in them than women would do if they became leaders. The only sense in which male dominance is "right" is that it expresses the free choices of individual men to strive for positions of power and the free choices of individual women to do other things.... [A]ttempts to eliminate patriarchy within a group must sharply limit the freedom of the group's members, and can only be undertaken from without by a stronger group of men....

THE FREE MARKET AND FEMINISM

Judged historically, the free market is the most successful economic arrangement. Permitting people to trade and associate freely for productive purposes has created unparalleled prosperity, along with support for the democratic institutions on which other forms of individual liberty have been found to depend. It is inevitable that feminists reject the free market, however, because they must interpret the expressions of sex differences facilitated by the freedom of the market as products of adverse socialization and discrimination.

Certainly, the observed differences between male and female labor market behavior are not in dispute; men and women do different sorts of work, and women earn lower average wages. It is also widely agreed that the immediate cause of these differences are differences in the motives which lead men and women into the labor market. Most married working women work to supplement their husband's income, which is regarded as the mainstay of the family budget. Working mothers are expected to care for their children as well, or at any rate to supervise the arrangements for their care, an expectation that does not fall nearly so heavily upon fathers. Unmarried women often see work as an interregnum between school and marriage. For these reasons, women gravitate to jobs permitting easy entry, exit and re-entry to and from the workforce. Nor, finally, is it seriously questioned that men tend to seek (although of course not always find) more prestigious jobs and to try to "get ahead" more than women do. In short, men and women invest their human capital differently.

As always, the question is why these things are so. Feminist theory takes them to be consequences of oppression....

This theory is contradicted by the close match between many of the major differences in skills brought by men and women to the workplace and a number of the innate differences discussed [earlier]. Together with the greater innate dominance-aggression of men, which manifests itself economically as greater competitiveness, this match strongly suggests that differences in workplace behavior are not best explained as products of the denial of equal opportunity....

Some innate sex differences correlate closely with aptitude for specific occupations, many of them prestigious, remunerative, and important in industrial society. Spatial ability is requisite for pipe fitting, technical drawing, and wood working, and is the most important component of mechanical ability. Only about 20 percent of girls in the elementary grades reach the average level of male performance on tests of spatial ability, and, according to the U.S. Employment Service, all classes of engineering and drafting as well as a high proportion of scientific and technical occupations require spatial ability in the top 10 percent of the U.S. population. While one should normally be chary of explaining any social phenomenon *directly* in terms of some innate gender dimorphism, male domination of the technical and engineering professions is almost certainly due to the male's innate cognitive advantage rather than to a culturally induced female disadvantage....

However, if one assumes that women would, given the opportunity, be as interested in and as suited for virtually the same work as men, one is compelled to interpret the continuing statistical segregation of the work force as evidencing discrimination....

QUOTAS

Once discrimination is separated from intent, and it is assumed that there should be as many women as men in some position, it becomes natural to seek to replace previously used criteria, including merit (or what employers have regarded as merit) with quotas. . . .

Gender quotas are at this writing the most pervasive influence of feminism on the American economy, although comparable worth has the potential to supersede them. Decisions about employment, union contracts, apprenticeships, admission to professional schools, and the casting and directing of motion pictures are made with an eye toward sex (and skin color). . . .

Quotas deny benefits and impose burdens on individuals not responsible for any wrongs. They cannot be justified as compensation, inspiration, or prevention, and they decrease economic efficiency. . . .

THE FAMILY

[According to feminism,] the family under patriarchy is a one-sided bargain in which the wife settles for exploitation, brutality, rape, incest, and madness. . . .

The idea that marriage is a spontaneous bond between naturally complementary partners is dismissed out of hand. There is nothing good whatever to be said about male impulses, and the asymmetries of marriage are understood exclusively in terms of the husband's superior physical strength. . . .

Only complete ignorance of male emotions can account for the belief that men invented marriage to force the sexual compliance of women. . . . For most men, sexual arousal vanishes without reciprocation. Even prostitutes find it useful to feign involvement. It would be psychologically impossible for the average man to meet his sexual needs by regularly forcing himself on an unwilling woman. . . .

After increasing for twenty years, the divorce rate has stabilized at the high rate of nearly 5 per 1,000 people in the U.S. One out of two new marriages ends in divorce. This phenomenon has many causes, of which feminism may itself be a further effect, but feminism's ongoing diabolization of marriage is almost certainly a factor. Divorce has been made socially and psychologically more acceptable by the idea that it is a reasonable response to a defective and dying institution. Increased rates of divorce create a feedback loop in which many divorced women embrace a theory which absolves them of blame for an emotional shambles. There are bound to be people for whom the normal frictions of marriage are made unendurable by the message that marriage is oppression. Finally, while I do not see how this could be verified statistically, it seems to me beyond doubt that many households of marriages and affairs vectoring toward marriage have been ruined as couples have tried to conform their sex lives to feminist imperatives. . . .

Feminist ideology encourages a variety of other pressures against marriage. Rates of childlessness, divorce and failure to marry rise steeply for women in careers; to the extent that women are encouraged to pursue careers and defer children, they are being encouraged to be single. There is the related message that women ought to learn to be independent of men. A prominent theme in rationales for non-traditional vocational training for girls is that women will be alone for a good part of their lives, that "millions of women are a divorce away from destitution," and that men are unreliable.

NO

Marilyn French

FEMINISM

Feminism is the only serious, coherent, and universal philosophy that offers an alternative to patriarchal thinking and structures. Feminists believe in a few simple tenets. They believe that women are human beings, that the two sexes are (at least) equal in all significant ways, and that this equality must be publicly recognized. They believe that qualities traditionally associated with women—the feminine principle—are (at least) equal in value to those traditionally associated with men—the masculine principle—and that this equality must be publicly recognized. (I modify these statements with *at least* because some feminists believe in the superiority of women and "feminine" qualities. Indeed, it is difficult not to stress the value of the "feminine" in our culture because it is so pervasively debased and diminished.) Finally, feminists believe the personal is the political—that is, that the value structure of a culture is identical in both public and private areas, that what happens in the bedroom has everything to do with what happens in the boardroom, and vice versa, and that, mythology notwithstanding, at present the same sex is in control in both places.

There are also those who believe they consider women equal to men, but see women as fettered by their traditional socialization and by the expectations of the larger world. These people see women as large children who have talent and energy, but who need training in male modes, male language, and an area of expertise in order to "fit in" in the male world. One philosopher, for example, has commented that women are *not yet ready* for top government posts. This is not just patronizing; it shows a lack of comprehension of feminism. For although feminists do indeed want women to become part of the structure, participants in public institutions; although they want access for women to decision-making posts, and a voice in how society is managed, *they do not want women to assimilate to society as it presently exists but to change it.* Feminism is not yet one more of a series of political movements demanding for their adherents access to existing structures and their rewards. This is how many people see it, however: as a strictly political movement through which women demand entry into the "male" world, a share of male prerogatives, and the chance to be like men. This perception of feminism alienates many nonfeminist women.

Feminism is a political movement demanding access to the rewards and responsibilities of the "male" world, but it is more: it is a revolutionary moral movement, intending to use political power to transform society, to "feminize" it. For such a movement, assimilation is death. The assimilation of women to society as it presently exists would lead simply to the inclusion of certain women (not all, because society as it presently exists is highly stratified) along with certain men in its higher echelons. It would mean continued stratification and continued contempt for "feminine" values. Assimilation would be the cooption of feminism. Yet it must be admitted that the major success of the movement in the past twenty years has been to increase the assimilation of women into the existing structure. This is not to be deplored, but it is only a necessary first step.

There have been many revolutions against various patriarchal forms over the past three or four thousand years, but in each case, what has succeeded an oppressive structure is another oppressive structure. This is inevitable because, regardless of the initial ideas and ideals of rebellious groups, they come to worship power above all: only power, they believe, can overwhelm power; only their greater power can bring them victory over an "enemy" that is the Father. But each victory has increased the power of the *idea* of power, thus each victory has increased human oppression. . . .

If women and men were seen as equal, if male self-definition no longer depended upon an inferior group, other stratifications would also become unnecessary. Legitimacy (which has no meaning without the idea of illegitimacy) would no longer be a useful concept, and its disappearance from human minds would lead to the establishment of new structures for social organization. These structures would blur the distinction between public and private spheres, a distinction that was originally created not only to exclude women from a male (public) arena, but to permit discourse which ignored and effectively eliminated from existence the parts of all lives that are bound to nature, that are necessary and nonvolitional. If public and private life were integrated, it would no longer seem incongruous to discuss procreation and weapons systems in the same paragraph. Since pleasure would be the primary value of both personal and public life, harmony (which produces pleasure) would be a universal societal goal, and would no longer have to be manufactured in the ersatz form of coerced uniformity, conformity. Love too would regain its innocence, since it would not be coerced into playing a role within a power structure and thus functioning as an oppression—as it often does in our world.

The foregoing is a sketch of feminist beliefs. It is difficult at present to provide more than a sketch, for to create truly feminist programs we must rid our heads of the power notions that fill them, and that cannot be done in a generation, or even several generations. The sketch may sound utopian: I think it is not. That is, I believe such a world is possible for humans to maintain, to live within, once it is achieved. What may be utopian is the idea that we can achieve it. For to displace power as the highest human value means to supersede patriarchal modes while eschewing traditional power maneuvers as a means. But it is impossible to function in the public world without using power maneuvers; and revolution does imply overthrow of current systems.

Two elements cast a friendly light on feminist goals. One is that the movement is not aimed at overthrow of any particular government or structure, but at the displacement of one way of thinking by another. The other is that feminism offers desirable goals. The first means that the tools of feminism are naturally nonviolent: it moves and will continue to move by influencing people, by offering a vision, by providing an alternative to the cul-de-sacs of patriarchy. The second means that feminism is in a state I call blessed: its ends and its means are identical. Feminism increases the wellbeing of its adherents, and so can appeal to others on grounds of the possibility of greater felicity. Integration of the self, which means using the full range of one's gifts, increases one's sense of well-being; if integration of one's entire life is not always possible because of the nature of the public world, it is a desirable goal. Patriarchy, which in all its forms requires some kind of self-sacrifice, denial, or repression in the name of some higher good which is rarely (if ever) achieved on earth, stresses nobility, superiority, and victory, the satisfaction of a final triumph. Feminism requires use of the entire self in the name of present well-being, and stresses integrity, community, and the *jouissance* of present experience....

It was probably Betty Friedan's *The Feminine Mystique*, published in 1963, that first galvanized American women into action. Women legislators had seen to it that laws passed to redress wrongs done to blacks were expanded to include women. The Equal Pay Act was passed in 1963; the Civil Rights Act in 1965. Title VII of the latter prohibited discrimination on grounds of sex, race, color, religion, or national origin. The word *sex* was included as a result of maneuvers by Representative Martha Griffiths, Senator Margaret Chase Smith, and a reporter, Mae Craig. In 1965 the Supreme Court held that laws banning contraceptives were unconstitutional, and in 1966 a federal court declared that an Alabama law barring women from juries violated the Fourteenth Amendment (guaranteeing equal protection under the law). In that year too, the National Organization for Woman was founded....

The decade that followed was enormously fertile; the seeds planted then are still bearing fruit. Women scholars began to delve into women's history, to break away from male interpretations and lay the groundwork for an alternative view of anthropology, psychology, sociology, philosophy, and language. Politically oriented groups pressed for legislation granting women equality in education, housing, credit, and promotion and hiring. Other women established feminist magazines, journals, publishing houses, and bookstores. Some strove for political office; some entered the newly open "male" world of business and industry. In the exhilaration of that period, women who had felt crippled found limbs, women who had felt marginal found a center, women who had felt alone found sisters.

It is now less than twenty years since the rising of the "second wave." The difference is astonishing. Women are now working in hundreds of jobs that were closed to them in the past. Women can sign leases, buy cars and houses, obtain credit; they cannot be denied telephone service because they are divorced. They can be seated in restaurants although they are dining without a man. Although some women's fashions still inhibit mobility, they are no longer *de rigueur*. Women are no longer expected to produce elaborate entertainments: life can be easier, more leisurely, for both sexes.

Most important of all, women now possess reproductive freedom. Although men have long had access to condoms, which were and are sold over the counter in every drugstore, women needed doctors' prescriptions to purchase diaphragms and, later, the birth control pill. This is still true, but such prescriptions are widely available now, and women do not have to be married to obtain them. (In France, where men can also obtain condoms easily, women could not purchase contraceptive devices in drugstores until 1967, and such purchases still require the authorization of the minister of social affairs.) Clearly, it is not birth control—or, more accurately, the prevention of conception—per se that is offensive to patriarchal culture, but the placing of that control in the hands of women. Despite continuing attempts to wrest it from them, American women are likely to hold on to this right over their own bodies. But in some Western nations—Ireland, for example—they still do not possess it.

The difference is great for a huge number of women, and because the difference permeates their lives, change may seem complete. But in the scale of things, the change is minimal. Capitalism, under great pressure for almost a hundred and fifty years, has yielded women about what socialism yielded them immediately. But it has managed—as has socialism—to retain its essential character. Capitalism has assimilated women, it has not broadened itself; it has swallowed women rather than alter itself. And it has done this in accordance with its traditional structures. Thus the women who have benefited most from

the changes are well-educated, white, middle-class women, often without children. Thus the divisiveness of racism has pervaded the women's movement itself. Thus women have by and large been kept out of the most sensitive and powerful areas of business and government, so that they have not achieved a voice in the running of our society. And thus women who have not managed to live like men, or with them, have been condemned to the lowest rank in our society: women are the new poor. It is not an exaggeration to say that although feminism in capitalist states has freed many women and improved the lives of others, it has had little effect on the patriarchy, which has simply absorbed a few women who appear acceptable to its purposes, and barred the door for the rest....

[T]he gap between male and female earnings has increased. According to the last census, the mean income of white females was $10,244 (59 cents of a white male dollar), of black females $9,476 (54 cents of a white male dollar), and of Hispanic females $8,466 (49 cents of a white male dollar). Despite differences in the concerns and approaches of women of color and white women, in the realm of economics, women as a caste comprise a lower class.

The poor of America are women: the poor of the world are women. In 1980, in America, the median adjusted income for men was $12,530, for women it was $4,920. In 1980 the poverty level was $8,414 for a nonfarm family of four, and nearly thirty million Americans live beneath it. Seventy percent of these are white, 30 percent black—and we may note that only 12 percent of the population is black—two thirds of them women and children. If we limit these figures to adults, two out of every three poor adults are female. If present trends continue, by the year 2000 the poor of America will be entirely its women.

There are a number of reasons for this. A presidential report published in 1981 claims that women are "systematically underpaid," that "women's work" pays about four thousand dollars a year less than men's work, and that occupational segregation is more pronounced by sex than by race: 70 percent of men and 54 percent of women are concentrated in jobs done only by those of their own sex.

Because women are still held responsible—by themselves and by men—for raising the children, they are forced to take jobs that are close to home, that offer flexible hours (like waitressing), or are part-time; jobs that do not require extended traveling or long hours. They are not able to "compete" in a job market that demands single-minded devotion to work, fast running on a narrow track. For some this is a tolerable situation: some women are not notably ambitious, prefer a balanced life, and have working husbands. But this is not the case for all, or even most, women.

More women than ever in the period covered by American record keeping on this point are living without men: they are single mothers, divorced mothers, and widows, as well as single working women. The reasons for this are complex. Two major reasons, however, are the movement for "sexual liberation" and the feminist movement.

The movement for "sexual liberation" begun in the 1950s was a male campaign, rooted in ideas that seem for the most part honest and beneficial: that sex was good, the body was good; that trading sexual access for financial support degraded sex and the body; that virginity was a ques-tionable good in women and not at all necessary in men; and that the requirement of sexual fidelity in marriage was an oppression. However, the campaign was also extremely self-serving: it was not based on a philosophy that saw a joyous sex life as one element in a life concerned with the pleasure and the good of self and others. It was not a responsible movement: in fact it "masculinized" sex by making it a commodity and by isolating sex from other elements intrinsic to it—affection, connection, and the potential for procreation. To speak lightly, what the sexual revolution accomplished was to change the price of sexual access to a woman from marriage to a dinner.

At the same time, the ties of marriage lost their force—for men. As of 1963, almost all divorces sought in America were initiated (whether openly or not) by men. Divorce—like marriage—is morally neutral. Insofar as it ends a relationship of misery, it is a good; insofar as it ends a long-term intimacy, it is to be lamented. Even when a marriage involves children, it cannot be pre-judged: divorce may be better for the children than the marriage was. It seems reasonable to assume that if one party to a marriage wants a divorce, divorce should occur. But marriage and divorce are both tied to responsibility, and it was this tie that was broken by the "sexual liberation" movement.

If a man—and society in general—requires a woman to set aside ideas of an individual life, and to accept the role of functionary—wife, mother, housekeeper—without payment, then that role must be structured to guarantee that woman a secure life despite her unpaid labor. In cognizance of this contract, traditional divorce laws stipulated alimony. Laws did not, of course, prevent men from abandoning their families completely, or failing in alimony payments. But the new sexual morality was growing in the sixties, a period when feminists were struggling to gain the right to paid employment above the national level, and when many women who had gained such work were initiating divorce themselves. The thinking of legislators and judges underwent an amazing swift change. The new assumption was that women worked, that they earned as much as men, and thus that they did not require alimony—which is rarely granted now, and even more rarely paid. In 1979, only 14 percent of all divorced or separated women were granted alimony or child support, and of those at least 30 percent did not receive what they were awarded.

This situation is unjust to women who have accepted lesser jobs to help their husbands through school, or given up fellowships or promotions to accompany a husband to his new job. It is appallingly unjust to women who have neglected their own potential careers to care for husbands and children. But it becomes outrageous when we consider the statistics (if we need statistics, many women are too well acquainted with the reality behind them) on men's support of their children after divorce.

Although some very rich men use the power of their wealth to take the children away from their mothers after divorce, most men who divorce leave not just a marriage but a family. Men father children; although the degree to which they participate in childraising varies, it seems likely that they have some love and concern for those children. Nevertheless, after divorce they often disappear: they contribute neither emotion, time, nor money to the care of their own children. More than 90 percent of children who live with one parent live with their mothers; in 1978 there were 7.1 million single mothers with custody of their children in the United States. The number of men raising children on their own declined in the decade of the seventies. "The result of divorce, in an overwhelming number of cases, is that men become singles and women become single mothers." Women's incomes decline by 73 percent in the first year after divorce; men's incomes *increase* by 42 percent. The father is better off, the children are often hungry.

In recent years judges have tended not to award child support to mothers with custody; they have denied it to 41 percent of such mothers. Studies of the amounts awarded vary, ranging from as low as an average of $539 per year to an average of $2,110. But over 50 percent of custodial mothers never receive the amounts due them. Lenore Weitzman's research in California shows that only 13 percent of women with custody of preschool children receive alimony; child support payments (even when they are made) are almost never enough to cover the cost of raising small children....

The women's movement under capitalism has worked almost unbelievably hard and made large gains. Those gains are changes in law and custom, and they affect all women, although they have their greatest effect on middle-class educated women. But feminism has not been able to budge an intransigent establishment bent on destroying the globe; it has not moved us one inch closer to the feminization of society. Indeed, it seems to lose ground with every decade, as the nourishing, procreative, communal, emotional dimensions of experience are increasingly ground into dust, as high technology and more intense pursuit of power are increasingly exalted.

This situation constitutes a quandary for feminists. Only by bringing great numbers of women with feminist values into the institutional structure of the nation can women achieve a voice in the way this country is run. Only by unified political action can women influence the course of the future. But at present, and for the foreseeable future, women are carefully screened, hired in small numbers, and watched for deviance. Women hired by institutions are far more likely to be coopted by institutional policy than to change it; they will assimulate or be fired

or quit. Some feminist groups oppose women's efforts to enter the establishment on the ground that women should not contribute to a structure that is sexist, racist, and dedicated to profit and power. On the other hand, to refuse to enter the establishment is to refuse even to try to change it from within and thus to accept the marginal position women have traditionally held. To refuse to enter American institutions may also be to doom oneself to poverty, and poverty is silent and invisible. It has no voice and no face.

For this problem, as for so many others, there is no clear right answer.

POSTSCRIPT

Is Feminism a Harmful Ideology?

"Feminism," says Levin, "is the thesis that males and females are already innately alike." Not so, says French. In her view, feminism insists that the sexes are *not* alike: there are distinctly "feminine values"—nurturance, cooperation, nonviolence—that are quite different from the aggressive ways of men, and feminism is an organized effort to force American institutions to give "the feminine principle" the recognition it deserves. But if that is so, how would French stand on the issue of the New York City fire department's entrance exam discussed by Levin? If there are inherent value differences between men and women that should be given institutional recognition, shouldn't our institutions also take cognizance of the inherent *physical* differences between the sexes? This is a problem for feminist theory, though perhaps not an insuperable one, for on some level all sides agree that there are gender differences; the question really turns upon *which* differences should be considered relevant in the workplace.

French advocates more than just equality. She demands the transformation of society to institutionalize feminine values. Levin, on the other hand, argues that the feminist agenda is "at variance with the ideals of a free society" because it "is a program for making different beings—men and women—turn out alike." As a result it uses the law to force equalizing changes that most women (as well as most men) do not want.

Over the past 30 years, there has been a deluge of books, articles, and periodicals devoted to expounding feminist positions. Among the earliest feminist publications was Betty Friedan's book *The Feminine Mystique* (W. W. Norton, 1963). Friedan later wrote *The Second Stage* (Summit Books, 1981), which was less antagonistic to men and more accepting of motherhood and traditional women's roles. An analysis of the current status of the women's movement is Susan Faludi's *Backlash: The Undeclared War on American Women* (Crown Publishers, 1991). An analytical and historical discussion of women's movements over the past century and a half is provided by Steven M. Buechler in *Women's Movements in the United States: Suffrage, Equal Rights, and Beyond* (Rutgers University Press, 1990). A general work on the position of women in American society is Jessie Bernard, *The Female World* (Free Press, 1981).

Antifeminist works are rarer. Nicholas Davidson charges that it is "extremely difficult to find a publisher for a work critical of feminism"; see Davidson's *The Failure of Feminism* (Prometheus Books, 1988). Still, anyone seeking antifeminist arguments may look to Maggie Gallagher's *Enemies of Eros* (Chicago, 1993), Midge Decter's *The New Chastity and Other Arguments Against Women's Liberation* (Putnam, 1974), George Gilder's *Sexual Suicide* (Times Books, 1973), and Phyllis Schlafly's *The Power of Positive Woman* (Arlington House, 1977).

ISSUE 4

Is Sexual Harassment a Pervasive Problem in America?

YES: Ellen Bravo and Ellen Cassedy, from *The 9to5 Guide to Combating Sexual Harassment* (John Wiley & Sons, 1992)

NO: Gretchen Morgenson, from "May I Have the Pleasure," *National Review* (November 18, 1991)

ISSUE SUMMARY

YES: Ellen Bravo, the executive director of 9to5, the National Association of Working Women, and her colleague Ellen Cassedy argue that women in every profession are subjected to sexual harassment and that corporations must take steps to curtail the problem.

NO: Gretchen Morgenson, senior editor of *Forbes* magazine, argues that the notion of pervasive sexual harassment in the workplace is largely the product of hype by an "anti-harassment industry" and its supporters.

Relations between the sexes and society's expectations concerning men's and women's roles have changed considerably over the past 30 years. Indeed, some sociologists argue that this area has witnessed some of the most significant social changes in our time. For women, one aspect of their changing roles has been increased participation in the paid labor force and the increased likelihood that they view their work experience as a career. It is within this work context that we look at the issue of sexual harassment—a relatively new term that came into popular usage in the period 1975–1980.

Rape and sexual assault have always been outlawed in the United States, but these offenses involve physical acts. Sexual harassment need not; it can consist of words, gestures, even facial expressions. Sexual harassment occupied headlines in the fall of 1991: during Senate confirmation hearings on Supreme Court justice nominee Judge Clarence Thomas, law professor Anita Hill charged that she had been sexually harassed by Thomas when she worked for him. Thomas had served for a time as head of the Equal Employment Opportunity Commission (EEOC), which over a decade ago was the federal agency responsible for developing workplace guidelines on sexual harassment. In 1980 the EEOC defined sexual harassment as any "unwelcome sexual conduct that is a term or condition of employment," and the EEOC ruled that it constituted a form of sexual discrimination outlawed by Title VII of the Civil Rights Act of 1964. This raises a tricky question: What is "unwelcome" behavior? It seems to vary with time, place, and social circles. Certain kinds of male behavior that were not uncommon in the 1950s—whistling, winking, or commenting on a woman's figure—are taboo in enlightened circles today, though perhaps not everywhere in America.

In defining sexual harassment, the EEOC delineated two basic types. The first type is the *quid pro quo* (something for something) variety, in which an employer or some other empowered individual in the workplace suggests to an employee that sexual favors will be rewarded while withholding sexual favors will be punished. The second general category of sexual harassment defined by the EEOC is the so-called *hostile environment:* The boss or co-workers engage in sexually oriented behavior that unreasonably interferes with an employee's job performance. Such behavior might include sexual ridicule, sexual pranks, and the use of sexually charged words or gestures that threaten or demean. The importance of this second form of sexual harassment was underscored by the U.S. Supreme Court in a 1986 decision, *Meritor Savings Bank v. Vinson.* The Court said that to win a sexual harassment suit, an employee does not have to prove quid pro quo; it is enough if she can prove that she was subjected to a hostile working environment.

The Court's conclusion caused little debate, yet even some of those whose business it is to guard against sexual harassment admit that there is danger of pushing its application too far. In its 1980 guidelines the EEOC warned, "Because sexual attraction may often play a role in the day-to-day social exchange between employees," the distinction between sexual conduct that is uninvited but not necessarily unwelcome and clearly unwelcome sexual conduct is sometimes difficult to discern, "but this distinction is essential because sexual conduct becomes unlawful only when it is unwelcome." The distinction is useful, but it raises questions of its own. *How* unwelcome must conduct be to constitute a violation? In what ways should "unwelcomeness" be expressed? If certain types of behavior are tolerated by the victims, does that mean that we can assume it to be welcome—or at least not too "unwelcome"—by EEOC standards?

Beyond the legal definition of sexual harassment is the larger question of how men and women should relate to one another in today's workplace. In the selections that follow, Ellen Bravo and Ellen Cassedy maintain that combating sexual harassment will help promote mutual respect among men and women and that the extent to which sexual harassment occurs in the workplace has only recently begun to come to light. Gretchen Morgenson argues that women are strong enough to handle dirty remarks, whistles, and requests for dates, and that the limits of the tolerable are being overly constricted by an "anti-harassment industry" and its supporters.

YES

Ellen Bravo and
Ellen Cassedy

THE 9TO5 GUIDE TO COMBATING SEXUAL HARASSMENT

INTRODUCTION

*A project manager went to her boss's office to pick up her paycheck. "Come and get it,"
he crooned and pointed to the envelope he'd tucked into the fly of his trousers.*

*A supervisor observed a group of male workers laughing over a postcard depicting a nude
woman having sex with a goat. Later he saw one of the men slip the postcard into the
locker of a new female hire. The supervisor didn't know what to do. "If I make an issue of
it," he said, "I'm afraid either her neck is going to be on the line or mine is."*

*A group of graphic artists couldn't believe their ears one evening. A coworker had turned
up the volume on his tape player and was broadcasting the gang rape scene from a
pornographic movie.*

The project manager, the supervisor, and the graphic artists are some of
the more than 100,000 employees and employers who have telephoned
the toll-free 9to5 Job Problem Hotline since it was established in 1989....
Among those reporting problems and receiving advice have been beauti-
cians, supervisors, sales representatives, medical assistants, factory workers,
teachers, cashiers, waitresses, library workers, computer operators, executive
secretaries, therapists, bartenders, bakers, and zookeepers—as well as one
symphony-orchestra manager, one oil-rig supervisor, and one topless dancer.

They call about unequal pay and unsafe computer equipment, pensions
and maternity leave, who serves the coffee, and how to get promoted. Some
tell of being asked to perform bizarre tasks—to sharpen 1,400 pencils, one
right after the other; or to snip the boss's nose hairs, to clean his dentures, or
to carry his urine specimen, still warm, to the lab.

And some call about sexual harassment. Ever since 9to5 was founded in
1973 to give voice to working women's concerns, unwelcome sexual attention
at the workplace has been viewed within the organization as a significant and
disturbing issue.

Harassment Goes Public

When 9to5 began, the problem of unwanted sexual attention at work had no name and little visibility. Neither corporate nor government leaders were expected to worry about what some men were doing to annoy some hapless (and, in their eyes, probably provocative) women. The issue was seen as a trivial matter involving nothing more than individual personality conflicts and office etiquette. The term *sexual harassment* didn't yet exist—the courts were years away from recognizing the concept.

But the two decades that followed saw big changes. Millions of women entered the workplace and stayed—because they had to. (A full 58 percent of women workers are single, divorced, widowed, separated, or married to men who earn less than $15,000.) Once women were firmly established in the labor force in large and growing numbers, the problem of sexual harassment began to come out of the closet.

The term itself was popularized in such books as Lin Farley's *Sexual Shakedown: The Sexual Harassment of Women on the Job* (McGraw-Hill, 1978) and Catharine A. MacKinnon's *Sexual Harassment of Working Women: A Case of Sex Discrimination* (Yale University Press, 1979). Pressure grew for a solution. Speakouts and public hearings were held. Women's magazines and other media sources publicized the issue. Lawsuits moved through the courts. The government, academia, and some corporate leaders began to take the problem seriously. Still, in most workplaces and across the nation as a whole, the issue remained nearly invisible—until October of 1991. Public awareness of sexual harassment then took a giant step forward.

The Clarence Thomas Hearings: Did He or Didn't He?

In October 1991, the Senate Judiciary Committee completed hearings to consider President Bush's nomination of conservative Appellate Judge Clarence Thomas to the Supreme Court. The nomination appeared headed for easy approval on the Senate floor. Then, two days before the scheduled vote, a startling challenge to Thomas's character arose. A radio reporter learned that the FBI had interviewed a former government lawyer, Anita Hill. She told investigators that, a decade earlier, when Thomas was her boss, he had repeatedly subjected her to unwelcome sexual attention. He'd insisted on discussing sex and pornographic movies, Hill said, and pressured her for dates.

Informed by the FBI of Hill's allegations, the Senate Judiciary Committee had decided not to pursue them. But once the story hit the media, a public outcry led the committee to reconvene. Throughout the Columbus Day weekend, millions of Americans spent hours in front of the television watching committee members contend with the graphic and gruesome details of sexual harassment.

Thomas steadfastly denied Hill's allegations, the Senate approved his nomination, and he was appointed Associate Justice of the Supreme Court. But the storm stirred up by Hill's charges wasn't over. Throughout the country, sexual harassment became a matter of heated discussion....

A Pervasive Problem

As a result of the hearings, even those who weren't sure what to think about Anita Hill and Clarence Thomas learned that sexual harassment is a pervasive problem. It happens to women in every profession from waitress to corporate executive. It occurs at every level of the corporate hierarchy and in every kind of business and industry. It's carried out by superiors and subordinates, coworkers and clients. Some men are also sexually harassed, though on a far smaller scale. (To avoid cumbersome language, the victim is often referred to here as "she" and the harasser and employer as "he.")

• In a survey of federal employees conducted by the U.S. Merit Protection Services Board in 1980, 42 percent of females and 15 percent of males said they'd been harassed on the job. A follow-up survey in 1987 yielded nearly identical results.

• Since 1980, more than 38,500 charges of sexual harassment have been filed with the federal government.

• In a 1990 study of 20,000 military employees conducted by the Department of Defense, 64 percent of the females and 17 percent of the males said they'd been harassed.

• In numerous corporate studies carried out by management consultant Freada Klein, at least 15 percent of women employees said they'd been harassed within the past 12 months.

• In a 1987 study, 37 percent of women at the Department of Labor said they'd been sexually harassed on the job.

• In a 1989 study, the National Law Journal found that of 3,000 women lawyers at 250 top law firms, 60 percent had been harassed at some point in their careers.

• A survey of United Nations employees showed 50 percent of women and 31 percent of men had experienced or witnessed harassment by higher-ups.

• Nearly half of the 832 working women in researcher Barbara Gutek's 1985 study said they'd been harassed. None had taken any legal action. Only 22 percent had ever told anybody about the harassment.

• In a 1988 survey of Fortune 500 companies conducted by *Working Woman* magazine, almost 90 percent of the respondents reported receiving complaints of harassment. More than a third had been sued.

• In a poll released in 1991 by the National Association for Female Executives, 53 percent of 1,300 respondents had either been harassed themselves or knew someone who had.

• More than half of the professional women surveyed in 1990 by *Working Smart*, a business newsletter, said they'd been harassed.

• In a 1986 study by the Association of American Colleges, 32 percent of tenured faculty women and 49 percent of untenured women at Harvard University had experienced harassment.

• So have 40 percent of undergraduate women students and 28 percent of female graduate students, according to consultant Freada Klein.

• In a survey conducted at the time of the Thomas hearings, *Newsweek* (10/21/91) found that 21 percent of women polled said they'd been harassed.

• At the same time, the *New York Times* (10/11/91) found that four out of ten women polled had been harassed and that five out of ten men reported they'd said or done something that could be construed as harassment.

Sexual Harassment in Context

Sexual harassment doesn't take place in a vacuum. It is the relatively low status of women in the work world that makes the problem so widespread and so persistent. And if harassment stems from women's inferior position on the job, it also functions to *keep* women there.

Despite laws against discrimination, Census Bureau figures show that women bring home less than two-thirds of the pay men receive. Women college graduates earn about the same salary as men who hold only a high school diploma. Furthermore, the Bureau of Labor Statistics reports that the segregation of women into lower-paying jobs is not a thing of the past—in some cases it's even getting worse. Fewer than 3 percent of the top jobs at Fortune 500 companies are held by women, according to a 1991 study by the Feminist Majority Foundation....

Unresolved Debate

The debate over sexual harassment, on the other hand, is nowhere near being resolved. People don't agree on what harassment is, how serious it is, and what steps should be taken to stop it.

Should the term *harassment* apply only to unwelcome *physical* advances? Or should it encompass other offensive statements and actions? Who defines *offensive*? Do women really mind the attention? If a man puts his arm around a woman at work or tells an off-color joke, should he be hauled into court? Should women learn to speak out against harassment or simply to live with it? How can a manager ban harassment without stifling all friendly banter on the job? What, if anything, should be done about the pinups in the men's room?

Sexual harassment is relatively simple to define—it is repeated, unwanted sexual attention on the job. In most cases, it's easy to tell when it's happening. Often, whether a particular kind of behavior is offensive or not depends on who's doing it, to whom, how often, with what tone of voice and facial expression, and on how the behavior is received.

Sexual harassment can be stopped. The majority of men are not harassers. Of those who are, most will stop once harassment becomes less acceptable and the consequences more severe. Many managers want a work environment that treats all employees with equal respect and an atmosphere free of harassment. But more companies need to promote these goals with clearly stated policies, and the laws must be strengthened. These are not simple goals—but they're not unattainable, either....

What 9to5 Is

The organization known as 9to5 began in 1973 when a group of ten women workers gathered after a Boston seminar and began to trade stories. The group grew into a nationwide effort that garnered the attention of management and the trade-union movement....

* * *

Louette Colombano was one of the first female police officers in her San Francisco district. While listening to the watch commander, she and the other officers stood at attention with their hands behind their backs. The officer behind her unzipped his fly and rubbed his penis against her hands.

Diane, a buyer, was preparing to meet an out-of-town client for dinner when she received a message: her boss had informed the client that she would spend the night with him. Diane sent word that she couldn't make it to dinner. The next day she was fired.

Few people would disagree that these are clear-cut examples of sexual harassment. Touching someone in a deliberately sexual way, demanding that an employee engage in sex or lose her job—such behavior is clearly out of bounds. (It's also *illegal....*)...

[T]he essence of combating sexual harassment—creating a workplace that is built on mutual respect. . . .

A Common-Sense Definition

Sexual harassment is not complicated to define. To harass someone is to bother him or her. Sexual harassment is bothering someone in a sexual way. The harasser offers sexual attention to someone who didn't ask for it and doesn't welcome it. The unwelcome behavior might or might not involve touching. It could just as well be spoken words, graphics, gestures or even looks (not any look— but the kind of leer or stare that says, "I want to undress you").

Who decides what behavior is offensive at the workplace? The recipient does. As long as the recipient is "reasonable" and not unduly sensitive, sexual conduct that offends him or her should be changed.

That doesn't mean there's a blueprint for defining *sexual harassment*. "Reasonable" people don't always agree. Society celebrates pluralism. Not everyone is expected to have the same standards of morality or the same sense of humor. Still, reasonable people will agree *much of the time* about what constitutes offensive behavior or will recognize that certain behavior or language can be expected to offend some others. Most people make distinctions between how they talk to their best friends, to their children, and to their elderly relatives. Out of respect, they avoid certain behavior in the presence of certain people. The same distinctions must be applied at work.

Sexual harassment is different from the innocent mistake—that is, when someone tells an off-color joke, not realizing the listener will be offended, or gives what is meant as a friendly squeeze

---

DEFINING SEXUAL HARASSMENT

Sexual harassment means bothering someone in a sexual way.

Sexual harassment is behavior that is not only unwelcome but in most cases *repeated*.

The goal of sexual harassment is not sexual pleasure but gaining power over another.

Some male harassers want to put "uppity women" in their place.

The essence of combating sexual harassment is fostering mutual respect in the workplace.

---

of the arm to a coworker who doesn't like to be touched. Such behavior may represent insensitivity, and that may be a serious problem, but it's usually not sexual harassment. In many cases, the person who tells the joke that misfires or who pats an unreceptive arm *knows right away* that he or she has made a mistake. Once aware or made aware, this individual will usually apologize and try not to do it again.

Do They Mean It?

Some offensive behavior stems from what University of Illinois psychologist Louise Fitzgerald calls "cultural lag." "Many men entered the workplace at a time when sexual teasing and innuendo were commonplace," Fitzgerald told the *New York Times*. "They have no idea there's anything wrong with it." Education will help such men change their behavior.

True harassers, on the other hand, *mean* to offend. Even when they know their talk or action is offensive, they continue. Sexual harassment is defined as behavior that is not only unwelcome but *repeated.* (Some kinds of behavior are *always* inappropriate, however, even if they occur only once. Grabbing someone's breast or crotch, for example, or threatening to fire a subordinate who won't engage in sexual activity does not need repetition to be deemed illegal.)

The true harasser acts not out of insensitivity but precisely because of the knowledge that the behavior will make the recipient uncomfortable. The harasser derives pleasure from the momentary or continuing powerlessness of the other individual. In some cases, the harasser presses the victim to have sex, but sexual pleasure itself is not the goal. Instead, the harasser's point is to dominate, to gain power over another. As University of Washington psychologist John Gottman puts it, "Harassment is a way for a man to make a woman vulnerable."

Some harassers target the people they consider the most likely to be embarrassed and least likely to file a charge. Male harassers are sometimes attempting to put "uppity women" in their place. In certain previously all-male workplaces, a woman who's simply attempting to do her job may be considered uppity. In this instance, the harassment is designed to make the woman feel out of place, if not to pressure her out of the job. Such harassment often takes place in front of an audience or is recounted to others afterwards ("pinch and tell")....

COUNTERING THE MYTHS ABOUT SEXUAL HARASSMENT

From the Senate chambers to the company mailroom, from the executive suite to the employee lounge, from the locker room to the bedroom, a debate is raging over sexual harassment. No matter what the forum, the same arguments arise. Here are some of the most common myths about harassment rebutted by the facts.

Myth: Sexual harassment doesn't deserve all the attention it's getting. It's a rare disorder unique to a few sick people.

Fact: No exact figures exist, but a large body of research conducted at workplaces and universities suggests that at least 50 percent of women—as well as a smaller percentage of men—have been sexually harassed, either on the job or on campus. Very few people are considered to be "chronic harassers," but most of these are not psychopaths. Many men in the workplace, whether intentionally or not, end up encouraging or condoning harassment.

Myth: Sexual harassment is a fact of life that people might as well get used to. It's so widespread that it's pointless to try to stamp it out.

Fact: To expect men to engage in abusive behavior is insulting. The notion that women should take responsibility for preventing harassers from behaving offensively at the workplace is also a myth. Like other forms of sexual abuse, harassment is usually a means of exerting power, not of expressing a biological urge. Yes, sexual harassment is widespread, but the answer is to stop it, not to accept it.

Myth: Most men accused of harassment don't really intend to offend women.

Fact: A small percentage of men are dead serious about engaging in abusive behavior on the job. They know their behavior makes women uncomfortable; that's why they do it.

Other men are surprised to find that what they intend as innocent teasing isn't received that way. They need to make some simple changes in behavior.

After all, beginning in early childhood, most people are taught that different settings require different codes of behavior. Children learn not to use swear words at Grandma's dinner table and not to insult the teacher. At the workplace, it's safest to assume that a coworker *won't* like sexual comments or gestures. If you find out you've offended someone, simply apologize.

Myth: If women want to be treated equally on the job, they can't expect special treatment—whether at the construction site or in the executive boardroom.

Fact: Women don't want special treatment. They want *decent* treatment—the same decent treatment most men want for themselves....

Myth: Many charges of sexual harassment are false—the women are either fantasizing or lying in order to get men in trouble.

Fact: According to a survey of Fortune 500 managers conducted by *Working Woman* magazine (December 1988), false reports are rare. "Every story I hear is very specific and very detailed," said one survey respondent, "too much so to be made up." Said another respondent, "More than 95 percent of our complaints have merit."

There's little incentive for women to come forward with false harassment charges. The real problem is not that reports are fraudulent but that women who *are* suffering severe harassment remain silent for fear of being humiliated and derailing their careers.

Myth: A man's career can be destroyed by an accusation of sexual harassment, while the woman who accuses him suffers no consequences.

Fact: A woman's *life* can be destroyed by sexual harassment, at least for a time.

Offensive behavior *should* bring consequences for the perpetrator. But most cases don't result in heavy penalties.

A good corporate policy, however, protects both the accuser and the accused by ensuring confidentiality and a fair hearing. A range of disciplinary action is needed—from warnings and reprimands to suspensions and terminations—depending on the severity of the offense.

As things stand now, it's usually the victim who suffers a career setback. Many harassers receive only a slap on the wrist or no reprisals at all, even for serious offenses.

Myth: You can't blame a guy for looking. Women bring harassment on themselves by the way they dress.

Fact: Truly provocative clothing doesn't belong at the workplace, and management shouldn't allow it. Yet under no circumstances does a woman's appearance give men license to break the law.

Many employers require women to dress in a way that calls attention to their physical appearance. Waitresses, for example, may be required to wear uniforms with short skirts or low necklines. In 1991, Continental Airlines reservation clerk Teresa Fischette was summarily fired when she refused to wear makeup on the job. Only after the *New York Times* publicized her case and she appeared on a television talk show did she win back her position.

Without questioning the importance of being well groomed, many women resent having to conform to a highly specific "look" for the benefit of clients or coworkers. Not only is it expensive and time-consuming, it can lead others to treat them like sex objects at the workplace.

Myth: Women send mixed signals. Half the time when they say no, they really mean yes.

Fact: Men can't assume they're the ones who know best what women "really want." Especially at the workplace, some women can't put up strong resistance to sexual pressure without fear of endangering their jobs. Dr. Michelle Paludi, a psychologist at Hunter College in New York City, finds that "90 percent of women who have been sexually harassed want to leave, but can't because they need their job." Take a no as a no.

Myth: Women who make clear that they don't welcome sexual attention don't get harassed. If a woman doesn't like what's happening, she can say so.

Fact: Most hard-core harassers know their conduct is unwelcome; that's why they continue. Some women do say no again and again and find that their resistance is simply ignored. Others hesitate to speak up because they fear being ridiculed or ostracized.

While women do have a responsibility to communicate when sexual attention is unwelcome, the employer has a prior legal responsibility: to create an environment where no woman is punished for refusing to accept offensive behavior.

Myth: All this attention to harassment will give women ideas, causing them to imagine problems where there are none.

Fact: In the short run, defining *sexual harassment* and providing women with ways to speak up probably *will* lead to an increase in the number of reports filed, most of them concerning legitimate, not imagined, offenses. In the long run, however, public discussion of the issue will cut down on unwelcome sexual attention on the job. The result will be fewer harassment complaints and a more harmonious and productive work world for all.

Myth: Cracking down on sexual harassment will lead to a boring and humorless workplace.

Fact: Antiharassment policies are aimed at repeated, unwelcome sexual attention, not at friendly relations among coworkers. Social interaction that's mutually enjoyable is fine, so long as it doesn't interfere with work or offend others.

The aim of a sexual-harassment policy is to eliminate *offensive* interactions, not *all* interactions. Most encounters defined as sexual harassment have nothing to do with a romantic agenda. They involve an assertion of power, not of affection.

But sex between managers and their subordinates—or between faculty and students—is a different story. Many employers and college administrators recognize that romantic relationships are fraught with danger when one party to the affair has economic or academic power over the other. Even when it seems that both parties have entered freely into the relationship, management is right to worry about the potential for exploitation and adverse effects on the workplace or academic setting.

NO

Gretchen Morgenson

MAY I HAVE THE PLEASURE

On October 11 [1991],in the middle of the Anita Hill/Clarence Thomas con-tretemps, the *New York Times* somberly reported that sexual harassment pervades the American workplace. The source for this page-one story was a *Times*/CBS poll conducted two days earlier in which a handful (294) of women were interviewed by telephone. Thirty-eight per cent of respondents confirmed that they had been at one time or another "the object of sexual advances, propositions, or unwanted sexual discussions from men who su-pervise you or can affect your position at work." How many reported the incident at the time it happened? Four per cent.

Did the *Times* offer any explanation for why so few actually reported the incident? Could it be that these women did not report their "harassment" because they themselves did not regard a sexual advance as harassment? Some intelligent speculation on this matter might shed light on a key point: the vague definitions of harassment that make it easy to allege, hard to identify, and almost impossible to prosecute. Alas, the *Times* was in no mood to enlighten its readers.

It has been more than ten years since the Equal Employment Opportu-nity Commission (EEOC) wrote its guidelines defining sexual harassment as a form of sexual discrimination and, therefore, illegal under Title VII of the Civil Rights Act of 1964. According to the EEOC there are two different types of harassment: so-called *quid pro quo* harassment, in which career or job advancement is guaranteed in return for sexual favors, and environmental harassment, in which unwelcome sexual conduct "unreasonably interferes" with an individual's working environment or creates an "intimidating, hos-tile, or offensive working environment."

Following the EEOC's lead, an estimated three out of four companies na-tionwide have instituted strict policies against harassment; millions of dollars are spent each year educating employees in the subtleties of Title VII etiquette. Men are warned to watch their behavior, to jettison the patronizing pat and excise the sexist comment from their vocabularies.

Yet, if you believe what you read in the newspapers, we are in the Stone Age where the sexes are concerned. A theme common to the media, plain-tiff's lawyers, and employee-relations consultants is that male harassment of women is costing corporations millions each year in lost productivity and low employee morale. "Sexual harassment costs a typical Fortune 500 Service or Manufacturing company $6.7 million a year" says a sexual-harassment survey conducted late in 1988 for *Working Woman* by Klein Associates. This Boston consulting firm is part of a veritable growth industry which has sprung up to dispense sexual-harassment advice to worried companies in the form of seminars, videos, and encounter groups.

But is sexual harassment such a huge problem in business? Or is it largely a product of hype and hysteria? The statistics show that sexual harassment is less prevalent today than it was five years ago. According to the EEOC, federal cases alleging harassment on the job totaled 5,694 in 1990, compared to 6,342 in 1984. Yet today there are 17 per cent more women working than there were then.

At that, the EEOC's figures are almost certainly too high. In a good many of those complaints, sexual harassment may be tangential to the case; the complaint may primarily involve another form of discrimination in Title VII territory: race, national origin, or religious discrimination, for example. The EEOC doesn't separate cases involving sexual harassment alone; any case where sexual harassment is mentioned, even in passing, gets lumped into its figures.

Many of the stories depicting sexual harassment as a severe problem spring from "consultants" whose livelihoods depend upon exaggerating its extent. In one year, DuPont spent $450,000 on sexual-harassment training programs and materials. Susan Webb, president of Pacific Resources Development Group, a Seattle consultant, says she spends 95 per cent

of her time advising on sexual harassment. Like most consultants, Miss Webb acts as an expert witness in harassment cases, conducts investigations for companies and municipalities, and teaches seminars. She charges clients $1,500 for her 35-minute sexual-harassment video program and handbooks.

UNFELT NEEDS

Corporations began to express concern on the issue back in the early Eighties, just after the EEOC published its first guidelines. But it was *Meritor Savings Bank v. Vinson*, a harassment case that made it to the Supreme Court in 1985, that really acted as an employment act for sex-harassment consultants. In *Vinson*, the Court stated that employers could limit their liability to harassment claims by implementing anti-harassment policies and procedures in the workplace. And so, the anti-harassment industry was born.

Naturally, the consultants believe they are filling a need, not creating one. "Harassment is still as big a problem as it has been because the workplace is not integrated," says Susan Webb. Ergo, dwindling numbers of cases filed with the EEOC are simply not indicative of a diminution in the problem.

Then what do the figures indicate? Two things, according to the harassment industry. First, that more plaintiffs are bringing private lawsuits against their employers than are suing through the EEOC or state civil-rights commissions. Second, that the number of cases filed is a drop in the bucket compared to the number of actual, everyday harassment incidents.

It certainly stands to reason that a plaintiff in a sexual-harassment case would prefer bringing a private action against her employer to filing an EEOC claim. EEOC and state civil-rights cases allow plaintiffs only compensatory damages, such as back pay or legal fees. In order to collect big money—punitive damages—from an employer, a plaintiff must file a private action.

Yet there's simply no proof that huge or increasing numbers of private actions are being filed today. No data are collected on numbers of private harassment suits filed, largely because they're brought as tort actions—assault and battery, emotional distress, or breach of contract. During the second half of the Eighties, the San Francisco law firm of Orrick, Herrington, and Sutcliffe monitored private sexual-harassment cases filed in California. Its findings: From 1984 to 1989, the number of sexual-harassment cases in California that were litigated through a verdict totaled a whopping 15. That's in a state with almost six million working women.

Of course, cases are often settled prior to a verdict. But how many? Orrick, Herrington partner Ralph H. Baxter Jr., management co-chairman of the American Bar Association's Labor Law Committee on Employee Rights and Responsibilities, believes the number of private sexual-harassment cases launched today is greatly overstated. "Litigation is not as big a problem as it's made out to be; you're not going to see case after case," says Mr. Baxter. "A high percentage of matters go to the EEOC and a substantial number of cases get resolved."

Those sexual-harassment actions that do get to a jury are the ones that really grab headlines. A couple of massive awards have been granted in recent years—five plaintiffs were awarded $3.8 million by a North Carolina jury—but most mammoth awards are reduced on appeal. In fact, million-dollar sexual-harassment verdicts are still exceedingly rare. In California, land of the happy litigator, the median jury verdict for all sexual-harassment suits cases litigated between 1984 and 1989 was $183,000. The top verdict in the sate was just under $500,000, the lowest was $45,000. And California, known for its sympathetic jurors, probably produces higher awards than most states.

Now to argument number two: that the number of litigated harassment cases is tiny compared to the number of actual incidents that occur. Bringing a sexual-harassment case is similar to filing a rape case, consultants and lawyers say; both are nasty proceedings which involve defamation, possible job loss, and threats to both parties' family harmony.

It may well be that cases of perceived harassment go unfiled, but is it reasonable to assume that the numbers of these unfiled cases run into the millions? Consider the numbers of cases filed that are dismissed for "no probable cause." According to the New York State human-rights commission, almost two-thirds of the complaints filed in the past five years were dismissed for lack of probable cause. Of the two hundred sexual-harassment cases the commission receives a year, 38 per cent bring benefits to the complainant.

What about private actions? No one keeps figures on the percentage of cases nationwide won by the plaintiff versus the percentage that are dismissed. However, the outcomes of private sexual-harassment suits brought in California from 1984 to 1989 mirror the public figures from New York. According to Orrick, Herrington, of the 15 cases litigated to a verdict in California from 1984 to 1989, slightly less than half were dismissed and slightly more than half (53 per cent) were won by the plaintiff.

Are California and New York anomalies? Stephen Perlman, a partner in labor law at the Boston firm of Ropes & Gray, who has 15 years' experience litigating sexual-harassment cases, thinks not: "I don't suppose I've had as many as a dozen cases go to litigation. Most of the cases I've seen—the vast majority—get dismissed. They don't even have probable cause to warrant further processing."

WHAT IS HARASSMENT?

A major problem is the vague definition of harassment. If "environmental harassment" were clearly defined and specifiable, lawyers would undoubtedly see more winnable cases walk through their doors. Asking a subordinate to perform sexual favors in exchange for a raise is clearly illegal. But a dirty joke? A pin-up? A request for a date?

In fact, behavior which one woman may consider harassment could be seen by another as a non-threatening joke. The closest thing to harassment that I have experienced during my 15-year career occurred in the early Eighties when I was a stockbroker-in-training at Dean Witter Reynolds in New York City. I had brought in the largest personal account within Dean Witter's entire retail brokerage system, an account which held roughly $20 million in blue-chip stocks. Having this account under my management meant I had a larger capital responsibility than any of my colleagues, yet I was relatively new to the business. My fellow brokers were curious, but only one was brutish enough to walk right up to me and pop the question: "How did you get that account? Did you sleep with the guy?"

Instead of running away in tears, I dealt with him as I would any rude person. "Yeah," I answered. "Eat your heart out." He turned on his heel and never bothered me again. Was my colleague a harasser, or just practicing Wall Street's aggressive humor, which is dished out to men in other ways? Apparently, I am in the minority in thinking the latter. But the question remains. Whose standards should be used to define harassment?

Under tort law, the behavior which has resulted in a case—such as an assault or the intent to cause emotional distress—must be considered objectionable by a "reasonable person." The EEOC follows this lead and in its guidelines defines environmental harassment as that which "unreasonably interferes with an individual's job performance."

Yet, sexual-harassment consultants argue that any such behavior—even that which is perceived as harassment only by the most hypersensitive employee—ought to be considered illegal and stamped out. In fact, they say, the subtler hostile-environment cases are the most common and cause the most anguish. Says Frieda Klein, the Boston consultant: "My goal is to create a corporate climate where every employee feels free to object to behavior, where people are clear about their boundaries and can ask that objectionable behavior stop."

Sounds great. But rudeness and annoying behavior cannot be legislated out of existence; nor should corporations be forced to live under the tyranny of a hypersensitive employee. No woman should have to run a daily gauntlet of sexual innuendo, but neither is it reasonable for women to expect a pristine work environment free of coarse behavior.

Susan Hartzoge Gray, a labor lawyer at Haworth, Riggs, Kuhn, and Haworth in Raleigh, North Carolina, believes that hostile-environment harassment shouldn't be actionable under Title VII. "How can the law say one person's lewd and another's nice?" she asks. "There are so many different taste levels.... We condone sexual jokes and innuendos in the media—a movie might get a PG rating—yet an employer can be called on the carpet because the same thing bothers someone in an office."

But changing demographics may do more to eliminate genuine sexual harassment than all the apparatus of law and consultancy. As women reach a critical mass in the workforce, the problem of sexual harassment tends to go away. Frieda Klein says the problem practically vanishes once 30 per cent of the workers in a department, an assembly line, or a company are women.

Reaching that critical mass won't take long. According to the Bureau of Labor Statistics, there will be 66 million women to 73 million men in the workplace by 2000. They won't all be running departments or heading companies, of course, but many will.

So sexual harassment will probably become even less of a problem in the years ahead than it is today. But you are not likely to read that story in a major newspaper anytime soon.

POSTSCRIPT

Is Sexual Harassment a Pervasive Problem in America?

The difficulty in nailing down exactly what sexual harassment is and how prevalent it is in society is reflected in these two selections. Bravo and Cassedy assert that sexual harassment has increased, or at least has become more visible, because more women have entered the workforce. Morgenson, however, maintains that the opposite occurs; that as "women reach a critical mass in the workforce, the problem of sexual harassment tends to go away." Also, Bravo and Cassedy indicate that sexual harassment involves a deliberate attempt by an individual to gain power over another individual or to make that person feel vulnerable, while Morgenson feels that so-called harassing behavior is better described as aggressive humor, rudeness, or simply annoying behavior.

Much has been written about the issue of sexual harassment. Michele A. Paludi, director of the women's studies program at Hunter College of the City University of New York, is the author of *Academic and Workplace Sexual Harassment: A Resource Manual* (State University of New York Press, 1991) and the editor of *Ivory Power: Sexual Harassment on Campus* (State University of New York Press, 1991). Catharine A. MacKinnon's *Sexual Harassment of Working Women: A Case of Sex Discrimination* (Yale University Press, 1979) was an early and highly influential argument for placing sexual harassment under the legal category of sexual discrimination. Like MacKinnon, Susan Faludi, in *Backlash: The Undeclared War Against American Women* (Random House, 1991), argues that sexual harassment is virtually pandemic in our society. This argument is disputed and defended by various writers in the May/June 1991 issue of *Society*, which features the topic of sexual harassment. Two sources for women's views on sexual harassment are Amber Coverdale Sumrall and Dena Taylor, eds., *Sexual Harassment: Women Speak Out* (Crossing Press, 1992), and Nancy Dodd McCann and Thomas A. McGinn, *Harassed: One Hundred Women Define Inappropriate Behavior in the Workplace* (Irwin, 1992).

There may be some signs of a backlash against charges of sexual harassment. Some men have already brought defamation suits, charging that their reputations have been seriously harmed. More than a dozen major corporations, including General Motors, AT&T, and DuPont, have been sued by male employees who were dismissed on grounds of sexual harassment. Few of the suits have been successful so far, perhaps in part because firms have pulled out all the stops in fighting them.

ISSUE 5

Should Homosexuality Be Accepted by Society?

YES: Richard D. Mohr, from "Gay Basics: Some Questions, Facts, and Values," in James Rachels, ed., *The Right Thing to Do* (Random House, 1989)

NO: Dennis Prager, from "Homosexuality, the Bible, and Us—A Jewish Perspective," *The Public Interest* (Summer 1993)

ISSUE SUMMARY

YES: Philosophy professor Richard D. Mohr argues that homosexuals suffer from unjust discrimination and that homosexuality is neither immoral nor unnatural.

NO: Author and publisher Dennis Prager contends that homosexuality is not morally equivalent to heterosexuality and should not be given the same legal status.

In Sioux Falls, South Dakota, in 1979, Randy Rohl and Grady Quinn became the first acknowledged homosexual couple in America to receive permission from their high school principal to attend the senior prom together. The National Gay Task Force hailed the event as a milestone in the progress of human rights. It is unclear what the voters of Sioux Falls thought about it, since it was not put up to a vote, but if their views were similar to those of voters in Dade County, Florida, Houston, Texas, Wichita, Kansas, and various localities in the state of Oregon, they probably were not as enthusiastic as the Gay Task Force. In referenda held in these and other areas, voters have reversed decisions by legislators and local boards to ban discrimination by sexual preference. Even in New York City, which is well known for its liberal attitudes, parents in some school districts have fought all-out battles against school administrators over curricula that promotes tolerance of gay lifestyles.

Yet the attitude of Americans toward gay rights is not easy to pin down. On one hand, voting majorities in many localities have defeated or overturned resolutions designating sexual orientation as a protected right. In 1993 alone, 19 localities passed measures that are considered antihomosexual by gay rights leaders. However, voters have also defeated resolutions like the one in California in 1978 that would have banned the hiring of gay schoolteachers, or the one on the Oregon ballot in 1992 identifying homosexuality as "abnormal, wrong, unnatural and perverse." In some states, notably Colorado, voters have approved initiatives widely perceived as antigay, but, almost invariably, these resolutions have been carefully worded so as to appear to be opposing "special" rights for gays. In general, polls show that a large majority of Americans believe that homosexuals should have equal rights with heterosexuals with regard to job opportunities. On the other hand, many persist in viewing homosexuality as morally wrong.

President Clinton experienced both of these views in 1992 and 1993. When he ran for president, Clinton caused no particular stir when he openly supported gay rights and promised that if elected he would issue an executive order lifting the ban on homosexuals in the military services. Once in office, however, and faced with demands from gay rights groups to deliver on his pledge, Clinton encountered bitter opposition. The locus of the opposition was the armed services and their supporters in Congress, but these vocal opponents also enjoyed considerable support from the public at large. Clinton ended up accepting a much-modified version of what he had promised—a "don't ask, don't tell, don't pursue" policy that fell far short of fully accepting homosexuality in the armed services.

Homosexuality was once commonly viewed as "deviant," and the adjective may still be acceptable by both sides of the controversy if it simply means behavior considered different by the majority. But in popular usage, "deviant" means considerably more than this. It carries the sense of "sick" and "immoral," which is why homosexuals are working hard to redefine homosexuality as normal, natural, and an acceptable lifestyle in a pluralist society. A more accepting attitude seems to be growing, especially among younger, college-educated Americans, but the recent referendum results suggest that widespread opposition to gay rights measures still exists.

In the selections that follow, Richard D. Mohr argues that the refusal to accept homosexuality is simply another form of bigotry, in the same category as racial or sexual discrimination, and that the time is long past due for granting full civil rights to homosexuals. Dennis Prager, on the other hand, argues that although he is not ready to punish people for homosexuality, neither is he prepared to give it the same legal status as heterosexuality.

YES

Richard D. Mohr

GAY BASICS: SOME QUESTIONS, FACTS, AND VALUES

I. WHO ARE GAYS ANYWAY?

A recent Gallup poll found that only one in five Americans reports having a gay or lesbian acquaintance. This finding is extraordinary given the number of practicing homosexuals in America. Alfred Kinsey's 1948 study of the sex lives of 12,000 white males shocked the nation: 37 percent had at least one homosexual experience to orgasm in their adult lives; an additional 13 percent had homosexual fantasies to orgasm; 4 percent were exclusively homosexual in their practices; another 5 percent had virtually no heterosexual experience and nearly 20 percent had at least as many homosexual as heterosexual experiences.

Two out of five men one passes on the street have had orgasmic sex with men. Every second family in the country has a member who is essentially homosexual and many more people regularly have homosexual experiences. Who are homosexuals? They are your friends, your minister, your teacher, your bank teller, your doctor, your mail carrier, your officemate, your room-mate, your congressional representative, your sibling, parent, and spouse. They are everywhere, virtually all ordinary, virtually all unknown.

Several important consequences follow. First, the country is profoundly ignorant of the actual experience of gay people. Second, social attitudes and practices that are harmful to gays have a much greater overall harmful impact on society than is usually realized. Third, most gay people live in hiding—in the closet—making the "coming out" experience the central fixture of gay consciousness and invisibility the chief characteristic of the gay community.

II. IGNORANCE, STEREOTYPE, AND MORALITY

Ignorance about gays, however, has not stopped people from having strong opinions about them. The void which ignorance leaves has been filled with stereotypes. Society holds chiefly two groups of anti-gay stereotypes; the two are an oddly contradictory lot. One set of stereotypes revolves around alleged mistakes in an individual's gender identity: lesbians are women that want to be, or at least look and act like, men—bull dykes, diesel dykes; while gay men are those who want to be, or at least look and act like, women—queens, fairies, limpwrists, nellies. These stereotypes of mismatched genders provide the materials through which gays and lesbians become the butts of ethniclike jokes. These stereotypes and jokes, though derisive, basically view gays and lesbians as ridiculous.

Another set of stereotypes revolves around gays as a pervasive, sinister, conspiratorial threat. The core stereotype here is the gay person as child molester, and more generally as sex-crazed maniac. These stereotypes carry with them fears of the very destruction of family and civilization itself....

III. ARE GAYS DISCRIMINATED AGAINST? DOES IT MATTER?

Partly because lots of people suppose they don't know any gay people and partly through willful ignorance of its own workings, society at large is unaware of the many ways in which gays are subject to discrimination in consequence of widespread fear and hatred. Contributing to this social ignorance of discrimination is the difficulty for gay people, as an invisible minority, even to complain of discrimination. For if one is gay, to register a complaint would suddenly target one as a stigmatized person, and so in the absence of any protections against discrimination, would simply invite additional discrimination....

[G]ays are subject to violence and harassment based simply on their perceived status rather than because of any actions they have performed. A recent extensive study by the National Gay Task Force found that over 90 percent of gays and lesbians had been victimized in some form on the basis of their sexual orientation. Greater than one in five gay men and nearly one in ten lesbians had been punched, hit, or kicked; a quarter of all gays had had objects thrown at them; a third had been chased; a third had been sexually harassed; and 14 percent had been spit on—all just for being perceived as gay.

The most extreme form of anti-gay violence is "queerbashing"—where groups of young men target a person who they suppose is a gay man and beat and kick him unconscious and sometimes to death amid a torrent of taunts and slurs. Such seemingly random but in reality socially encouraged violence has the same origin and function as lynchings of blacks—to keep a whole stigmatized group in line. As with lynchings of the recent past, the police and courts have routinely averted their eyes, giving their implicit approval to the practice.

Few such cases with gay victims reach the courts. Those that do are marked by inequitable procedures and results. Frequently judges will describe "queerbashers" as "just all-American boys." Recently a District of Columbia judge handed suspended sentences to queerbashers whose victim had been stalked, beaten, stripped at knife point, slashed, kicked, threatened with castration, and pissed on, because the judge thought the bashers were good boys at heart—after all, they went to a religious prep school.

Police and juries will simply discount testimony from gays; they typically construe assaults on and murders of gays as "justified" self-defense—the killer need only claim his act was a panicked response to a sexual overture. Alternatively, when guilt seems patent, juries will accept highly implausible "diminished capacity" defenses, as in the case of Dan White's 1978 assassination of openly gay San Francisco city councilman Harvey Milk: Hostess Twinkies made him do it....

Gays are subject to widespread discrimination in employment—the very means by which one puts bread on one's table and one of the chief means by which individuals identify themselves to themselves and achieve personal dignity. Governments are leading offenders here. They do a lot of discriminating themselves, require that others do it (e.g., government contractors), and set precedents favoring discrimination in the private sector. The federal government explicitly discriminates against gays in the armed forces, the CIA, FBI, National Security Agency, and the state department. The federal government refuses to give security clearances to gays and so forces the country's considerable private sector military and aerospace contractors to fire known gay employees. State and local governments regularly fire gay teachers, policemen, firemen, social workers, and anyone who has contact with the public. Further, through licensing laws states officially bar gays from a vast array of occupations and professions—everything from doctors, lawyers, accountants, and nurses to hairdressers, morticians, and used car dealers. The American Civil Liberties Union's handbook *The Rights of Gay People* lists 307 such prohibited occupations.

Gays are subject to discrimination in a wide variety of other ways, including private-sector employment, public accommodations, housing, immigration and naturalization, insurance of all types, custody and adoption, and zoning regulations that bar "singles" or "nonrelated" couples. All of these discriminations affect central components of a meaningful life; some even reach to the means by which life itself is sustained. In half the states, where gay sex is illegal, the central role of sex to meaningful life is officially denied to gays....

IV. BUT AREN'T THEY IMMORAL?

Many people think society's treatment of gays is justified because they think gays are extremely immoral. To evaluate this claim, different senses of "moral" must be distinguished. Sometimes by "morality" is meant the overall beliefs affecting behavior in the society—its mores, norms, and customs. On this understanding, gays certainly are not moral: lots of people hate them and social customs are designed to register widespread disapproval of gays. The problem here is that this sense of morality is merely a *descriptive* one. On this understanding *every* society has a morality—even Nazi society, which had racism and mob rule as central features of its "morality," understood in this sense. What is needed in order to use the notion of morality to praise or condemn behavior is a sense of morality that is *prescriptive* or *normative*—a sense of morality whereby, for instance, the descriptive morality of the Nazis is found wanting....

Furthermore, recent historical and anthropological research has shown that opinion about gays has been by no means universally negative. Historically, it has varied widely even within the larger part of the Christian era and even within the church itself. There are even societies—current ones—where homosexuality is not only tolerated but a universal compulsory part of social maturation....

If popular opinion and custom are not enough to ground moral condemnation of homosexuality, perhaps religion can....

One of the more remarkable discoveries of recent gay research is that the Bible may not be as univocal in its condemnation of homosexuality as has been usually believed. Christ never mentions homosexuality. Recent interpreters of the Old Testament have pointed out that the story of Lot at Sodom is probably intended to condemn inhospitality rather than homosexuality. Further, some of the Old Testament condemnations of homosexuality seem simply to be ways of tarring those of the Israelites' opponents who happened to accept homosexual practices when the Israelites themselves did not. If so, the condemnation is merely a quirk of history and rhetoric rather than a moral precept....

Even if a consistent portrait of condemnation could be gleaned from the Bible, what social significance should it be given? One of the guiding principles of society, enshrined in the Constitution as a check against the government, is that decisions affecting social policy are not made on religious grounds. If the real ground of the alleged immorality invoked by governments to discriminate against gays is religious (as it has explicitly been even in some recent court cases involving teachers and guardians), then one of the major commitments of our nation is violated.

V. BUT AREN'T THEY UNNATURAL?

... Though the accusation of unnaturalness looks whimsical, in actual ordinary discourse when applied to homosexuality, it is usually delivered with venom aforethought. It carries a high emotional charge, usually expressing disgust and evincing queasiness. Probably it is nothing but an emotional charge. For people get equally disgusted and queasy at all sorts of things that are perfectly natural—to be expected in nature apart from artifice—and that could hardly be fit subjects for moral condemnation. Two typical examples in current American culture are some people's responses to mothers' suckling in public and to women who do not shave body hair. When people have strong emotional reactions, as they do in these cases, without being able to give good reasons for them, we think of them not as operating morally, but rather as being obsessed and manic. So the feelings of disgust that some people have to gays will hardly ground a charge of immorality. People fling the term "unnatural" against gays in the same breath and with the same force as when they call gays "sick" and "gross." When they do this, they give every appearance of being neurotically fearful and incapable of reasoned discourse.

When "nature" is taken in *technical* rather than ordinary usages, it looks like the notion also will not ground a charge of homosexual immorality. When unnatural means "by artifice" or "made by humans," it need only be pointed out that virtually everything that is good about life is unnatural in this sense, that the chief feature that distinguishes people from other animals is their very ability to make over the world to meet their needs and desires, and that their well-being depends upon these departures from nature. On this understanding of human nature and the natural, homosexuality is perfectly unobjectionable.

Another technical sense of natural is that something is natural and so, good, if it fulfills some function in nature. Homosexuality on this view is unnatural because it allegedly violates the function of genitals, which is to produce babies. One problem with this view is that lots of bodily parts have lots of functions and just because some one activity can be fulfilled by only one organ (say, the mouth for eating) this activity does not condemn other functions of the organ to immorality (say the mouth for talking, licking stamps, blowing bubbles, or having sex). So the possible use of the genitals to produce children does not, without more, condemn the use of the genitals for other purposes, say, achieving ecstasy and intimacy....

Further, ordinary moral attitudes about childbearing will not provide the needed supplement which in conjunction with the natural function view of bodily parts would produce a positive obligation to use the genitals for procreation. Society's attitude toward a childless couple is that of pity not censure—even if the couple could have children.... The couple who discovers they cannot have children are viewed not as having thereby had a debt canceled, but rather as having to forgo some of the richness of life, just as a quadriplegic is viewed not as absolved from some moral obligation to hop, skip, jump, but as missing some of the richness of life. Consistency requires then that, at most, gays who do not or cannot have children are to be pitied rather than condemned. What *is* immoral is the willful preventing of people from achieving the richness of life. Immorality in this regard lies with those social customs, regulations, and statutes that prevent lesbians and gay men from establishing blood or adoptive families, not with gays themselves....

If one looks to people... for a model—and looks hard enough—one finds amazing variety, including homosexuality as a social ideal (upper-class fifth-century Athens) and even as socially mandatory (Melanesia today). When one looks to people, one is simply unable to strip away the layers of social custom, history, and taboo in order to see what's really there to any degree more specific than that people are the creatures that make over their world and are capable of abstract thought. That this is so should raise doubts that neutral principles are to be found in human nature that will condemn homosexuality.

On the other hand, if one looks to nature apart from people for models, the possibilities are staggering. There are fish that change gender over their lifetimes: should we "follow nature" and be operative transsexuals? Orangutans, genetically our next of kin, live completely solitary lives without social organization of any kind: ought we to "follow nature" and be hermits? There are many species where only two members per generation reproduce: should we be bees? The search in nature for people's purpose, far from finding sure models for action, is likely to leave one morally rudderless.

VI. BUT AREN'T GAYS WILLFULLY THE WAY THEY ARE?

It is generally conceded that if sexual orientation is something over which an individual—for whatever reason—has virtually no control, then discrimination against gays is especially deplorable, as it is against racial and ethnic classes, because it holds people accountable without regard for anything they themselves have done. And to hold a person accountable for that over which the person has no control is a central form of prejudice.

Attempts to answer the question whether or not sexual orientation is something that is reasonably thought to be within one's own control usually appeal simply to various claims of the biological or "mental" sciences. But the ensuing debate over genes, hormones, twins, early childhood development, and the like, is as unnecessary as it is currently inconclusive. All that is needed to answer the question is to look at the actual experience of gays in current society and it becomes fairly clear that sexual orientation is not likely a matter of choice. For coming to have a homosexual identity simply does not have the same sort of structure that decision making has.

On the one hand, the "choice" of the gender of a sexual partner does not seem to express a trivial desire that might be as easily well fulfilled by a simple substitution of the desired object. Picking the gender of a sex partner is decidedly dissimilar, that is, to such activities as picking a flavor of ice cream. If an ice-cream parlor is out of one's flavor, one simply picks another. And if people were persecuted, threatened with jail terms, shattered careers, loss of family and housing, and the like, for eating, say, rocky road ice cream, no one would ever eat it; everyone would pick another easily available flavor. That gay people abide in being gay even in the face of persecution shows that being gay is not a matter of easy choice.

On the other hand, even if establishing a sexual orientation is not like making a relatively trivial choice, perhaps it is nevertheless relevantly like making the central and serious life choices by which individuals try to establish themselves as being of some type. Again, if one examines gay experience, this seems not to be the case. For one never sees anyone setting out to become a homosexual, in the way one does see people setting out to become doctors, lawyers, and bricklayers. One does not find "gays-to-be" picking some end—"At some point in the future, I want to become a homosexual"—and then setting about planning and acquiring the ways and means to that end, in the way one does see people deciding that they want to become lawyers, and then sees them plan what courses to take and what sort of temperaments, habits, and skills to develop in order to become lawyers. Typically gays-to-be simply find themselves having homosexual encounters and yet at least initially resisting quite strongly the identification of being homosexual.... Only with time, luck, and great personal effort, but sometimes never, does the person gradually come to accept her or his orientation, to view it as a given material condition of life, coming as materials do with certain capacities and limitations. The person begins to act in accordance with his or her orientation and its capacities, seeing its actualization as a requisite for an integrated personality and as a central component of personal well-being. As a result, the experience of coming out to oneself has for gays the basic structure of a discovery, not the structure of a choice....

VII. HOW WOULD SOCIETY AT LARGE BE CHANGED IF GAYS WERE SOCIALLY ACCEPTED?

Suggestions to change social policy with regard to gays are invariably met with claims that to do so would invite the destruction of civilization itself: after all, isn't that what did Rome in? Actually Rome's decay paralleled not the flourishing of homosexuality but its repression under the later Christianized emperors. Predictions of American civilization's imminent demise have been as premature as they have been frequent. Civilization has shown itself rather resilient here, in large part because of the country's traditional commitments to a respect for privacy, to individual liberties, and especially to people minding their own business....

Half the states have decriminalized homosexual acts. Can you guess which of the following states still have sodomy laws: Wisconsin, Minnesota; New Mexico, Arizona; Vermont, New Hampshire; Nebraska, Kansas. One from each pair does and one does not have sodomy laws. And yet one would be hard pressed to point out any substantial difference between the members of each pair. (If you're interested, it is the second of each pair with them.) Empirical studies have shown that there is no increase in other crimes in states that have decriminalized. Further, sodomy laws are virtually never enforced. They remain on the books not to "protect society" but to insult gays, and for that reason need to be removed.

Neither has the passage of legislation barring discrimination against gays ushered in the end of civilization. Some 50 counties and municipalities, including some of the country's largest cities (like Los Angeles and Boston), have passed such statutes and among the states and colonies Wisconsin and the District of Columbia have model protective codes. Again, no more brimstone has fallen in these places than elsewhere. Staunchly anti-gay cities, like Miami and Houston, have not been spared the AIDS crisis.

Berkeley, California, has even passed domestic partner legislation giving gay couples the same rights to city benefits as married couples, and yet Berkeley has not become more weird than it already was.

Seemingly hysterical predictions that the American family would collapse if such reforms would pass proved false, just as the same dire predictions that the availability of divorce would lessen the ideal and desirability of marriage proved completely unfounded. Indeed if current discriminations, which drive gays into hiding and into anonymous relations, were lifted, far from seeing gays raze American families, one would see gays forming them.

Virtually all gays express a desire to have a permanent lover. Many would like to raise or foster children—perhaps those alarming numbers of gay kids who have been beaten up and thrown out of their "families" for being gay. But currently society makes gay coupling very difficult. A life of hiding is a pressure-cooker existence not easily shared with another. Members of non-gay couples are here asked to imagine what it would take to erase every trace of their own sexual orientation for even just a week....

Finally..., in extending to gays the rights and benefits it has reserved for its dominant culture, America would confirm its deeply held vision of itself as a morally progressing nation, a nation itself advancing and serving as a beacon for others—especially with regard to human rights. The words with which our national pledge ends—"with liberty and justice for all"—are not a description of the present but a call for the future. Ours is a nation given to a prophetic political rhetoric which acknowledges that morality is not arbitrary and that justice is not merely the expression of the current collective will. It is this vision that led the black civil rights movement to its successes. Those congressmen who opposed that movement and its centerpiece, the 1964 Civil Rights Act, on obscurantist grounds, but who lived long enough and were noble enough, came in time to express their heartfelt regret and shame at what they had done. It is to be hoped and someday to be expected that those who now grasp at anything to oppose the extension of that which is best about America to gays will one day feel the same.

NO

Dennis Prager

HOMOSEXUALITY, THE BIBLE, AND US—A JEWISH PERSPECTIVE

Of all the issues that tear at our society, few provoke as much emotion, or seem as complex, as the question of homosexuality.

Most homosexuals and their heterosexual supporters argue that homosexuality is an inborn condition, and one, moreover, that is no less valid than heterosexuality. They maintain that to discriminate in any way against a person because of his or her sexual orientation is the moral equivalent of discrimination against a person on the basis of color or religion; that is to say, bigotry plain and simple.

On the other hand there are those who feel, no less passionately, that homosexuality is wrong, that society must cultivate the heterosexual marital ideal, or society's very foundations will be threatened.

In the middle are many who are torn between these two claims. I have been one of them. Generally speaking, I do not concern myself with the actions of consenting adults in the privacy of their homes, and I certainly oppose government involvement with what consenting adults do in private. In addition, both lesbians and homosexual men have been part of my life as friends and relatives.

At the same time, I am a Jew who reveres Judaism. And my religion not only prohibits homosexuality, it unequivocally, unambiguously, and in the strongest language at its disposal, condemns it. Judaism—and Christianity—hold that marital sex must be the ideal to which society aspires. Thus my instinct to tolerate all non-coercive behavior runs counter to the deepest moral claims of my source of values.

This is not all. Adding to the seeming complexity are the questions of choice and psychopathology. Current homosexual doctrine holds that homosexuals are born homosexual, and that homosexuality is in no way a psychological or emotional deviation. Are these claims true? And if they are, what are we to do with Western society's (i.e., Judaism's and Christianity's) opposition to homosexuality? What are we to do with our gut instinct that men and women should make love and marry each other, not their own sex? Have Judaism and Christianity been wrong? Is our instinctive reaction no more

Excerpted from Dennis Prager, "Homosexuality, the Bible, and Us—A Jewish Perspective," *The Public Interest*, no. 112 (Summer 1993), pp. 60–61, 69–71, 76–82. Copyright © 1993 by Dennis Prager. Reprinted by permission. Notes omitted.

than a heterosexual bias? And what about those of us who have two gut instincts—one that favors heterosexual love, and one that believes "live and let live"? These two feelings seem irreconcilable, and they have caused me and millions of others anguish and confusion.

After prolonged immersion in the subject, I continue to have anguish about the subject of homosexuality, but, to my great surprise, much less confusion. I hope that the reader will undergo a similar process, and it is to this end that I devote this article. . . .

Men Need Women

God's first declaration about man (the human being generally, and the male specifically) is, "It is not good for man to be alone." Now, presumably, in order to solve the problem of man's aloneness, God could have made another man, or even a community of men. However, God solved man's aloneness by creating one other person, a woman—not a man, not a few women, not a community of men and women. Man's solitude was not a function of his not being with other people; it was a function of his being without a woman.

Of course, Judaism also holds that women need men. But both the Torah statement and Jewish law have been more adamant about men marrying than about women marrying. Judaism is worried about what happens to men and to society when men do not channel their drives into marriage. In this regard, the Torah and Judaism were highly prescient: The overwhelming majority of violent crimes are committed by unmarried men.

In order to become fully human, male and female must join. In the words of Genesis, "God created the human . . . male and female He created them." The

union of male and female is not merely some lovely ideal; it is the essence of the biblical outlook on becoming human. To deny it is tantamount to denying a primary purpose of life.

The Family

Throughout their history, one of the Jews' most distinguishing characteristics has been their commitment to family life. To Judaism, the family—not the nation, and not the individual—is to be the fundamental unit, the building block of society. Thus, when God blesses Abraham, He says, "Through you all the families of the earth will be blessed."

Homosexuality's Effect on Women

Yet another reason for Judaism's opposition to homosexuality is homosexuality's negative effect on women. There appears to be a direct correlation between the prevalence of male homosexuality and the relegation of women to a low societal role. At the same time, the emancipation of women has been a function of Western civilization, the civilization least tolerant of homosexuality.

In societies where men sought out men for love and sex, women were relegated to society's periphery. Thus, for example, ancient Greece, which elevated homosexuality to an ideal, was characterized, in [Norman] Sussman's words, by "a misogynistic attitude." Homosexuality in ancient Greece, he writes, "was closely linked to an idealized concept of the man as the focus of intellectual and physical activities."

Classicist Eva Keuls describes Athens at its height of philosophical and artistic greatness as "a society dominated by men who sequester their wives and daughters, denigrate the female role in reproduction, erect monuments to the male genitalia, have sex with the sons of their peers...."

In medieval France, when men stressed male-male love, it "implied a corresponding lack of interest in women. In the *Song of Roland*, a French mini-epic given its final form in the late eleventh or twelfth century, women appear only as shadowy, marginal figures: 'The deepest signs of affection in the poem, as well as in similar ones, appear in the love of man for man....'"

The women of Arab society, wherein male homosexuality has been widespread, have a notably low status. In traditional Chinese culture, as well, the low state of women has been linked to widespread homosexuality.

While traditional Judaism is not as egalitarian as many late twentieth century Jews would like, it was Judaism, very much through its insistence on marriage and family and its rejection of infidelity and homosexuality, that initiated the process of elevating the status of women. While other cultures were writing homoerotic poetry, the Jews wrote the *Song of Songs*, one of the most beautiful poems depicting male-female sensual love ever written.

The Male Homosexual Lifestyle

A final reason for opposition to homosexuality is the homosexual lifestyle. While it is possible for male homosexuals to live lives of fidelity comparable to those of heterosexual males, it is usually not the case. While the typical lesbian has had fewer than ten sexual partners, the typical male homosexual in America has had over 500. In general, neither homosexuals nor heterosexuals confront the fact that it is this male homosexual lifestyle, more than the specific act, that disturbs most people.

This is probably why less attention is paid to female homosexuality. When male sexuality is not controlled, the consequences are considerably more destructive than when female sexuality is not controlled. Men rape. Women do not. Men, not women, engage in fetishes. Men are more frequently consumed by their sex drive, and wander from sex partner to sex partner. Men, not women, are sexually sadistic.

The indiscriminate sex that characterizes much of male homosexual life represents the antithesis of Judaism's goal of elevating human life from the animal-like to the God-like....

DECRIMINALIZING HOMOSEXUALITY

Before dealing with areas where discriminating on behalf of marital heterosexuality may be proper, let us deal with the areas where discrimination is not morally defensible.

Twenty-three states in the United States continue to have laws against private homosexual relations. I am opposed to these laws. Whatever my misgivings about homosexuality may be, they do not undo my opposition to the state's interference in private consensual relations between adults. Those who wish to retain such laws need to explain where, if ever, they will draw their line. Should we criminalize adultery? After all, adultery is prohibited by the Ten Commandments.

What should be permitted in private, however, does not have to be permitted in all areas of society. Thus, for example, while I am for decriminalizing prostitution, I would not allow the transactions to take place in public or permit prostitutes to advertise on billboards, radio, or television.

To decriminalize an act is not to deem it as socially acceptable as any other act. But social acceptance is precisely what gay liberation aims for—and also where the majority of society disagrees with gay liberation.

I suspect that in this regard most people feel as I do—antipathy to gay-baiting, gay-bashing, and to the criminalizing of private gay behavior, while simultaneously holding that homosexuality is not an equally viable alternative. Given these admittedly somewhat contradictory positions, what are we to do?

I believe that we ought to conduct public policy along two guidelines:

1) We may distinguish between that which grants homosexuals basic rights and that which honors homosexuality as a societally desirable way to live.

2) Therefore, we may discriminate on behalf of the heterosexual marital ideal, but not against the individual homosexual in the private arena—for example, where and how a homosexual lives....

HOMOSEXUAL MARRIAGE

Gay activists and some liberal groups such as the ACLU [American Civil Liberties Union] argue for the right of homosexuals to marry. Generally, two arguments are advanced—that society should not deny anyone the right to marry, and that if male homosexuals were given the right to marry, they would be considerably less likely to cruise [search for sexual partners].

The first argument is specious because there is no "right to marry." There is no right to marry more than one partner at a time, or to marry an immediate member of one's family. Society does not allow either practice. Though the ACLU and others believe that society has no rights,

only individuals do, most Americans feel otherwise. Whether this will continue to be so, as Judaism and Christianity lose their influence, remains to be seen.

The second argument may have some merit, and insofar as homosexual marriages would decrease promiscuity among gay men, it would be a very positive development for both gays and society. But homosexual marriage would be unlikely to have such an effect. The male propensity to promiscuity would simply overwhelm most homosexual males' marriage vows. It is women who keep most heterosexual men monogamous, or at least far less likely to cruise, but gay men have no such brake on their cruising natures. Male nature, not the inability to marry, compels gay men to wander from man to man. This is proven by the behavior of lesbians, who, though also prevented from marrying each other, are not promiscuous.

HOMOSEXUAL EMPLOYMENT

In general, not hiring a person because he or she is gay is morally indefensible. There are, however, at least two exceptions which necessitate the use of the qualifier, "in general."

In some rare cases in which sexual attraction, or non-attraction, is an absolutely relevant aspect of a job, a case can be made for discrimination against gays in hiring. The armed forces are one possible example. One reason for not admitting gays into combat units is the same reason for not allowing women and men to share army barracks. The sexual tension caused by individuals who may be sexually interested in one another could undermine effectiveness.

Big Brothers provides a second example. Just as heterosexual men are not allowed to serve as Big Brothers to girls, gay men should not be allowed to serve as Big Brothers to boys. The reason is not anti-homosexual any more than not allowing heterosexual men to be Big Brothers to girls is anti-heterosexual; it is common sense. We do not want Big Brothers to be potentially sexually attracted to the young people with whom they are entrusted. It is not because we trust homosexual men less; it is because we do not trust male sexual nature with any minor to whom a male may be sexually attracted.

My own view is that, in general, if employees work responsibly, their off-duty hours are their own business. This is not the view of many liberals and conservatives today, however. Off-hours "womanizing" ended the career of the leading contender for the Democratic Party's presidential nomination of 1988. And it was a major reason for not approving a secretary of defense-designate. Ironically, the voting public often seems far more tolerant of "manizing" than of womanizing. Rep. Barney Frank's male lover ran a male prostitution ring from the congressman's apartment, yet Frank seems to be as popular with his constituency as ever. Such behavior on the part of a heterosexual would doubtless have led to his resignation from Congress.

BEHAVIOR TOWARD HOMOSEXUALS

Violence against homosexuals has claimed numerous lives over the past decade, and too often the law seems to regard it as less of a crime than the murder of heterosexuals. In 1976, when a gay college student was beaten to death by teenagers in front of a Tucson bar, the judge imposed no penalty. In 1984,

a Bangor, Maine, judge released to custody of their parents three teenage boys who had beaten and thrown a young gay man into a stream. In 1988, a Texas judge eased the sentence of a man who murdered two homosexuals because, in the judge's words, "I put prostitutes and gays at about the same level, and I'd be hard put to give somebody life for killing a prostitute."

According to a National Gay Task Force study, one-fourth to one-third of gay men have been assaulted or threatened with violence. Even if the figures are exaggerated by a factor of two, they are terrible. And they may actually be understated, since many homosexuals do not wish to report such crimes for fear of embarrassment.

Unfortunately, religious opponents of homosexuality can abet this type of behavior. It should go without saying, but, unfortunately, it needs to be said that the homosexual is created in God's image as much as every other person, and that a homosexual can be as decent a human being as anyone else.

It should also go without saying but, again, it needs to be said that to hurt a homosexual, to be insensitive to a homosexual because of the person's homosexuality, is despicable. Likewise, I believe that when a parent severs relations with a child because of the child's homosexuality, it is a terrible and mutually destructive act.

Gay-bashing, gay-baiting, and jokes that mock (as opposed to poking good-natured fun at) homosexuals have no place in a decent society.

I can confirm from personal experience the truth of the gay activist claim that nearly all of us know or come into regular contact with gay people. From childhood, I was aware that a member of our family circle, one of my mother's cousins, was a gay man; my closest friend during my college year in England was a homosexual; and a proofreader of my journal for two years, one of my closest co-workers, was a lesbian.

I have regarded these people as no less worthy of friendship than my priest friends whose celibacy I do not agree with, or my bachelor friends whose decisions not to marry I disagree with.

"HOMOPHOBIA"

Just as we owe homosexuals humane, decent, and respectful conduct, homosexuals owe the same to the rest of us. Homosexuals' use of the term "homophobic," however, violates this rule as much as heterosexuals' use of the term "faggot" does.

When the term "homophobic" is used to describe anyone who believes that heterosexuality should remain Western society's ideal, it is quite simply a contemporary form of McCarthyism. In fact, it is more insidious than the late senator's use of "communist." For one thing, there was and is such a thing as a communist. But "homophobia" masquerades as a scientific description of a phobia that does not exist in any medical list of phobias.

Yet the insidiousness of the term really lies elsewhere. It abuses psychology in order to dismiss a human being whose values the name-caller does not like. It dismisses a person's views as being the product of unconscious pathological fears. It is not only demeaning, it is unanswerable. Indeed, the more one denies it, the more the label sticks.

Whenever I hear the term, unless it is used to describe thugs who beat innocent homosexuals, I know that the user of the term has no argument, only McCarthy-like demagoguery, with which to rebut others. To hold that heterosexual marital sex is preferable to all other expressions of sexuality is no more "homophobic" than it is "incest-phobic" to oppose incest, or "beast-phobic" to want humans to make love only to their own species.

Finally, those who throw around the term "homophobic" ought to recognize the principle of "that which goes around comes around." We can easily descend into name-calling. Shall we start by labeling male homosexuals "women-phobic" and "vagina-phobic," and lesbians "men-phobic" and "penis-phobic"? It makes as much sense, and it is just as filthy a tactic.

Good people can differ about the desirability of alternate modes of sexual expression. There are many good people who care for homosexuals, and yet fear the chiseling away of the West's family-centered sex-in-marriage ideal. They merit debate, not the label "homophobic." And there are good homosexuals who argue otherwise. They, too, merit debate, not the label "faggot."

WHAT IS AT STAKE

The creation of Western civilization has been a terribly difficult and unique thing. It took a constant delaying of gratification, and a rechanneling of natural instincts; and these disciplines have not always been well received. There have been numerous attempts to undo Judeo-Christian civilization, not infrequently by Jews (through radical politics) and Christians (through antisemitism).

And the bedrock of this civilization, and of Jewish life, of course, has been the centrality and purity of family life. But the family is not a natural unit so much as it is a *value* that must be cultivated and protected. The Greeks assaulted the family in the name of beauty and Eros. The Marxists assaulted the family in the name of progress. And, today, gay liberation assaults it in the name of compassion and equality. I understand why gays would do this. Life has been miserable for many of them. What I have not understood is why Jews and Christians would join the assault.

I do now. They do not know what is at stake. At stake is our civilization. It is very easy to forget what Judaism has wrought and what Christians have created in the West. But those who loathe this civilization never forget. The radical Stanford University faculty and students who chanted, "Hey, hey, ho, ho, Western civ has got to go," were referring to much more than their university's syllabus.

And no one is chanting that song more forcefully than those who believe and advocate that sexual behavior doesn't play a role in building or eroding a civilization.

POSTSCRIPT

Should Homosexuality Be Accepted by Society?

Mohr concedes that many Americans consider gays to be immoral and that if the term *moral* is taken to mean "the overall beliefs affecting behavior in the society," then they are right. But he then demonstrates that homosexuality does not violate the norms of many other societies, and in some it is considered desirable. His point is that sexual norms have no universal application. This prompts a number of questions: Are there any sexual practices that deserve universal condemnation, such as rape, pedophilia, or clitoridectomy? Does the acceptance of certain practices by other societies or in other times mean that they should be any less condemned in this country today? What about society's traditional prohibition against infanticide? Like homosexuality, it too was commonly accepted in ancient Greece. Should we treat traditions that are merely relative differently from those that have universal meaning?

Mohr's *Gay Ideas: Outing and Other Controversies* (Beacon, 1992) is a collection of essays on the gay male community. *After the Ball: How America Will Conquer Its Fear and Hatred of Gays in the '90s*, by Marshall Kirk and Hunter Madsen (Doubleday, 1989), documents the abuses of gays in America and proposes strategies for making homosexuality more acceptable. Randy Shilts, in *Conduct Unbecoming: Gays and Lesbians in the U.S. Military* (St. Martin's Press, 1993), investigates the situation of lesbians and gays in the military over the last three decades, relying on more than 1,000 interviews and documents that Shilts obtained under the Freedom of Information Act. Eugene T. Gomulka, in "Why No Gays?" *Proceedings* (December 1992), makes the case for maintaining the ban on gays in the military. John D'Emilio's *Making Trouble* (Routledge, 1992) is a collection of essays on gay liberation that combine argument with autobiography. For a history of Christianity and homosexuality, see John Boswell, *Christianity, Social Tolerance, and Homosexuality: Gay People in Western Europe from the Beginning of the Christian Era to the Fourteenth Century* (University of Chicago Press, 1980). In addition to their fight against discrimination, some gay rights groups are pushing for societal recognition of gay marriages. In the November 22, 1992, edition of *Commonweal*, Brent Hartinger, in "A Case for Gay Marriage: In Support of Loving and Monogamous Relationships," argues in favor of legalizing gay marriage, while Dennis O'Brien, in "Against Gay Marriage: What Heterosexuality Means," and Jean Bethke Elshtain, in "Against Gay Marriage: Accepting Limits," argue that homosexuality goes against the purpose and meaning of the institution of marriage.

ISSUE 6

Should Traditional Families Be Preserved?

YES: David Popenoe, from "Breakup of the Family: Can We Reverse the Trend?" *USA Today Magazine*, a publication of the Society for the Advancement of Education (May 1991)

NO: Judith Stacey, from *Brave New Families: Stories of Domestic Upheaval in Late Twentieth Century America* (Basic Books, 1990)

ISSUE SUMMARY

YES: Sociologist David Popenoe decries the demise of the traditional nuclear family, explains its causes, and recommends corrective actions.

NO: Sociologist Judith Stacey argues that the falsely labeled traditional family, with the wife confined to the home, is not an option for many women and is not the preferred family practice for a majority of women.

The crisis of the American family deeply concerns many Americans. About 50 percent of marriages end in divorce, and only 27 percent of children born in 1990 are expected to be living with both parents by the time they reach age 17. Most Americans, therefore, are affected personally or are close to people who are affected by structural changes in the family. Few people can avoid being exposed to the issue: violence in the family and celebrity divorces are standard fare for news programs, and magazine articles decrying the breakdown of the family appear frequently. Most politicians today try to address the problems of the family. Academics have affirmed that the family crisis has numerous significant negative effects on children, spouses, and the larger society.

Sociologists pay attention to the role that the family plays in the functioning of society. For a society to survive, its population must reproduce (or take in many immigrants), and its young must be trained to perform adult roles and to have the values and attitudes that will motivate them to contribute to society. Procreation and socialization are two vital roles that families traditionally have performed. In addition, the family provides economic and emotional support for its members, which is vital to their effective functioning in society.

Today the performance of the family is disappointing in all these areas. Procreation outside of marriage has become rather common, and it often leads to less than ideal conditions for raising children. The scorecard on American family socialization is hard to assess, but complaints are common about such issues as parents' declining time with and influence on their children and the large population of latchkey children, or children whose parents work and who must therefore spend part of the day unsupervised. The prevalence of poverty among single-parent families and the potential for financial difficulties within families that have only one income earner indicate that the modern family will fail economically unless both spouses work. The high divorce rate and the frequency of child and spouse abuse indicate that the modern family fails to provide adequate social and emotional support.

Although most experts agree that the American family is in crisis, there is little agreement about what, if anything, should be done about it. After all, most of these problems result from the choices that people make to increase their happiness. People end unhappy marriages. Married women work for fulfillment or money that is perceived as needed. Unwed mothers decide to keep their children. The number of couples who choose to remain childless is growing rapidly. More people are also choosing to have sex before marriage, which further redefines the role of marriage in a way that pleases individuals but weakens the institutions of marriage and family. The widespread practice of abortion has similar effects.

Individual choices are not the only factors that have contributed to the weakening of the family (economic and legal changes have also played an important role), but this trend cannot be changed unless people start choosing differently. There is no sign, however, that people are going to choose differently. Does this mean that the weakening of the family is desirable? Few would advocate such an idea, but it is a reasonable position if free choice is a leading value. Sociologists recognize that the free choices of individuals do not always produce good results at the aggregate or societal level. For example, people smoke, drink, and take drugs by choice for their pleasure, but the costs in lost production, medical services, and socially harmful behaviors are immense. Is the family crisis this type of problem?

In the readings that follow, David Popenoe argues that the weakening of the traditional family is a trend that *must* be reversed. He describes the extent of the problems of the family and identifies the social consequences of current trends. He concludes by suggesting what needs to be done to strengthen families and family life. Judith Stacey argues that the traditional family needed to change. She does not applaud all the changes that have taken place, but she supports many of the choices (and the right to make those choices) that have resulted in the variety of family structures that exist in the United States today.

YES
David Popenoe

BREAKUP OF THE FAMILY: CAN WE REVERSE THE TREND?

As a social institution, the family has been "in decline" since the beginning of world history. It gradually has been becoming weaker through losing social functions and power to other institutions such as church, government, and school. Yet, during the past 25 years, family decline in the U.S., as in other industrialized societies, has been both steeper and more alarming than during any other quarter-century in our history. Although they may not use the term decline, most scholars now agree—though for many this represents a recent change of viewpoint—that the family has undergone a social transformation during this period. Some see "dramatic and unparalleled changes," while others call it "a veritable revolution."

I believe, in short, that we are witnessing the end of an epoch. Today's societal trends are bringing to a close the cultural dominance of the traditional nuclear family—one situated apart from both the larger kin group and the workplace, and focused on procreation. It consists of a legal, lifelong, sexually exclusive, heterosexual, monogamous marriage, based on affection and companionship, in which there is a sharp division of labor (separate spheres), with the female as full-time housewife and the male as primary provider and ultimate authority. Lasting for only a little more than a century, this family form emphasized the male as "good provider," the female as "good wife and mother," and the paramount importance of the family for childbearing. (Of course, not all families were able to live up to these cultural ideals.) During its heyday, the terms family, home, and mother ranked extraordinarily high in the hierarchy of cultural values.

In certain respects, this family form reached its apogee in the middle of the 20th century. By the 1950's—fueled in part by falling maternal and child mortality rates, greater longevity, and a high marriage rate—a larger percentage of children than ever before were growing up in stable, two-parent families. Similarly, this period witnessed the highest-ever proportion of women who married, bore children, and lived jointly with their husbands until at least age 50.

In the 1960's, however, four major social trends emerged to signal a widespread "flight" from both the ideal and the reality of the traditional nuclear family: rapid fertility decline, the sexual revolution, the movement of mothers into the labor force, and the upsurge in divorce. None of these changes was new to the 1960's; each represents a tendency that already was in evidence in earlier years. What happened in the 1960's was a striking acceleration of the trends, made more dramatic by the fact that, during the 1950's, they had leveled off and, in some cases, even reversed direction.

First, fertility declined in the U.S. by almost 50% between 1960 and 1989, from an average of 3.7 children per woman to only 1.9. Although births have been diminishing gradually for several centuries (the main exception being the two decades following World War II), the level of fertility during the past decade was the lowest in U.S. history and below that necessary for the replacement of the population.

A growing dissatisfaction with parenthood is now evident among adults in our culture, along with a dramatic decrease in the stigma associated with childlessness. Some demographers predict that 20–25% of today's young women will remain completely childless, and nearly 50% will be either childless or have only one offspring.

Second, the sexual revolution has shattered the association of sex and reproduction. The erotic has become a necessary ingredient of personal well-being and fulfillment, both in and outside of marriage, as well as a highly marketable commodity. The greatest change has been in the area of premarital sex. From 1971 to 1982 alone, the proportion of unmarried females in the U.S. aged 15–19 who engaged in premarital sexual intercourse jumped up from 28 to 44%. This behavior reflects a widespread change in values; in 1967, 85% of Americans condemned premarital sex as morally wrong, compared to 37% in 1979.

The sexual revolution has been a major contributor to the striking increase in unwed parenthood. Nonmarital births jumped from five percent of all births in 1960 (22% of black births) to 22% in 1985 (60% of black births). This is the highest rate of nonmarital births ever recorded in the U.S.

Third, although unmarried women long have been in the labor force, the past quarter-century has witnessed a striking movement into the paid work world of married women with children. In 1960, only 19% of married women with children under the age of six were in the labor force (39% with children between six and 17); by 1986, this figure had climbed to 54% (68% of those with older children).

Fourth, the divorce rate in the U.S. over the past 25 years (as measured by the number of divorced persons per 1,000 married persons) has practically quadrupled, going from 35 to 130. This has led many to refer to a divorce revolution. The probability that a marriage contracted today will end in divorce ranges from 44 to 66%, depending upon the method of calculation.

These trends signal a widespread retreat from the traditional nuclear family in its dimensions of a lifelong, sexually exclusive unit, focused on children, with a division of labor between husband and wife. Unlike most previous change, which reduced family functions and diminished the importance of the kin group, that of the past 25 years has tended to break up the nucleus of the family unit—the bond between husband and wife. Nuclear units, therefore, are losing ground to single-parent households, serial and step-families, and unmarried and homosexual couples.

The number of single-parent families, for example, has grown sharply—the result not only of marital breakup, but also of marriage decline (fewer persons who bear children are getting married) and widespread male abandonment. In 1960, only nine percent of U.S. children under 18 were living with a lone parent; by 1986, this figure had climbed to nearly one-quarter of all children. (The comparable figures for blacks are 22 and 53%.) Of children born during 1950–54, only 19% of whites (48% of blacks) had lived in a single-parent household by the time they reached age 17. For children born in 1990, however, the figure is projected to be 70% (94% for blacks).

The psychological character of the marital relationship also has changed substantially over the years. Traditionally, marriage has been understood as a social obligation—an institution designed mainly for economic security and procreation. Today, marriage is understood mainly as a path toward self-fulfillment. One's self-development is seen to require a significant other, and marital partners are picked primarily to be personal companions. Put another way, marriage is becoming deinstitutionalized. No longer comprising a set of norms and social obligations that are enforced widely, marriage today is a voluntary relationship that individuals can make and break at will. As one indicator of this shift, laws regulating marriage and divorce have become increasingly more lax.

As psychological expectations for marriage grow ever higher, dashed expectations for personal fulfillment fuel our society's high divorce rate. Divorce also feeds upon itself. With more divorce, the more "normal" it becomes, with fewer negative sanctions to oppose it and more potential partners available. In general, psychological need, in and of itself, has proved to be a weak basis for stable marriage.

Trends such as these dramatically have reshaped people's lifetime connectedness to the institution of the family. Broadly speaking, the institution of the family has weakened substantially over the past quarter-century in a number of respects. Individual members have become more autonomous and less bound by the group, and the latter has become less cohesive. Fewer of its traditional social functions are now carried out by the family; these have shifted to other institutions. The family has grown smaller in size, less stable, and with a shorter life span; people are, therefore, family members for a smaller percentage of their lives. The proportion of an average person's adulthood spent with spouse and children was 62% in 1960, the highest in our history. Today, it has dropped to a low of 43%.

The outcome of these trends is that people have become less willing to invest time, money, and energy in family life. It is the individual, not the family unit, in whom the main investments increasingly are made.

These trends are all evident, in varying degrees, in every industrialized Western society. This suggests that their source lies not in particular political or economic systems, but in a broad cultural shift that has accompanied industrialization and urbanization. In these societies, there clearly has emerged an ethos of radical individualism in which personal autonomy, individual rights, and social equality have gained in supremacy as cultural ideals. In keeping with these ideals, the main goals of personal behavior have shifted from commitment to social units of all kinds (families, communities, religions, nations) to personal choices, lifestyle options, self-fulfillment, and personal pleasure.

SOCIAL CONSEQUENCES

How are we to evaluate the social consequences of recent family decline? Certainly, one should not jump immediately to the conclusion that it is necessarily bad for our society. A great many positive aspects to the recent changes stand out as noteworthy. During this same quarter-century women and many minorities clearly have improved their status and probably the overall quality of their lives. Much of women's status gain has come through their release from family duties and increased participation in the labor force. In addition, given the great emphasis on psychological criteria for choosing and keeping marriage partners, it can be argued persuasively that those marriages today which do endure are more likely than ever before to be true companionships that are emotionally rewarding.

This period also has seen improved health care and longevity, as well as widespread economic affluence that has produced, for most people, a material standard of living that is historically unprecedented. Some of this improvement is due to the fact that people no longer are dependent on their families for health care and economic support or imprisoned by social class and family obligation. When in need, they now can rely more on public care and support, as well as self-initiative and self-development.

Despite these positive aspects, the negative consequences of family decline are real and profound. The greatest negative effect of recent trends, in the opinion of nearly everyone, is on children. Because they represent the future of a society, any negative consequences for them are especially significant. There is substantial, if not conclusive, evidence that, partly due to family changes, the quality of life for children in the past 25 years has worsened. Much of the problem is of a psychological nature, and thus difficult to measure quantitatively.

Perhaps the most serious problem is a weakening of the fundamental assumption that children are to be loved and valued at the highest level of priority. The general disinvestment in family life that has occurred has commonly meant a disinvestment in children's welfare. Some refer to this as a national "parent deficit." Yet, the deficit goes well beyond parents to encompass an increasingly less child-friendly society.

The parent deficit is blamed all too easily on newly working women. Yet, it is men who have left the parenting scene in large numbers. More than ever before, fathers are denying paternity, avoiding their parental obligations, and absent from home. (At the same time, there has been a slow, but not offsetting, growth of the "house-father" role.)

The breakup of the nuclear unit has been the focus of much concern. Virtually every child desires two biological parents for life, and substantial evidence exists that childrearing is most successful when it involves two parents, both of whom are strongly motivated to the task. This is not to say that other family forms can not be successful, only that, as a group, they are not as likely to be so. This also is not to claim that the two strongly motivated parents must be organized in the patriarchal and separate-sphere terms of the traditional nuclear family.

Regardless of family form, there has been a significant change over the past quarter-century in what can be called the social ecology of childhood. Advanced societies are moving ever further from what many hold to be a highly desirable childrearing environment, one consisting of a relatively large family that does a lot of things together, has many routines and traditions, and provides a great deal of quality contact time between adults and children; regular contact with relatives, active neighboring in a supportive neighborhood, and contact with the adult world of work; little concern on the part of children that their parents will break up; and the coming together of all these ingredients in the development of a rich family subculture that has lasting meaning and strongly promulgates such values as cooperation and sharing.

AGENDAS FOR CHANGE

What should be done to counteract or remedy the negative effects of family decline? This is the most controversial question of all, and the most difficult to answer. Among the agendas for change that have been put forth, two extremes stand out as particularly prominent in the national debate. The first is a return to the structure of the traditional nuclear family characteristic of the 1950's; the second is the development of extensive governmental policies.

Aside from the fact that it probably is impossible to return to a situation of an earlier time, the first alternative has major drawbacks. It would require many women to leave the workforce and, to some extent, become "de-liberated," an unlikely occurrence indeed. Economic

conditions necessitate that even more women take jobs, and cultural conditions stress ever greater equality between the sexes.

In addition to such considerations, the traditional nuclear family form, in today's world, may be fundamentally flawed. As an indication of this, one should realize that the young people who led the transformation of the family during the 1960's and 1970's were brought up in 1950's households. If the 1950's families were so wonderful, why didn't their children seek to emulate them? In hindsight, the 1950's seem to have been beset with problems that went well beyond patriarchy and separate spheres. For many families, the mother-child unit had become increasingly isolated from the kin group, the neighborhood and community, and even from the father, who worked a long distance away. This was especially true for women who were fully educated and eager to take their place in work and public life. Maternal childrearing under these historically unprecedented circumstances became highly problematic.

Despite such difficulties, the traditional nuclear family is still the one of choice for millions of Americans. They are comfortable with it, and for them it seems to work. It is reasonable, therefore, at least not to place roadblocks in the way of couples with children who wish to conduct their lives according to the traditional family's dictates. Women who freely desire to spend much of their lives as mothers and housewives, outside of the labor force, should not be penalized economically by public policy for making that choice. Nor should they be denigrated by our culture as second-class citizens.

The second major proposal for change that has been stressed in national debate is the development of extensive governmental programs offering monetary support and social services for families, especially the new "non-nuclear" ones. In some cases, these programs assist with functions these families are unable to perform adequately; in others, the functions are taken over, transforming them from family to public responsibilities.

This is the path followed by the European welfare states, but it has been less accepted by the U.S. than by any other industrialized nation. The European welfare states have been far more successful than the U.S. in minimizing the negative economic impact of family decline, especially children. In addition, many European nations have established policies making it much easier for women (and increasingly men) to combine work with childrearing. With these successes in mind, it seems inevitable that the U.S. will (and I believe should) move gradually in the European direction with respect to family policies, just as we are now moving gradually in that direction with respect to medical care.

There are clear drawbacks, however, in moving too far down this road. If children are to be served best, we should seek to make the family stronger, not to replace it. At the same time that welfare states are minimizing some of the consequences of decline, they also may be causing further breakup of the family unit. This phenomenon can be witnessed today in Sweden, where the institution of the family probably has grown weaker than anywhere else in the world. On a lesser scale it has been seen in the U.S. in connection with our welfare programs. Fundamental to successful welfare state programs, therefore, is keeping uppermost in mind that the ultimate goal is to strengthen families.

While each of the above alternatives has some merit, I suggest a third one. It is premised on the fact that we can not return to the 1950's family, nor can we depend on the welfare state for a solution. Instead, we should strike at the heart of the cultural shift that has occurred, point up its negative aspects, and seek to reinvigorate the cultural ideals of family, parents, and children within the changed circumstances of our time. We should stress that the individualistic ethos has gone too far, that children are getting woefully shortchanged, and that, over the long run, strong families represent the best path toward self-fulfillment and personal happiness. We should bring again to the cultural forefront the old ideal of parents living together and sharing responsibility for their children and for each other.

What is needed is a new social movement whose purpose is the promotion of families and their values within the new constraints of modern life. It should point out the supreme importance to society of strong families, while at the same time suggesting ways they can adapt better to the modern conditions of individualism, equality, and the labor force participation of both women and men. Such a movement could build on the fact that the overwhelming majority of young people today still put forth as their major life goal a lasting, monogamous, heterosexual relationship which includes the procreation of children. It is reasonable to suppose that this goal is so pervasive because it is based on a deep-seated human need.

The time seems ripe to reassert that strong families concerned with the needs of children are not only possible, but necessary.

NO

Judith Stacey

THE POSTMODERN FAMILY, FOR BETTER AND WORSE

BACKWARD TOWARD THE POSTMODERN FAMILY

Two centuries ago leading white, middle-class families in the newly united American states spearheaded a family revolution that replaced the premodern gender order with a modern family system. But "modern family" was an oxymoronic label for the peculiar institution, which dispensed modernity to white, middle-class men only by withholding it from women. The former could enter the public sphere as breadwinners and citizens, because their wives were confined to the newly privatized family realm. Ruled by an increasingly absent patriarchal landlord, the modern, middle-class family, a woman's domain, soon was sentimentalized as "traditional."

It took most of the subsequent two centuries for substantial numbers of white working-class men to achieve the rudimentary economic passbook to "modern" family life—a male family wage. By the time they had done so, however, a second family revolution was well underway. Once again middle-class, white families appeared to be in the vanguard. This time women were claiming the benefits and burdens of modernity, a status we could achieve only at the expense of the "modern" family itself. Reviving a long-dormant feminist movement, frustrated middle-class homemakers and their more militant daughters subjected modern domesticity to a sustained critique. At times this critique displayed scant sensitivity to the effects our antimodern family ideology might have on women for whom full-time domesticity had rarely been feasible. Thus, feminist family reform came to be regarded widely as a white, middle-class agenda, and white, working-class families its most resistant adversaries.

I shared these presumptions before my fieldwork among Silicon Valley families radically altered my understanding of the class basis of the postmodern family revolution. White, middle-class families, I have come to believe, are less the innovators than the propagandists and principal beneficiaries of contemporary family change. African-American women and white, working-class women have been the genuine postmodern family pioneers, even though they also suffer most from its most negative effects. Long denied the mixed benefits that the modern family order offered middle-class women, less privileged women quietly forged alternative models of femininity to that of full-time domesticity and mother-intensive child rearing. Struggling creatively, often heroically, to sustain oppressed families and to escape the most oppressive ones, they drew on "traditional" premodern kinship resources and crafted untraditional ones, lurching backward and forward into the postmodern family.

Rising divorce and cohabitation rates, working mothers, two-earner households, single and unwed parenthood, and matrilineal, extended, and fictive kin support networks appeared earlier and more extensively among poor and working-class people. Economic pressures more than political principles governed these departures from domesticity, but working women... soon found additional reasons to appreciate paid employment. Eventually white, middle-class women, sated and even sickened by our modern family privileges, began to emulate, elaborate, and celebrate many of these alternative family practices....

FAMILY QUARRELS

Recent books with such titles as *Falling from Grace* and *Fear of Falling* convey widespread suffering and anxiety among once-settled, middle-class Americans. And Americans, as historian Linda Gordon noted, recurrently frame social anxieties in familial terms. Sociologists may attempt to reassure an anxious populace that family life is "here to stay,"

but, as political analyst Andrew Hacker once observed, "it is hardly news that families are not what they used to be." The modern family system has lost the cultural and statistical dominance it long enjoyed, and no new family order has arisen to supplant it. The postmodern family is a site of disorder instead, a contested domain.

The passionate public response to the [Daniel Patrick] Moynihan report [on minority families] of the 1960s signaled a prolonged era of national conflict and confusion over which gender and kinship relationships are to count as "families" in postindustrial America. And in this family quarrel, gender and sexual politics occupy pride of place. Which relationships between and among women and men will receive legal recognition, social legitimacy, institutional and cultural support? In the postmodern period, a truly democratic gender and kinship order, one that does not favor male authority, heterosexuality, a particular division of labor, or a singular household or parenting arrangement became thinkable for the first time in history. And during the past several decades, family visionaries and reformers have been organizing struggles to bring it to fruition. They have met, however, with fierce resistance, and, as feminists have learned with great pain, it is not men alone who resist.

Why do many people of both genders recoil from the prospect of a fully democratic family regime? While there are multiple motives, including theological ones, this [selection] suggests compelling sociological sources of popular ambivalence about family reform. Not only would a democratic kinship system threaten vested gender and class interests, but even under the most benevolent of social orders, it promises also to bring its own kind of costs. A fully voluntary marriage system, as this century's experience with divorce rates indicates,... institutionalizes conjugal and thus parental instability. A normless gender order, one in which parenting arrangements, sexuality, and the distribution of work, responsibility, and resources all are negotiable and constantly renegotiable, can also invite considerable conflict and insecurity. These inescapable "burdens of freedom" have been magnified monstrously, however, under the far-from-benevolent social conditions of this turbulent, conservative period.

Many men, African-American men most of all, have suffered from postindustrialization and the eroding modern family order, while, thanks to feminism, numerous women, particularly white, middle-class ones, have achieved substantial gains. The resilient gender inequality of the transitional period, however, places the vast majority of women at disproportionate risk. In exchange for subordination and domestic service, the modern family promised women a number of customary protections and privileges, principal among these, lifelong support from a male breadwinner. Scarcely had working-class women... achieved access to this "patriarchal bargain," however, before it collapsed in a postindustrial deluge. With few social protections provided to replace the precarious "private" ones that the modern family once offered, many women have found good cause to mistrust the terms postmodern conditions appear to offer in its place. Women have been adding the burdens and benefits of paid labor to their historic domestic responsibilities, but men seem less eager

to share the responsibilities and rewards of child rearing and housework. Moreover, as feminists have demonstrated in depressing detail, women have suffered numerous unexpected, and disturbing, consequences of egalitarian family reforms, such as no-fault divorce, joint custody provisions, shared parenting, and sexual liberation. Consequently, as Deirdre English, former editor of *Mother Jones* once observed, many women have come to "fear that feminism will free men first."

The insecure and undemocratic character of postmodern family life fuels nostalgia for the fading modern family, now recast as the "traditional" family. Capitalizing on this nostalgia, a vigorous, antifeminist "profamily" movement was able to score impressive political victories in the 1980s. It successfully, if incorrectly, identified feminism as the primary cause of the demise of the modern family, rather than the mopping-up operation for postindustrial transformations that were long underway. Defining the ERA [Equal Rights Amendment] and abortion rights as threats to the family, it placed feminists in the same defensive posture that housewives had come to assume. And partly because the profamily movement could draw on the volunteer labors of the disproportionate numbers of housewives it attracted to its political ranks, the backlash movement was able to achieve political visibility and victories far in excess of its numerical strength. Former President Reagan assured this movement a profound and lasting political legacy by rewarding its contribution to his "revolution" with antifeminist appointments to the Supreme Court and the federal judiciary who promise to inhibit the progress of democratic family reform well into the twenty-first century.

Many feminists, like myself, were caught off guard by the retreat from feminist activism and the resurgence of profamilialism that characterized the 1980s. During the 1970s family instability seemed to swell the ranks of the women's liberation movement. Feminist ideology, disseminated not only by the media but in flourishing grass-roots community activities and women's reentry programs, served [many] women... well to ease the exit from, or the reform of, unhappy modern marriages. Even older women in successful long-term marriages... employed feminist principles to improve their relationships. Second-wave feminism also supported women's efforts to develop independent work lives and career goals. With high divorce rates and women's paid work continuing throughout the eighties, feminist activism and family reforms might have been expected to progress apace.

Yet optimistic projections like these did not reckon with the ravages of post-industrialism. Neither feminism nor other progressive family reform movements have been as useful in addressing the structural inequalities of postindustrial occupational structure or the individualist, fast-track culture that makes all too difficult the formation of stable intimate relations on a democratic, or any other basis....

WHOSE FAMILY CRISIS?

Ironically, while women are becoming the new proletariat and some men are increasing their participation in housework and childwork, the postmodern family, even more than the modern family it is replacing, is proving to be a woman-tended domain. There is some empirical basis for the enlightened father imagery celebrated by films like "Kramer versus Kramer." Indeed my fieldwork corroborates evidence that the determined efforts by many working women and feminists to reintegrate men into family life have had some success. There are data, for example, indicating that increasing numbers of men would sacrifice occupational gains in order to have more time with their families, just as there are data documenting actual increases in male involvement in child care. The excessive media attention which the faintest signs of new paternity enjoy, however, may be symptomatic of a deeper, far less comforting reality it so effectively obscures. We are experiencing, as demographer Andrew Cherlin aptly puts it, "the feminization of kinship." Demographers report a drastic decline in the average numbers of years that men live in households with young children. Few of the women who assume responsibility for their children in 90 percent of divorce cases in the United States today had to wage a custody battle for this privilege. We hear few proposals for a "daddy track." And few of the adults providing care to sick and elderly relatives are male. Yet ironically, most of the alarmist, nostalgic literature about contemporary family decline impugns women's abandonment of domesticity, the flipside of our tardy entry into modernity. Rarely do the anxious outcries over the destructive effects on families of working mothers, high divorce rates, institutionalized child care, or sexual liberalization scrutinize the family behaviors of men. Anguished voices, emanating from all bands on the political spectrum, lament state and market interventions that are weakening "the family." But whose family bonds are fraying? Women have amply demonstrated our continuing commitment to sustaining kin ties. If there is a family crisis, it is a male family crisis.

The crisis cannot be resolved by reviving the modern family system. While nostalgia for an idealized world of *Ozzie and Harriet* and *Archie Bunker* families abounds, little evidence suggests that most Americans genuinely wish to return to the gender order these symbolize. On the contrary, the vast majority ... are actively remaking family life. Indeed a 1989 survey conducted by *The New York Times* found more than two-thirds of women, including a substantial majority of even those living in "traditional"— that is to say, "modern"—households, as well as a majority of men agreeing that "the United States continues to need a strong women's movement to push for changes that benefit women." Yet many seem reluctant to own their family preferences.... [T]hey cling to images of themselves as "back from the old days," while venturing ambivalently but courageously into the new.

Responding to new economic and social insecurities as well as to feminism, higher percentages of families in almost all income groups have adopted a multiple-earner strategy. Thus, the household form that has come closer than any other to replacing the modern family with a new cultural and statistical norm consists of a two-earner, heterosexual married couple with children. It is not likely, however, that any single household type will soon achieve the measure of normalcy that the modern family long enjoyed. Indeed, the postmodern success of the voluntary principle of the modern family system precludes this. The routinization of divorce and remarriage generates a diversity of family patterns even greater than was characteristic of the premodern period when death

prevented family stability or household homogeneity. Even cautious demographers judge the new family diversity to be "an intrinsic feature ... rather than a temporary aberration" of contemporary family life.

"The family" is *not* "here to stay." Nor should we wish it were. On the contrary, I believe that all democratic people, whatever their kinship preferences, should work to hasten its demise. An ideological concept that imposes mythical homogeneity on the diverse means by which people organize their intimate relationships, "the family" distorts and devalues this rich variety of kinship stories. And, along with the class, racial, and heterosexual prejudices it promulgates, this sentimental fictional plot authorizes gender hierarchy. Because the postmodern family crisis ruptures this seamless modern family script, it provides a democratic opportunity. Efforts to expand and redefine the definition of family by feminists and gay liberation activists and by many minority rights organizations are responses to this opportunity, seeking to extend social legitimacy and institutional support to the diverse patterns of intimacy that Americans have already forged.

If feminist identity threatens many and seems out of fashion, struggles to reconstitute gender and kinship on a just and democratic basis are more popular than ever. If only a minority of citizens are willing to grant family legitimacy to gay domestic partners, an overwhelming majority subscribe to the postmodern definition of a family by which the New York Supreme Court validated a gay man's right to retain his deceased lover's apartment. "By a ratio of 3-to-1" people surveyed in a Yale University study defined the family as "a group of people who love and care for each other." And while a majority of those surveyed gave negative ratings to the quality of American family life in general, 71 percent declared themselves "at least very satisfied" with their own family lives.

There is bad faith in the popular lament over family decline. Family nostalgia deflects social criticism from the social sources of most "personal troubles." Supply-side economics, governmental deregulation, and the right-wing assault on social welfare programs have intensified the destabilizing effects of recent occupational upheavals on flagging modern families and emergent postmodern ones alike. This [selection] is not the first to expose the bitter irony of right-wing politicians manipulating nostalgia for eroding working-class families while instituting policies that deepened their distress. Indeed, the ability to provide financial security was the chief family concern of most surveyed in the Yale study. If the postmodern family crisis represents a democratic opportunity, contemporary economic and political conditions enable only a minority to realize its tantalizing potential.

The bad faith revealed in the discrepant data reported in the Yale study indicates how reluctant most Americans are to fully own the genuine ambivalence we feel about family and social change. Yet ambivalence, as sociologist Alan Wolfe suggests, is an underappreciated but responsible moral stance, and one well suited for democratic citizenship: "Given the paradoxes of modernity, there is little wrong, and perhaps a great deal right, with being ambivalent—especially when there is so much to be ambivalent about."

Certainly... there are good grounds for ambivalence about postmodern family conditions. Even were a feminist family revolution to succeed, it could never eliminate all family distress. At best, it would foster a social order that could invert Tolstoy's aphorism by granting happy families the freedom to differ, and even to suffer. Truly postfeminist families, however, would suffer only the "common unhappiness" endemic to intimate human relationships; they would be liberated from the "hysterical misery" generated by social injustice. No nostalgic movement to restore the modern family can offer as much. For better and/or worse, the postmodern family revolution is here to stay.

POSTSCRIPT

Should Traditional Families Be Preserved?

It is important to understand how each author uses the terminology to describe different family forms. Stacey describes the white, middle-class family model as the "modern family system," while Popenoe refers to the same model as the "traditional nuclear family," a term that has declined in use since the 1950s. Also, what Stacey calls the "postmodern family"—represented by a variety of family styles, including single-mother, two-earner, and unwed-parent families—Popenoe calls the "recent" or "modern" family system. Therefore, Stacey and Popenoe use the word *modern* in opposite ways.

Popenoe admits that there are many positive aspects to the recent changes that have affected families, but he sees the negative consequences, especially for children, as necessitating actions to counter them. He recognizes that it is impossible to return to the family pattern that predominated in the 1950s and that a government welfare approach would weaken family values further, as has been found where it has been tried. Instead he recommends a propaganda campaign to sell family values and preach against the individualistic ethos. He hopes for a family-oriented social movement. Is this a pie-in-the-sky solution? Remember that social movements arise spontaneously. Governments can encourage them, but they cannot manufacture them. Remember also that social movements (the women's movement and the sexual revolution) created the crisis of the family in the first place, and many join Stacey in applauding these changes. Finally, one cannot be encouraged by a theory that maintains that the only acceptable solution requires a change of heart of the American people because such a widespread and thoroughgoing change is generally unlikely.

Both authors agree that great changes have taken place in the American family, but this observation has not gone uncontested. Theodore Caplow and others replicated a study first conducted in the 1920s in Muncie, Indiana, and found many continuities and relatively few changes in family patterns. See *Middletown Families: Fifty Years of Change and Continuity* (University of Minnesota Press, 1983). Mary Jo Bane, in *Here to Stay: American Families in the Twentieth Century* (Basic Books, 1976), upholds Caplow et al.'s conclusion that there is little evidence that the family as an institution has disintegrated. Continuity is also the theme in the collection of essays on women's familial roles entitled *Women and the Family: Two Decades of Change* (Haworth Press, 1984), edited by Beth B. Hess and Marvin B. Sussman. Arlene Skolnick argues that the family is in a crisis in *Embattled Paradise: The American Family in an Age of Uncertainty* (Basic Books, 1991). In contrast to the family crisis view, Andrew M. Greeley presents a positive portrait of the family in *Faithful Attraction* (Tor Books, 1991). Change is emphasized in Andrew Cherlin's two books *Marriage, Divorce, Remarriage* (Harvard University Press, 1981) and *The Changing American Family and Public Policy* (Urban Institute Press, 1988). For a major statistical analysis of changing family patterns, see James A. Sweet and Larry L. Bumpass, *American Families and Households* (Russell Sage Foundation, 1987). For a long-term view of changes in the American family, see Steven Mintz and Susan Kellogg, *Domestic Revolutions: A Social History of American Family Life* (Free Press, 1989). For a discussion of equality in the family and society, see Mary Frances Berry, *The Politics of Parenthood* (Viking Penguin, 1993).

PART 3

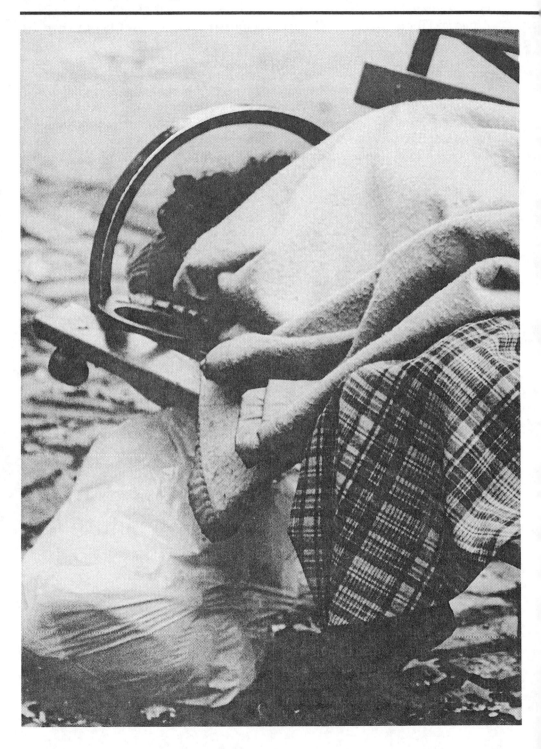

Stratification and Inequality

Although the ideal of equal opportunity for all is strong in the United States, many charge that the American political and economic system is unfair. Various affirmative action programs have been implemented to remedy unequal opportunities, but some argue that this is discrimination in reverse. Others argue that minorities should depend on themselves, not the government, to overcome differences in equality. Does poverty continue to exist in the United States despite public assistance programs because it has become a deeply ingrained way of life for individuals? Or is poverty as well as homelessness a result of the failure of policymakers to live up to U.S. egalitarian principles? Social scientists debate these questions in this part.

- Is Economic Inequality Beneficial
  to Society?

- Does "Lower-Class" Culture
  Perpetuate Poverty?

- Is Black Self-Help the Solution to Racial
  Inequality?

- Is Affirmative Action Reverse Discrimination?

- Do Social and Mental Pathologies Largely
  Account for Homelessness?

ISSUE 7

Is Economic Inequality Beneficial to Society?

YES: George Gilder, from *Wealth and Poverty* (Basic Books, 1981; Reissue, ICS Press, 1993)

NO: William Ryan, from *Equality* (Pantheon Books, 1981)

ISSUE SUMMARY

YES: Social critic George Gilder praises the American political economy because it provides many incentives for people to get ahead and make money. He maintains that the economy is dynamic and that all classes of people benefit.

NO: Professor of psychology William Ryan contends that income inequalities in America are excessive and immoral because they vastly exceed differences of merit and result in tremendous hardship for the poor.

Few people think that the president of the United States should be paid the same salary as a professor of sociology or a teaching assistant. Everyone benefits when the financial rewards for being president are large enough to motivate the most capable members of society to compete for the job. A society is better off with income inequality than with income equality as long as everyone has an equal opportunity to compete for the high-paying jobs. Pay differentials are needed to get the best possible fit between people and jobs. But how much income inequality is desirable? On this issue, people strongly disagree, and they carry their disagreement into the political arena.

Income inequality should be viewed as only one type of inequality. Four other essential dimensions of equality/inequality are opportunity, legal rights, political power, and social status. In principle, America is fully committed to equality of opportunity and equality of legal and political rights. Americans believe that everyone should have an equal opportunity to compete for jobs and awards. Laws that forbid discrimination and free public school education are two major means for providing equal opportunities to U.S. citizens. Whether or not society should also compensate for handicaps such as disadvantaged family backgrounds or the ravages of past discrimination, however, is a knotty issue that has divided the country. Policies such as the Head Start compensatory education program for poor preschoolers, income-based scholarships, quotas, and affirmative action are hotly debated. Equality of legal rights has been promoted by the civil rights and women's movements. A major debate in this area, of course, is the Equal Rights Amendment (ERA). However, the disagreement is not over the principle of equality but over whether the ERA is good or bad for women. America's commitment to political equality is strong in principle, though less strong in practice. Everyone over 18 years old gets one vote, and all votes are counted equally, but the political system tilts in the direction of special interest groups; those who do not belong to such groups are seldom heard. Furthermore, money plays an increasingly important role in political campaigns. Clearly, there is room for improvement here. The final dimension of equality/inequality is status. Inequality of status involves differences in prestige, and it is arguable as to whether or not it can or should be eliminated. Ideally, the people who contribute the most to society are the most highly esteemed. The reader can judge the extent to which this principle holds true in the United States.

The Declaration of Independence proclaims that "all men are created equal," and the Founding Fathers who wrote the Declaration of Independence went on to base the laws of the land on the principle of equality. The equality they were referring to was equality of opportunity and legal and political rights for white, property-owning males. They did not mean equality of income or status, though they recognized that too much inequality of income would jeopardize democratic institutions. In the two centuries following the signing of the Declaration, nonwhites and women struggled for and won considerable equality of opportunity and rights. Meanwhile, income gaps in the United States have been widening (except from 1929 to 1945, when the stock market crash harmed the wealthy and wartime full employment favored the poor).

Should America now move toward greater income equality? Must this dimension of inequality be rectified in order for society to be just? George Gilder strongly believes that people must try hard, work hard, innovate, compete, aspire, accept risks, and be rewarded for their efforts. He maintains that welfare, public enterprise, highly progressive taxes, and many other egalitarian measures are sapping American initiative, crippling American enterprise, slowing the American economy, and perpetuating the poverty of the poor. According to Gilder, the free enterprise system, with all of its inequalities, stimulates individual effort and enterprise, and this is what makes America great and prosperous. On the other hand, William Ryan makes the case that the existing income inequalities are obscene and offensive to moral sensibilities. He believes that some reduction of inequalities is essential to social justice. According to Ryan, the rich and their propagandists justify existing inequalities by claiming that the system is fair and that the inequalities result largely from differential effort, skill, and achievement. He argues that this justification is weak.

YES

George Gilder

THE DIRGE OF TRIUMPH

The most important event in the recent history of ideas is the demise of the socialist dream. Dreams always die when they come true, and fifty years of socialist reality, in every partial and plenary form, leave little room for idealistic reverie. In the United States socialism chiefly rules in auditoria and parish parlors, among encounter groups of leftist intellectuals retreating from the real world outside, where socialist ideals have withered in the shadows of Stalin and Mao, Sweden and Tanzania, gulag and bureaucracy.

The second most important event of the recent era is the failure of capitalism to win a corresponding triumph. For within the colleges and councils, governments and churches where issue the nebulous but nonetheless identifiable airs and movements of new opinion, the manifest achievements of free enterprise still seem less comely than the promise of socialism betrayed....

A prominent source of trouble is the profession of economics. Smith entitled Book One of *The Wealth of Nations,* "Of the Causes of Improvement in the productive Powers of Labour and the Order according to which its Produce is naturally distributed among the different Ranks of the people." He himself stressed the productive powers, but his followers, beginning with David Ricardo, quickly became bogged down in a static and mechanical concern with distribution. They all were forever counting the ranks of rich and poor and assaying the defects of capitalism that keep the poor always with us in such great numbers. The focus on distribution continues in economics today, as economists pore balefully over the perennial inequalities and speculate on brisk "redistributions" to rectify them.

This mode of thinking, prominent in foundation-funded reports, best-selling economics texts, newspaper columns, and political platforms, is harmless enough on the surface. But its deeper effect is to challenge the golden rule of capitalism, to pervert the relation between rich and poor, and to depict the system as "a zero-sum game" in which every gain for someone implies a loss for someone else, and wealth is seen once again to create poverty. As Kristol has said, a free society in which the distributions are widely seen as unfair cannot long survive. The distributionist mentality thus strikes at the living heart of democratic capitalism.

Whether of wealth, income, property, or government benefits, distributions always, unfortunately, turn out bad: highly skewed, hugely unequal,

From George Gilder, *Wealth and Poverty* (Basic Books, 1981; Reissue, ICS Press, 1993). Copyright © 1981 by George Gilder. Reprinted by permission of Georges Borchardt, Inc., for the author.

presumptively unfair, and changing little, or getting worse. Typical conclusions are that "the top 2 percent of all families own 44 percent of all family wealth, and the bottom 25 percent own none at all"; or that "the top 5 percent get 15.3 percent of the pretax income and the bottom 20 percent get 5.4 percent." ...

Statistical distributions, though, can misrepresent the economy in serious ways. They are implicitly static, like a picture of a corporate headquarters, towering high above a city, that leaves out all the staircases, escalators, and elevators, and the Librium® on the executive's desk as he contemplates the annual report. The distribution appears permanent, and indeed, like the building, it will remain much the same year after year. But new companies will move in and out, executives will come and go, people at the bottom will move up, and some at the top will leave their Librium® and jump. For example, the share of the tobacco industry commanded by the leading four firms has held steady for nearly thirty years, but the leader of the 1950s is now nearly bankrupt. The static distributions also miss the simple matter of age; many of the people at the bottom of the charts are either old, and thus beyond their major earning years, or young, and yet to enter them. Although the young and the old will always be with us, their low earnings signify little about the pattern of opportunity in a capitalist system.

Because blacks have been at the bottom for centuries now, economists often miss the dynamism within the American system. The Japanese, for example, were interned in concentration camps during World War II, but thirty years later they had higher per capita earnings than any other ethnic group in America except the Jews. Three and one-half million

Jewish immigrants arrived on our shores around the turn of the century with an average of nine dollars per person in their pockets, less than almost any other immigrant group. Six decades later the mean family income of Jews was almost double the national average. Meanwhile the once supreme British Protestants (WASPs) were passed in per capita earnings after World War II not only by Jews and Orientals but also by Irish, Italians, Germans, and Poles (which must have been the final Polish joke), and the latest generation of black West Indians.

It is a real miracle that learned social scientists can live in the midst of these continuing eruptions and convulsions, these cascades and cataracts of change, and declare in a tone of grim indignation that "Over the last fifty years there has been no shift in the distribution of wealth and income in this country." ...

The income distribution tables also propagate a statistical illusion with regard to the American rich. While the patterns of annual income changed rather little in the 1970s, there was a radical shift in the distribution of wealth. In order to understand this development, it is crucial to have a clear-eyed view of the facts and effects of inflation, free of the pieties of the Left and the Right: the familiar rhetoric of the "cruelest tax," in which all the victims seem to be widows and orphans. In fact, widows and orphans—at least the ones who qualified for full social security and welfare benefits—did rather well under inflation. Between 1972 and 1977, for example, the median household income of the elderly rose from 80 to 85 percent of the entire population's. As Christopher Jencks of Harvard University and Joseph Minarek of the Brookings Institution, both men of the Left, discovered in the late 1970s, inflation hit hardest at savers and investors, largely the rich....

Wealth consists of assets that promise a future stream of income. The flows of oil money do not become an enduring asset of the nation until they can be converted into a stock of remunerative capital—industries, ports, roads, schools, and working skills—that offer a future flow of support when the oil runs out. Four hundred years ago, Spain was rich like Saudi Arabia, swamped by a similar flood of money in the form of silver from the mines of Potosi in its Latin American colonies. But Spain failed to achieve wealth and soon fell back into its previous doldrums, while industry triumphed in apparently poorer parts of Europe.

A wealthy country must be able to save as well as to consume. Saving is often defined as deferred consumption. But it depends on investment: the ability to produce consumable goods at that future date to which consumption has been deferred. Saving depends on having something to buy when the deposit is withdrawn. For an individual it sounds easy; there must always be *something* to buy after all. But for a nation, with many savers, real wealth is hard work, requiring prolonged and profitable production of goods....

Work, indeed, is the root of wealth, even of the genius that mostly resides in sweat. But without a conception of goals and purposes, well-paid workers consume or waste all that they earn. Pop singers rocking and rolling in money, rich basketball stars who symbolize wealth to millions, often end up deep in debt with nothing solid to show for their efforts, while the poorest families can often succeed in saving enough to launch profitable businesses. The old adages on the importance of thrift are true not only because they signify a quantitative rise in investible funds, but because they betoken imagination and purpose, which make wealth. Few businesses begin with bank loans, and small businesses almost never do. Instead they capitalize labor.

For example, ten years ago a Lebanese family arrived in Lee, Massachusetts, with a few dollars and fewer words of English. The family invested the dollars in buying a woebegone and abandoned shop beside the road at the edge of town, and they started marketing vegetables. The man rose at five every morning to drive slowly a ramshackle truck a hundred miles to farms in the Connecticut Valley, where he purchased the best goods he could find as cheaply as possible to sell that morning in Lee. It was a classic entrepreneurial performance, arbitrage, identifying price differentials in different markets, and exploiting them by labor. But because both the labor and the insight was little compensated, it was in a sense invisibly saved and invested in the store. All six children were sources of accumulating capital as they busily bustled about the place. The store remained open long hours, cashed checks of locals, and began to build a clientele. A few years later one had to fight through the crowds around it in summer, when the choice asparagus or new potted plants went on sale. Through the year it sold flowers and Christmas trees, gas and dry goods, maple syrup and blackberry jam, cider and candies, and wines and liquors, in the teeth of several supermarkets, innumerable gas stations, and other shops of every description, all better situated, all struggling in an overtaxed and declining Massachusetts economy.

The secret was partly in the six children (who placed the family deep in the statistics of per capita poverty for long after its arrival) and in the entrepreneurial vision of the owner, which eluded all the charts. Mr. Michael Zabian is the man's name, and he recently bought the biggest office building in the town, a three-story structure made of the same Lee marble as the national capitol building. He owns a large men's clothing store at street level and what amounts to a small shopping center at his original site; and he preens in three-piece suits in the publicity photos at the Chamber of Commerce.

As extraordinary as may seem his decade of achievement, though, two other Lebanese have performed similar marvels in the Berkshires and have opened competing shops in the area. Other immigrants in every American city—Cubans in Miami, Portuguese in Providence and Newark, Filipinos in Seattle, Koreans in Washington, D.C., and New York, Vietnamese in Los Angeles, to mention the more recent crop—have performed comparable feats of commerce, with little help from banks or government or the profession of economics.

Small firms, begun by enterprising men, can rise quickly to play important roles in the national economy. Berkshire Paper Company, for example, was started by Whitmore (Nick) Kelley of Glendale, Massachusetts, as a maker of scratch pads in the rural town of Great Barrington. One of the array of paper manufacturers along the Housatonic River, the firm endured repeated setbacks, which turned into benefits, and, by 1980, it was providing important capital and consumer goods to some of the nation's largest and fastest growing corporations, though Kelley himself had no inherited wealth or outside support.

From the onset, the company's capital consisted mostly of refuse. Like the copper and steel companies thriving on the contents of slag heaps, Berkshire Paper Company employed paper, machinery, and factory space rejected as useless by other companies. Berkshire Paper, in fact, was launched and grew with almost no recourse to resources or capital that was accorded by any value at all in any national economic accounts. Yet the company has now entered the semiconductor industry and holds virtual monopolies in three sophisticated products. The story of its rise from scratch pads to semiconductor products shows the irrelevance of nearly all the indices of economic value and national wealth employed by the statisticians of our economy.

As a sophomore in college, Nick Kelley used to visit his stepfather at Clark-Aiken, a manufacturer of papermaking machine tools in Lee, Massachusetts. Within and around the factory, he noticed random piles of paper and asked his stepfather what was done with them. He was told they were leftovers from machinery tests and would be loaded into a truck and taken to the Lee dump. Kelley asked whether he could have them instead.

He took a handful of paper to an office-supply store, Gowdy's in Pittsfield, and asked the proprietor what such paper was good for. Scratch pads, he was told. After long trial and error, and several visits to a scratch pad factory in the guise of a student, he figured out how to make the pads. With the help of his stepfather he purchased and repaired a broken paper-cutting machine, and he even found a new method of applying glue, replacing the usual paintbrush with a paint roller. He then scoured much of the Northeast for markets and created a thriving scratch pad business that, again with his stepfather's help, even survived

Kelley's stint in Southeast Asia during the Vietnam War.

In every case, setbacks led to innovation and renewed achievement. Deprived of paper from Clark-Aiken, he learned how to purchase it from jobbers in New York. Discovering that it cost two cents a pound more in sheets than in rolls (nine cents rather than seven cents), he computed that the two pennies represented a nearly 30 percent hike in cost and determined to contrive a sheeter out of old equipment. Finally, his worst setback drove him out of the scratch pad business altogether and allowed him to greatly expand his company.

Attempting to extend his marketing effort to Boston, Kelley approached the buyer for a large office-supply firm. The buyer said he doubted that Kelley could meet the competition. Kelley demanded to know how anyone could sell them for less, when the raw materials alone cost some fourteen cents a pound, and he sold the pads for eighteen cents. He went off to investigate his rival, a family firm run by Italians in Somerville. Kelley found a factory in an old warehouse, also filled with old equipment, but organized even more ingeniously than Kelley's own. He had to acknowledge that the owner was "the best." "He had me beat." Kelley said, "I decided then and there to go out of scratch pad manufacturing." Instead he resolved to buy pads from the Somerville factory and use his own marketing skills to sell them. He also purchased printing equipment and began adding value to the pads by printing specified lines and emblems on them.

This effort led to a request from Schweitzer, a large paper firm in the Berkshires, that Kelley print up legal pads, and then later, in a major breakthrough, that he cut up some tea bag paper that the Schweitzer machines could not handle. Although Kelley had only the most crude cutting machinery, he said sure, he could process tea bags. He took a pile of thin paper and spent several days and nights at work on it, destroying a fourth of the sheets before his machine completely jammed and pressed several of the layers together so tightly that he found he could easily cut them. This accident gave Kelley a reputation as a worker of small miracles with difficult and specialized papermaking tasks, and the large companies in the area began channeling their most difficult production problems to him.

These new assignments eventually led to three significant monopolies for the small Berkshire firm. One was in making women's fingernail mending tissue (paper with long fibers that adhere to the nail when it is polished) for cosmetic firms from Avon to Revlon. Another was in manufacturing facial blotting tissue (paper that cleans up dirt and makeup without rubbing) for such companies as Mary Kaye and Bonne Belle. His third and perhaps most important project, though—a task that impelled Kelley to pore endlessly through the literature of semiconductor electronics, trafficking in such concepts as microns (one-thousandth of a centimeter) and angstroms (one thousandth of a micron)—was production of papers for use in the manufacture of microprocessors and other semiconductor devices. This required not only the creation of papers sufficiently lint free to wrap a silicon wafer in (without dislodging an electron), but also a research effort to define for the companies precisely what impurities and "glitches" might remain. Kelley now provides this paper, along with the needed information, to all leading semiconductor companies, from National Semiconductor to Intel and Motorola, and he continues research to perfect his product.

Throughout his career, Kelley had demonstrated that faith and imagination are the most important capital goods in the American economy, that wealth is a product less of money than of mind.

The official measures miss all such sources of wealth. When Heilbroner and Thurow claim that 25 percent of American households owned zero net wealth in 1969, they are speaking of families that held above 5 billion dollars' worth of automobiles, 16 billion dollars of other consumer durables, such as washers and television sets, 11 billion dollars' worth of housing (about one-third had cars and 90 percent TVs), as well as rights in Medicaid, social security, housing, education, and other governmental benefits. They commanded many billions of dollars' worth of human capital, some of it rather depreciated by age and some by youthful irresponsibilities (most of these poor households consisted either of single people or abandoned mothers and their offspring). Their net worth was zero, because their debts exceeded their calculable worth. Yet some 80 percent of these people who were poor in 1969 escaped poverty within two years, only to be replaced in the distributions by others too young, too old, too improvident, or too beset with children to manage a positive balance in their asset accounts.

Now it may be appropriate to exclude from the accounting such items as rights in government welfare and transfer programs, which often destroy as much human worth as they create. But the distribution tables also miss the assets of the greatest ultimate value. For example, they treated as an increment of poverty, bereft of net worth, the explosive infusion of human capital that arrived on our shores from Lebanon in the guise of an unlettered family.

Families of zero wealth built America. Many of the unincorporated businesses that have gained some 500 billion dollars in net value since World War II (six times more than all the biggest corporations combined) were started in households of zero assets according to the usual accounts. The conception of a huge and unnegotiable gap between poverty and wealth is a myth. In the Berkshires, Zabian moving up passed many scions of wealth on their way down....

In the second tier of wealth-holders, in which each member would average nearly 2 million dollars net worth in 1970 dollars, 71 percent reported no inherited assets at all, and only 14 percent reported substantial inheritance. Even in the top group of multimillionaires, 31 percent received no inherited assets, and 9 percent only small legacies. Other studies indicate that among the far larger and collectively more important group of wealth-holders of more than $60,000 in 1969, 85 percent of the families had emerged since 1953. With a few notable exceptions, which are always in the news, fast movement up or down in two generations has been the fate of the American rich....

In attacking the rich, tax authorities make great use of the concept of "unearned income," which means the returns from money earned earlier, heavily taxed, then saved or invested. Inheritances receive special attention, since they represent undemocratic transfers and concentrations of power. But they also extend the time horizons of the economy (that is, business), and retard the destruction of capital. That inheritance taxes are too high is obvious from the low level of revenue they collect and the huge industry of tax avoidance they sustain. But politically these levies have long been regarded as too attractive to forgo at a time of hostility toward the rich.

Nonetheless, some of the most catalytic wealth in America is "unearned." A few years before Michael Zabian arrived on our shores, Peter Sprague, now his Berkshire neighbor, inherited 400,000 dollars, largely from the sale of Sprague Electric Company stock. Many heirs of similar legacies have managed to lose most of it in a decade or so. But Sprague set out on a course that could lose it much faster. He decided on a career in venture capital. To raise the odds against him still further, he eventually chose to specialize in companies that faced bankruptcy and lacked other sources of funds.

His first venture was a chicken hatchery in Iran, which taught him the key principles of entrepreneurship—chiefly that nothing happens as one envisions it in theory. The project had been based on the use of advanced Ralston-Purina technology, widely tested in Latin America, to tap the rapidly growing poultry markets of the Middle East. The first unexpected discovery was two or three feet of snow; no one had told him that it *snowed* in Iran. Snow ruined most of the Ralston-Purina equipment. A second surprise was chicanery (and sand) in the chicken feed business. "You end up buying two hundred pounds of stone for every hundred pounds of grain." But after some seven years of similar setbacks, and a growing capital of knowledge, Sprague began to make money in Iran; growing a million trees fertilized with chicken manure, cultivating mushrooms in abandoned ice houses, and winding

up with the largest cold storage facilities in the country. The company has made a profit through most of the seventies.

In 1964, three years after starting his Iranian operations, Sprague moved in on a failing electronics company called National Semiconductor. Sprague considered the situation for a week, bought a substantial stake, and became its chairman. The firm is now in the vanguard of the world-wide revolution in semiconductor technology and has been one of America's fastest growing firms, rising from 300 employees when Sprague joined it to 34,000 in 1980.

Also in the mid-sixties Sprague bought several other companies, including the now fashionable Energy Resources, and rescued Design Research from near bankruptcy (the firm finally folded in 1976). In 1969, he helped found Auton Computing Company, a firm still thriving in the business of detecting and analyzing stress in piping systems in nuclear and other power plants, and in 1970 he conducted a memorably resourceful and inventive but finally unsuccessful Republican campaign for the New York City congressional seat then held by Edward Koch....

He then entered the latest phase of his career rescuing collapsing companies. A sports car buff, he indicated to some friends an interest in reviving Aston-Martin, which had gone out of business six months earlier, in mid-1974. Arriving in England early in 1975 with a tentative plan to investigate the possibilities, he was besieged by reporters and TV cameras. Headlines blared: MYSTERY YANK FINANCIER TO SAVE ASTON MARTIN. Eventually he did, and the company is now securely profitable....

A government counterpart of Sprague's investment activity was Wedgewood Benn's National Enterprise Board in England, which spent some 8 billion dollars attempting to save various British companies by drowning them in money. Before Sprague arrived in England Benn had adamantly refused to invest in Aston-Martin—dismissing the venerable firm as a hopeless case—and instead subsidized a large number of other companies, most of which, unlike Aston, still lose money, and some of which ended up bankrupt. The British, however, did find 104 million dollars—fifty times more than Sprague had to invest in Aston-Martin—to use in luring John DeLorean's American luxury car project to Northern Ireland and poured 47.8 million dollars into the effort to create Ininos, a British nationalized semiconductor firm that has yet to earn any money and technologically remains well in the wake of Sprague's concern. With 400,000 dollars inheritance and his charismatic skills, Sprague has revived many times more companies than Wedgewood Benn with the British Treasury. One entrepreneur with energy, resolution, and charisma could turn 400,000 dollars into a small fortune for himself and a bonanza for the economy, accomplishing more than any number of committee-bound foundations, while a government agency usually requires at least 400,000 dollars to so much as open an office.

Nonetheless, considering the sometimes unedifying spectacle of the humpty-dumpty heirs of wealth—and often focusing on the most flamboyant and newsworthy consumers of cocaine and spouses—it is all too easy to forget that the crucial role of the rich in a capitalist economy is not to entertain and titillate the classes below, but to invest: to provide unencumbered and unbureaucratized cash. The broad class of rich

does, in fact, perform this role. Only a small portion of their money is consumed. Most of it goes to productive facilities that employ labor and supply goods to consumers. The rich remain the chief source of discretionary capital in the economy.

These are the funds available for investment outside the largely sterile channels of institutional spending. This is the money that escapes the Keynesian trap of compounded risk, created by the fact that a bank, like an entrepreneur, may lose most of its investment if an enterprise fails, but only the entrepreneur can win the large possible payoff that renders the risk worthwhile. Individuals with cash comprise the wild card—the mutagenic germ—in capitalism, and it is relatively risky investments that ultimately both reseed the economy and unseat the rich....

The risk-bearing role of the rich cannot be performed so well by anyone else. The benefits of capitalism still depend on capitalists. The other groups on the pyramid of wealth should occasionally turn from the spectacles of consumption long enough to see the adventure on the frontiers of the economy above them—an adventure not without its note of nobility, since its protagonist families will almost all eventually fail and fall in the redeeming struggle of the free economy.

In America the rich should not be compared to the Saudi Arabians or be seen in the image of Midas in his barred cage of gold.... Under capitalism, when it is working, the rich have the anti-Midas touch, transforming timorous liquidity and unused savings into factories and office towers, farms and laboratories, orchestras and museums—turning gold into goods and jobs and art. That is the function of the rich: fostering opportunities for the classes below them in the continuing drama of the creation of wealth and progress....

THE NATURE OF POVERTY

To get a grip in the problems of poverty, one should also forget the idea of overcoming inequality by redistribution. Inequality may even grow at first as poverty declines. To lift the incomes of the poor, it will be necessary to increase the rates of investment, which in turn will tend to enlarge the wealth, if not the consumption, of the rich. The poor, as they move into the work force and acquire promotions, will raise their incomes by a greater percentage than the rich; but the upper classes will gain by greater absolute amounts, and the gap between the rich and the poor may grow. All such analyses are deceptive in the long run, however, because they imply a static economy in which the *numbers* of the rich and the middle class are not growing.

In addition, inequality may be favored by the structure of a modern economy as it interacts with demographic changes. When the division of labor becomes more complex and refined, jobs grow more specialized; and the increasingly specialized workers may win greater rents for their rare expertise, causing their incomes to rise relative to common labor. This tendency could be heightened by a decline in new educated entrants to the work force, predictable through the 1990s, and by an enlarged flow of immigration, legal and illegal. Whatever the outcome of these developments, an effort to take income from the rich, thus diminishing their investment, and to give it to the poor, thus reducing their work incentives, is sure to cut American productivity, limit job opportunities, and perpetuate poverty.

Among the beneficiaries of inequality will be the formerly poor. Most students of the problems of poverty consider the statistics of success of previous immigrant groups and see a steady incremental rise over the years, accompanied by the progressive acquisition of educational credentials and skills. Therefore, programs are proposed that foster a similar slow and incremental ascent by the currently poor. But the incremental vision of the escape from poverty is mostly false, based on a simple illusion of statistical aggregates that conceals everything important about upward mobility. Previous immigrants earned money first by working hard; their children got the education.

The rising average incomes of previous groups signify not the smooth progress of hundreds of thousands of civil-service or bureaucratic careers, but the rapid business and professional successes of a relative few, who brought their families along and inspired others to follow. Poor people tend to rise up rapidly and will be damaged by a policy of redistribution that will always hit new and unsheltered income and wealth much harder than the elaborately concealed and fortified winnings of the established rich. The poor benefit from a dynamic economy full of unpredictable capital gains (they have few capital losses!) more than from a stratified system governed by educational and other credentials that the rich can buy.

The only dependable route from poverty is always work, family, and faith. The first principle is that in order to move up, the poor must not only work, they must work harder than the classes above them. Every previous generation of the lower class has made such efforts. But the current poor, white even more than black, are refusing to work hard. Irwin

Garfinkel and Robert Haveman, authors of an ingenious and sophisticated study of what they call *Earning Capacity Utilization Rates*, have calculated the degree to which various income groups use their opportunities—how hard they work outside the home. This study shows that, for several understandable reasons, the current poor work substantially less, for fewer hours and weeks a year, and earn less in proportion to their age, education, and other credentials (even *after* correcting the figures for unemployment, disability, and presumed discrimination) than either their predecessors in American cities or those now above them on the income scale (the study was made at the federally funded Institute for Research on Poverty at the University of Wisconsin and used data from the census and the Michigan longitudinal survey). The findings lend important confirmation to the growing body of evidence that work effort is the crucial unmeasured variable in American productivity and income distribution, and that current welfare and other subsidy programs substantially reduce work. The poor choose leisure not because of moral weakness, but because they are paid to do so.

A program to lift by transfers and preferences the incomes of less diligent groups is politically divisive—and very unlikely—because it incurs the bitter resistance of the real working class. In addition, such an effort breaks the psychological link between effort and reward, which is crucial to long-run upward mobility. Because effective work consists not in merely fulfilling the requirements of labor contracts but "in putting out" with alertness and emotional commitment, workers have to understand and feel deeply that what they are given depends on what they

give—that they must supply work in order to demand goods. Parents and schools must inculcate this idea in their children both by instruction and example. Nothing is more deadly to achievement than the belief that effort will not be rewarded, that the world is a bleak and discriminatory place in which only the predatory and the specially preferred can get ahead. Such a view in the home discourages the work effort in school that shapes earnings capacity afterward. As with so many aspects of human performance, work effort begins in family experiences, and its sources can be best explored through an examination of family structure.

Indeed, after work the second principle of upward mobility is the maintenance of monogamous marriage and family. Adjusting for discrimination against women and for child-care responsibilities, the Wisconsin study indicates that married men work between two and one-third and four times harder than married women, and more than twice as hard as female family heads. The work effort of married men increases with their age, credentials, education, job experience, and birth of children, while the work effort of married women steadily declines. Most important in judging the impact of marriage, husbands work 50 percent harder than bachelors of comparable age, education, and skills.

The effect of marriage, thus, is to increase the work effort of men by about half. Since men have higher earnings capacity to begin with, and since the female capacity-utilization figures would be even lower without an adjustment for discrimination, it is manifest that the maintenance of families is the key factor in reducing poverty.

Once a family is headed by a woman, it is almost impossible for it to greatly raise its income even if the woman is highly educated and trained and she hires day-care or domestic help. Her family responsibilities and distractions tend to prevent her from the kind of all-out commitment that is necessary for the full use of earning power. Fewer women with children make earning money the top priority in their lives.

A married man, on the other hand, is spurred by the claims of family to channel his otherwise disruptive male aggressions into his performance as a provider for a wife and children. These sexual differences alone, which manifest themselves in all societies known to anthropology, dictate that the first priority of any serious program against poverty is to strengthen the male role in poor families.

These narrow measures of work effort touch on just part of the manifold interplay between family and poverty. Edward Banfield's *The Unheavenly City* defines the lower class largely by its lack of an orientation to the future. Living from day to day and from hand to mouth, lower class individuals are unable to plan or save or keep a job. Banfield gives the impression that short-time horizons are a deep-seated psychological defect afflicting hundreds of thousands of the poor.

There is no question that Banfield puts his finger on a crucial problem of the poor and that he develops and documents his theme in an unrivaled classic of disciplined social science. But he fails to show how millions of men, equally present oriented, equally buffeted by impulse and blind to the future, have managed to become farseeing members of the middle classes. He also fails to explain how mil-

lions of apparently future-oriented men can become dissolute followers of the sensuous moment, neglecting their jobs, dissipating their income and wealth, pursuing a horizon no longer than the most time-bound of the poor.

What Banfield is in fact describing in his lower-class category is largely the temperament of single, divorced, and separated men. The key to lower-class life in contemporary America is that unrelated individuals, as the census calls them, are so numerous and conspicuous that they set the tone for the entire community. Their congregation in ghettos, moreover, magnifies greatly their impact on the black poor, male and female (though, as Banfield rightly observes, this style of instant gratification is chiefly a male trait).

The short-sighted outlook of poverty stems largely from the breakdown of family responsibilities among fathers. The lives of the poor, all too often, are governed by the rhythms of tension and release that characterize the sexual experience of young single men. Because female sexuality, as it evolved over the millennia, is psychologically rooted in the bearing and nurturing of children, women have long horizons within their very bodies, glimpses of eternity within their wombs. Civilized society is dependent upon the submission of the short-term sexuality of young men to the extended maternal horizons of women. This is what happens in monogamous marriage; the man disciplines his sexuality and extends it into the future through the womb of a woman. The woman gives him access to his children, otherwise forever denied him; and he gives her the product of his labor, otherwise dissipated on temporary pleasures. The woman gives him a unique link to the future and a vision of it; he gives her faithfulness and a commitment to a lifetime of hard work. If work effort is the first principle of overcoming poverty, marriage is the prime source of upwardly mobile work.

It is love that changes the short horizons of youth and poverty into the long horizons of marriage and career. When marriages fail, the man often returns to the more primitive rhythms of singleness. On the average, his income drops by one-third and he shows a far higher propensity for drink, drugs, and crime. But when marriages in general hold firm and men in general love and support their children, Banfield's lower-class style changes into middle-class futurity....

Adolph A. Berle, contemplating the contrast between prosperous and dominantly Mormon Utah and indigent, chiefly secular Nevada next door, concluded his study of the American economy with the rather uneconomic notion of a "transcendental margin," possibly kin to Leibenstein's less glamorous X-efficiency and Christopher Jencks's timid "luck." Lionel Tiger identifies this source of unexplained motion as "evolutionary optimism—the biology of hope," and finds it in the human genes. Ivan Light, in his fascinating exploration of the sources of difference between entrepreneurial Orientals and less venturesome blacks, resolved on "the spirit of moral community." Irving Kristol, ruminating on the problems of capitalism, sees the need for a "transcendental justification." They are all addressing, in one way or another, the third principle of upward mobility, and that is faith.

Faith in man, faith in the future, faith in the rising returns of giving, faith in the mutual benefits of trade, faith in the providence of God are all essential to successful capitalism. All are necessary to sustain the spirit of work and enterprise against the setbacks and frustrations it inevitably meets in a fallen world; to inspire trust and cooperation in an economy where they will often be betrayed; to encourage the forgoing of present pleasures in the name of a future that may well go up in smoke; to promote risk and initiative in a world where the rewards all vanish unless others join the game. In order to give without the assurance of return, in order to save without the certainty of future value, in order to work beyond the requirements of the job, one has to have confidence in a higher morality: a law of compensations beyond the immediate and distracting struggles of existence.

NO

William Ryan

EQUALITY

It should not surprise us... that the clause "all men are created equal" can be interpreted in quite different ways. Today, I would like to suggest, there are two major lines of interpretation: one, which I will call the "Fair Play" perspective, stresses the individual's right to pursue happiness and obtain resources; the other, which I will call the "Fair Shares" viewpoint, emphasizes the right of access to resources as a necessary condition for equal rights to life, liberty and happiness.

Almost from the beginning, and most apparently during the past century or so, the Fair Play viewpoint has been dominant in America. This way of looking at the problem of equality stresses that each person should be equally free from all but the most minimal necessary interferences with his right to "pursue happiness."... Given significant differences of interest, of talents, and of personalities, it is assumed that individuals will be variably successful in their pursuits and that society will consequently propel to its surface what Jefferson called a "natural aristocracy of talent," men who because of their skills, intellect, judgment, character, will assume the leading positions in society that had formerly been occupied by the hereditary aristocracy—that is, by men who had simply been born into positions of wealth and power. In contemporary discussions, the emphasis on the individual's unencumbered pursuit of his own goals is summed up in the phrase "equality of opportunity." Given at least an approximation of this particular version of equality, Jefferson's principle of a natural aristocracy—spoken of most commonly today as the idea of "meritocracy"—will insure that the ablest, most meritorious, ambitious, hardworking, and talented individuals will acquire the most, achieve the most, and become the leaders of society. The relative inequality that this implies is seen not only as tolerable, but as fair and just. Any effort to achieve what proponents of Fair Play refer to as "equality of results" is seen as unjust, artificial, and incompatible with the more basic principle of equal opportunity.

The Fair Shares perspective, as compared with the Fair Play idea, concerns itself much more with equality of rights and of access, particularly the implicit rights to a reasonable share of society's resources, sufficient to sustain life at a decent standard of humanity and to preserve liberty and freedom from compulsion. Rather than focusing on the individual's pursuit of his own happiness, the advocate of Fair Shares is more committed to the principle that all members of the society obtain a reasonable portion of the goods that society produces. From his vantage point, the overzealous pursuits of private goals on the part of some individuals might even have to be bridled. From this it follows, too, that the proponent of Fair Shares has a different view of what constitutes fairness and justice, namely, an appropriate distribution throughout society of sufficient means for sustaining life and preserving liberty.

So the equality dilemma is built into everyday life and thought in America; it comes with the territory. Rights, equality of rights—or at least interpretations of them—clash. The conflict between Fair Play and Fair Shares is real, deep, and serious, and it cannot be easily resolved. Some calculus of priorities must be established. Rules must be agreed upon. It is possible to imagine an almost endless number of such rules:

• Fair Shares until everyone has enough; Fair Play for the surplus

• Fair Play until the end of a specified "round," then "divvy up" Fair Shares, and start Fair Play all over again (like a series of Monopoly games)

• Fair Play all the way, except that no one may actually be allowed to starve to death.

The last rule is, I would argue, a perhaps bitter parody of the prevailing one in the United States. Equality of opportunity and the principle of meritocracy are the clearly dominant interpretation of "all men are created equal," mitigated by the principle (usually defined as charity rather than equality) that the weak, the helpless, the deficient will be more or less guaranteed a sufficient share to meet their minimal requirements for sustaining life.

FAIR PLAY AND UNEQUAL SHARES

The Fair Play concept is dominant in America partly because it puts forth two most compelling ideas: the time-honored principle of distributive justice and the cherished image of America as the land of opportunity. At least since Aristotle, the principle that rewards should accrue to each person in proportion of his worth or merit has seemed to many persons one that warrants intuitive acceptance. The more meritorious person—merit being some combination of ability and constructive effort—*deserves* a greater reward. From this perspective it is perfectly consistent to suppose that *unequal* shares could well be *fair* shares; moreover, within such a framework, it is very unlikely indeed that equal shares could be fair shares, since individuals are not equally meritorious.

The picture of America as the land of opportunity is also very appealing. The idea of a completely open society, where each person is entirely free to advance in his or her particular fashion, to become whatever he or she is inherently capable of becoming, with the sky the limit, is a universally inspiring one. This is a picture that makes most Americans proud.

But is it an accurate picture? Are these two connected ideas—unlimited opportunity and differential rewards fairly distributed according to differences in individual merit—congruent with the facts of life? The answer, of course, is yes and no. Yes, we see some vague congruence here and there—some evidence of upward mobility, some kinds of inequalities that can appear to be justifiable. But looking at the larger picture, we must answer with an unequivocal "No!" The fairness of unequal shares and the reality of equal opportunity are wishes and dreams, resting on a mushy, floating, purely imaginary foundation. Let us look first at the question of unequal shares.

Fair Players and Fair Sharers disagree about the meaning, but not about the fact, of unequal shares and of the significant degree of inequality of wealth and income and of everything that goes along with wealth and income—general life conditions, health, education, power, access to services and to cultural and recreational amenities, and so forth. Fair Sharers say that this fact is the very *essence* of inequality, while Fair Players define the inequalities of condition that Fair Sharers decry as obvious and necessary *consequences* of equality of opportunity. Fair Players argue, furthermore, that such inequalities are for the most part roughly proportional to inequalities of merit....

There [are] some patterns of ownership that are reasonably consistent with the Fair Play paradigm. In the distribution of such items as automobiles, televisions, appliances, even homes, there are significant inequalities, but they are not extreme. And if the Fair Player is willing to concede that many inequities remain to be rectified—and most Fair Players are quite willing, even eager, to do so—these inequalities can, perhaps, be swallowed.

It is only when we begin to look at larger aspects of wealth and income— aspects that lie beyond our personal vision—that the extreme and, I believe, gross inequalities of condition that prevail in America become evident. Let us begin with income. How do we divide up the shares of what we produce annually? In 1977 about one American family in

ten had an income of less than $5,000 and about one in ten had an income of $35,000 a year and up ("up" going all the way to some unknown number of millions). It is difficult to see how anyone could view such a dramatic disparity as fair and justified. One struggles to imagine any measure of merit, any sign of membership in a "natural aristocracy," that would manifest itself in nature in such a way that one sizable group of persons would "have" eight or ten or twenty times more of it—whatever "it" might be—than another sizeable group has.

Income in the United States is concentrated in the hands of a few: one-fifth of the population gets close to half of all the income, and the top 5 percent of this segment get almost one-fifth of it. The bottom three-fifths of the population—that is, the majority of us—receive not much more than one-third of all income....

As we move [to] the reality of living standards, the pertinent questions are: How much do people spend and on what? How do the groups at the different tables, that is, different income groups in America, live? Each year the Bureau of Labor Statistics [BLS] publishes detailed information on the costs of maintaining three different living standards, which it labels "lower," "intermediate," and "higher"; in less discreet days it used to call the budgets "minimum," "adequate," and "comfortable." The adequate, intermediate budget is generally considered to be an index of a reasonably decent standard of living. It is on this budget, for example, that newspapers focus when they write their annual stories on the BLS budgets.

To give some sense of what is considered an "intermediate" standard of living, let me provide some details about this budget as it is calculated for a family of four—mother, father, eight-year-old boy, and thirteen-year-old girl. As of the autumn of 1978, for such a family the budget allows $335 a month for housing, which includes rent or mortgage, heat and utilities, household furnishings, and all household operations. It allows $79 a week for groceries, which extends to cleaning supplies, toothpaste, and the like. It allows $123 a month for transportation, including car payments. It allows $130 a month for clothing, clothing care or cleaning, and all personal-care items.

In his book *The Working Class Majority*, Andrew Levinson cites further details about this budget from a study made by the UAW:

A United Auto Workers study shows just how "modest" that budget is: The budget assumes, for example, that a family will own a toaster that will last for thirty-three years, a refrigerator and a range that will each last for seventeen years, a vacuum cleaner that will last for fourteen years, and a television set that will last for ten years. The budget assumes that a family will buy a two-year-old car and keep it for four years, and will pay for a tune-up once a year, a brake realignment every three years, and front-end alignment every four years.... The budget assumes that the husband will buy one year-round suit every four years... and one topcoat every eight and a half years.... It assumes that the husband will take his wife to the movies once every three months and that one of them will go to the movies alone once a year. The average family's two children are each allowed one movie every four weeks. A total of two dollars and fifty-four cents per person per year is allowed for admission to all other events, from football and baseball games to plays or concerts.... The budget allows nothing whatever for savings.

This budget, whether labeled intermediate, modest, or adequate, is perhaps more accurately described by those who call it "shabby but respectable."...

In 1978 the income needs by an urban family of four in order to meet even this modest standard of living was $18,622. This is a national average; for some cities the figure was much higher: in Boston, it was $22,117, in metropolitan New York, $21,587, in San Francisco, $19,427. More than *half* of all Americans lived *below* this standard. As for the "minimum" budget (which, by contrast with the "intermediate" budget, allows only $62 rather than $79 for groceries, $174 rather than $335 for housing, $67 rather than $123 for transportation, and $93 rather than $130 for clothing and personal care), the national average cost for an urban family in 1978 was $11,546. Three families out of ten could not afford even *that* standard, and one family in ten had an income below $5,000 which is *less than half enough* to meet minimum standards.

These dramatically *unequal* shares are—it seems to me—clearly *unfair* shares. Twenty million people are desperately poor, an additional forty million don't get enough income to meet the minimal requirements for a decent life, the great majority are just scraping by, a small minority are at least temporarily comfortable, and a tiny handful of persons live at levels of affluence and luxury that most persons cannot even imagine.

The myth that America's income is symmetrically distributed—an outstanding few at the top getting a lot, an inadequate few at the bottom living in poverty, and the rest clustered around the middle—could hardly be more false. The grotesquely lopsided distribution of our yearly production of goods and services is well illustrated by Paul Samuelson's famous image:

A glance at the income distribution in the United States shows how pointed is the income pyramid and how broad its base. "There's always room at the top" is certainly true; this is so because it is hard to get there, not easy. If we make an income pyramid out of a child's blocks, with each layer portraying $1000 of income, the peak would be far higher than the Eiffel Tower, but almost all of us would be within a yard of the ground.

When we move from income to wealth—from what you *get* to what you *own*—the *degree* of concentration makes the income distribution look almost fair by comparison. About one out of every four Americans owns *nothing*. Nothing! In fact, many of them *owe* more than they have. Their "wealth" is actually negative. The persons in the next quarter own about 5 percent of all personal assets. In other words, half of us own 5 percent, the other half own 95 percent. But it gets worse as you go up the scale. Those in the top 6 percent own half of all the wealth. Those in the top 1 percent own one-fourth of all the wealth. Those in the top 1/2 percent own one-fifth of all the wealth. That's one-half of 1 percent—about one million persons, or roughly 300,000 families.

And even this fantastic picture doesn't tell the whole story, because "assets" include homes, cars, savings accounts, cash value of life insurance policies—the kinds of assets that the very rich don't bother with very much. The very rich put their wealth into the ownership of things that produce more wealth—corporate stocks and bonds, mortgages, notes, and the like. Two-thirds of their wealth is in

this form and the top 1 percent owns 60 percent of all that valuable paper. The rest of it is owned by only an additional 10 percent, which means that nine people out of ten own none of it—and, if they're like me, they probably have never seen a real stock certificate in their lives.

America, we are sometimes told, is a nation of capitalists, and it is true that an appreciable minority of its citizens have a bank account here, a piece of land there, along with a few shares of stock. But quantitative differences become indisputably qualitative as one moves from the ownership of ten shares of General Motors to the ownership of ten thousand. There are capitalists, and then there are capitalists....

Another way of grasping the extreme concentration of wealth in our society is to try to imagine what the ordinary person would have if that wealth were evenly distributed rather than clumped and clotted together in huge piles. Assuming that all the personal wealth was divided equally among all the people in the nation, we would find that every one of us, man, woman, and child, would *own* free and clear almost $22,000 worth of goods: $7,500 worth of real estate, $3,500 in cash, and about $5,000 worth of stocks and bonds. For a family of four that would add up to almost $90,000 in assets, including $30,000 equity in a house, about $14,000 in the bank, and about $20,000 worth of stocks and bonds. That much wealth would also bring in an extra $3,000 or $4,000 a year in income.

If you have any doubts about the reality of grossly unequal shares, compare the utopian situation of that imaginary "average" family with your own actual situation. For most of us, the former goes beyond our most optimistic fantasies of competing and achieving and getting ahead. Actually only about ten million persons in the country own as much as that, and, as I suggested before, the majority of us have an *average* of less than $5,000 per family including whatever equity we have in a home, our car and other tangible assets, and perhaps $500 in the bank.

Still another way of thinking about this is to remark that the fortunate few at the top, and their children, are more or less guaranteed an opulent standard of living because of what they own, while the majority of American families are no more than four months' pay away from complete destitution.

All of this, of course, takes place in the wealthiest society the world has ever known. If we extended our horizons further and began to compare the handful of developed, industrial nations with the scores of underdeveloped, not to say "over-exploited," nations, we would find inequalities that are even more glaring and appalling....

THE VULNERABLE MAJORITY

Stripped down to its essentials, the rule of equal opportunity and Fair Play requires only that the best man win. It doesn't necessarily specify the margin of victory, merely the absence of unfair barriers. The practical test of equal opportunity is *social mobility*—do talented and hardworking persons, whatever their backgrounds, actually succeed in rising to higher social and economic positions?

The answer to that of course, is that they do. Remaining barriers of discrimination notwithstanding, it is plain that many persons climb up the social and economic ladder and reach much higher rungs than those their parents attained and than those from which they started.

Fair Players prize these fortunate levitations as the ultimate justification of their own perspective and as phenomena that must be protected against any erosion caused by excessive emphasis upon Fair Shares.

It is necessary, then, to look seriously at the question of mobility. Among the questions to be asked are the following:

• How much mobility can we observe? No matter how rigidly hierarchical it might be, every society permits some mobility. How much movement up and down the scale is there in ours?

• How far do the mobile persons move?

• Is mobility evident across the whole social and economic range? Do the very poor stay poor, or do they, too, have an equal chance to rise? Are the very rich likely to slide *down* the ladder very often?

Given our great trove of rags-to-riches mythology, our creed that any child (well, any man-child) can grow up to be president—if not of General Motors, at least of the United States—we clearly assume that our society is an extraordinarily open one. And everyone knows, or has a friend who knows, a millionaire or someone on the way to that envied position: the patient, plodding peddler who transformed his enterprise into a great department store; the eccentric tinkerer in his garage whose sudden insight produced the great invention that everyone had been saving his pennies to buy.

At lesser levels of grandeur, we all know about the son of the illiterate cobbler who is now a wealthy neurosurgeon, the daughter of impoverished immigrants who sits in a professional chair at Vassar or Smith—or even Princeton. In America social mobility is an unquestioned fact.

But how many sons of illiterate cobblers become physicians, on the other hand, and how many become, at best, literate cobblers? And how many settle for a job on the assembly line or in the sanitation department? And all of those daughters of impoverished immigrants—how many went on to get Ph.D.'s and become professors? Very few. A somewhat larger number may have gone to college and gotten a job teaching sixth grade. But many just finished high school and went to work for an insurance company for a while, until they married the sons of other impoverished immigrants, most of them also tugging at their bootstraps without much result.

About all of these facts there can be little dispute. For most people, there is essentially no social mobility—for them, life consists of rags to rags and riches to riches. Moreover, for the relatively small minority who do rise significantly in the social hierarchy, the *distance* of ascent is relatively short. Such a person may start life operating a drill press and eventually become a foreman or even move into the white-collar world by becoming a payroll clerk or perhaps an accountant. Or he may learn from his father to be a cobbler, save his money, and open a little cobbler shop of his own. He hardly ever starts up a shoe factory. It is the son of the owner of the shoe factory who gets to do that. So there is mobility—it is rather common, but also rather modest, with only an occasional dramatic rise from rags to riches.

To provide some specific numbers, it has been calculated that for a young man born into a family in which the father does unskilled, low-wage manual work, the odds against his rising merely to the point of his becoming a nonmanual white-collar worker are at least three or four to one; the odds against his rising to

the highest level and joining the wealthy upper class are almost incalculable. For the son of a middle-level white-collar worker, the odds against his rising to a higher-level professional or managerial occupation are two or three to one. On the other hand, the odds are better than fifty to one that the son of a father with such a high-level occupation will not descend the ladder to a position as an unskilled or semiskilled manual worker. Upward mobility is very limited and usually involves moving only one or two levels up the hierachy....

Finally, we have to look carefully to see that, for all our social mobility, the very rich almost all stay at the top and welcome only a select handful to their ranks. The rich of one generation are almost all children of the rich of the previous generation, partly because more than half of significant wealth is inherited, partly because all the other prerogatives of the wealthy are sufficient to assure a comfortable future for Rockefeller and Du Pont toddlers. It may well take more energy, ingenuity, persistence, and single-mindedness for a rich youngster to achieve poverty than for a poor one to gain wealth.

The dark side of the social-mobility machine is that it is, so to speak, a reciprocating engine—when some parts go up, others must come *down*. Downward mobility is an experience set aside almost exclusively for the nonrich, and it is grossly destructive of the quality of life.

The majority of American families are constantly vulnerable to economic disaster—to downward mobility to the point where they lack sufficient income to meet their most basic needs—food, shelter, clothing, heat, and medical care. Included in this vulnerable majority, who have at least an even chance of spending some portion of their lives in economic distress, are perhaps three out of four Americans.

This does not accord with the common view of poverty. We have been given to understand that "the poor" form a fairly permanent group in our society and that those who are above the poverty line are safe and perhaps even on their way up. This thought is comforting but false. A number of small studies have raised serious questions about this static picture; recently we have received massive evidence from one of the most comprehensive social and economic investigations ever mounted. This study, under the direction of James Morgan, has traced the life trajectories of five thousand American families over a period, to date, of eight years, concentrating on the nature of and possible explanations for economic progress or the lack of it.

Five Thousand American Families indicates that over a period of eight years, although only one in ten families is poor during *every one* of the eight years, over one-third of American families are poor for *at least one* of those eight years.

From the Michigan study, the census data, and other sources, we can readily estimate that a few are permanently protected against poverty because they *own things*—property, stocks, bonds—that provide them with income sufficient to meet their needs whether or not they work or have any other source of income. Another small minority of Americans own only *rights*—virtual job tenure, a guaranteed pension—but these rights also give effective protection against poverty. At the bottom of the pyramid, there are a few who might be called permanently poor. Between these extremes come persons whose income is primarily or wholly dependent on salaries or wages. This is the core of the vulnerable majority—not poor now, but in jeopardy. In any given year one family out of six in that vulnerable majority will suffer income deficit, will go through a year of poverty. Over a five-year period nearly half of them will be poor for at least one year. If we project this over ten or fifteen years, we find that well over half will be poor for at least one year. On adding this group to the permanently poor, we arrive at the startling fact that a *substantial majority* of American families will experience poverty at some point during a relatively short span of time.

Several elements in our socioeconomic structure help account for income deficiency. Let us consider, for example, those who are more or less permanently poor. Why do they stay mired in poverty? The answer in most cases is simple: they remain poor because it has been deliberately *decided* that they should remain poor. They are, for the most part, dependent on what we impersonally call transfer payments—mostly Social Security, some private pensions, some welfare. To put it as simply as possible, these transfer payments are not enough to live on, not enough to meet basic needs. Countrywide, public assistance payments provide income that is only 75 percent of what is required to pay for sufficient food, adequate shelter, clothing, and fuel; the percentage decreases as the size of the family increases. For very large families, welfare provides only half of what is needed to live on. The poverty of the permanently poor is thus easily explained by the fact that the income assistance that we provide them is simply too small.

For the vulnerables, however, economic hills and valleys are created by the job situation. Economic status, progress, and deficit are determined by what social scientists call "family composition and participation in the labor force." In plain English that means they depend on the number of mouths to be fed and on the number of people working—that is, on how many children there are, on whether both wife and husband are working, and so forth. But this, of course, is only synonymous with the natural ebb and flow in the life of almost any family. It should not be an economic catastrophe, after all, when people get married and have children.... So, children are born and they grow up, sometimes work awhile, and then leave home. One parent, usually the mother, is tied to the home during some periods, free to work during others. A family member finds a job, loses a job, gets sick or injured, sometimes dies tragically young. All of these events are the landmarks in the life of a family, most of them are common enough, and some are inevitable sources of joy or sorrow. Yet these ordinary occurrences have a drastic impact on families, because they lead to greater changes in one or both sides of the ratio of income and needs. In most cases they are direct causes of most of the economic progress or distress that a family experiences....

WHY NOT FAIR SHARES?

I have been trying to show, in a preliminary way, that the beliefs and assumptions associated with the Fair Play rendering of equality are quite inconsistent with the facts of life as we know them, although its principles are paraded as a version—in fact, the correct version—of equality and are widely accepted as quite plausible, indeed obvious. To the extent that there is any competition between Fair Players and Fair Sharers for the mind of the public, the former usually win hands down. Yet, as we have seen, the Fair Play idea appears to condone and often to endorse conditions of inequality that are blatant and, I would say, quite indefensible. Such equal opportunities for advancing in life as do exist are darkly overshadowed by the many head starts and advantages provided to the families of wealth and privilege. As for the workings out of the solemnly revered principles of meritocracy, they are—like many objects of reverence—invisible to most persons and rarely discernible in the lives of the vulnerable majority of us. Barely two centuries after its most persuasive formulation, the Fair Play concept of equality has shriveled to little more than the assertion that a few thousand individuals are fully licensed to gather and retain wealth at the cost of the wasteful, shameful, and fraudulent impoverishment of many millions....

A Fair Shares egalitarian would hold that all persons have a *right* to a reasonable share of material necessities, a right to do constructive work, and a right of unhindered access to education, to gratifying social memberships, to participation in the life and decisions of the community, and to all the major amenities of society. This principle doesn't lend itself to the calculation of "equal results," and it certainly doesn't imply a demand for uniformity of resources. No one in his right mind would entertain some cockeyed scheme in which everyone went to school for precisely thirteen years; consumed each year 19,800 grams of protein and 820,000 calories; read four works of fiction and six of non-fiction; attended two concerts, one opera, and four basketball games, and voted in 54 percent of the elections.... Unfortunately, many persons who are upset about the present state of inequality tend to talk vaguely about the need "to redistribute income" or even "to redistribute wealth." When such ideas are tossed out without consideration of the fact that they will then be discussed within the framework of Fair Play, we have a surefire prescription for disaster. From that viewpoint, which is, after all, the dominant one in America, such ideas appear both extremely inpracticable and not particularly desirable. For example, are we to take redistribution of income to mean that every individual will somehow receive the same compensation, no matter what work he or she does or whether he works at all? And would we try to redistribute wealth by giving every person, say, a share of stock in GM, Exxon, IBM, and the local paper-bag factory? Hardly. Fair Players can make mincemeat of such silly ideas, and they love to pretend that that's what Fair Share egalitarians are proposing. I don't think many of us have strong objections to inequality of monetary income as such. A modest range, even as much as three or four to one, could, I suspect, be tolerable to almost everybody. (And one would suppose that, given some time for adjustment and perhaps some counseling and training in homemaking and budgeting skills, those who now get a lot more could learn to scrape by on something like eight or nine hundred dollars a week.) The current range in annual incomes—from perhaps $3,000 to some unknown number of *millions*—is, however, excessive and intolerable, impossible to justify rationally, and plain inhuman. The problem of wealth is more fundamental. Most of the evils of inequality derive from the reality that a few thousand families control almost all the necessities and amenities of life,

indeed the very conditions of life. The rest of us, some 200 million, have to pay tribute to them if we want even a slight illusion of life, liberty, and the pursuit of happiness. But the solution to this problem is certainly not simply the fragmentation of ownership into tiny units of individual property. This naive solution has been well criticized by serious proponents of equality, perhaps most gracefully by R. H. Tawney:

> It is not the division of the nation's income into eleven million fragments, to be distributed, without further ado, like cake as a school treat, among its eleven million families. It is, on the contrary, the pooling of its surplus resources by means of taxation, and use of the funds thus obtained to make accessible to all, irrespective of their income, occupation, or social position, the conditions of civilization which, in the absence of such measures, can only be enjoyed by the rich....
>
> It can generalize, by collective action, advantages associated in the past with ownership of property.... It can secure that, in addition to the payments made to them for their labour, its citizens enjoy a social income, which is provided from the surplus remaining after the necessary cost of production and expansion have been met, and is available on equal terms for all its members....

The central problem of inequality in America—the concentration of wealth and power in the hands of a tiny minority—cannot, then, be solved, as Tawney makes clear, by any schemes that rest on the process of long division. We need, rather, to accustom ourselves to a different method of holding resources, namely, holding them in common, to be *shared* amongst us all—not divided up and parceled out, but shared. That is the basic principle of Fair Shares, and it is not at all foreign to our daily experience. To cite a banal example, we share the air we breathe, although some breathe in penthouses or sparsely settled suburbs and others in crowded slums. In a similar fashion, we share such resources as public parks and beaches, although, again, we cannot overlook the gross contrast between the size of vast private waterfront holdings and the tiny outlets to the oceans that are available to the public. No one in command of his senses would go to a public beach, count the number of people there, and suggest subdividing the beach into thirty-two-by-twenty-six-foot lots, one for each person. Such division would not only be unnecessary, it would ruin our enjoyment. If I were assigned to Lot No. 123, instead of enjoying the sun and going for a swim, I might sit and watch that sneaky little kid with the tin shovel to make sure he did not extend the sand castle onto my beach. We own it in common; it's *public*; and we just plain *share* it.

We use this mode of owning and sharing all the time and never give it a second thought. We share public schools, streets, libraries, sewers, and other public property and services, and we even think of them as being "free" (many libraries even have the word in their names). Nor do we need the "There's no such thing as a free lunch" folks reminding us that they're not really free; everyone is quite aware that taxes support them. We don't feel any need to divide up all the books in the library among all the citizens. And there's no sensible way of looking at the use of libraries in terms of "equal opportunity" as opposed to "equal results." Looking at the public library as a tiny example of what Fair Shares equality is all about, we note that it satisfies the principle of equal access if no one is *excluded* from the library on the irrelevant grounds of not owning enough or of having spent twelve years in school learning how not to read. And "equal results" is clearly quite meaningless. Some will withdraw many books; some, only a few; some will be so unwise as to never even use the facility.

The *idea* of sharing, then, which is the basic idea of equality, and the *practice* of sharing, which is the basic methodology of Fair Shares equality, are obviously quite familiar and acceptable to the American people in many areas of life. There are many institutions, activities, and services that the great majority believe should be located in the public sector, collectively owned and paid for, and equally accessible to everyone. We run into trouble when we start proposing the same system of ownership for the resources that the wealthy have corralled for themselves....

Most of the good things of life have either been provided free by God (nature, if you prefer) or have been produced by the combined efforts of many persons, sometimes many generations. As all share in the making, so all should share in the use and the enjoyment. This may help convey a bit of what the Fair Shares idea of equality is all about.

POSTSCRIPT

Is Economic Inequality Beneficial to Society?

The spirit of personal initiative seems to be alive in the hearts of Michael Zabian, the vegetable stand owner, Nick Kelley, the scratch pad dealer, and Peter Sprague, the venture capitalist, whose success stories are related by Gilder. But how typical are their experiences? What about the government's bail-outs of Lockheed and Chrysler and the trials of U.S. Steel, General Motors, and many other corporations? What about the limitation of individual initiative in countless corporations guided by decisions made by committees and teams of experts? And what about the issues of fairness raised by Ryan? Perhaps the basic question is, Can the system be made more just, fair, and humane without squelching enterprise and drive?

Stratification and social mobility are two of the central concerns of sociology, and much literature discussing these issues has been produced. Two major publications of research on census statistics are Peter M. Blau and Otis Dudley Duncan's *The American Occupational Structure* (John Wiley & Sons, 1967) and Robert M. Hauser and David L. Featherman's *The Process of Social Stratification* (Academic Press, 1972). For general works, see Gerhard Lenski's *Power and Privilege* (McGraw-Hill, 1966) and Leonard Beeghley's *Social Stratification in the United States* (Goodyear, 1978). Many have written about the rich and their power, including Ferdinand Lundberg, *The Rich and the Super Rich* (Lyle Stuart, 1968); E. Digby Baltzell, *The Protestant Establishment* (Random House, 1964); G. William Dornhoff, *The Power Elite and the State* (Aldine de Gruyter, 1990); and Michael Patrick Allen, *The Founding Fortunes* (E. P. Dutton, 1989). A number of important works look at the poor and their disadvantages, including Michael Harrington, *The New American Poverty* (Holt, Rinehart & Winston, 1984); William Wilson, *The Truly Disadvantaged* (University of Chicago Press, 1987); Elliot Liebow, *Tally's Corner* (Little, Brown, 1967); Lawrence M. Mead, *The New Politics of Poverty* (Basic Books, 1992); Richard H. Ropers, *Persistent Poverty* (Plenum, 1992); Mickey Kaus, *The End of Inequality* (Basic Books, 1992); and Jonathan Kozol, *Savage Inequalities: Children in America's Schools* (Harper Perennial, 1992).

One study of the social origins of elites is Suzanne Keller's *Beyond the Ruling Class* (Random House, 1963). An interesting study of how the rich view themselves and the poor and income inequalities is *Equality in America: The View from the Top*, by Sidney Verber and Gary Orren (Harvard University Press, 1985). Two valuable resources on stratification are *Research in Social Stratification and Mobility: A Research Annual* and *Research in Inequality and Social Conflict: A Research Annual*.

ISSUE 8

Does "Lower-Class" Culture Perpetuate Poverty?

YES: Edward Banfield, from *The Unheavenly City* (Little, Brown, 1970; Reissue, Waveland Press, 1990)

NO: William Ryan, from *Blaming the Victim* (Pantheon Books, 1971)

ISSUE SUMMARY

YES: Sociologist Edward Banfield asserts that it is the cultural outlook of the poor that tends to keep them in poverty.

NO: Professor of psychology William Ryan argues that attacking the culture of the poor for the conditions that surround them is a form of "blaming the victim."

The Declaration of Independence proclaims the right of every human being to "life, liberty, and the pursuit of happiness." It never defines happiness, but Americans have put their own gloss on the term. Whatever else happiness means, Americans tend to agree that it includes doing well financially, getting ahead in life, and maintaining a comfortable standard of living.

The fact is that millions of Americans do not do well and do not get ahead. They are mired in poverty and seem unable to get out of it. On the face of it, this fact poses no contradiction to America's commitment to the pursuit of happiness. To pursue is not necessarily to catch; it certainly does not mean that everyone should feel entitled to a life of material prosperity. "Equality of opportunity," the prototypical American slogan, is vastly different from the socialist dream of "equality of condition," which perhaps is one reason socialism has so few adherents in America.

The real difficulty in reconciling the American ideal with American reality is not the problem of income differentials but the *persistence* of poverty from generation to generation. Often, parent, child, and grandchild seem to be locked into a hopeless cycle of destitution and dependence. One explanation is that a large segment of the poor do not really try to get out of poverty. In its more vicious form this view portrays these people as lazy, stupid, or base. Their poverty is not to be blamed on defects of American society but on their own defects. After all, many successful Americans have worked their way up from humble beginnings, and many immigrant groups have made progress in one generation. Therefore, the United States provides opportunities for all who will work hard and make something of themselves. Another explanation, however, could be that the poor have few opportunities and many obstacles to overcome to climb out of poverty. If so, then America is not the land of opportunity for the poor, and the American dream is reserved for the more fortunate.

The first explanation for the persistence of poverty holds that among some groups there is a *culture* that breeds poverty because it is antithetical to the self-discipline and hard work that enable others to climb out of their poverty. In other words, the poor have a culture all their own that is at variance with middle-class culture and hinders their success. Although it may keep people locked into what seems to be an intolerable life, this culture nevertheless has its own compensations and pleasures: It is full of "action," and it does not demand that people postpone pleasure, save money, or work hard. And it is, for the most part, tolerable to those who live in it. Furthermore, according to this argument, not all poor people embrace the culture of poverty, and those who embrace middle-class values should be given every workable form of encouragement—material and spiritual—for escaping poverty. But for those poor who embrace the lower-class culture, very little can be done. These poor will always be with us.

According to the second explanation of poverty, most of the poor will become self-supporting if they are given a decent chance. Their most important need is for decent jobs that can go somewhere. But often they cannot find jobs, and when they do, the jobs are dead-end or degrading. Some need job training or counseling to give them more self-confidence before navigating the job market. Others need temporary help such as rent supplements, inexpensive housing, income supplements, protection from crime, medical services, or better education to help them help themselves.

The culture of poverty thesis shields the economic system from blame for poverty and honors Americans who are better off. But most of the poor are as committed to taking care of themselves and their families through hard work as is the middle class, and a sense of dignity is common to all classes. Critics judge the culture of poverty thesis to be a smug, self-righteous justification by spokesmen for the middle and upper classes for the economic system that rewards them so handsomely while subjecting the poor to an intolerable existence. The culture of the poor is similar to the culture of the middle class. Where they do differ, however, the difference is because the culture of the poor is materially different. Change their material conditions and their culture will change rather quickly.

Edward Banfield, a proponent of the culture of poverty thesis, maintains that it is not the material that controls the culture but the other way around; only the abandonment of lower-class culture will get the poor out of poverty. On the other side, William Ryan charges that Banfield's approach is a typical case of "blaming the victim."

YES   Edward Banfield

THE FUTURE OF THE LOWER CLASS

So long as the city contains a sizable lower class, nothing basic can be done about its most serious problems. Good jobs may be offered to all, but some will remain chronically unemployed. Slums may be demolished, but if the housing that replaces them is occupied by the lower class it will shortly be turned into new slums. Welfare payments may be doubled or tripled and a negative income tax instituted, but some persons will continue to live in squalor and misery. New schools may be built, new curricula devised, and the teacher-pupil ratio cut in half, but if the children who attend these schools come from lower-class homes, they will be turned into blackboard jungles, and those who graduate or drop out from them will, in most cases, be functionally illiterate. The streets may be filled with armies of policemen, but violent crime and civil disorder will decrease very little. If, however, the lower class were to disappear—if, say, its members were overnight to acquire the attitudes, motivations, and habits of the working class—the most serious and intractable problems of the city would all disappear with it.

[The] serious problems of the city all exist in two forms—a normal-class and a lower-class form—which are fundamentally different from each other. In its normal-class form, the employment problem, for example, consists mainly of young people who are just entering the labor market and who must make a certain number of trials and errors before finding suitable jobs; in its lower-class form, it consists of people who prefer the "action" of the street to any steady job. The poverty problem in its normal-class form consists of people (especially the aged, the physically handicapped, and mothers with dependent children) whose only need in order to live decently is money; in its lower-class form it consists of people who live in squalor and misery even if their incomes were doubled or tripled. The same is true with the other problems—slum housing, schools, crime, rioting; each is really two quite different problems.

The lower-class forms of all problems are at bottom a single problem: the existence of an outlook and style of life which is radically present-oriented and which therefore attaches no value to work, sacrifice, self-improvement, or service to family, friends, or community. Social workers, teachers, and law-enforcement officials—all those whom Gans calls "caretakers"—cannot achieve their goals because they can neither change nor circumvent this cultural obstacle....

Robert Hunter described it in 1904:

> They lived in God only knows what misery. They ate when there were things to eat; they starved when there was lack of food. But, on the whole, although they swore and beat each other and got drunk, they were more contented than any other class I have happened to know. It took a long time to understand them. Our Committees were busy from morning until night in giving them opportunities to take up the fight again, and to become independent of relief. They always took what we gave them; they always promised to try; but as soon as we expected them to fulfill any promises, they gave up in despair, and either wept or looked ashamed, and took to misery and drink again,—almost, so it seemed to me at times, with a sense of relief.

In Hunter's day these were the "undeserving," "unworthy," "depraved," "debased," or "disreputable" poor; today, they are the "troubled," "culturally deprived," "hard to reach," or "multi-problem." In the opinion of anthropologist Oscar Lewis, their kind of poverty "is a way of life, remarkably stable and persistent, passed down from generation to generation among family lines." This "culture of poverty," as he calls it, exists in city slums in many parts of the world, and is, he says, an adaptation made by the poor in order to defend themselves against the harsh realities of slum life.

The view that is to be taken here [is that] there is indeed such a culture, but that poverty is its effect rather than its cause. (There are societies even poorer than the ones Lewis has described—primitive ones, for example—in which nothing remotely resembling the pattern of behavior here under discussion exists.) Extreme present-orientedness, not lack of income or wealth, is the principal cause of poverty in the sense of "the culture of poverty." Most of those caught up in this culture are unable or unwilling to plan for the future, to sacrifice immediate gratifications in favor of future ones, or to accept the disciplines that are required in order to get and to spend. Their inabilities are probably culturally given in most cases—"multi-problem" families being normal representatives of a class culture that is itself abnormal. No doubt there are also people whose present-orientedness is rationally adaptive rather than cultural, but these probably comprise only a small part of the "hard core" poor.

Outside the lower class, poverty (in the sense of hardship, want, or destitution) is today almost always the result of external circumstances—involuntary unemployment, prolonged illness, the death of a breadwinner, or some other misfortune. Even when severe, such poverty is not squalid or degrading. Moreover, it ends quickly once the (external) cause of it no longer exists. Public or private assistance can sometimes remove or alleviate the cause—for example, by job retraining or remedial surgery. Even when the cause cannot be removed, simply providing the nonlower-class poor with sufficient income is enough to enable them to live "decently."

Lower-class poverty, by contrast, is "inwardly" caused (by psychological inability to provide for the future, and all that this inability implies). Improvements in external circumstances can affect this poverty only superficially: One problem of a "multiproblem" family is no sooner solved than another arises. In principle, it is possible to eliminate the poverty (material lack) of such a family, but only at great expense, since the capacity of the radically improvident to waste money is almost unlimited. Raising such a family's income would not necessarily improve its way of life, moreover, and could conceivably even make things worse. Consider, for example, the H. family:

Mrs. H. seemed overwhelmed with the simple mechanics of dressing her six children and washing their clothes. The younger ones were running around in their underwear; the older ones were unaccounted for, but presumably were around the neighborhood. Mrs. H. had not been out of the house for several months; evidently her husband did the shopping. The apartment was filthy and it smelled. Mrs. H. was dressed in a bathrobe, although it was mid-afternoon. She seemed to have no plan or expectations with regard to her children; she did not know the names of their teachers and she did not seem to worry about their school work, although one child had been retained one year and another two years. Mrs. H. did seem to be somewhat concerned about her husband's lack of activity over the weekend—his continuous drinking and watching baseball on television. Apparently he and she never went out socially together nor did the family ever go anywhere as a unit.

If this family had a very high income—say, $50,000 a year—it would not be considered a "culture of poverty" case. Mrs. H. would hire maids to look after the small children, send the others to boarding schools, and spend her time at fashion shows while her husband drank and watched TV at his club. But with an income of only moderate size—say 100 percent above the poverty line—they would probably be about as badly off as they are now. They might be even worse off, for

Mrs. H. would be able to go to the dog races, leaving the children alone, and Mr. H. could devote more time to his bottle and TV set....

Welfare agencies, recognizing the difference between "internally" and "externally" caused poverty, have long been trying first by one means and then another to improve the characters or, as it is now put, to "bring about personal adjustment" of the poor. In the nineteenth century, the view was widely held that what the lower class individual needed was to be brought into a right relation with God or (the secular version of the same thing) with the respectable (that is, middle- and upper-class) elements of the community. The missionary who distributed tracts door to door in the slums was the first caseworker; his—more often, her—task was to minister to what today would be called "feelings of alienation."

The stranger, coming on a stranger's errand, becomes a friend, discharging the offices and exerting the influence of a friend....

Secularized, this approach became the "friendly visitor" system under which "certain persons, under the direction of a central board, pledge themselves to take one or more families who need counsel, if not material help, on their visiting list, and maintain personal friendly relations with them." The system did not work; middle- and upper-class people might be "friendly," but they could not sympathize, let alone communicate, with the lower class. By the beginning of the twentieth century the friendly visitor had been replaced by the "expert." The idea now was that the authority of "the facts" would bring about desired changes of attitude, motive, and habit. As it happened, however, the lower class did not recognize the authority of the facts. The expert then became a supervisor, using his (or her) power to confer or withhold material benefits in order to force the poor to do the things that were supposed to lead to "rehabilitation" (that is, to a middle-class style of life). This method did not work either; the lower class could always find ways to defeat and exploit the system. They seldom changed their ways very much and they never changed them for long. Besides, there was really no body of expertise to tell caseworkers how to produce the changes desired. As one caseworker remarked recently in a book addressed to fellow social service professionals:

> Despite years of experience in providing public aid to poor families precious little is yet known about how to help truly inadequate parents make long term improvements in child care, personal maturity, social relations, or work stability.

Some people understood that if the individual's style of life was to be changed at all, it would be necessary to change that of the group that produced, motivated, and constrained him. Thus, the settlement house. As Robert A. Woods explained:

> The settlements are able to take neighborhoods in cities, and by patience bring back to them much of the healthy village life, so that the people shall again know and care for one another....

When it became clear that settlement houses would not change the culture of slum neighborhoods, the group approach was broadened into what is called "community action." In one type of community action ("community development"), a community organizer tries to persuade a neighborhood's in-formal leaders to support measures (for instance, measures for delinquency control) that he advances. In another form of it ("community organization"), the organizer tries to promote self-confidence, self-respect, and attachment to the group (and, hopefully, to normal society) among lower-class people. He attempts to do this by encouraging them in efforts at joint action, or by showing them how to conduct meetings, carry on discussions, pass resolutions, present requests to politicians, and the like. In still another form ("community mobilization"), the organizer endeavors to arouse the anger of lower-class persons against the local "power structure," to teach them the techniques of mass action—strikes, sit-ins, picketing, and so on—and to show them how they may capture power. The theory of community organization attributes the malaise of the poor to their lack of self-confidence (which is held to derive largely from their "inexperience"); community mobilization theory, by contrast, attributes it to their feelings of "powerlessness." According to this doctrine, the best cure for poverty is to give the poor power. But since power is not "given," it must be seized.

The success of the group approach has been no greater than that of the caseworker approach. Reviewing five years of effort on the part of various community action programs, Marris and Rein conclude:

> ... the reforms had not evolved any reliable solutions to the intractable problems with which they struggled. They had not discovered how in general to override the intransigent autonomy of public and private agencies, at any level of government; nor how to use the social sciences practically to formulate and evaluate policy; nor how, under the sponsorship of

government, to raise the power of the poor. Given the talent and money they had brought to bear, they had not even reopened very many opportunities.

If the war on poverty is judged by its ability "to generate major, meaningful and lasting social and economic reforms in conformity with the expressed wishes of poor people," writes Thomas Gladwin, "... it is extremely difficult to find even scattered evidence of success." ...

Although city agencies have sent community organizers by the score into slum neighborhoods, the lower-class poor cannot be organized. In East Harlem in 1948, five social workers were assigned to organize a five-block area and to initiate a program of social action based on housing, recreation, and other neighborhood needs. After three years of effort, the organizers had failed to attract a significant number of participants, and those they did attract were upwardly mobile persons who were unrepresentative of the neighborhood. In Boston a "total community" delinquency control project was found to have had "negligible impact," an outcome strikingly like that of the Cambridge-Somerville experiment— a "total caseworker" project—a decade earlier. Even community mobilization, despite the advantages of a rhetoric of hate and an emphasis on "action," failed to involve lower-class persons

to a significant extent. Gangsters and leaders of youth gangs were co-opted on occasion, but they did not suffer from feelings of powerlessness and were not representative of the class for which mobilization was to provide therapy. No matter how hard they have tried to appeal to people at the very bottom of the scale, community organizers have rarely succeeded. Where they have appeared to succeed, as, for example, in the National Welfare Rights Organization, it has been by recruiting people who had some of the *outward* attributes of the lower class—poverty, for example—but whose outlook and values were not lower class; the lower-class person (as defined here) is incapable of being organized. Although it tried strenuously to avoid it, what the Mobilization for Youth described as the general experience proved to be its own experience as well:

> Most efforts to organize lower-class people attract individuals on their way up the social-class ladder. Persons who are relatively responsible about participation, articulate and successful at managing organizational "forms" are identified as lower-class leaders, rather than individuals who actually reflect the values of the lower-class groups. Ordinarily the slum's network of informal group associations is not reached.

NO
William Ryan

BLAMING THE VICTIM

Twenty years ago, Zero Mostel used to do a sketch in which he impersonated a Dixiecrat Senator conducting an investigation of the origins of World War II. At the climax of the sketch, the Senator boomed out, in an excruciating mixture of triumph and suspicion, "What was Pearl Harbor *doing* in the Pacific?" This is an extreme example of Blaming the Victim.

Twenty years ago, we could laugh at Zero Mostel's caricature. In recent years, however, the same process has been going on every day in the arena of social problems, public health, anti-poverty programs, and social welfare. A philosopher might analyze this process and prove that, technically, it is comic. But it is hardly ever funny.

Consider some victims. One is the miseducated child in the slum school. He is blamed for his own miseducation. He is said to contain within himself the causes of his inability to read and write well. The shorthand phrase is "cultural deprivation," which, to those in the know, conveys what they allege to be inside information: that the poor child carries a scanty pack of cultural baggage as he enters school. He doesn't know about books and magazines and newspapers, they say. (No books in the home: the mother fails to subscribe to *Reader's Digest*.) They say that if he talks at all—an unlikely event since slum parents don't talk to their children—he certainly doesn't talk correctly. Lower-class dialect spoken here, or even—God forbid!—Southern Negro. *(Ici on parle nigra.)* If you can manage to get him to sit in a chair, they say, he squirms and looks out the window. (Impulse-ridden, these kids, motoric rather than verbal.) In a word he is "disadvantaged" and "socially deprived," they say, and this, of course, accounts for his failure (*his* failure, they say) to learn much in school.

Note the similarity to the logic of Zero Mostel's Dixiecrat Senator. What is the culturally deprived child *doing* in the school? What is wrong with the victim? In pursuing this logic, no one remembers to ask questions about the collapsing buildings and torn textbooks, the frightened, insensitive teachers, the six additional desks in the room, the blustering, frightened principals, the relentless segregation, the callous administrator, the irrelevant curriculum, the bigoted or cowardly members of the school board, the insulting history book, the stingy taxpayers, the fairy-tale readers, or the self-serving faculty of the local teachers' college. We are encouraged to confine our attention to the child and to dwell on all his alleged defects. Cultural deprivation becomes an omnibus explanation for the educational disaster area known as the inner-city school. This is Blaming the Victim.

Pointing to the supposedly deviant Negro family as the "fundamental weakness of the Negro community" is another way to blame the victim. Like "cultural deprivation," "Negro family" has become a shorthand phrase with stereotyped connotations of matriarchy, fatherlessness, and pervasive illegitimacy. Growing up in the "crumbling" Negro family is supposed to account for most of the racial evils in America. Insiders have the word, of course, and know that this phrase is supposed to evoke images of growing up with a long-absent or never-present father (replaced from time to time perhaps by a series of transient lovers) and with bossy women ruling the roost, so that the children are irreparably damaged. This refers particularly to the poor, bewildered male children, whose psyches are fatally wounded and who are never, alas, to learn the trick of becoming upright, downright, forthright all-American boys. Is it any wonder the Negroes cannot achieve equality? From such families! And, again, by focusing our attention on the Negro family as the apparent *cause* of racial inequality, our eye is diverted. Racism, discrimination, segregation, and the powerlessness of the ghetto are subtly, but thoroughly, downgraded in importance.

The generic process of Blaming the Victim is applied to almost every American problem. The miserable health care of the poor is explained away on the grounds that the victim has poor motivation and lacks health information. The problems of slum housing are traced to the characteristics of tenants who are labeled as "Southern rural migrants" not yet "acculturated" to life in the big city. The "multiproblem" poor, it is claimed, suffer the psychological effects of impoverishment, the "culture of poverty," and the deviant value system of the lower classes; consequently, though unwittingly, they cause their own troubles. From such a viewpoint, the obvious fact that poverty is primarily an absence of money is easily overlooked or set aside.

The growing number of families receiving welfare are fallaciously linked together with the increased number of illegitimate children as twin results of promiscuity and sexual abandon among members of the lower orders. Every important social problem—crime, mental illness, civil disorder, unemployment—has been analyzed within the framework of the victim-blaming ideology. In the following pages, I shall present in detail nine examples that relate to social problems and human services in urban areas.

It would be possible for me to venture into other areas—one finds a perfect example in literature about the underdeveloped countries of the Third World, in which the lack of prosperity and technological progress is attributed to some aspect of the national character of the people, such as lack of "achievement motivation"—but I plan to stay within the confines of my own personal and professional experience, which is, generally, with racial injustice, social welfare, and human services in the city.

I have been listening to the victim-blamers and pondering their thought processes for a number of years. That process is often very subtle. Victim-blaming is cloaked in kindness and concern, and bears all the trappings and statistical furbelows of scientism; it is obscured by a perfumed haze of humanitarianism. In observing the process of Blaming the Victim, one tends to be confused and disoriented because those who practice this art display a deep concern for the victims that is quite genuine. In this way, the new ideology is very different from the open prejudice and reactionary tactics of the old days. Its adherents include sympathetic social scientists with social consciences in good working order, and liberal politicians with a genuine commitment to reform. They are very careful to dissociate themselves from vulgar Calvinism or crude racism; they indignantly condemn any notions of innate wickedness or genetic defect. "The Negro is *not born* inferior," they shout apoplectically. "Force of circumstance," they explain in reasonable tones, "has *made* him inferior." And they dismiss with self-righteous contempt any claims that the poor man in America is plainly unworthy or shiftless or enamored of idleness. No, they say, he is "caught in the cycle of poverty." He is trained to be poor by his culture and his family life, endowed by his environment (perhaps by his ignorant mother's outdated style of toilet training) with those unfortunately unpleasant characteristics that make him ineligible for a passport into the affluent society.

Blaming the Victim is, of course, quite different from old-fashioned conservative ideologies. The latter simply dismissed victims as inferior, genetically defective, or morally unfit; the emphasis is on the intrinsic, even hereditary, defect. The former shifts its emphasis to the environmental causation. The old-fashioned conservative could hold firmly to the belief that the oppressed and the victimized were born that way—that way being defective or inadequate in character or ability. The new ideology attributes defect and inadequacy to the malignant nature of poverty, injustice, slum life, and racial difficulties. The stigma that marks the victim and accounts for his victimization is an acquired stigma, a stigma of social, rather than genetic, origin. But the stigma, the defect, the fatal difference—though derived in the past from environmental forces—is still located *within* the victim, inside his skin. With such an elegant formulation, the humanitarian can have it both ways. He can, all at the same time, concentrate his charitable interest on the defects of the victim, condemn the vague social and environmental stresses that produced the defect (some time ago), and ignore the continuing effect of victimizing social forces (right now). It is a brilliant ideology for justifying a perverse form of social action designed to change, not society, as one might expect, but rather society's victim.

As a result, there is a terrifying sameness in the programs that arise from this kind of analysis. In education, we have programs of "compensatory education" to build up the skills and attitudes of the ghetto child, rather than structural changes in the schools. In race relations, we have social engineers who think up ways of "strengthening" the Negro family, rather than methods of eradicating racism. In health care, we develop new programs to provide health information (to correct the supposed ignorance of the poor) and to reach out and discover cases of untreated illness and disability (to compensate for their supposed unwillingness to seek treatment). Meanwhile, the gross inequities of our medical care delivery systems are left completely unchanged. As we might expect, the logical outcome of analyzing social problems in terms of the deficiencies of the victim is the development of programs aimed at correcting those deficiencies. The formula for action becomes extraordinarily simple: change the victim.

All of this happens so smoothly that it seems downright rational. First, identify a social problem. Second, study those affected by the problem and discover in what ways they are different from the rest of us as a consequence of deprivation and injustice. Third, define the differences as the cause of the social problem itself. Finally, of course, assign a government bureaucrat to invent a humanitarian action program to correct the differences.

Now no one in his right mind would quarrel with the assertion that social problems are present in abundance and are readily identifiable. God knows it is true that when hundreds of thousands of poor children drop out of school—or even graduate from school—they are barely literate. After spending some ten thousand hours in the company of professional educators, these children appear to have learned very little. The fact of failure in their education is undisputed. And the racial situation in America is usually acknowledged to be a number one item on the nation's agenda. Despite years of marches, commissions, judicial decisions, and endless legislative remedies, we are confronted with unchanging or even widening racial differences in achievement. In addition, despite our assertions that Americans get the best health care in the world, the poor stubbornly remain unhealthy. They lose more work because of illness, have more carious teeth, lose more babies as a result of both miscarriage and infant death,

and die considerably younger than the well-to-do.

The problems are there, and there in great quantities. They make us uneasy. Added together, these disturbing signs reflect inequality and a puzzlingly high level of unalleviated distress in America totally inconsistent with our proclaimed ideals and our enormous wealth. This thread—this rope—of inconsistency stands out so visibly in the fabric of American life, that it is jarring to the eye. And this must be explained, to the satisfaction of our conscience as well as our patriotism. Blaming the Victim is an ideal, almost painless, evasion.

The second step in applying this explanation is to look sympathetically at those who "have" the problem in question, to separate them out and define them in some way as a special group, a group that is *different* from the population in general. This is a crucial and essential step in the process, for that difference is in itself hampering and maladaptive. The Different Ones are seen as less competent, less skilled, less knowing—in short, less human....

The ultimate effect is always to distract attention from the basic causes and to leave the primary social injustice untouched. And, most telling, the proposed remedy for the problem is, of course, to work on the victim himself. Prescriptions for cure, [are] invariably conceived to revamp and revise the victim, never to change the surrounding circumstances. They want to change his attitudes, alter his values, fill up his cultural deficits, energize his apathetic soul, cure his character defects, train him and polish him and woo him from his savage ways.

... The old, reactionary exceptionalistic formulations are replaced by new progressive, humanitarian exceptionalistic formulations. In education, the outmoded and unacceptable concept of racial or class differences in basic inherited intellectual ability simply gives way to the new notion of cultural deprivation: there is very little functional difference between these two ideas. In taking a look at the phenomenon of poverty, the old concept of unfitness or idleness or laziness is replaced by the newfangled theory of the culture of poverty. In race relations, plain Negro inferiority—which was good enough for old-fashioned conservatives—is pushed aside by fancy conceits about the crumbling Negro family. With regard to illegitimacy, we are not so crass as to concern ourselves with immorality and vice, as in the old days; we settle benignly on the explanation of the "lower-class pattern of sexual behavior," which no one condemns as evil, but which is, in fact, simply a variation of the old explanatory idea. Mental illness is no longer defined as the result of hereditary taint or congenital character flaw; now we have new causal hypotheses regarding the ego-damaging emotional experiences that are supposed to be the inevitable consequence of the deplorable child-rearing practices of the poor.

In each case, of course, we are persuaded to ignore the obvious: the continued blatant discrimination against the Negro, the gross deprivation of contraceptive and adoption services to the poor, the heavy stresses endemic in the life of the poor. And almost all our make-believe liberal programs aimed at correcting our urban problems are off target; they are designed either to change the poor man or to cool him out....

But, in any case, are the poor really all that different from the middle class? Take a common type of study, showing that ninety-one percent of the upper class, compared to only sixty-eight percent of the poor, prefer college education for their children. What does that tell us about the difference in values between classes?

First, if almost seventy percent of the poor want their children to go to college, it doesn't make much sense to say that the poor, as a group, do not value education. Only a minority of them—somewhat less than one-third— fail to express a *wish* that their children attend college. A smaller minority—one in ten—of the middle class give similar responses. One might well wonder why this small group of the better-off citizens of our achieving society reject higher education. They have the money; many of them have the direct experience of education; and most of them are aware of the monetary value of a college degree. I would suggest that the thirty percent of the poor who are unwilling to express a wish that their children go to college are easier to understand. They know the barriers—financial, social, and for black parents, racial—that make it very difficult for the children of the poor to get a college education. That seven out of ten of them nevertheless persist in a desire to see their children in a cap and gown is, in a very real sense, remarkable. Most important, if we are concerned with cultural or subcultural differences, it seems highly illogical to emphasize the values of a small minority of one group and then to attribute these values to the whole group. I simply cannot accept the evidence. If seventy percent of a group values education, then it is completely illogical to say that the group as a whole does *not* value education.

A useful formulation is to be found in Hyman Rodman's conception of the "lower class value stretch" which, to give a highly oversimplified version, proposes that members of the lower class *share* the dominant value system but *stretch* it to include as much as possible of the variations that circumstances force upon them. Rodman says:

Lower class persons in close interaction with each other and faced with similar problems do not long remain in a state of mutual ignorance. They do not maintain a strong commitment to middle class values that they cannot attain, and they do not continue to respond to others in a rewarding or punishing way simply on the basis of whether these others are living up to the middle class values. A change takes place. They come to tolerate and eventually to evaluate favorably certain deviations from the middle class values. In this way they need not be continually frustrated by their failure to live up to unattainable values. The resultant is a stretched value system with a low degree of commitment to all the values within the range, including the dominant, middle class values.

In Rodman's terms, then, differences in range of values and commitments to specific elements within that range occur primarily as an *adaptive* rather than as a *cultural* response....

The most recent, and in many ways the best information on [the related issue of child rearing] comes to us from the Hylan Lewis child-rearing studies, which I have mentioned before. Lewis has demonstrated (finally, one hopes) that there really *is* no "lower class child-rearing pattern." There are a number of such patterns—ranging from strict and overcontrolled parenting, to permissiveness, to down-right neglect—just as in Lewis' sample there are a variety of different kinds of families—ranging from those with rigid, old-fashioned standards of hard work, thrift, morality and obsessive cleanliness, to the disorganized and disturbed families that he calls the "clinical poor." Lewis says:

... it appears as a broad spectrum of pragmatic adjustments to external and internal stresses and deprivation.... Many low income families appear here as, in fact, the frustrated victims of what are thought of as middle class values, behavior and aspirations.

We return, finally, to where we began: the concept of Deferred Need Gratification. The simple idea that lower class folk have, as a character trait, a built-in deficiency in ability to delay need gratification has been explored, analyzed and more or less blown apart by Miller, Riessman, and Seagull. They point out that the supposed commitment of the middle classes to the virtues of thrift and hard work, to the practices of planning and saving for every painfully-chosen expenditure is, at this point in time, at best a surviving myth reflecting past conditions of dubious prevalence. The middle classes of today are clearly consumption-minded and debt-addicted. So the comparison group against which the poor are judged exists largely as a theoretical category with a theoretical behavior pattern. They go on to raise critical questions, similar to those I have raised earlier in this chapter. For example, on the question of what one would do with a two thousand dollar windfall, there was a difference between class groups of only five percent—about seventy percent of the middle class said they would save most of it, compared with about sixty-five percent of the lower class. On the basis of this small difference (which was statistically, but not practically, significant), the researchers, you will remember, had concluded that working-class people had less ability to defer need gratification. This conclusion may reflect elegant research methodology, but it fails the test of common sense. . . .

As for the idea that the poor share a culture in the sense that they subscribe to and follow a particular, deviant prescription for living—a poor man's blueprint for choosing and decision-making which accounts for the way he lives—this does not deserve much comment. Every study—with the exception of the egregious productions of Walter Miller—shows that, at the very least, overwhelming numbers of the poor give allegiance to the values and principles of the dominant American culture.

A related point—often the most overlooked point in any discussion of the culture of poverty—is that there is not, to my knowledge, *any evidence whatever* that the poor perceive their way of life as good and preferable to that of other ways of life. To make such an assertion is to talk pure nonsense. . . .

Perhaps the most fundamental question to ask of those who are enamored of the idea that the poor have one culture and the rich another is to ask, simply, "So what?" Suppose the mythical oil millionaire behaves in an unrefined "lower class" manner, for example. What difference does that make as long as he owns the oil wells? Is the power of the Chairman of the Ways and Means Committee in the state legislature diminished or enhanced in any way by his taste in clothing or music? And suppose every single poor family in America set as its long-range goal that its sons and daughters would get a Ph.D.—who would pay the tuition?

The effect of tastes, child-rearing practices, speech patterns, reading habits, and other cultural factors is relatively small in comparison to the effect of wealth and influence. What I am trying to suggest is that the inclusion in the analytic process of the elements of social stratification that are usually omitted—particularly economic class and power—would produce more significant insights into the circumstances of the poor and the pressures and deprivations with which they live. The simplest—and at the same time, the most significant—proposition in understanding poverty is that it is caused by lack of money. The overwhelming majority of the poor are poor because they have, first: insufficient income; and second: no access to methods of increasing that income—that is, no power. They are too young, too old, too sick; they are bound to the task of caring for small children, or they are simply discriminated against. The facts are clear, and the solution seems rather obvious—raise their income and let their "culture," whatever it might be, take care of itself.

The need to avoid facing this obvious solution—which is very uncomfortable since it requires some substantial changes and redistribution of income—provides the motivation for developing the stabilizing ideology of the culture of poverty which acts to sustain the *status quo* and delay change. The function of the ideology of lower class culture, then, is plainly to maintain inequality in American life.

The millionaire, freshly risen from the lower class, whose crude tongue and appalling table manners betray the newness of his affluence, is a staple of American literature and folklore. He comes on stage over and over, and we have been taught exactly what to expect with each entrance. He will walk into the parlor in his undershirt, gulp tea from a saucer, spit into the Limoges flower pot, and, when finally invited to the society garden party, disgrace his wife by saying "bullshit" to the president of the bank. When I was growing up, we had daily lessons in this legend from Jiggs and Maggie in the comic strip.

This discrepancy between *class* and *status*, between possession of economic resources and life style, has been a source of ready humour and guaranteed fascination for generations. The centrality of this mythical strain in American thought is reflected again in the strange and perverse ideas emerging from the mouths of many professional Pauper Watchers and Victim Blamers.

In real life, of course, Jiggs' character and behavior would never remain so constant and unchanging over the decades. The strain between wealth and style is one that usually tends to be quickly resolved. Within a fairly short time, Jiggs would be coming into the parlor first with a shirt, then with a tie on, and, finally, in one of his many custom-made suits. He would soon be drinking tea from a Limoges cup, and for a time he would spit in an antique cuspidor, until he learned not to spit at all. At the garden party, he would confine his mention of animal feces to a discussion of the best fertilizer for the rhododendron. In real life, style tends to follow close on money, and money tends to be magnetized and attracted to power. Those who try to persuade us that the process can be reversed, that a change in style of life can lead backward to increased wealth and greater power, are preaching nonsense. To promise that improved table manners can produce a salary increase; that more elegant taste in clothes will lead to the acquisition of stock in IBM; that an expanded vocabulary will automatically generate an enlargement of community influence—these are pernicious as well as foolish. There is no record in history of any *group* having accomplished this wondrous task. (There may be a few clever individuals who have followed such artful routes to money and power, but they are relatively rare.) The whole idea is an illusion of fatuous social scientists and welfare bureaucrats blinded by the ideology I have painstakingly tried to dissect in the previous chapters.

POSTSCRIPT

Does "Lower-Class" Culture Perpetuate Poverty?

The debate over the culture of poverty thesis is as strong today as it was over 20 years ago when Banfield and Ryan were debating. In 1981 George Gilder incorporated the culture of poverty thesis in his book *Wealth and Poverty* (Basic Books) and argued that hard work is the tried and true path from poverty to wealth. He also agrees that many welfare programs perpetuate poverty by breeding dependence and supporting the culture of poverty. This criticism of welfare has been forcefully argued with ample statistics by Charles Murray in *Losing Ground* (Basic Books, 1984). Both Gilder and Murray view the welfare system as an important contributor to the culture of poverty, whereas Banfield sees the culture of poverty as being virulent long before welfare became a major factor in the lives of poor people.

There are countless works that describe the crushing and numbing conditions of the poor. The nineteenth-century English novelist Charles Dickens was a crusader for the poor, and many of his novels, still in print and certainly considered classics, graphically depict the wretchedness of poverty. Michael Harrington (1929–1989), a prominent political theorist and socialist, is one example of a more contemporary writer whose works call attention to the poor in our society. He described poverty in America in his influential nonfiction book *The Other America* (Macmillan, 1963) at a time when most of the country was increasingly affluent. He also helped launch the War on Poverty of the Kennedy and Johnson administrations. Thomas Gladwin, in *Poverty USA* (Little, Brown, 1967), and Nick Katz, in *Let Them Eat Promises* (Prentice Hall, 1969), sought to maintain national concern about poverty in the late 1960s by documenting its prevalence even though the poverty rate had dropped from 30 percent in 1950 to 13 percent in 1970.

The antipoverty crusaders have new concerns with more recent developments, such as the increase in the number of female-headed single-parent families living below the poverty line and the increase throughout the 1980s in the number of homeless people. Michael Harrington chronicled these changes in the condition of the poor in *The New American Poverty* (Holt, Rinehart & Winston, 1984). More recently, William Julius Wilson has written about the macroeconomic forces at work on the poor in *The Truly Disadvantaged* (University of Chicago Press, 1987). The most vigorous proponent of the culture of poverty thesis today is Lawrence E. Harrison, who wrote *Who Prospers? How Cultural Values Shape Economic and Political Success* (Basic Books, 1992).

ISSUE 9

Is Black Self-Help the Solution to Racial Inequality?

YES: Glenn C. Loury, from "A Prescription for Black Progress," *The Christian Century* (April 30, 1986)

NO: John E. Jacob, from "The Future of Black America," *Vital Speeches of the Day* (August 1, 1988)

ISSUE SUMMARY

YES: Professor of economics Glenn C. Loury contends that government programs aimed at relieving black poverty often become job programs for middle-class professionals, and he argues that, historically and today, self-help has been the key to black progress.

NO: National Urban League president John E. Jacob argues that the notion of blacks pulling themselves out of poverty by their own bootstraps is a myth without basis in fact or in history.

In 1968, following four years of urban riots by blacks in several major U.S. cities, a presidential commission headed by Illinois governor Otto Kerner tried to determine the causes of the disorders. In its report the Kerner Commission offered this conclusion: "Our nation is moving toward two societies, one black, one white—separate and unequal." Ironically, this gloomy diagnosis came near the close of one of the most progressive periods in American race relations, for within the four previous years, between 1964 and 1968, Congress passed three major civil rights bills and added a new civil rights amendment to the Constitution. These new laws banned racial discrimination in employment, public accommodations, and housing, and removed the remaining obstacles to black voting rights. Federal judges began to vigorously enforce laws against racial discrimination, in some cases ordering busing and other actions to remedy the long-term effects of discrimination. Yet this great rights revolution, launched with vigor and high hopes, was culminating in violence, arson, and looting. Why?

The Kerner Commission attributed it to a combination of white racism and black frustration. Racism, the Commission said, produced the ghettos where crime, drug addiction, and welfare dependency flourished; it also lay behind the white suburban exodus that sapped the cities of funds and services needed by blacks. White racism produced the "frustrated hopes" and "the frustrations of powerlessness," which in turn produced the black riots. To cure what it saw as the underlying malaise, the Kerner Commission urged a massive new program of state and federal involvement in the black community: job creation, education, training, urban aid, welfare, housing, and new studies.

The Kerner Commission report was startling at the time, but today most major civil rights organizations have incorporated its conclusions into their platforms. Like the Kerner Commission, they say that civil rights must go much further than the attainment of legal equality. They focus upon the persistence of social inequality between the races, as measured in the statistics on everything from joblessness to maternal and child health. They conclude, as did the Kerner Commission, that white racism created these problems and that only a massive commitment by government can solve them.

There exists, however, another perspective. It was also foreshadowed by a report written in the 1960s, although this report began with a different set of premises and pointed toward a different conclusion than that of the Kerner Commission. In 1965, Assistant Secretary of Labor Daniel Patrick Moynihan, now a U.S. senator from New York, wrote a report entitled *The Negro Family: The Case for National Action,* in which he suggested that one reason for the persistence of social inequality between the races was the breakdown of the black family. Early pregnancies, illegitimate children, and the absence of a father were factors that he claimed contributed to a culture of poverty and dependency among urban blacks. Moynihan emphasized that these pathologies were ultimately rooted in a history of high unemployment and racial discrimination, but he suggested that they had taken on a life of their own. Although Moynihan urged the government to play a role in helping the black family, as the subtitle of his report makes clear, the Moynihan report has been widely interpreted as suggesting the need for black self-help.

At the time, the Moynihan report provoked angry denunciation—critics saw it as a classic case of "blaming the victim"—but in recent years the theme of black self-help has won support from some black writers and activists. Robert L. Woodson, head of the National Center for Neighborhood Enterprise (NCNE), and Roy Innis, director of the Congress of Racial Equality (CORE), are outspoken self-help activists. Even some black liberals, such as law professor Eleanor Holmes Norton, have endorsed the Moynihan report (Norton notes that the deterioration of the black family has become much worse since the report was written) and have urged a rediscovery of what Norton calls the "enduring values" of black America: hard work, education, and respect for family. Many civil rights spokespersons, however, worry that simplistic theories of "self-help" may be used as excuses for abandoning social programs that help poor blacks.

In the selections that follow, Glenn C. Loury makes the case for self-help, while John E. Jacob insists on the need for a major government role in narrowing the social differences between the races in the United States.

YES
Glenn C. Loury

A PRESCRIPTION FOR BLACK PROGRESS

Black Americans confront a great challenge, and an enormous opportunity. The black struggle for equality, born in the dark days of slavery and nurtured with the courage and sacrifices of generations who would not silently accept second-class citizenship, now threatens to falter and come to a stop—short of its historic goal. Throughout America, in the rural counties of the Black Belt, in the slums of Harlem, in North Philadelphia, on the west side of Chicago, on the east side of Detroit, in south-central Los Angeles, in East St. Louis, Illinois, in the ghettos of Houston, Oakland, Newark and scores of smaller cities and towns, literally millions of blacks live in poverty and, all too often, despair.

Of course, it is not only blacks who experience poverty or who deserve our concern. I focus on this group for two reasons. First, the problems associated with civic exclusion are especially severe for blacks and originate from a unique history of central importance to our nation. Second, I am convinced that group cohesion, identity and mutual concern are key assets in the struggle for equality. So I address the situation of this particular group—my group. Undoubtedly much of what I say can be applied to other groups as well.

The great challenge facing black America today is the task of taking control of its own future by exerting the necessary leadership, making the required sacrifices, and building the needed institutions so that black social and economic development becomes a reality. No matter how windy the debate becomes among white liberals and conservatives as to what should be done, meeting this self-creating challenge ultimately depends on black action.

It is unwise (and dangerous) to suppose that any state or federal government would, over the long haul, remain sufficiently committed to such a program of black revitalization. It is to make a mockery of the ideal of freedom to hold that, as free men and women, blacks must sit back and wait for white Americans, of whatever political persuasion, to come to the rescue. A people who languish in dependency, while the means through which they might work for their advancement exist, have surrendered their claim to dignity. A genuinely free people must accept responsibility for their fate. Black

America's political leaders have too often failed to face up to this fact.

One way of framing the choice now confronting blacks is to ask, "What does it mean today to be an advocate for the poor?" I propose a different answer to this question than one could infer from the historic practices of those now most widely recognized as "black leaders." My central theme is that poor black people have the wherewithal to begin to make fundamental improvements in their lives, given the opportunity. An advocate for the poor, from this perspective, is one who provides the means for poor people to help themselves develop to their full potential. An advocate for the poor is not someone who perpetuates the dependency of poor people, teaching them by example that their only option is to hold out their hands to accept gifts from others.

In order for the black self-help movement to flourish and prosper, several forces which work to impede or distract this effort must be recognized. As a case in point, some elected officials at the state and federal level are unwilling to consider efforts that would spur self-help activities because of their attachment to past, misguided programs. These legislators retard progress when, for example, they oppose even trying urban enterprise zones in areas of high urban unemployment, but instead urge a return to massive Great Society schemes which have no chance of passage in this era of $200 billion deficits.

Another impediment and distraction is the array of groups who graft their interests on to those of the economically disenfranchised. A poor people's march is seldom held without the participation of radical feminists, gay rights activists, environmentalists and communist apologists, who have twisted the misfortune of the inner-city poor to their own ends.

Yet another major obstacle to the goal of black empowerment is the quality of leadership supplied by many black elected officials. In local, state and federal elections around the country, the black masses are constantly told that sending a black elected official to the mayor's office, the state capital or Congress will lead to the solution of their plight, simply because the candidate is black. Yet, in many cities around the country where blacks are in positions of power, the same lack of economic development can be observed in the black ghettos (which constitute the politicians' key political base) that can be seen in white-controlled cities. It is not suggested that all black politicians are unworthy of their people's support; but there should be mechanisms to evaluate and discipline indifferent political leaders so that they would be forced to adopt positions and pursue programs that contribute to the economic and social advancement of their constituents. The sad fact is that these disciplining forces are few in number.

Unfortunately, poor blacks seldom seem willing to exercise this kind of critical judgment of the performance of their leaders. Black elected officials who have done little, other than parrot the lines of white liberals, seem to be re-elected regularly. Because of the long history of racism, many blacks mistakenly place group solidarity and considerations of loyalty above a common-sense evaluation of a politician's on-the-job performance. Many black incumbents seem immune to challenge by another black, since it is easy to cast the challenger as somehow being "a white man's nigger."

Some of these rascal incumbents should be voted out of office. But even before that, poor blacks should structure an ongoing system of monitoring a politician's day-to-day performance. Regularly scheduled public political forums and community-based newsletters are but two examples of how to match deed with need.

* * *

John L. McKnight, associate director of the Center for Urban Affairs and Policy Research at Northwestern University, has made an accurate assessment of how our society views its poor: "What we have done for many poor people is to say to them you are sentenced to be a consumer and a client, you are denied the privileges to create, to solve problems, and to produce; you have the most degraded status our society will provide."

McKnight, recounting an experience he had in a low-income community during the 1960s, tells of "poverty experts" who came into a town of 20,000 residents to conduct "needs surveys." All too predictably, they discovered there were severe problems in the areas of housing, education, jobs, crime and health.

In his role as a community organizer, McKnight took note of the "public-policy experts" from both the public and private sectors who were sent in to "solve" the community's problems. They included public housing officials, land clearance experts, housing development counselors, daily-living skills advisers, rodent removal experts, weatherization counselors, teacher's aides, audiovisual specialists, urban curriculum developers, teacher trainers, school security advisers, civil rights consultants, job developers, job counselors, job classifiers, job location specialists, relocation program specialists, job trainees, small business advisers, police aides, correctional system designers, rehabilitation specialists, a juvenile counselor, diversion specialists, social workers, psychologists, psychiatrists, health outreach workers, health educators, sex educators, environmental reform workers, caseworkers, home-budget management trainers, lead inspectors, skills trainers, and administrators and managers to coordinate all of these activities. In short, overkill. McKnight termed this situation an example of an economic development plan for people who *don't* live in the neighborhood.

McKnight concluded his observation by remarking with bull's-eye accuracy:

I know from years in the neighborhoods that we can rely on community creativity. You have heard about it today over and over again. It is the most exciting thing that's happening in America. America is being reinvented little by little in the little places, but there is much more wealth that could be freed up, made available, if we understood that we have a big investment in the poor but their income is radically misdirected into the hands of service professionals [*Revitalizing Our Cities: New Approaches to Solving Urban Problems*, ed. Marc Lipsitz (Fund for American Renaissance and the National Center for Neighborhood Enterprise, 1986) pp. 101–102].

McKnight's example is all too familiar to those who are aware of the profusion of misdirected and misinformed approaches to "solving" the problems of the country's low-income citizens. This miscalculation of black capabilities is not by any means restricted to white America.

Some of the most eminent black thinkers, with close links to the civil rights establishment, no longer voice the same confidence they once did regarding the capabilities of black people. A great turning point was reached in the history of black Americans when, in 1934, the brilliant black thinker W. E. B. DuBois was dismissed from the editorship of *Crisis*, the journal of the National Association for the Advancement of Colored People, because of his view that the drive for integration at all costs undermined black people's confidence in their own institutions and capacities. Fearing that the fight against segregation (which he often led) had become a crusade to mix with whites for its own sake, DuBois wrote: "Never in the world should our fight be against association with ourselves because by that very token we give up the whole argument that we are worth association with."

Just 20 years after these words were written, however, black psychologist Kenneth Clark managed to convince the justices of the Supreme Court that segregation was inherently damaging to the personalities of black children. Unless whites were willing to mix with blacks, Clark seemed to argue, the result would inevitably be that black children would suffer self-image problems. The belief that development and self-respect for blacks is inherently impossible without "integration" might itself be considered damaging to the personalities of black children. As famed civil rights leader Floyd McKissick noted sarcastically, it seems to mean "if you put Negro with Negro you get stupidity." Such apparent expressions of black insecurity and inferiority bore out DuBois's fears. When the civil rights struggle moved from ending de facto segregation to forcing racial mixing, blacks often seemed to be rejecting the very possibility of beneficial association with themselves.

* * *

This lack of confidence voiced by the black intelligentsia about their own people extended to the capacity of black institutions to confront successfully the development problems that black people face. Many examples of this could be given, but one in the area of education should make the point. Recent experience in Chicago, Philadelphia and Washington, D.C., confirms the potential of developing independent black schools in the inner cities. These schools show that the education of poor black children can be improved with very limited resources, when there are parents and teachers willing to make the children's education an urgent priority. Yet so deeply entrenched is the civil rights mentality that in some communities black children are permitted to languish with limited skills while their "advocates" seek ever more far-fetched versions of "integration," tacitly rejecting the option of positively promoting the education of their children themselves.

In 1977, black parents in Ann Arbor, Michigan, faced a difficult educational problem. Their children in the early grades were not learning how to read, though white students were. A group of civil rights lawyers and educators convinced these parents to sue the public schools, alleging discrimination, because white teachers in Ann Arbor failed to take due account of the fact that the black children spoke a distinct dialect of the English language called "black English." Two years later, a federal judge ordered the Ann Arbor schools to provide reading teachers with sensitivity training in "black English" so as to better teach reading to the black students. Now, seven years after the court order, it appears that young blacks in Ann Arbor continue to lag far behind their white counterparts in reading ability—but they have won their discrimination lawsuit, and are duly instructed by teachers "sensitized" to their "foreign" dialect.

All of this would be amusing if it weren't so tragically sad. Civil rights advocates won themselves a symbolic victory, but what did they do for those children? While years of legal wrangling went on, the opportunity of the Ann Arbor community to address directly the needs of the poor black students went unexploited. Apparently, it never occurred to those parents or their "advocates" that, rather than cast their problem as one of discrimination, their children might benefit more from a straightforward effort to tutor them in reading. With 35,000 students at the University of Michigan's Ann Arbor campus, a sizable number of whom are black, one imagines that sufficient volunteers for such a tutoring effort could have been found. That such an effort was rejected in favor of the far-fetched "black English" argument suggests the kind of intellectual malaise of which DuBois warned a half-century ago.

Blacks must examine their past objectively, taking what is valuable from it and rejecting those notions that have proven unworkable. Over many decades and under much more adverse circumstances than exist today, blacks have made impressive progress—without the benefit of the civil rights laws and welfare transfers that now exist. I do not suggest repeal of those laws. I merely urge that we not permit ourselves to become wholly dependent on them.

There are many examples of the impressive accomplishments which our ancestors managed under difficult conditions. The literacy rate among blacks rose steadily after emancipation, though free public schools were virtually unknown in the South. Independent black businesses and entire black towns flourished in the late 19th century. Modern research has shown that despite the terrible economic and social oppression to which the slaves were subjected, they created a vibrant familial, religious and cultural tradition which continues to enrich black America.

Among the black migrant communities in the North in the early years of this century, the kind of social dislocation and family instability that plagues today's black ghettos was virtually unknown. In 1925 in Harlem, 85 per cent of black families were intact, and single, teenage mothers were virtually unknown. In Buffalo, New York, in 1910, blacks exhibited similarly strong family structures, despite the virulent racism which they faced at that time. The point is that without liberal apologists to tell them what little they could do for themselves or how inevitable their misery, poor black folk in years past were able to maintain their communities and establish a firm foundation for their children's progress.

This heritage is the underpinning of a collective black strength waiting to be tapped today. To revive a value system that nurtured and enriched the lives of yesterday's black America, a dynamic and continuing process of economic, political and social development must be initiated to furnish the soil in which the seeds of black pride and accomplishment can take root and sprout. Some activists, like Robert Woodson of the National Center for Neighborhood Enterprise in Washington, D.C., have begun to explore the components of an economic rejuvenation process that could launch such a large-scale self-help movement. To be successful, however, these suggested programs must be built upon, expanded, revised and adapted to the varying conditions of local communities. We must, in the words of Chairman Mao, "let a hundred flowers bloom!" The time is now ripe for blacks to spearhead such an effort. With everything to gain and little to lose, a spirit of black adventurism could lift the community beyond dependency to self-sufficiency.

It is important to understand that I am *not* arguing here against the ancient and still valid notion that there is a public responsibility in a decent society to contribute to the alleviation of poverty, black or otherwise. In the areas of education, employment training, and provision of minimal subsistence to the impoverished, the government must be involved. Some of the most innovative and useful private efforts are sustained by public funds. There are publicly supported programs—preschool education, for one—which are expensive, but which research has shown pay an even greater dividend. It is a tragic error that those of us who make the self-help argument in dialogue concerning alternative development strategies for blacks are often construed by the political right as making a case for "benign neglect."

Black America cannot lift itself by its bootstraps into great wealth overnight. But there is a great unexploited potential for change at the level of the black individual and the local black community. In the current environment it is evident that blacks must exploit this dormant opportunity. The self-help approach—more a philosophy of life than a list of specific projects—must be initiated as a matter of necessity, not ideology.

Religious leadership at the grass-roots level, through committed ministries and active church congregations, can play a useful role in the process of collective uplift that I envision. It is the natural province of the religious institutions within a community to provide moral leadership, to set and enforce standards of behavior. In *Where Do We Go from Here: Chaos or Community?* (Beacon, 1968) Martin Luther King, Jr., recognized the crucial role that the then-emerging black middle class, through its churches, would have to play in the process of improving conditions for the group as a whole. He wrote:

It is time for the Negro haves to join hands with the Negro have-nots and, with compassion, journey into that other country of hurt and denial. It is time for the Negro middle class to rise up from its stool of indifference, to retreat from its flight into unreality and to bring its full resources— its heart, its mind and its checkbook— to the aid of the less fortunate brother [p. 132].

Concerning moral leadership King added:

It is not a sign of weakness, but a sign of high maturity, to rise to the level of self-criticism. Through group unity we must convey to one another that our women must be respected, and that life is too precious to be destroyed in a Saturday night brawl, or a gang execution. Through community agencies and religious institutions we must develop a positive program through which Negro youth can become adjusted to urban living and improve their general level of behavior [p. 125].

I believe that, were King at the helm of the civil rights movement today, it is in this direction that he would be taking us.

The task of narrowing class schisms within the black community should have priority. Blacks must not be afraid to make judgments about faults and failings in their community. Blacks must abandon the pernicious and self-destructive tendency arbitrarily to empower the "man" with ultimate control over their destiny. This is an almost criminal abdication of responsibility. Precisely because racism is a fact of life not likely to disappear soon, *all* blacks are "in the same lifeboat." This being the case, it is in the individual black's interest to contribute time and resources to the advancement of those least well off in the community. It is politically and morally irresponsible to sit back in disgust, as so many veterans of past struggles are fond of doing, constantly decrying the problems, doing little or nothing to solve them, shouting epithets and threats at whites who grow weary of being "generous and understanding," while the black poor sink deeper and deeper into despair.

It is crucial that blacks not become so caught up in seeking welfare state hand-outs that we lose our own souls. The very important, but essentially private, matter of the indignities our ancestors suffered due to their race must not be allowed to become a vehicle for cheap brokering with the welfare state. The generations of blacks who suffered under Jim Crow deserve something more than simply having their travails used as an excuse for current failures. Our work today is not to change the *minds* of white people, but to involve ourselves in the *lives* of black people. Past black sufferings should not be hauled out to gain guilt money. Such a posture is pitiful and unbecoming of black America's proud heritage. Dependency, even when one is dependent on sympathetic and generous souls, is destructive of dignity—and dignity is a necessary precondition of genuine freedom and equality.

NO   John E. Jacob

THE FUTURE OF BLACK AMERICA

I'm honored to be here and I look forward to this opportunity to present my views on the future prospects for black Americans and to engage in some dialogue with you.

Today I want to begin by briefly sketching what the Urban League is, and going on from there to discuss the plight of black citizens. Along the way, I'd like to look back at some of the things America has done to deal with its racial problems. And I'd like to look ahead as well, to suggest some of the things we can do to secure the future for black people and for all Americans.

Most of you are familiar with the work of the National Urban League. We have affiliates in 112 cities—and that means most of your districts and states include at least one Urban League.

We're based on three principles—and we've held fast to them since our founding 78 years ago.

One is advocacy on behalf of black citizens and all poor people. We are a repository of research, ideas, and experiences that the nation needs in framing policies that affect the third of our population that is black or poor.

Second, we are a community-based service delivery organization. Urban League job and skills training programs, education and health and housing programs, and a host of others, serve one-and-a-half million people who come to Urban League offices each year.

Currently, we are concentrating on mobilizing black and minority communities around a national Education Initiative designed to radically improve black students' academic achievement. We are also concentrating resources on the plight of female-headed households, teenage pregnancy, crime, and citizenship education.

Third, the National Urban League is a bridge-builder between the races. We are believers in an open, integrated, pluralistic society, and our activities support that goal. Our staffs and boards are integrated, and we work very hard at improving race relations in America.

I am clearly here today in our advocacy role, and I have to tell you that the state of black Americans is very bad. In fact, our future is at risk.

In January [1988], the National Urban League published its annual State of Black America report. It documents continuing black disadvantage.

Let me share with you some of the facts about black life in America. I know that this knowledgeable audience is familiar with them—but I also know that they cannot be repeated often enough.

- Half of all black children grow up in poverty.

- Over a third of all blacks are poor—two million more blacks became poor in the past dozen years.

- Almost two million black workers are jobless—over twelve percent of the black work force, and a rate two-and-a-half times that for whites.

- Black family income is only 58 percent that of whites; the typical black family earns less than the government itself says is needed for a decent but modest living standard.

- Black households have less than one-tenth the wealth of white households.

In this high-tech, information age, black dropout rates in some cities are higher than black graduation rates, and there has been an alarming decline in the numbers of blacks entering college.

In virtually all of those areas, black disadvantage is worse than it has been at any time since the mid-1970s.

At the same time, I should acknowledge the fact that some blacks have made extraordinary progress.

Today, black judges preside over court rooms where civil rights demonstrators were once sentenced in the 1950s. Black executives now help shape policies of corporations that once wouldn't hire blacks. Black professionals live in formerly all-white suburbs and earn middle class incomes.

But they share with their poorer brothers and sisters the bond of blackness—the fact that whether affluent or disadvantaged, all blacks suffer from racism.

Racism need not be violent, like the murder of a black truck driver in Texas by police officers, or the actions of a mob in Howard Beach.

It can take subtler forms that affect all blacks—from the teenage kid denied a job in a downtown store because of racial stereotypes to the son of the black doctor who's stopped by police because he's driving his Dad's Mercedes and they just assume a young black behind the wheel of that kind of car stole it.

Recently, we've seen surveys that document the harassment of black managers in corporate America, and their perceptions of a racial ceiling that limits their potential.

So despite the often-proclaimed statements that we are finally a color-blind society, I have to tell you that we are very far... very far... from achieving that goal.

And let me take this opportunity to say that Congress' action last week in overriding the veto of the Civil Rights Restoration Act helps move us just that little bit closer to our goal.

Your vote to override is important for the future of black people and the entire nation. It endorsed the proposition that federal money should not subsidize discrimination in any of its forms.

And it sends a bi-partisan message that when it comes to civil rights, America will allow no loopholes.

To the extent that black people have made progress, we have to credit the civil rights revolution of the 1960s and the effects of the Great Society programs that are now out of fashion.

The laws, executive orders and judicial decisions of the 1960s empowered black people and removed many of the barriers in their way. Social welfare programs assisted many black people to get the incomes, health and nutrition care, and education they needed to enter the mainstream.

Some of those programs may not have worked as well as they should. Too often, programs were not targeted sharply enough and resources intended by Congress for the poorest of the poor found their way into middle-class neighborhoods instead.

The Urban League carefully monitored training programs and urban aid programs, and we found a consistent pattern of diverting funds away from community-based programs that could have helped those most in need.

Part of the problem has been the lack of patience with those programs—the drive for instant results. So we had a lot of skimming—helping people who would be likely to succeed anyway so the numbers look better, rather than attempting to work with the most impacted of the poor.

Other programs worked well by any standard. The Job Corps, Head Start, Chapter One remedial education, nutrition programs, and others.

Where those programs did not work as well as they should, it was most often due to underfunding and restrictive eligibility procedures that prevented them from reaching all in need. It is notorious that such proven programs as Medicaid, food stamps and others reached only about half of the poor. Head Start enrolls only about a fifth of eligible children—and similar figures apply to nutrition and training and health programs.

In the 1980s, there was an extraordinary increase in poverty, in homelessness, and in other indexes of disadvantaged among blacks and other minorities.

This was due to two factors.

One was the deep cuts in government social programs. The Center on Budget and Policy Priorities studied funding for low-income programs other than entitlements and found that spending was cut by 54 percent after inflation since 1981. Subsidized housing was cut by 81 percent and training and employment services by 68 percent.

A second factor is the economic shift in our society.

The elimination of a substantial part of America's manufacturing base has hit black workers hardest. Studies show they are concentrated in the most vulnerable industries and are more likely to be laid off and less likely to find comparable jobs.

And there has been an extraordinary shrinkage in lower level jobs available to people without high educational credentials. That is the single most important factor in the troubles of the black family.

Twenty-five years ago, three out of four black men in America were working and three out of four black families were intact. Today, just a little over half of all black men are working and just over half of all black families are intact.

Anyone concerned about the rise of single-parent families in the black community doesn't have to look further for the reason. Unemployment and underemployment is tearing black families apart. And it is responsible for the inability of many young people to begin families.

Last year [1987], the Children's Defense Fund released a study that further confirms this thesis. In the early 1970s about 60 percent of all young men earned enough to lift a family of three above the poverty line. By the mid-1980s, only about 40 percent earned that much. Between the mid-1970s and the mid-1980s, the marriage rate for young men was cut by one-half.

And those are overall, national figures for all races. For blacks, and especially for young black men who do not finish school, the figures are far worse. Only one out of nine black dropouts, for example, earns enough to support a family of three above the poverty line.

So there have been worsening economic prospects for a majority of young blacks at the same time that the props of federal education, training and social supports have been cut or removed.

We've found that black people with skills, education and strong family backgrounds are able to enter the mainstream today. But the other half—blacks without skills and suffering from educational deficiencies and social deficits, are increasingly locked out.

There is a powerful myth today that the answer to such problems is self-help—that it is the sole responsibility of the black community to eradicate dysfunctional behavior and to pull itself into the mainstream.

That's just a myth—without basis in fact or in history. I have little patience with the people who tell us to look at other groups that are making it. Black people did not come here voluntarily. No other group came in chains. Today's successful immigrant groups came to these shores with education, with a belief in the American Dream, and with substantial internal community financial resources.

Black people have made it in America despite overwhelming odds—the rise of the new black middle class is proof of that. But far too many of us are trapped in the hopelessness and despair of urban ghettos with little hope to escape. Too many of our kids are seduced by the underground economy and sucked into crack and crime.

While many ask why they don't stop such behavior, I have to ask what kind of society creates an environment of hopelessness and despair that drives young children into self-destructive behavior.

The Urban League knows all about self-help and pulling yourself up by your bootstraps. That's what we've been about for 78 years. But we also know that conditions have changed in many of our communities—changed to the point where our efforts cannot possibly succeed without government intervention.

It's all right to talk about pulling yourself by your bootstraps but not when you're talking to people who don't have boots. The conditions that allowed previous generations of black people to pull themselves up have changed. Today's young generation is too concerned with simple survival to think about long-term career choices.

In Chicago's Cabrini public housing project, the big question for kids is: have the gangs stopped shooting so I can go out of the house. We're talking about kids whose parents keep them away from the windows so they won't be hit by stray bullets. We're talking about kids whose classmates tote automatic weapons.

It's a new ball game out there, and those people in positions of power who won't do anything about it and who preach self-help are adding to the problem, not solving it.

The black community today is mobilizing to deal with those issues. Last week I attended a meeting of community leaders drawn from across the nation to find ways to save young black men—America's most endangered group.

The Urban League and other community-based agencies and groups are working very hard to turn things around—but we're just whistling in the dark unless government is on our side.

The problem is simply not amenable to solution through self-help alone. Let me give you two examples drawn from the *New York Times* of March 16th.

Page One headline: "Reliance on Temporary Jobs Hints at Economic Fragility." The story went on to talk about the shift to part-time and temporary jobs that are likely to disappear at the first hint of recession. The dark side of the well-publicized job boom is that many of those jobs are low-paying, and are temporary.

Black people who used to get steady work at low-skill jobs are now either unemployed or working part-time and unable to support their families or to serve as role models for their kids.

Another page one headline the same day: "Carnegie Report Urges Crusade for Bypassed Urban Schools."

That story reported that the school reforms of the past five years have bypassed ghetto schools, which are still sunk in a morass of failure. It reports about students there—our black kids— quote: "No one notices if they drop out because no one noticed when they dropped in."

Twenty years after the Kerner Commission [which, under the chairmanship of Illinois governor Otto Kerner, was established in 1967 to study the increasing number of civil disorders in America; the resulting report indicated that the nation was moving toward "two societies, separate and unequal"], we're finding not only that we're moving to two separate societies—one black, one white—but also two societies within the black community—one middle class and aspiring, the other desperately poor and increasingly without hope.

That is not simply a problem for black people—this is a national problem that will affect the future of our economy.

In the past, America could write off young black people... relegate them to the margins... deny them training and opportunities.

In the future, doing that will amount to committing economic suicide.

The Labor Department's Workforce 2000 study says that there will be 25 percent fewer young adults entering the workforce than there were in the 1980s. The least-skilled jobs will disappear and the most highly skilled jobs will grow rapidly.

And up to a third of new workers will be minority—in other words, the core of our future workforce will come from groups that are most at-risk today.

We face a surplus of people without the skills to be productive in a post-industrial, information-based economy. And we face a shortage of people to fill the growing number of jobs required to remain competitive in a global marketplace.

David Kearns is chairman and CEO of the Xerox Corporation and a former chairman of the National Urban League. David is concerned about the huge training costs imposed on industry just to bring people up to the point where they can hold entry-level jobs.

And he's asking the question: "Who is going to do the work that needs to be done to keep this economy running?"

The demographics are putting America at a competitive disadvantage in this global economy. Unless we take the problems of minority youth seriously— unless we assure that each and every young black and brown person has the education and skills our economy needs—we're going to wind up colonized by foreign competitors.

At this point, I suppose I'm expected to present a shopping list of solutions—a want list that you as Congresspeople would be asked to legislate and fund.

The only problem with that is that the Reagan Revolution has created such awesome deficits and such a huge national debt that any proposals for new funding initiatives are unlikely.

But I'd like to suggest that ducking the problems we face by pointing to the deficits is irresponsible. Inaction won't save endangered black youth... won't make us more competitive in the future... won't prevent the inequalities in our society from growing to the point where they endanger our democracy.

Who among us can expect the homeless to remain silent forever... the unemployed to accept their lot quietly forever... the despairing to contain their anger forever?

We're sitting on a social and economic powderkeg, and future generations will be harsh on those who did nothing, when they had the power and the responsibility to act constructively.

Frankly, I see those huge deficits as an *excuse* to do nothing, not as a reason.

I find it incredible to hear that a trillion dollar budget can't accommodate investments that cut poverty and create opportunities. I find it incredible that a five trillion dollar economy can't support programs that cut inequality and invest in the human resources that represent our best hope for the future.

Politics and governing are based on reasoned choices among alternatives. One choice we have is to redirect spending away from areas that are marginal to areas that are crucial.

We found it within our capabilities, for example, to spend some two trillion dollars on the Pentagon over the past eight years. As one expert has written: "We manufacture weapons that are not needed, that cost too much, and that don't work, while we fail to meet other, more basic defense needs."

We need to tailor military spending to a realistic defense posture in a multi-polar world. That would most likely result in savings that could be diverted to domestic investment in human capital.

Those people programs are cheap by comparison. The B-1B bomber cost $28 billion for a fleet of 100 planes that don't do what they were supposed to do. That's more than enough to assure training every disadvantaged young person in marketable skills.

A nation with the lowest rates in the industrial world can increase taxes to levels commensurate with its needs. A modest tax on oil would not only keep the OPEC cartel at bay—it would finance Head Start and Chapter One remedial education programs for every disadvantaged child, and enough would be left over to beef up child health programs.

With a 28 percent top tax rate, can anyone really argue that a surtax or a third bracket at 35 percent is unreasonable at a time of huge national needs?

Any prudent person invests in the future and any responsible government does the same. There's a strange notion around that when government builds a bridge it is making a capital investment in the future, but when it invests in a job training program, it is current spending. It's not—it is a long-term investment in human capital.

By not making those investments today, we're increasing tomorrow's deficits. Between 700,000 and 900,000 kids drop out of school every year, and the ultimate cost to society in lost earnings and lost tax revenues comes to $240 billion over their lifetimes! And that doesn't even include the bill for crime, social welfare programs, and other costs.

I find it hard to explain why so many businessmen understand that while others do not. The Committee for Economic Development includes some of the top corporate leaders, and they've urged heavy investments in child development programs and in education.

They point out that one dollar spent in child health programs—the same programs the Administration wants to cut—saves almost $5 in expenditures down the road.

When hard-nosed businessmen start talking about the need for nutrition, health, and education programs, you know the message is beginning to get across that government action is necessary. Only government can train and educate our young people, keep them healthy, and give them access to the social services they've got to have if they're to make decent lives for themselves.

That should also be clear to people in government and to the public. In fact, we're seeing a shift in the public's mood today—toward greater compassion and more realism about enabling all Americans to be more productive and more competitive.

We're really confronted with two scenarios today. One is based on the continuation of present policies. That will inevitably lead to greater inequality and the formation of a permanent underclass that threatens America's social stability and economic foundations.

A second scenario would be an activist government role in equipping disadvantaged people to make it in our society.

That scenario would shrink the poverty population, and increase the numbers of young blacks entering college and moving into the middle class. The result would be a stronger black community and an America that retains its world primacy.

That second scenario could be implemented by a number of steps:

One, a national effort to create jobs or training opportunities for every disadvantaged person.

Two, a national education program that fully funds early childhood education for the disadvantaged, and provides incentives to local school districts to provide whatever assistance is necessary to bring quality education to disadvantaged students.

Three, transformation of the welfare system to provide decent living standards for the poor and incentives to work and to get the education and training necessary to be productive.

There are further unmet needs in housing, health and other areas that must also be addressed.

This is hardly the time or the place to go into detailed specifics of such programs. The National Urban League has a Washington Operations Office headed by our Vice President, Doug Glasgow, and we'd be very happy to work with you and with your staffs to help you address the specifics of such issues. We have already worked with some of you on key legislation in the past and hope to continue and expand that relationship.

But today, I do want to suggest that such investments in the nation's future make sense . . . are do-able . . . and should cross party and ideological lines.

Winston Churchill is the model of a conservative statesman, and he once said: "There is no finer investment for any community than putting milk into babies."

And George Will, the conservative columnist, wrote: "It is cheaper to feed the child than jail the man. Persons who do not understand this are not conservatives, just dim."

So I don't want to see the fate of black Americans embroiled in false liberal versus conservative ideological disputes. I would hope that all of us have the sense to understand that government has the responsibility and the ability to solve the social problems that endanger our economy and our society.

And I would hope that all of us have the compassion and the human concern to want to do something about children who face bleak futures and adults who have no jobs, no homes, no hope.

Social and economic policy has been in a state of paralysis over the past decade.

We now find ourselves having to make up for lost time and lost resources. A generation of young black people was lost in the 1980s—doomed to failure and to marginality because they didn't have access to the opportunities they needed to become functioning members of our changing society.

We can't let that wastage of human resources continue. We can't let our society continue to drift apart, separated by unbridgeable gaps in education, income, skills, class and race.

We are at a period in time when the currents of the past and future converge... when we are positioned to make decisions and implement policies that determine whether future generations of poor and black people are consigned to the outer borders of society or are drawn into the mainstream.

As Congressmen, as leaders, and as citizens, you have the power to make the right choices and the right decisions.

I have faith that you will.

POSTSCRIPT

Is Black Self-Help the Solution to Racial Inequality?

Both Loury and Jacob seem to agree that government transfer payments are not the solution in the long term to the problem of social inequality. Both also agree that, in Loury's words, "there is a public responsibility in a decent society to contribute to the alleviation of poverty." Clearly, both favor government investment in education and training for the poor, especially for young people. (Both praise Operation Head Start, a program for disadvantaged preschoolers.) But Loury insists that private volunteer work is the real key to helping the black poor, while Jacob insists that government involvement is essential. It seems beyond dispute that both approaches are needed; the question is where to place the emphasis.

Loury quotes with approval some of the advice given by Martin Luther King, Jr., and W. E. B. Du Bois, but one black leader from the early years of the twentieth century whose views (or at least some of them) he might have quoted was Booker T. Washington. Much praised during his lifetime, scorned later as an "Uncle Tom," Washington has made something of a comeback in recent years because of his philosophy—and personal example—of black self-help. His autobiographical *Up From Slavery* (1900), available in a number of editions, is still inspirational. Du Bois was an early critic of Washington; see *The Souls of Black Folk* (1903; Reprint, New American Library, 1969). Shelby Steele is a major spokesman for black self-help today; see *The Content of Our Character* (St. Martin's Press, 1990). Also see John Sibley Butler's *Entrepreneurship and Self-Help Among Black Americans* (SUNY Press, 1991), in which Butler shows that blacks have a good record of self-help and entrepreneurship. Two seminal historical studies that may lend support to the conclusion that black family breakdown is a relatively new phenomenon that was not caused by slavery or segregation are *Roll, Jordan, Roll,* by Eugene Genovese (Random House, 1976), and Herbert G. Gutman's *The Black Family in Slavery and Freedom* (Random House, 1977). In contrast, Jay R. Mandle, in *Not Slave Not Free* (Duke University Press, 1992), ties current black poverty to slavery and the subsequent economic oppression of blacks. Still another perspective, not necessarily contradictory, is provided by J. Owens Smith in *The Politics of Racial Inequality* (Greenwood Press, 1987), which stresses the importance of a legal framework guaranteeing civil rights. Reynolds Farley and Walter Allen use census data to demonstrate the progress of blacks and the remaining gap between the races in *The Color Line and the Quality of Life in America* (Russell Sage, 1987).

ISSUE 10

Is Affirmative Action Reverse Discrimination?

YES: Shelby Steele, from *The Content of Our Character* (St. Martin's Press, 1990)

NO: Stanley Fish, from "Reverse Racism, or How the Pot Got to Call the Kettle Black," *The Atlantic Monthly* (November 1993)

ISSUE SUMMARY

YES: Associate professor of English Shelby Steele contends that, instead of solving racial inequality problems, affirmative action mandates have undermined black initiative and self-help and that they have generated racial discrimination in reverse.

NO: Professor of law Stanley Fish argues that equating affirmative action with reverse racism requires the fallacious assumption that the playing field is level and the view that a terrifying and punishing racism is comparable to minor efforts to remedy some of the harms of that racism.

In America, equality is a political principle as basic as liberty. "All men are created equal" is perhaps the most well known phrase in the Declaration of Independence. More than half a century after the signing of the Declaration, the French social philosopher Alexis de Tocqueville examined democracy in America and concluded that its most essential ingredient was the equality of condition. Today we know that the "equality of condition" that de Tocqueville perceived did not exist for women, blacks, Native Americans, and other racial minorities, nor for other disadvantaged social classes. Nevertheless, the ideal persisted. When slavery was abolished after the Civil War, the Constitution's newly ratified Fourteenth Amendment proclaimed: "No State shall... deny to any person within its jurisdiction the equal protection of the laws."

Equality has been a long time coming. For nearly a century after the abolition of slavery, American blacks were denied equal protection by law in some states and by social practice nearly everywhere. One-third of the states either permitted or forced schools to become racially segregated, and segregation was achieved elsewhere through housing policy and social behavior. In 1954 the Supreme Court reversed a 58-year-old standard that had found "separate but equal" schools compatible with equal protection of the law. A unanimous decision in *Brown v. Board of Education* held that separate is *not* equal for the members of the discriminated-against group when the segregation "generates a feeling of inferiority as to their status in the community that may affect their hearts and minds in a way unlikely ever to be undone." The 1954 ruling on public elementary education has been extended to other areas of both governmental and private conduct, including housing and employment.

Even if judicial decisions and congressional statutes could end all segregation and racial discrimination, would this achieve equality—or simply perpetuate the status quo? The unemployment rate for blacks today is more than twice that of whites. Disproportionately higher numbers of blacks experience poverty, brutality, broken homes, physical and mental illness, and early deaths, while disproportionately lower numbers of them reach positions of affluence and prestige. It seems likely that much of this inequality has resulted from 300 years of slavery and segregation. Is termination of this ill treatment enough to end the injustices? No, say the proponents of affirmative action.

Affirmative action—the effort to improve the educational and employment opportunities for minorities—has had an uneven history in U.S. federal courts. In *Regents of the University of California v. Allan Bakke* (1978), which marked the first time the Supreme Court directly dealt with the merits of affirmative action, a 5–4 majority ruled that a white applicant to a medical school had been wrongly excluded in favor of a less qualified black applicant due to the school's affirmative action policy; yet the majority also agreed that "race-conscious" policies may be used in admitting candidates—as long as they do not amount to fixed quotas. The ambivalence of *Bakke* has run through the Court's treatment of the issue since 1978. Decisions have gone one way or the other depending on the precise circumstances of the case (such as whether it was a federal or state policy, whether or not it was mandated by a congressional statute, and whether quotas were required or simply permitted). Recent decisions suggest that the Court is beginning to take a dim view of affirmative action. In 1989, for example, the Court ruled that a city council could *not* set aside a fixed percentage of public construction projects for minority contractors.

Affirmative action is hotly debated outside the courts, and white males have recently been complaining loudly on talk shows and in print about being treated unjustly because of affirmative action policies. In the following selections, Shelby Steele and Stanley Fish debate the merits of affirmative action. In Steele's view, affirmative action represents a distortion of the original aims of the civil rights revolution and is often counterproductive for blacks. Fish, on the other hand, considers it an essential means for undoing some of the effects of white racism.

YES
Shelby Steele

AFFIRMATIVE ACTION:
THE PRICE OF PREFERENCE

In a few short years, when my two children will be applying to college, the affirmative action policies by which most universities offer black students some form of preferential treatment will present me with a dilemma. I am a middle-class black, a college professor, far from wealthy, but also well-removed from the kind of deprivation that would qualify my children for the label "disadvantaged." Both of them have endured racial insensitivity from whites. They have been called names, have suffered slights, and have experienced firsthand the peculiar malevolence that racism brings out in people. Yet, they have never experienced racial discrimination, have never been stopped by their race on any path they have chosen to follow. Still, their society now tells them that if they will only designate themselves as black on their college applications, they will likely do better in the college lottery than if they conceal this fact. I think there is something of a Faustian bargain [sacrificing values for material gain] in this.

Of course, many blacks and a considerable number of whites would say that I was sanctimoniously making affirmative action into a test of character. They would say that this small preference is the meagerest recompense for centuries of unrelieved oppression. And to these arguments other very obvious facts must be added. In America, many marginally competent or flatly incompetent whites are hired everyday—some because their white skin suits the conscious or unconscious racial preference of their employer. The white children of alumni are often grandfathered into elite universities in what can only be seen as a residual benefit of historic white privilege. Worse, white incompetence is always an individual matter, while for blacks it is often confirmation of ugly stereotypes. The Peter Principle [which states that in a hierarchy, every employee tends to rise to the level of his or her incompetence] was not conceived with only blacks in mind. Given that unfairness cuts both ways, doesn't it only balance the scales of history that my children now receive a slight preference over whites? Doesn't this repay, in a small way, the systematic denial under which their grandfather lived out his days?

So, in theory, affirmative action certainly has all the moral symmetry that fairness requires—the injustice of historical and even contemporary white advantage is offset with black advantage; preference replaces prejudice, inclusion answers exclusion. It is reformist and corrective, even repentant and redemptive. And I would never sneer at these good intentions. Born in the late forties in Chicago, I started my education (a charitable term in this case) in a segregated school and suffered all the indignities that come to blacks in a segregated society. My father, born in the South, only made it to the third grade before the white man's fields took permanent priority over his formal education. And though he educated himself into an advanced reader with an almost professorial authority, he could only drive a truck for a living and never earned more than ninety dollars a week in his entire life. So yes, it is crucial to my sense of citizenship, to my ability to identify with the spirit and the interests of America, to know that this country, however imperfectly, recognizes its past sins and wishes to correct them.

Yet good intentions, because of the opportunity for innocence they offer us, are very seductive and can blind us to the effects they generate when implemented. In our society, affirmative action is, among other things, a testament to white goodwill and to black power, and in the midst of these heavy investments, its effects can be hard to see. But after twenty years of implementation, I think affirmative action has shown itself to be more bad than good and that blacks—whom I will focus on in this essay—now stand to lose more from it than they gain.

In talking with affirmative action administrators and with blacks and whites in general, it is clear that supporters of affirmative action focus on its good intentions while detractors emphasize its negative effects. Proponents talk about "diversity" and "pluralism"; opponents speak of "reverse discrimination," the unfairness of quotas and set-asides. It was virtually impossible to find people outside either camp. The closest I came was a white male manager at a large computer company who said, "I think it amounts to reverse discrimination, but I'll put up with a little of that for a little more diversity." I'll live with a little of the effect to gain a little of the intention, he seemed to be saying. But this only makes him a half-hearted supporter of affirmative action. I think many people who don't really like affirmative action support it to one degree or another anyway.

I believe they do this because of what happened to white and black Americans in the crucible of the sixties when whites were confronted with their racial guilt and blacks tasted their first real power. In this stormy time white absolution and black power coalesced into virtual mandates for society. Affirmative action became a meeting ground for these mandates in the law, and in the late sixties and early seventies it underwent a remarkable escalation of its mission from simple anti-discrimination enforcement to social engineering by means of quotas, goals, timetables, set-asides and other forms of preferential treatment.

Legally, this was achieved through a series of executive orders and EEOC [Equal Employment Opportunity Commission] guidelines that allowed racial imbalances in the workplace to stand as proof of racial discrimination. Once it could be assumed that discrimination explained racial imbalances, it became easy to justify group remedies to presumed discrimination, rather than the normal case-by-case redress for proven discrimination. Preferential treatment through quotas, goals, and so on is designed to correct imbalances based on the assumption that they always indicate discrimination. This expansion of what constitutes discrimination allowed affirmative action to escalate into the business of social engineering in the name of anti-discrimination, to push society toward statistically proportionate racial representation, without any obligation of proving actual discrimination.

What accounted for this shift, I believe, was the white mandate to achieve a new racial innocence and the black mandate to gain power. Even though blacks had made great advances during the sixties without quotas, these mandates, which came to a head in the very late sixties, could no longer be satisfied by anything less than racial preferences. I don't think these mandates in themselves were wrong, since whites clearly needed to do better by blacks and blacks needed more real power in society. But, as they came together in affirmative action, their effect was to distort our understanding of racial discrimination in a way that allowed us to offer the remediation of preference on the basis of mere color rather than actual injury. By making black the color of preference, these mandates have reburdened society with the very marriage of color and preference (in reverse) that we set out to eradicate. The old sin is reaffirmed in a new guise.

But the essential problem with this form of affirmative action is the way it leaps over the hard business of developing a formerly oppressed people to the point where they can achieve proportionate representation on their own (given equal opportunity) and goes straight for the proportionate representation. This may satisfy some whites of their innocence and some blacks of their power, but it does very little to truly uplift blacks.

A white female affirmative action officer at an Ivy League university told me what many supporters of affirmative action now say: "We're after diversity. We ideally want a student body where racial and ethnic groups are represented according to their proportion in society." When affirmative action escalated into social engineering, diversity became a golden word. It grants whites an egalitarian fairness (innocence) and blacks an entitlement to proportionate representation (power). *Diversity* is a term that applies democratic principles to races and cultures rather than to citizens, despite the fact that there is nothing to indicate that real diversity is the same thing as proportionate representation. Too often the result of this on campuses (for example) has been a democracy of colors rather than of people, an artificial diversity that gives the appearance of an educational parity between black and white students that has not yet been achieved in reality. Here again, racial preferences allow society to leapfrog over the difficult problem of developing blacks to parity with whites and into a cosmetic diversity that covers the blemish of disparity—a full six years after admission, only about 26 percent of black students graduate from college.

Racial representation is not the same thing as racial development, yet affirmative action fosters a confusion of these very different needs. Representation can be manufactured; development is always hard-earned. However, it is the music of innocence and power that we hear in affirmative action that causes us to cling to it and to its distracting emphasis on representation. The fact is that after twenty years of racial preferences, the gap between white and black median income is greater than it was in the seventies. None of this is to say that blacks don't need policies that ensure our right to equal opportunity, but what we need more is the development that will let us take advantage of society's efforts to include us.

I think that one of the most troubling effects of racial preferences for blacks is a kind of demoralization, or put another way, an enlargement of self-doubt. Under affirmative action the quality that earns us preferential treatment is an implied inferiority. However this inferiority is explained—and it is easily enough explained by the myriad deprivations that grew out of our oppression—it is still inferiority. There are explanations, and then there is the fact. And the fact must be borne by the individual as a condition apart from the explanation, apart even from the fact that others like himself also bear this condition. In integrated situations where blacks must compete with whites who may be better prepared, these explanations may quickly wear thin and expose the individual to racial as well as personal self-doubt.

All of this is compounded by the cultural myth of black inferiority that blacks have always lived with. What this means in practical terms is that when blacks deliver themselves into integrated situations, they encounter a nasty little reflex in whites, a mindless, atavistic reflex that responds to the color black with alarm. Attributions may follow this alarm if the white cares to indulge them, and if they do, they will most likely be negative—one such attribution is intellectual ineptness. I think this reflex and the attributions that may follow it embarrass most whites today, therefore,

it is usually quickly repressed. Nevertheless, on an equally atavistic level, the black will be aware of the reflex his color triggers and will feel a stab of horror at seeing himself reflected in this way. He, too, will do a quick repression, but a lifetime of such stabbings is what constitutes his inner realm of racial doubt.

The effects of this may be a subject for another essay. The point here is that the implication of inferiority that racial preferences engender in both the white and black mind expands rather than contracts this doubt. Even when the black sees no implication of inferiority in racial preferences, he knows that whites do, so that—consciously or unconsciously—the result is virtually the same. The effect of preferential treatment—the lowering of normal standards to increase black representation—puts blacks at war with an expanded realm of debilitating doubt, so that the doubt itself becomes an unrecognized preoccupation that undermines their ability to perform, especially in integrated situations. On largely white campuses, blacks are five times more likely to drop out than whites. Preferential treatment, no matter how it is justified in the light of day, subjects blacks to a midnight of self-doubt, and so often transforms their advantage into a revolving door.

Another liability of affirmative action comes from the fact that it indirectly encourages blacks to exploit their own past victimization as a source of power and privilege. Victimization, like implied inferiority, is what justifies preference, so that to receive the benefits of preferential treatment one must, to some extent, become invested in the view of one's self as a victim. In this way, affirmative action nurtures a victim-focused identity in blacks. The obvious irony here is that we become inadvertently invested in the very condition we are trying to overcome. Racial preferences send us the message that there is more power in our past suffering than our present achievements—none of which could bring us a *preference* over others.

When power itself grows out of suffering, then blacks are encouraged to expand the boundaries of what qualifies as racial oppression, a situation that can lead us to paint our victimization in vivid colors, even as we receive the benefits of preference. The same corporations and institutions that give us preference are also seen as our oppressors. At Stanford University minority students—some of whom enjoy as much as $15,000 a year in financial aid—recently took over the president's office demanding, among other things, more financial aid. The power to be found in victimization, like any power, is intoxicating and can lend itself to the creation of a new class of super-victims who can feel the pea of victimization under twenty mattresses. Preferential treatment rewards us for being underdogs rather than for moving beyond that status—a misplacement of incentives that, along with its deepening of our doubt, is more a yoke than a spur.

But, I think, one of the worst prices that blacks pay for preference has to do with an illusion. I saw this illusion at work recently in the mother of a middle-class black student who was going off to his first semester of college. "They owe us this, so don't think for a minute that you don't belong there." This is the logic by which many blacks, and some whites, justify affirmative action—it is something "owed," a form of reparation. But this logic overlooks a much harder and less digestible reality, that it is impossible to repay blacks living today for the historic suffering of the race. If all blacks were given a million dollars tomorrow morning it would not amount to a dime on the dollar of three centuries of oppression, nor would it obviate the residues of that oppression that we still carry today. The concept of historic reparation grows out of man's need to impose a degree of justice on the world that simply does not exist. Suffering can be endured and overcome, it cannot be repaid. Blacks cannot be repaid for the injustice done to the race, but we can be corrupted by society's guilty gestures of repayment.

Affirmative action is such a gesture. It tells us that racial preferences can do for us what we cannot do for ourselves. The corruption here is in the hidden incentive *not* to do what we believe preferences will do. This is an incentive to be reliant on others just as we are struggling for self-reliance. And it keeps alive the illusion that we can find some deliverance in repayment. The hardest thing for any sufferer to accept is that his suffering excuses him from very little and never has enough currency to restore him. To think otherwise is to prolong the suffering....

The mandates of black power and white absolution out of which preferences emerged were not wrong in themselves. What was wrong was that both races focused more on the goals of these mandates than on the means of the goals. Blacks can have no real power without taking responsibility for their own educational and economic development. Whites can have no racial innocence without earning it by eradicating discrimination and helping the disadvantaged to develop. Because we ignored the means, the goals have not been reached, and the real work remains to be done.

NO

Stanley Fish

REVERSE RACISM, OR HOW THE POT GOT TO CALL THE KETTLE BLACK

I take my text from George Bush, who, in an address to the United Nations on September 23, 1991, said this of the UN resolution equating Zionism with racism: "Zionism... is the idea that led to the creation of a home for the Jewish people.... And to equate Zionism with the intolerable sin of racism is to twist history and forget the terrible plight of Jews in World War II and indeed throughout history." What happened in the Second World War was that six million Jews were exterminated by people who regarded them as racially inferior and a danger to Aryan purity. What happened after the Second World War was that the survivors of that Holocaust established a Jewish state—that is, a state centered on Jewish history, Jewish values, and Jewish traditions: in short, a Jewocentric state. What President Bush objected to was the logical sleight of hand by which these two actions were declared equivalent because they were both expressions of racial exclusiveness. Ignored, as Bush said, was the *historical* difference between them—the difference between a program of genocide and the determination of those who escaped it to establish a community in which they would be the makers, not the victims, of the laws.

Only if racism is thought of as something that occurs principally in the mind, a falling-away from proper notions of universal equality, can the desire of a victimized and terrorized people to band together be declared morally identical to the actions of their would-be executioners. Only when the actions of the two groups are detached from the historical conditions of their emergence and given a purely abstract description can they be made interchangeable. Bush was saying to the United Nations, "Look, the Nazis' conviction of racial superiority generated a policy of systematic genocide; the Jews' experience of centuries of persecution in almost every country on earth generated a desire for a homeland of their own. If you manage somehow to convince yourself that these are the same, it is you, not the Zionists, who are morally confused, and the reason you are morally confused is that you have forgotten history."

A KEY DISTINCTION

What I want to say, following Bush's reasoning, is that a similar forgetting of history has in recent years allowed some people to argue, and argue persuasively, that affirmative action is reverse racism. The very phrase "reverse racism" contains the argument in exactly the form to which Bush objected: In this country whites once set themselves apart from blacks and claimed privileges for themselves while denying them to others. Now, on the basis of race, blacks are claiming special status and reserving for themselves privileges they deny to others. Isn't one as bad as the other? The answer is no. One can see why by imagining that it is not 1993 but 1955, and that we are in a town in the South with two more or less distinct communities, one white and one black. No doubt each community would have a ready store of dismissive epithets, ridiculing stories, self-serving folk myths, and expressions of plain hatred, all directed at the other community, and all based in racial hostility. Yet to regard their respective racisms—if that is the word—as equivalent would be bizarre, for the hostility of one group stems not from any wrong done to it but from its wish to protect its ability to deprive citizens of their voting rights, to limit access to educational institutions, to prevent entry into the economy except at the lowest and most menial levels, and to force members of the stigmatized group to ride in the back of the bus. The hostility of the other group is the result of these actions, and whereas hostility and racial anger are unhappy facts wherever they are found, a distinction must surely be made between the ideological hostility of the oppressors and the experience-based hostility of those who have been oppressed.

Not to make that distinction, is adapting George Bush's words, to twist history and forget the terrible plight of African-Americans in the more than 200 years of this country's existence. Moreover, to equate the efforts to remedy that plight with the actions that produced it is to twist history even further. Those efforts, designed to redress the imbalances caused by long-standing discrimination, are called affirmative action; to argue that affirmative action, which gives preferential treatment to disadvantaged minorities as part of a plan to achieve social equality, is no different from the policies that created the disadvantages in the first place is a travesty of reasoning. "Reverse racism" is a cogent description of affirmative action only if one considers the cancer of racism to be morally and medically indistinguishable from the therapy we apply to it. A cancer is an invasion of the body's equilibrium, and so is chemotherapy; but we do not decline to fight the disease because the medicine we employ is also disruptive of normal functioning. Strong illness, strong remedy: the formula is as appropriate to the health of the body politic as it is to that of the body proper.

At this point someone will always say, "But two wrongs don't make a right; if it was wrong to treat blacks unfairly, it is wrong to give blacks preference and thereby treat whites unfairly." This objection is just another version of the forgetting and rewriting of history. The work is done by the adverb "unfairly," which suggests two more or less equal parties, one of whom has been unjustly penalized by an incompetent umpire. But blacks have not simply been treated unfairly; they have been subjected first to decades of slavery, and then to decades of second-class citizenship, widespread legalized discrimination, economic persecution, educational deprivation, and cultural stigmatization. They have been bought, sold, killed, beaten, raped, excluded, exploited, shamed, and scorned for a very long time. The word "unfair" is hardly an adequate description of their experience, and the belated gift of "fairness" in the form of a resolution no longer to discriminate against them legally is hardly an adequate remedy for the deep disadvantages that the prior discrimination has produced. When the deck is stacked against you in more ways than you can even count, it is small consolation to hear that you are now free to enter the game and take your chances.

A TILTED FIELD

The same insincerity and hollowness of promise infect another formula that is popular with the anti-affirmative-action crowd: the formula of the level playing field. Here the argument usually takes the form of saying "It is undemocratic to give one class of citizens advantages at the expense of other citizens; the truly democratic way is to have a level playing field to which everyone has access and where everyone has a fair and equal chance to succeed on the basis of his or her merit." Fine words—but they conceal the facts of the situation as it has been given to us by history: the playing field is already tilted in favor of those by whom and for whom it was constructed in the first place. If mastery of the requirements for entry depends upon immersion in the cultural experiences of the mainstream majority, if the skills that make for success are nurtured by institutions and cultural practices

from which the disadvantaged minority has been systematically excluded, if the language and ways of comporting oneself that identify a player as "one of us" are alien to the lives minorities are forced to live, then words like "fair" and "equal" are cruel jokes, for what they promote and celebrate is an institutionalized unfairness and a perpetuated inequality. The playing field is already tilted, and the resistance to altering it by the mechanisms of affirmative action is in fact a determination to make sure that the present imbalances persist as long as possible.

One way of tilting the field is the Scholastic Aptitude Test. This test figures prominently in Dinesh D'Souza's book *Illiberal Education* (1991), in which one finds many examples of white or Asian students denied admission to colleges and universities even though their SAT scores were higher than the scores of some others—often African-Americans—who were admitted to the same institution. This, D'Souza says, is evidence that as a result of affirmative-action policies colleges and universities tend "to depreciate the importance of merit criteria in admissions." D'Souza's assumption—and it is one that many would share—is that the test does in fact measure *merit*, with merit understood as a quality objectively determined in the same way that body temperature can be objectively determined.

In fact, however, the test is nothing of the kind. Statistical studies have suggested that test scores reflect income and socioeconomic status. It has been demonstrated again and again that scores vary in relation to cultural background; the test's questions assume a certain uniformity in educational experience and lifestyle and penalize those who, for whatever reason, have had a different experience and lived different kinds of lives. In short, what is being measured by the SAT is not absolutes like native ability and merit but accidents like birth, social position, access to libraries, and the opportunity to take vacations or take SAT prep courses.

Furthermore, as David Owen notes in *None of the Above: Behind the Myth of Scholastic Aptitude* (1985), the "correlation between SAT scores and college grades... is lower than the correlation between weight and height; in other words you would have a better chance of predicting a person's height by looking at his weight than you would of predicting his freshman grades by looking only at his SAT scores." Everywhere you look in the SAT story, the claims of fairness, objectivity, and neutrality fall away, to be replaced by suspicions of specialized measures and unfair advantages.

Against this background a point that in isolation might have a questionable force takes on a special and even explanatory resonance: the principal deviser of the test was an out-and-out racist. In 1923 Carl Campbell Brigham published a book called *A Study of American Intelligence*, in which, as Owen notes, he declared, among other things, that we faced in America "a possibility of racial admixture... infinitely worse than that faced by any European country today, for we are incorporating the Negro into our racial stock, while all of Europe is comparatively free of this taint." Brigham had earlier analyzed the Army Mental Tests using classifications drawn from another racist text, Madison Grant's *The Passing of the Great Race*, which divided American society into four distinct racial strains, with Nordic, blue-eyed, blond people at the pinnacle and the Ameri-

can Negro at the bottom. Nevertheless, in 1925 Brigham became a director of testing for the College Board, and developed the SAT. So here is the great SAT test, devised by a racist in order to confirm racist assumptions, measuring not native ability but cultural advantage, an uncertain indicator of performance, an indicator of very little except what money and social privilege can buy. And it is in the name of this mechanism that we are asked to reject affirmative action and reaffirm "the importance of merit criteria in admissions."

THE REALITY OF DISCRIMINATION

Nevertheless, there is at least one more card to play against affirmative action, and it is a strong one. Granted that the playing field is not level and that access to it is reserved for an already advantaged elite, the disadvantages suffered by others are less racial—at least in 1993—than socioeconomic. Therefore shouldn't, as D'Souza urges, "universities... retain their policies of preferential treatment, but alter their criteria of application from race to socioeconomic disadvantage," and thus avoid the unfairness of current policies that reward middle-class or affluent blacks at the expense of poor whites? One answer to this question is given by D'Souza himself when he acknowledges that the overlap between minority groups and the poor is very large—a point underscored by the former Secretary of Education Lamar Alexander, who said, in response to a question about funds targeted for black students, "Ninety-eight percent of race-specific scholarships do not involve constitutional problems." He meant, I take it, that 98 percent of race-specific scholarships were also scholarships to the economically disadvantaged.

Still, the other two percent—nonpoor, middle-class, economically favored blacks—are receiving special attention on the basis of disadvantages they do not experience. What about them? The force of the question depends on the assumption that in this day and age race could not possibly be a serious disadvantage to those who are otherwise well positioned in the society. But the lie was given dramatically to this assumption in a 1991 broadcast of the ABC program *PrimeTime Live.* In a stunning fifteen-minute segment reporters and a camera crew followed two young men of equal education, cultural sophistication, level of apparent affluence, and so forth around St. Louis, a city where neither was known. The two differed in only a single respect: one was white, the other black. But that small difference turned out to mean everything. In a series of encounters with shoe salesmen, record-store employees, rental agents, landlords, employment agencies, taxicab drivers, and ordinary citizens, the black member of the pair was either ignored or given a special and suspicious attention. He was asked to pay more for the same goods or come up with a larger down payment for the same car, was turned away as a prospective tenant, was rejected as a prospective taxicab fare, was treated with contempt and irritation by clerks and bureaucrats, and in every way possible was made to feel inferior and unwanted.

The inescapable conclusion was that alike though they may have been in almost all respects, one of these young men, because he was black, would lead a significantly lesser life than his white counterpart: he would be housed less well and at greater expense; he would pay more for services and products when and if he was given the opportunity to buy them; he would have difficulty establishing credit; the first emotions he would inspire on the part of many people he met would be distrust and fear; his abilities would be discounted even before he had a chance to display them; and, above all, the treatment he received from minute to minute would chip away at his self-esteem and self-confidence with consequences that most of us could not even imagine. As the young man in question said at the conclusion of the broadcast, "You walk down the street with a suit and tie and it doesn't matter. Someone will make determinations about you, determinations that affect the quality of your life."

Of course, the same determinations are being made quite early on by kindergarten teachers, grade school principals, high school guidance counselors, and the like, with results that cut across socioeconomic lines and place young black men and women in the ranks of the disadvantaged no matter what the bank accounts of their parents happen to show. Racism is a cultural fact, and although its effects may to some extent be diminished by socioeconomic variables, those effects will still be sufficiently great to warrant the nation's attention and thus the continuation of affirmative-action policies. This is true even of the field thought to be dominated by blacks and often cited as evidence of the equal opportunities society now affords them. I refer, of course, to professional athletics. But national self-congratulation on this score might pause in the face of a few facts: A minuscule number of African-Americans ever receive a paycheck from a professional team. Even though nearly 1,600 daily newspapers report on the exploits of black athletes, they employ only seven full-time black sports columnists. Despite repeated pledges and resolutions, major-league teams have managed to put only a handful of blacks and Hispanics in executive positions.

WHY ME?

When all is said and done, however, one objection to affirmative action is unanswerable on its own terms, and that is the objection of the individual who says, "Why me? Sure, discrimination has persisted for many years, and I acknowledge that the damage done has not been removed by changes in the law. But why me? I didn't own slaves; I didn't vote to keep people on the back of the bus; I didn't turn water hoses on civil-rights marchers. Why, then, should I be the one who doesn't get the job or who doesn't get the scholarship or who gets bumped back to the waiting list?"

I sympathize with this feeling, if only because in a small way I have had the experience that produces it. I was recently nominated for an administrative post at a large university. Early signs were encouraging, but after an interval I received official notice that I would not be included at the next level of consideration, and subsequently I was told unofficially that at some point a decision had been made to look only in the direction of women and minorities. Although I was disappointed, I did not conclude that the situation was "unfair," because the policy was obviously not directed at me—at no point in the proceedings did someone say, "Let's find a way to rule out Stanley Fish." Nor was it directed even at persons of my race and sex—the policy was not intended to disenfranchise white

males. Rather, the policy was driven by other considerations, and it was only as a by-product of those considerations—not as the main goal—that white males like me were rejected. Given that the institution in question has a high percentage of minority students, a very low percentage of minority faculty, and an even lower percentage of minority administrators, it made perfect sense to focus on women and minority candidates, and within that sense, not as the result of prejudice, my whiteness and maleness became disqualifications.

I can hear the objection in advance: "What's the difference? Unfair is unfair: you didn't get the job; you didn't even get on the short list." The difference is not in the outcome but in the ways of thinking that led up to the outcome. It is the difference between an unfairness that befalls one as the unintended effect of a policy rationally conceived and an unfairness that is pursued as an end in itself. It is the difference between the awful unfairness of Nazi extermination camps and the unfairness to Palestinian Arabs that arose from, but was not the chief purpose of, the founding of a Jewish state.

THE NEW BIGOTRY

The point is not a difficult one, but it is difficult to see when the unfairness scenarios are presented as simple contrasts between two decontextualized persons who emerge from nowhere to contend for a job or a place in a freshman class. Here is student A; he has a board score of 1,300. And here is student B; her board score is only 1,200, yet she is admitted and A is rejected. Is that fair? Given the minimal information provided, the answer is of course no. But if we expand our horizons and consider fairness in relation to the cultural and institutional histories that have brought the two students to this point, histories that weigh on them even if they are not the histories' authors, then both the question and the answer suddenly grow more complicated.

The sleight-of-hand logic that first abstracts events from history and then assesses them from behind a veil of willed ignorance gains some of its plausibility from another key word in the anti-affirmative-action lexicon. That word is "individual," as in "The American way is to focus on the rights of individuals rather than groups." Now, "individual" and "individualism" have been honorable words in the American political vocabulary, and they have often been well employed in the fight against various tyrannies. But like any other word or concept, individualism can be perverted to serve ends the opposite of those it originally served, and this is what has happened when in the name of individual rights, millions of individuals are enjoined from redressing historically documented wrongs. How is this managed? Largely in the same way that the invocation of fairness is used to legitimize an institutionalized inequality. First one says, in the most solemn of tones, that the protection of individual rights is the chief obligation of society. Then one defines individuals as souls sent into the world with equal entitlements as guaranteed either by their Creator or by the Constitution. Then one pretends that nothing has happened to them since they stepped onto the world's stage. And then one says of these carefully denatured souls that they will all be treated in the same way, irrespective of any of the differences that history has produced. Bizarre as it may seem, individualism in this argument turns out to mean that everyone is or should be the *same*. This dismissal of individual difference in the name of the individual would be funny were its consequences not so serious: it is the mechanism by which imbalances and inequities suffered by millions of people through no fault of their own can be sanitized and even celebrated as the natural workings of unfettered democracy.

"Individualism," "fairness," "merit"—these three words are continually misappropriated by bigots who have learned that they need not put on a white hood or bar access to the ballot box in order to secure their ends. Rather, they need only clothe themselves in a vocabulary plucked from its historical context and made into the justification for attitudes and policies they would not acknowledge if frankly named.

POSTSCRIPT

Is Affirmative Action Reverse Discrimination?

Much of the argument between Steele and Fish turns on the question of color blindness. To what extent should U.S. laws be color-blind? During the 1950s and early 1960s, civil rights leaders were virtually unanimous on this point. "I have a dream," said Martin Luther King, "[that white and black people] will not be judged by the color of their skin, but by the content of their character." This was the consensus view in 1963, but today Fish seems to be suggesting that the statement needs to be qualified. In order to *bring about* color blindness, it may be necessary to become temporarily color conscious. But for how long? And is there a danger that this temporary color consciousness may become a permanent policy?

The writings on this subject are diverse and numerous. Robert M. O'Neil, in *Discriminating Against Discrimination: Preferential Admissions and the DeFunis Case* (Indiana, 1975), reports his studies of preferential admission to universities and argues in support of preferential treatment without racial quotas. Steven L. Carter's *Reflections of an Affirmative Action Baby* (Basic Books, 1991) is based on the author's own experiences under affirmative action. Frederick R. Lynch's *Invisible Victims: White Males and the Crisis of Affirmative Action* (Greenwood Press, 1989) traces some of the effects of affirmative action on society and other groups within it. Andrew Hacker argues that affirmative action has relatively minor adverse consequences for whites in *Two Nations: Black and White, Separate, Hostile, Unequal* (Charles Scribner's Sons, 1992). Lee Sigleman and Susan Welch, in *Black American's Views of Racial Inequality: The Dream Deferred* (Cambridge University Press, 1991), argue that blacks and whites have basically different perspectives of the racial situation, though they also note that there is little agreement in the black community about how government should address the problem of inequality. The focus of Allan P. Sindler's *Bakke, DeFunis, and Minority Admissions* (Longman, 1978) is on affirmative action in higher education.

Whatever the Supreme Court says today or in the future, it will not be easy to lay to rest the issue of affirmative action. There are few issues on which opposing sides are more intransigent. It appears as if there is no easily found compromise that can satisfy the passionately held convictions of both sides.

ISSUE 11

Do Social and Mental Pathologies Largely Account for Homelessness?

YES: Myron Magnet, from *The Dream and the Nightmare: The Sixties' Legacy to the Underclass* (William Morrow, 1993)

NO: Jonathan Kozol, from *Rachel and Her Children: Homeless Families in America* (Crown Publishers, 1988)

ISSUE SUMMARY

YES: Essayist Myron Magnet argues that the vast majority of the permanently homeless are people who belong in institutions, not low-income housing.

NO: Social commentator Jonathan Kozol maintains that homelessness results from the lack of affordable housing, not from the personal problems of the homeless people themselves.

The number of America's homeless has become a national scandal. No one knows for certain exactly how many homeless there are—estimates have ranged from a low of 250,000 to a high of 3 million—but anyone walking through the streets of America's cities is likely to encounter them.

A generation ago, it was rare to see anyone begging and living on the streets of an American city. Why are there so many homeless people on the streets of America now? The answer seems to vary according to the ideology of the analyst. Leftists attribute homelessness to the structural failures of American capitalism. Liberals blame it on the Reagan and Bush administrations, which produced cutbacks in federal spending on low-income housing. Social conservatives say it comes from the breakdown of families and the unwise policy of "deinstitutionalizing" the mentally ill, which releases patients from institutional care and into the community. And fiscal conservatives blame rent control and similar government interventions in the market economy, which, as they see it, caused the deterioration and ultimate abandonment of residential buildings.

All of these explanations may shed some light on the problem of homelessness. The U.S. economy has not been able to suppress its cyclical ups and downs, and during recession periods the homelessness problem gets worse. Even during good times, policymakers have not been able to find a satisfactory answer to the problem of the "underclass," or the chronically unemployed and dependent. Even for those who do work there is a shortage of affordable housing in some major American cities. But homelessness has other roots as well. The mentally ill have been deinstitutionalized in large numbers since the 1960s. The major purpose of this policy was to improve the quality of life of the patients, but for many of these former inmates the results turned out to be disastrous. Assumptions about the kind of care that they could receive in the community proved false, or the released patients failed to avail themselves of the services provided. Drug addicts also swelled the population of the homeless (some estimates put them at a third of New York City's homeless population), adding to the sense that homelessness is a kind of social disease and increasing much of the public's desire to solve the problem by "sweeping the streets" of the homeless.

There is no one simple solution to the tragedy of homelessness. The police could be ordered to sweep the streets of the homeless, but where would they be kept? In jail? In mental institutions? Both are overcrowded to begin with, and jailing or otherwise confining people who have committed no crime hardly seems just. At the other end of the spectrum is a seemingly compassionate solution: build more shelters and low-income housing. But the experiences of Washington, D.C., and New York City in this area indicate that shelter building and the policy of giving the homeless priority in getting low-income housing may cause even more homelessness. Moreover, many of the homeless are unable to afford even low-income housing, and others are unable to function without supervision even in free housing.

A clear-eyed, objective study of the varying needs of the homeless seems necessary. But even before that, perhaps researchers should listen to the many voices of those who are touched by homelessness—the homeless themselves, advocates for the homeless, local officials confronted with the problem, and people who are not homeless but who encounter homeless people every day.

Two of these voices are presented in the following selections. Myron Magnet argues that homelessness has become a national problem because of public shelter building and other forms of state-run charity. He maintains that these programs have encouraged a small minority of pathological individuals to live on the streets. Jonathan Kozol, however, contends that the homeless mostly consist not of weird social misfits but of individuals and families who are too poor to afford private housing. In Kozol's view, mass homelessness has resulted from a combination of market forces in the 1980s that forced the poor out of their neighborhoods and a cutback in government support for low-income housing.

YES   Myron Magnet

THE SIXTIES' LEGACY TO THE UNDERCLASS

Here is a man moving his bowels on the Seventy-ninth Street sidewalk in the pouring afternoon rain. Behind him rises the Beaux Arts splendor of the Apthorp Apartments, an opulent relic of New York's vanished age of civic confidence. The squatting man, his smile sheepishly vacant, slowly tears up a newspaper and wipes himself with great deliberateness. Passing along this busy thoroughfare, embarrassed and dismayed, I can't keep at bay a discordantly uncharitable thought: what a fitting end to years—years!—of preposterously muddleheaded reporting on the problem of homelessness.

This is not kind, I know. But the shocking actuality of homelessness is so utterly different from the picture journalists have drawn that it's hard to keep patience with their almost mystifying distortion and misrepresentation of the unsettling truth. Can all of today's reporters commute from the suburbs? If you live in a city, after all, you can't help glimpsing the painful reality, as here on Seventy-ninth Street, before averting your eyes in shame. You get used to reassuring children after they've seen such sights—after they've been startled by sleeping bundles of rags at first indistinguishable from the trash by which the sleeper lies, after they've been frightened by aggressively insistent beggars or implacably angry, wild-eyed mutterers pushing refuse-laden shopping carts.

We urban dwellers have had to meditate on sights like these black plastic garbage bags, laid out last night like rotund soldiers in neat platoons of twenty or thirty beside each apartment building. This morning, like so many mornings, they are slashed open, their contents wildly strewn all over the pavement in a sickening riot of rot and disorder.

Dogs? hazarded a visitor from out-of-town.

No. The homeless have been scavenging. Once I saw magazines I had thrown away spread out in rows on a busy sidewalk, offered for sale by a homeless entrepreneur.

Of course it's especially raw in my borderline neighborhood, by turns gentrifying and degentrifying. Here—one block from a park where the homeless live, three blocks from the mostly underclass housing project into whose windows my old apartment looked, around the corner from a crack house—the poor are real, not the figment of a reporter's or advocate's imagination. Just look: you can't help seeing the true texture of life at the bottom.

The evidence of your senses shows you firsthand what scientific studies have been revealing with ever-increasing insistence: the homeless are radically different from the picture the advocates and the press painted all through the eighties and beyond. The fictitious picture is, to be sure, a dramatic attention-grabber. For starters, its scale is heroic: homelessness is a big, big problem. The advocates claim that three million Americans—over 1 percent of the total population—have no roof over their heads. Many more are allegedly so precariously housed that they might find themselves out on the street tomorrow. Already urgent, the homelessness problem can only intensify.

But like so many of the "facts" about the homeless, these numbers are pure fantasy. They were pulled out of the air by the wildest of advocates, the late Mitch Snyder, a troubled, stubble-bearded radical activist who headed an antiquated Washington antiwar commune grandiosely styled the Community for Creative Non-Violence. The commune sheltered the homeless, and Snyder, available right down the street whenever legislators needed an "expert," was asked by a congressional committee in 1980 exactly how many Americans were homeless. He simply made up a number: exactly 2.2 million fellow citizens, one American out of every hundred, lacked homes, he pronounced. Two years later he upped his estimate to 3 million. Snyder always declined to debate these figures; getting numbers right, he haughtily remarked, could only concern "Americans with little Western minds that have to quantify everything in sight."

Networks, newsweeklies, and most national dailies readily swallowed this fabrication. For a decade, "three million homeless" became a journalistic mantra.

But this number isn't just false: it is grotesquely, outrageously false. Responsible scientific investigators went out looking for Snyder's huddled masses. Guided by experienced policemen, social workers, and local homeless people, researchers combed major cities after dark, searching out the homeless in alleys, cellars, vacant buildings, thickets, all-night movies, and parked cars, including those rented out at fifty cents a night by an enterprising Washington garage attendant. The evidence they turned up after such diligence suggests a number around *one tenth* of Snyder's—probably 300,000 to 360,000. This is a lot of people, but it is hardly the apocalyptic catastrophe requiring total national mobilization that Snyder and his fellow advocates, supported by a credulous press, have depicted.

It's not merely the size of the problem that the advocates have misrepresented. More important, they have hopelessly muddled the larger question of who the homeless are and how they landed in their deplorable plight. In particular, listening to the advocates' insistence that increasing numbers of the homeless are families rather than unattached individuals, you'd think that Ozzie and Harriet were out on the street with their frightened kids clinging to their knees. Turning on the TV news to see what congressional advocates for the homeless are up to only strengthens that impression. Says advocate Robert Hayes, an ex–Wall Street lawyer who heads the National Coalition for the Homeless: "I can't tell you how often a congressional committee has called and said, 'We need a witness for a hearing. Can you get us a homeless family: mother, father—father out of work in the past four months from an industrial plant—white?'" Though such families can be found among the homeless—and could especially be found in the very early eighties, when the first wave of America's successful industrial restructuring painfully dislocated Rust Belt, logging, and oil patch workers—they are most untypical and are never homeless for long.

The broad intention of this distortion is to make viewers sympathize by identification, even if that entails shading the truth. But within that general intention is a sharply focused political point. Here are mainstream citizens doing everything right but nevertheless struck down by the homelessness plague—as you could be. The advocates have no doubt whatever about the source of the contagion. Says Hayes: "The homeless are indeed the most egregious symbol of a cruel economy, an unresponsive government, a festering value system." They are the victims of a ferocious, unjust economic Darwinism that has made the rich opulently richer at the calamitous expense of the poor, that has swept away jobs through "deindustrialization," that has gentrified affordable housing off the face of the earth for the benefit of self-cherishing yuppies. Indeed, the homeless are a moral thermometer, registering in their numbers and degradation the rising heartlessness and inequality of the American social order.

By now even the homeless themselves have incorporated these sentiments into their begging jingles. One drug-wasted regular on my downtown subway wove it into a craftily up-to-the-minute fabric of rock music and "concerned" politics

as he lurched through the train jingling his cup each morning.

> "We got a problem, [he rather
>   woozily sang]
> We gotta address it,
> It needs a so-lu-tion—
> It could happen to you or meeee...."

Throughout the eighties, many turned the indictment explicitly partisan. A Case Western Reserve professor "of family and child welfare," to take only one example, confidently predicted in *The New York Times* a rash of Hoovervilles that he dubbed Reaganvilles. As an academic expert on the homeless, sociologist Peter Rossi, sums up: "The advocates want you to say, 'There but for the grace of God—and the fact that Reagan didn't look at me directly—go I.'"

And then it became George Bush's turn. As columnist Anna Quindlen pronounced: "If empty shelves became a symbol for the failure of Communism in the Soviet Union, people living in cardboard boxes are the most visible sign that America is on the skids. They are living, breathing symbols of an economy that, no matter what the Astigmatism president says, is a mess."

You don't have to live in my neighborhood to know that this whole farrago just isn't so. All you have to do is go home by train or subway and pay attention. What you see, if you stop to look, is craziness, drunkenness, dope, and danger. Far from being the index of the nation's turpitude, the homeless are an encyclopedia of social pathology and mental disorder.

And what has produced homelessness is by no means Reaganomics or yuppification or any other primarily economic dislocation. What the homeless encamped in the streets, parks, and train stations in the heart of our cities really embody is the most extreme and catastrophic failure of the cultural revolution of the Haves and the social policies that resulted from it.

Look at who the homeless really are. The various subgroups of them overlap, so that separating them into categories yields only approximations. But the overall picture is clear.

In outline, it looks like this. Homeless families account for a little over a quarter of all homeless persons. These aren't conventional or ordinary families: put aside the image of Beaver Cleaver and his folks scouring the country for work. Instead, homeless families—almost *all* of them—consist of a single mother and her children. Almost *all* such families are on welfare. Half of them, according to one authoritative study, are headed by women under twenty-five years old, many themselves the illegitimate daughters of single mothers.

Homeless families, in other words, are an extension of the underclass. For the most part, they are headed by a subgroup of welfare mothers who haven't succeeded in keeping a roof over their children's heads. They live in welfare hotels and shelters, and they are homeless not in the sense of having been living on the streets but rather having been evicted from their own apartments or having been thrown out by friends. Or they have declared themselves homeless—no one checks to see if they really are—in order to get bumped to the head of the waiting list for permanent subsidized housing.

By contrast with homeless families, single homeless individuals are mostly men—at least three of them for each single homeless woman. Not as young as homeless welfare mothers, they are still youngish, with an average age in the mid- to late thirties. A majority of the single homeless are blacks and other minorities, with the proportion of minority persons ranging from 89 percent in New York to 23 percent in Portland, Oregon.

The single homeless are an even more pathological population than the underclass. Around one third of them are alcoholics, and the majority use drugs. In New York City shelters, 65 percent of the homeless singles tested by urinalysis showed positive results for drugs or alcohol, with 83 percent of that group testing positive for cocaine.

A startling number of them are criminals. Checking the records of several homeless beggars recently arrested for misdemeanors in New York's Pennsylvania Station, for example, police were taken aback to discover that two of the men were wanted for murder. Half of those arrested for rape in Santa Monica, California, in 1991 were homeless men. At least 40 percent of the single homeless nationwide have been in jail, for an average of two years. Somewhere between 13 and 26 percent of the incarcerated, depending on which study you pick, served their time for major crimes or felonies. While some of the criminal homeless landed in jail for crimes committed after they became homeless, the majority—63 percent—were criminals first and homeless second. So for most of this group, one can't argue that homelessness drove them to crime. Putting it mildly, all this adds up to something very different from the mainstream impression the advocates have tried to evoke.

It's a tough stretch to follow the advocates in seeing the criminal or drug-taking homeless as victims deserving compassion; but for one of the largest, most conspicuous groups of the homeless, those who are mentally ill, compassion is properly in order.

These disturbing figures—the lumpish shopping-bag ladies, the muttering men in rags pushing grocery carts—did not create their deplorable fate. They are the involuntary victims not only of their disease but also of a society that mocks them with a benefit they don't need in place of one they need desperately.

Ten National Institute of Mental Health studies of different large cities consistently show that around one third of the homeless—well over 100,000 souls if the homeless total 350,000—suffer from serious mental illnesses. If anything, the number may be higher: a recent, authoritative psychiatric study of the homeless in Baltimore found that almost half the women and 42 percent of the men suffered from a major mental disorder. Add in alcohol and drug abuse, and you account for 80 percent of the homeless single women and 91 percent of the homeless men in Baltimore. A 1988 Los Angeles study showed that 44 percent of the single homeless in that city had been hospitalized for psychiatric reasons. Two thirds of the New York homeless who live on the streets, rather than in the shelters, are schizophrenic, another study found....

It shouldn't be possible to be so protected from the natural consequences of your own self-destructive actions as to have a taxpayer-provided roof over your head with no questions asked and no conditions imposed. Take your meals at the soup kitchen, panhandle unmolested at the railroad station for crack or wine money—you can usually make at least a tax-free twelve dollars in a few hours, not much worse than the minimum wage—and you have achieved the life of a significant fraction of the homeless. This life is squalid, to be sure, but it insulates those who live it from the most immediate bad consequences of their behavior and removes an extremely effective deterrent to such behavior.

Public shelters, open to all comers, may cause at least as much homelessness as they cure. They draw more people out of housing than off the street. It's not just that they give people the option of not paying rent; they also allow people who've been doubled up with family or friends to move out—or to be shoved out with less guilt. That's one reason why cities and counties with liberal shelter admissions policies have larger homeless populations than jurisdictions with less "generous" policies, and why homeless populations suddenly grow as provision for the homeless is liberalized. A scant two years after Washington voters passed Initiative 17, guaranteeing shelter to all District of Columbia residents, for instance, homeless families in D.C. shelters increased by 500 percent. One woman phoned from Hong Kong as soon as she heard of the guarantee to say that she had just enough money for plane fare, so would the authorities please reserve space for her and her children.

Right-to-shelter policies promote dependency. Take the case of Lowell, a twenty-seven-year-old I met in New York's Catherine Street family shelter. With winning smile and ingratiating manner, he formerly made $350 a week as a manager of a Burger King; his wife, who lived in the shelter with him, was earning $160 at one of the chain's other branches. He landed in the shelter when an aunt evicted him from his little apartment in her house. Within several weeks, after getting back from work late enough to be locked out of the shelter several times, he quit his job. Too much hassle.

He told me he could easily find another job, but the idea left him cold. "If you get a job, you're going to be abused financially," he said. "No one has ever paid me what I'm worth." So he was spending his time lettering signs for the shelter and feasting on grandiose fantasies of becoming a famous graphic artist. Alas, his signs plastered on every wall showed no trace of the requisite talent. Meanwhile, he had no complaints. "You know what we had for dinner last night?" he asked. "Steak! We have a TV, a video room. I see more movies here than I ever saw outside. You really can't ask for more." If he had less, he would bestir himself quickly and soon be neither homeless nor a dropout from the labor force.

I don't at all mean to say that you won't find genuine distress being relieved in shelters. Of course some of those taking refuge there have been driven from their homes by fire, job loss, domestic violence. People do suffer misfortunes that overwhelm them, or they lose their way, grow confused, lose heart, and temporarily stop struggling. I have talked to them in shelters, seen the fear and humiliation that breaks through the armor of rigid reserve and haughty impassivity. But such people are seldom homeless long, and they are a very small minority of the public shelter population.

Public shelters don't distinguish among the unfortunate, the malingerers like Lowell, and the truly asocial. At Catherine Street, for instance, you look in one large, messy, fourteen-bed room housing four or five families and discover a malevolent-looking young man and his sixteen- or seventeen-year-old wife lying in adjoining beds at noon. A few doors down the hall you come upon four beds drawn close together to mark out one family's turf, each bed made up with military precision, each pillow surmounted by a handmade stuffed animal, a goldfish swimming in a bowl on the nightstand—all this betokening a far different mode of life, far higher aspirations. But to the shelter, all are equally homeless, all equally deserving of being housed at the taxpayers' cost.

At the very least, it would make sense for public shelter systems to institute much more discriminating admissions policies and house far fewer people. They would create less dependency if they also offered only temporary, not open-ended, shelter.

Even so, privately supported and privately run shelters are vastly preferable to public ones. Private shelters resist turning into huge, ravenously expensive, permanent bureaucracies with specious "entitlements" that continually expand the clientele and sink clients into permanent dependency. What's more, private shelters have a purposefulness that public ones lack. They have standards and values. They aim to change lives and save souls, to rescue the sinner and redeem the irredeemable. Laudable and necessary in a humane community, these goals nevertheless move beyond the scope of the state.

Suppose the following reversals occurred: what would happen? Picture for a moment the public shelters of the great cities shrunk or closed, the mentally ill in appropriate treatment, private shelters relieving temporary distress and trying to rehabilitate such drunks, drug takers, and dropouts as they deem salvageable, public places swept of beggars and sleepers, and a sense of public order restored. Would the sum total of distress be greater? Would thousands upon thousands of the homeless who formerly slept in the public shelters or in the subways now be freezing under bridges and starving on skid rows?

I think not. Were it to stop being so easy to drop out into a truly dead-end life—were compassionate citizens to stop sympathetically viewing the alcoholic, the drug-addicted, and the idle as poor, downtrodden victims to whom giving handouts is a public necessity—this variety of homelessness would become far less attractive. And in an intact social order, where petty lawlessness and self-destructive irresponsibility are not suffered to flourish in the heart of the city, many fewer would feel tempted to fall into such a fate.

We have misconceived every part of the homelessness problem—who the homeless are, how they got that way, what our own responsibility for their plight really is, what help to give them. We have abandoned the mad to the streets in the name of a liberty that mocks them. We take the sympathy we owe them and lavish it indiscriminately upon those who happen to look like them and be standing near them. If our public spaces are hijacked and despoiled, that somehow helps assuage the vague guilt we feel but can't quite bring into focus. If that erodes our social order, who are we—the guilty—to call others to account?

Enough. It's time to stop kidding ourselves and clean up the mess that a specious liberation has made.

NO

Jonathan Kozol

HOMELESS FAMILIES IN AMERICA

OVERVIEW: A CAPTIVE STATE

Since 1980 homelessness has changed its character. What was once a theater of the grotesque (bag ladies in Grand Central Station, winos sleeping in the dusty sun outside the Greyhound station in El Paso) has grown into the common misery of millions.

"This is a new population," said a homeless advocate in Massachusetts. "Many are people who were working all their lives. When they lose their jobs they lose their homes. When they lose their homes they start to lose their families too."

Even in New York City, with its permanent population of the long-term unemployed, 50 percent of individuals served at city shelters during 1984 were there for the first time. The same percentage holds throughout the nation.

The chilling fact, from any point of view, is that small children have become the fastest-growing sector of the homeless. At the time of writing there are 28,000 homeless people in emergency shelters in the city of New York. An additional 40,000 are believed to be unsheltered citywide. Of those who are sheltered, about 10,000 are homeless individuals. The remaining 18,000 are parents and children in almost 5,000 families. The average homeless family includes a parent with two or three children. The average child is six years old, the average parent twenty-seven.

In Massachusetts, three fourths of all homeless people are now children and their parents. In certain parts of Massachusetts (Plymouth, Attleboro, and Northampton) 90 to 95 percent of those who have no homes are families with children.

Homeless people are poor people. Four out of ten poor people in America are children, though children make up only one fourth of our population. The number of children living in poverty has grown to 14 million—an increase of 3 million over 1968—while welfare benefits to families with children have declined one third.

From Jonathan Kozol, *Rachel and Her Children: Homeless Families in America* (Crown Publishers, 1988). Copyright © 1988 by Jonathan Kozol. Reprinted by permission of Crown Publishers, Inc.

Seven hundred thousand poor children, of whom 100,000 have no health insurance, live in New York City. Approximately 20 percent of New York City's children lived in poverty in 1970, 33 percent in 1980, over 40 percent by 1982....

How Many Are Homeless in America? The U.S. Department of Health and Human Services (HHS), relying on groups that represent the homeless, suggested a figure of 2 million people in late 1983. Diminished numbers of low-income dwelling units and diminished welfare grants during the four years since may give credence to a current estimate, accepted by the Coalition for the Homeless, of 3 to 4 million people.

There is much debate about the numbers; the debate has a dreamlike quality for me because it parallels exactly the debates about the numbers of illiterate Americans. Government agencies again appear to contradict each other and attempt to peg the numbers low enough to justify inaction—or, in this case, negative action in the form of federal cuts.

Officials in the U.S. Department of Housing and Urban Development (HUD) puzzled congressional leaders during hearings held in 1984 by proposing a low estimate of 250,000 to 350,000 homeless people nationwide. The study from which HUD's estimate was drawn had contemplated as many as 586,000 people, but this number was discredited in its report.

A House subcommittee revealed serious flaws in the HUD study. Subsequent investigations indicated HUD had "pressured its consultants to keep the estimates low." HUD's researchers, for example, suggested a "reliable" low estimate of 12,000 homeless persons in New York City on a given night in January 1984. Yet, on the night in question, over 16,000 people had been given shelter in New York; and this, of course, does not include the larger number in the streets who had received no shelter. U.S. Representative Henry Gonzalez termed HUD's study intentionally deceptive.

Estimates made by shelter operators in twenty-one selected cities in October 1986 total about 230,000 people. This sampling does not include Chicago, San Francisco, Houston, Cleveland, Philadelphia, Baltimore, Atlanta, Pittsburgh, St. Paul, San Diego, or Detroit. With estimates from these and other major cities added, the total would exceed 400,000.

Even this excludes the metropolitan areas around these cities and excludes those middle-sized cities—Lawrence, Lowell, Worcester, Brockton, Attleboro, for example, all in Massachusetts—in which the loss of industrial jobs has marginalized hundreds of thousands of the working poor. Though technically not unemployed, most of these families live in economic situations so precarious that they cannot meet the basic costs of life, particularly rent, which in all these cities has skyrocketed. Nor does this include the rural areas of the Midwest and the Plains states, the oil towns of the Southwest, the southern states from which assembly plants and textile industries have fled, lumber counties such as those in Oregon and their New England counterparts in northern Maine. The homeless in these areas alone, if added to the major-city totals, would bring a cautious national count above 1.5 million.

We would be wise, however, to avoid the numbers game. Any search for the "right number" carries the assumption that we may at last arrive at an acceptable number. There is no acceptable number. Whether the number is 1 million or 4 million or the administration's estimate of less than a million, there are too many homeless people in America.[1]

Homeless people are, of course, impossible to count because they are so difficult to find. That is intrinsic to their plight. They have no address beyond a shelter bed, room number, tent or cave. In this book I follow my own sense that the number is between 2 and 3 million. If we include those people housing organizers call the "hidden homeless"—families doubled up illegally with other families, with the consequent danger that both families may be arbitrarily evicted—we are speaking of much larger numbers.

In 1983, 17,000 families were doubled up illegally in public housing in New York City. The number jumped to 35,000 by spring of 1986. Including private as well as public housing, the number had risen above 100,000 by November 1986. If we accept the New York City estimate of three to four family members in each low-income household, the total number of people (as opposed to families) doubled up in public and private housing in New York is now above 300,000.

The line from "doubling up" to homelessness is made explicit in a study by Manhattan's borough president: At least 50 percent of families entering New York City shelters (1986) were previously doubled up. Nationwide, more than 3 million families now are living doubled up.

It is, however, not only families doubled up or tripled up who are in danger of eviction. Any poor family paying rent or mortgage that exceeds one half of monthly income is in serious danger. Over 6 million American households pay half or more of income for their rent. Of these, 4.7 million pay 60 percent or more.

Of mortgaged homeowners, 2 million pay half or more of income for their housing. Combining these households with those who are doubled up, it appears that well above 10 million families may be living near the edge of homelessness in the United States.

Why Are They Without Homes?

Unreflective answers might retreat to explanations with which readers are familiar: "family breakdown," "drugs," "culture of poverty," "teen pregnancies," "the underclass," etc. While these are precipitating factors for some people, they are not the cause of homelessness. *The cause of homelessness is lack of housing.*

Half a million units of low-income housing are lost every year to condominium conversion, abandonment, arson, demolition. Between 1978 and 1980, median rents climbed 30 percent for those in the lowest income sector. Half these people paid nearly three quarters of their income for their housing. Forced to choose between housing and food, many of these families soon were driven to the streets. That was only a beginning. After 1980, rents rose at even faster rates. In Boston, between 1982 and 1984, over 80 percent of housing units renting below $300 disappeared, while the number of units renting above $600 more than doubled.

Hard numbers, in this instance, may be of more help than social theory in explaining why so many of our neighbors end up in the streets. By the end of 1983, vacancies averaged 1 to 2 percent in San Francisco, Boston and New York. Vacancies in *low-income* rental units averaged less than 1 percent in New York City by 1987. In Boston they averaged .5 percent. Landlords saw this seller's market as an invitation to raise rents.

Evictions grew. In New York City, with a total of nearly 2 million rental units, there were half a million legal actions for eviction during 1983.[2] Half of these actions were against people on welfare, four fifths of whom were paying rents above the maximum allowed by welfare. Rent ceilings established by welfare in New York were frozen for a decade at the levels set in 1975. They were increased by 25 percent in 1984; but rents meanwhile had nearly doubled.

During these years the White House cut virtually all federal funds to build or rehabilitate low-income housing. Federal support for low-income housing dropped from $28 billion to $9 billion between 1981 and 1986. "We're getting out of the housing business. Period," said a HUD deputy assistant secretary in 1985.

The consequences now are seen in every city of America.

What Distinguishes Housing from Other Basic Needs of Life? Why, of Many Essentials, Is It the First to Go?

Housing has some unique characteristics, as urban planning specialist Chester Hartman has observed. One pays for housing well in advance. The entire month's rent must be paid on the first day of any rental period. One pays for food only a few days before it is consumed, and one always has the option of delaying food expenditures until just prior to eating. Housing is a nondivisible and not easily adjustable expenditure. "One cannot pay less rent for the next few months by not using the living room," Hartman observes. By contrast, one can rapidly and drastically adjust one's food consumption: for example, by buying less expensive food, eating less, or skipping meals. "At least in the short run," Hartman notes, "the consequences of doing so are not severe." The cost of losing housing and then paying for re-entry to the housing system, on the other hand, is very high, involving utility and rent deposits equal sometimes to twice or three times the cost of one month's rent. For these reasons, one may make a seemingly "rational" decision to allocate scarce funds to food, clothing, health care, transportation, or the search for jobs—only to discover that one cannot pay the rent. "Some two and a half million people are displaced annually from their homes," writes Hartman. While some find other homes and others move in with their friends or relatives, the genesis of epidemic and increasing homelessness is there.

Is This a Temporary Crisis?

As families are compelled to choose between feeding their children or paying their rent, homelessness has taken on the characteristics of a captive state. Economic recovery has not relieved this crisis. Adults whose skills are obsolete have no role in a revived free market. "The new poor," according to the U.S. Conference of Mayors, "are not being recalled to their former jobs, because their former plants are not being reopened.... Their temporary layoffs are from dying industries."

Two million jobs in steel, textiles, and other industries, according to the AFL-CIO, have disappeared each year since 1979. Nearly half of all new jobs created from 1979 to 1985 pay poverty-level wages.

Increased prosperity among the affluent, meanwhile, raises the profit motive for conversion of low-income properties to upscale dwellings. The Conference of Mayors reported in January 1986 that central-city renewal has accelerated homelessness by dispossession of the poor. The illusion of recovery, therefore, has the ironic consequence of worsening the status of the homeless and near-homeless, while diluting explanations for their presence and removing explanations for their indigence.

But it is not enough to say that this is not a "temporary" crisis: Congressional research indicates that it is likely to grow worse. The House Committee on Government Operations noted in April 1985 that, due to the long advance-time needed for a federally assisted housing program to be terminated, the United States has yet to experience the full impact of federal cuts in housing aid. "The committee believes that current federal housing policies, combined with the continuing erosion of the private inventory of low-income housing, will add to the growth of homelessness...." The "harshest consequences," the committee said, are "yet to come."...

DISTANCING OURSELVES FROM PAIN AND TEARS

... "A Cold-Blooded Assault on Poor People." This headline in the *Washington Post* precedes an article by William Raspberry. "Programs for low-income Americans," he writes, represent "just over a tenth of the federal budget," but are "ticketed" for one third of the 1987 Reagan budget cuts. "Are appropriations for low-income housing so excessively generous," he asks, "that it makes sense to cut them by a third?" Do indigent people waste so many of our dollars on "imagined illness," he asks, "that a $20 billion cut in Medicaid over the next five years" is justified? "Do housing repair grants, rural housing programs, emer-

gency food assistance, legal services and the Work Incentive Program" represent such foolishly misguided policies that "they should be terminated altogether, as the president proposes?"...

"A continuously rising level of child abuse and homelessness," writes New York City Council President Andrew Stein, "is not a force of nature...." This is a point he is compelled to make because we tend so easily to speak of homelessness as an unauthored act: something sad, perhaps the fault of those who have no homes, more likely that of chance. Homelessness "happens," like a flood or fire or a devastating storm—what legal documents, insurance forms, might call "an act of God." But homelessness is not an act of God. It is an act of man. It is done by people like ourselves....

Phrases such as "no quick fix" do more than to dilute a sense of urgency; they also console us with the incorrect impression that we are, no matter with what hesitation, moving in the right direction. All available statistics make it clear that this is not the case.

"Federal housing assistance programs have been cut a full 64 percent since 1980," according to Manhattan Borough President David Dinkins in a study released in March of 1987, "from $32 billion to $9 billion in the current fiscal year."

In 1986, the Department of Housing and Urban Development subsidized construction of only 25,000 housing units nationwide. When Gerald Ford was president, 200,000 units were constructed. Under President Carter, 300,000 units were constructed.

"For each dollar authorized for national defense in 1980, nineteen cents were authorized for subsidized housing programs," according to another recent study. In 1984, only *three* cents were authorized for housing for each military dollar. This is neither a "quick fix" nor a "slow fix." It is an aggressive fix against the life and health of undefended children.

Mr. Stein poses a challenging scenario. "Imagine the mayor of New York calling an urgent news conference," he writes, "to announce that the crisis of the city's poor children had reached such proportions that he was mobilizing the city's talents for a massive rescue effort. . . ." Some such drastic action, he asserts, is warranted "because our city is threatened by the spreading blight of a poverty even crueler in some ways than that of the Great Depression half a century ago."

We hear this voice of urgency too rarely. Instead, we are told that all these children we have seen—those who cannot concentrate in school because they are too hungry and must rest their heads against their desks to stifle stomach pains, those who sleep in "pigpens," those who travel sixty miles twice a day to glean some bit of education from a school at which they will arrive too late for breakfast and may find themselves denied a lunch because of presidential cuts—must wait a little while and be patient and accept the fact that there is "no quick fix" for those who are too young to vote and whose defeated parents have no lobbyists in Washington or City Hall.

There is a degree of cruelty at stake when those who aren't in pain assume the privilege to counsel moderation in addressing the despair of those who are, or when those who have resources to assuage such pain urge us to be patient in denial of such blessings to the poor. It is still more cruel when those who make such judgments are, as they are bound to be, articulate adults and those who are

denied are very frail and very small and very young. . . .

The debate persists as to how many homeless people are the former patients of large mental hospitals, deinstitutionalized in the 1970s. Many homeless *individuals* may have been residents of such institutions. In cities like New York, however, where nearly half the homeless people are small children, with an average age of six, such suppositions obviously make little sense. Six-year-olds were not deinstitutionalized before their birth. Their parents, with an average age of twenty-seven, are not likely to have been the residents of mental hospitals when they were still teenagers. But there is a reason for the repetition of such arguments in face of countervailing facts. In a sense, when we refer to "institutions"—those from which we think some of the homeless come, those to which we think they ought to be consigned—we are creating a new institution of our own: the abstract institution of an airtight capsule ("underclass," "behavioral problem," "nonadaptive" or "psychotic") that will not allow their lives to touch our own. Few decent people or responsible physicians wish to do this; but the risk is there. The homeless are a nightmare. . . . It is natural to fear and try to banish nightmares. It is not natural to try to banish human beings.

The distancing we have observed receives its most extreme expression in the use of language such as "undeserving." This is, in some sense, the ultimate act of disaffiliation and the most decisive means of placing all these families and their children in a category where they can't intrude upon our dreams. . . .

[Charles Murray] argues that a thorough extirpation of the social benefactions that evolved from Franklin

Roosevelt's time into our own would remove unnatural incentives to unadmirable behavior: "Take away all governmentally-sponsored subsidies for irresponsible behavior.... The natural system will produce the historically natural results."

Murray's ideas have been received well in the [Reagan] White House. The harshness of the wording he employs reflects a mood that may be dangerous for our society. "Some people are better than others," he writes. "They deserve more of society's rewards...." The obverse of this statement, when applied to children such as Benjamin, is chilling.

Why is it that views like these, so alien to our American tradition and Judeo-Christian roots, should have received acceptance in this decade? Weariness and frustration, I have said, may lead some people to impatience and, at length, to anger at some of the mothers whom we have described. The fear of seeing our own nightmares acted out upon the sidewalk right before our eyes may be another reason for our willingness to place the indigent at a safe distance from our lives.

NOTES

1. One reason for discrepancies in estimates derives from various ways of counting. Homeless advocates believe that all who ask for shelter during any extended period of time ought to be termed homeless. The government asks: "How many seek shelter on a given day?" If the HUD study, cited above, had considered those who asked for shelter in the course of one full year, its upper estimate would have exceeded 1.7 million.

2. Half a million families, of course, were not evicted in one year. Many of these legal actions are "repeats." Others are unsuccessful. Still others are settled with payment of back rent.

POSTSCRIPT

Do Social and Mental Pathologies Largely Account for Homelessness?

Part of the argument between Kozol and Magnet concerns the number of homeless. Is it, as Kozol thinks, 2 to 3 million, or 360,000 at the most, as Magnet claims? The numbers issue ties in with the larger question of whether most of the homeless are ordinary people victimized by the economy or pathological types who have been motivated by misplaced compassion to live on the streets. If the number of people living in the streets is in the millions, then that would indicate that the American economy has indeed gone awry. But if the number of homeless is relatively small, it is more plausible to think of them as a pathological fringe element.

It is not easy to resolve this numbers argument. Much research has been done, so far without producing a consensus. Two articles on how estimates of the homeless are done are Peter H. Rossi, "The Urban Homeless: Estimating Size and Composition," *Science* (March 13, 1987), and Constance Holden, "Homelessness: Experts Differ on Root Causes," *Science* (May 2, 1986). For a review of the literature and empirical studies on homelessness, see Anne B. Shlay and Peter H. Rossi, "Social Science Research and Contemporary Studies of Homelessness," *Annual Review of Sociology* (vol. 18, 1992).

Some of the major efforts to explain the causes of homelessness are: Peter H. Rossi, *Down and Out in America: The Origins of Homelessness* (University of Chicago Press, 1988); James D. Wright, *Address Unknown: The Homeless in America* (Aldine de Gruyter, 1989); Karin Ringheim, *At Risk of Homelessness: The Role of Income and Rent* (Praeger, 1990); Richard P. Appelbaum, "The Affordability Gap," *Social Policy* (May/June 1989); and Alice S. Baum and Donald W. Burnes, *A Nation in Denial: The Truth About Homelessness* (Westview, 1993). Charles Hoch and Robert A. Slayton carefully examine the differences between homelessness today and homelessness in the 1960s in *New Homelessness and Old: Community and the Skid Row Hotel* (Temple University Press, 1989). Useful collections of articles that analyze homelessness include Carol L. M. Catton, ed., *Homelessness in America* (Oxford University Press, 1990), and Jamsid A. Momeni, ed., *Homelessness in the United States, Vol. 2: Data and Issues* (Greenwood Press, 1990). For a useful discussion of solutions, see Peter Dreier and John Atlas, "Grassroots Strategies for the Housing Crisis: A National Agenda," *Social Policy* (Winter 1989). For a sensitive examination of the ambivalent feelings that Americans have about the homeless, see Peter Marin, "Helping and Hating the Homeless," *Harper's* (January 1987). Finally, for two deeply moving portrayals of the lives of the homeless, see the award-winning *Rachel and Her Children: Homeless Families in America*, by Jonathan Kozol (Anchor Press, 1985) and *Tell Them Who I am: The Lives of Homeless Women*, by Elliott Liebow (Free Press, 1993).

PART 4

Political Economy

Are political power and economic power merged within a "power elite" that dominates the U.S. political system? The first issue in this part explores that debate. The second issue concerns the proper role of government in the economy. Some believe that the government must correct for the many failures of the market, while others think that the government usually complicates the workings of the free market. The next debate concerns public policy: How should we assess the impact and efficacy of welfare programs? Finally, in the last issue in this part, we examine the present and future condition of and role played by central cities.

- Is Government Dominated by Big Business?

- Should Government Intervene in a Capitalist Economy?

- Does Welfare Do More Harm Than Good?

- Are Central Cities Becoming Obsolete?

ISSUE 12

Is Government Dominated by Big Business?

YES: Thomas Byrne Edsall, from *The New Politics of Inequality: How Political Power Shapes Economic Policy* (W. W. Norton, 1984)

NO: Jeffrey M. Berry, from "Citizen Groups and the Changing Nature of Interest Group Politics in America," *The Annals of the American Academy of Political and Social Science* (July 1993)

ISSUE SUMMARY

YES: Political reporter Thomas Byrne Edsall argues that the power of big business is stronger than ever because of the increasing political sophistication of big business coupled with the breakdown of political parties.

NO: Jeffrey M. Berry, a professor of political science, contends that public interest pressure groups that have entered the political arena since the end of the 1960s have effectively challenged the political power of big business.

Since the framing of the U.S. Constitution in 1787, there have been periodic charges that America is unduly influenced by wealthy financial interests. Richard Henry Lee, a signer of the Declaration of Independence, spoke for many Anti-Federalists (those who opposed ratification of the Constitution) when he warned that the proposed charter shifted power away from the people and into the hands of the "aristocrats" and "moneyites." Before the Civil War, Jacksonian Democrats denounced the eastern merchants and bankers who, they charged, were usurping the power of the people. After the Civil War, a number of radical parties and movements revived this theme of antielitism. The ferment—which was brought about by the rise of industrial monopolies, government corruption, and economic hardship for western farmers—culminated in the founding of the People's party at the beginning of the 1890s. The Populists, as they were more commonly called, wanted economic and political reforms aimed at transferring power away from the rich and back to "the plain people."

By the early 1900s the People's party had disintegrated, but many writers and activists have continued to echo the Populists' central thesis: that the U.S. democratic political system is in fact dominated by business elites. Yet the thesis has not gone unchallenged. During the 1950s and the early 1960s, many social scientists subscribed to the *pluralist* view of America. Pluralists argue that because there are many influential elites in America, each group has a tendency to counterbalance the power of the others. Labor groups are often opposed to business groups; conservative interests challenge liberal interests, and vice versa; organized civil libertarians sometimes fight with groups that seek government-imposed bans on pornography or groups that demand tougher criminal laws. No single group, the pluralists argue, can dominate the political system

Pluralists readily acknowledg that American government is not democratic in the full sense of the word; it is not driven by the majority. But neither, they insist, is it run by a conspiratorial "power elite." In the pluralist view, the closest description of the American form of government would be neither majority rule nor minority rule but *minorities* rule. (Note that in this context, "minorities" does not necessarily refer to racial or ethnic minorities but to any organized group of people with something in common—including race, religion, and social concerns—not constituting a majority of the population.) Each organized minority enjoys some degree of power in the making of public policy. In extreme cases, when a minority's back is to the wall, its power may take a purely negative form: the power to derail policy. When the majority—or, more accurately, a coalition of other minorities—attempts to pass some measure that threatens the vital interests of some organized minority, that group may use its power to disrupt the policy-making process. (Often cited in this connection is the use of the Senate filibuster, which is the practice of using tactics during the legislative process that cause extreme delays or prevent action, thus enabling a group to "talk to death" a bill that threatens its vital interests.) But in the pluralist view, these interests possess more than negative power: they often work together and reach consensus on certain issues, which results in new laws and policy initiatives that enjoy broad public support. Pluralism, then, does not have to produce gridlock. It may produce temporary gridlock when a group fears that it is about to be steamrolled by the majority, but ultimately it leads to compromise, consensus, and moderation.

Critics of pluralism argue that pluralism is an idealized, prettified depiction of a political system that is in the grip of powerful elite groups. Critics fault pluralist theory for what they consider to be its failure to acknowledge that big business dominates the policy-making process. They question the pluralist premise that interest groups contend with one another on a level playing field, believing instead that it is tilted in favor of big business. In the selections that follow, Thomas Byrne Edsall supports this view and argues that well-financed business groups, having learned from challengers to their power in the 1970s, now know how to more or less control the political process. Jeffrey M. Berry, in opposition, argues that thanks to new consumer, environmental, and other citizen groups, big business no longer enjoys the cozy relationship it once had with Washington policymakers.

YES

Thomas Byrne Edsall

THE NEW POLITICS OF INEQUALITY

In the United States in recent years there has been a significant erosion of the power of those on the bottom half of the economic spectrum, an erosion of the power not only of the poor but of those in the working and middle classes. At the same time, there has been a sharp increase in the power of economic elites, of those who fall in the top 15 percent of the income distribution.

This transfer of power has coincided with an economic crisis: productivity growth, which for the three decades following the Second World War had been the source of a continuing rise in the standard of living, slowed to zero by the end of the 1970s; the median family income, which had doubled in real, uninflated dollars from 1950 to 1973, declined during the next ten years, paralleling a decline in the average factory worker's weekly earnings; and inflation and unemployment, instead of acting as counterbalancing forces, rose simultaneously.

This mounting economic crisis provided an opportunity for newly ascendant representatives of the interests of the business community and of the affluent to win approval of a sea change in economic policy. For nearly fifty years, since the formation of the New Deal coalition in the 1930s, there had been a sustained base of support for both social spending programs and a tax system that modestly redistributed income and restricted the concentration of wealth in the hands of the few. These deeply rooted liberal traditions were abandoned during the late 1970s in favor of policies calling for a major reduction of the tax burden on income derived from capital, and for reductions in domestic spending programs directed toward the poor and the working poor. These shifts in tax and spending policies, in combination with inflation, have had enormous distributional consequences, resulting, for the period from 1980 through 1984, in losses for every income group except the very affluent.

Although the election of Ronald Reagan to the presidency has been the catalyst for much of this alteration of policy, its roots run far deeper. The delicate balance of power between elites and larger groups seeking representation in the political process has been changing in almost all quarters, including the Democratic party, the Republican party, the business lobbying community, organized labor, and the intellectual establishment. These changes have been both accelerated and exacerbated throughout the entire electorate by increasingly class-skewed voting patterns. In each of these areas, the changes are resulting in a diminution of the representation of the majority in the development of economic policy, and in the growing leverage of the well-to-do.

Underlying this shift in the balance of political power among economic groups is a changed economic environment that has forced fundamental revisions in political strategies for both political parties. The economic crisis of the past decade has cut to the heart of a tradition in American politics, particularly in Democratic politics, playing havoc with that party's tradition of capitalizing on a growing and thriving economy in order to finance a continuing expansion of benefits for those toward the bottom of the income distribution. Past economic growth had provided the federal government with a fiscal dividend in additional tax revenues with which to finance growth in such broad-based programs as Social Security and Medicare, while simultaneously maintaining popular support, as all wage earners benefited from rising real incomes.

Altered economic circumstances have turned politics into what Lester Thurow has termed a zero-sum process. The balance of power in the competition for the benefits of government has shifted increasingly in favor of those in the top third of the income distribution. In many respects these shifts have pushed the national debate well to the right of its locus ten or twenty years ago. In 1964, the Republican presidential nominee, Senator Barry Goldwater, was decisively defeated while advocating a major reduction in domestic federal spending and a sharp increase in military spending; sixteen years later, Ronald Reagan, one of Goldwater's most ardent supporters, was elected to the presidency on a platform remarkably similar to Goldwater's and succeeded in persuading Congress, including a Democratic House of Representatives, to act into law legislation that would have been politically inconceivable at any time during the previous fifty years.

The roots of this shift to the right are by now deeply imbedded in the political system, severely restricting the scope of choices available to either party particularly to the Democratic party. Just as the shift to the left in public policy in the early 1960s resulted from fundamental alterations in the balance of power—ranging from rapid postwar economic growth, to the cohesiveness of the liberal-labor coalition, to the political vitality of the civil rights movement—the shift to the right over the past decade has resulted from complex, systemic alterations in the terms of the political and economic debate and in the power of those participating in the debate.

... [C]onservative forces,... are not only within the Republican party, the right-wing ideological groups, and the business community but within the Democratic party itself. Not only are these forces present in all major elements of the political system; even with economic recovery, lowered inflation, declining unemployment, and growth in the gross national product, the shape of economic and political pressures on the electorate at large would appear to preclude, for at least the near future, the emergence of a consensus in support of a revived liberal agenda....

During the 1970s, the political wing of the nation's corporate sector staged one of the most remarkable campaigns in the pursuit of political power in recent history. By the late 1970s and the early 1980s, business, and Washington's corporate lobbying community in particular, had gained a level of influence and leverage approaching that of the boom days of the 1920s. What made the acquisition of power in the 1970s remarkable was that business achieved its goals without any broad public-political mandate such as that of the 1920s, when probusiness values were affirmed in the elections of 1920, 1924, and 1928. Rather, business in the 1970s developed the ability to dominate the legislative process under adverse, if not hostile, circumstances. Corporate leaders had been closely associated with Watergate and its related scandals, and a reform-minded Democratic party with strong ties to the consumer and environmental movements had gained increasingly large majorities in Congress.

Despite these devastating odds, the political stature of business rose steadily from the early 1970s, one of its lowest points in the nation's history, until, by the end of the decade, the business community had achieved virtual dominance of the legislative process in Congress. The rise of the corporate sector is a case study in the ability of an economic elite to gain power by capitalizing on changes in the political system. In the case of the Democratic party, the shift in the balance of power toward the affluent, the erosion of the labor union movement, and the vastly increased importance of money in campaigns all combined to make Democratic politicians more vulnerable to pressures from the right. In the case of the Republican party, a de facto alliance has emerged between the GOP and much of the business community, a relationship paralleling the ties between the Democratic party and labor but lacking the inherent conflicts characteristic of that

liaison. The political ascendancy of the business community, furthermore, has coincided with a sustained and largely successful attack upon organized labor, an attack conducted both in private-sector union representation fights and in legislative battles on Capitol Hill.

In 1978, in the midst of the corporate political revival, R. Heath Larry, president of the National Association of Manufacturers, contended that the single most important factor behind the resurgence of business was "the decline in the role of the party, yielding a new spirit of independence among congressmen—independent of each other, of the president, of the party caucus." Larry's perception of the role of the decline in political parties in the revival of the stature of business was accurate, but his contention that this decline produced increased independence is wrong. In fact, the collapse of political parties and of traditional political organizations, especially those at the local level that formerly had the power to assure or to deny reelection, has been a key factor in a network of forces and developments undermining the independence of politicians and augmenting the strength of the business community....

By the mid-1970s, ... the decline of party loyalties, congressional reforms weakening the power of committee chairmen, and the diffusion of power to junior members of Congress forced a major alteration in lobbying strategies. "As long as you could go and get the cooperation of the committee chairman and the ranking members, and maybe a few others, you didn't have to have the vast network we are talking about now," [Ford Motor Company executive Wayne H.] Smithey noted. Smithey's reference to a "vast network" describes both the development of grass-roots lobbying as a legislative tactic and a much more pervasive effort to set the terms of the legislative debate in the nation's capital. Not only have the targets of lobbyists changed over the past generation, but the technology of public opinion molding has undergone changes of unprecedented magnitude, producing computerized direct-mail communications in which much of the nation's adult population has been broken down into demographic and "psychographic" profiles. A group or institution seeking to mobilize support or opposition on any issue can seek out ready-made lists of allies in the general public from computer specialists who can then communicate almost instantaneously with any selected constituency via letters produced on high-speed laser printers. If lobbying during the 1950s, in the words of one of the most eminent Washington lobbyists, Charles E. Walker, consisted of personal access to four natives of Texas—President Dwight Eisenhower, House Speaker Sam Rayburn, Senate Majority Leader Lyndon Baines Johnson, and Treasury Secretary Robert Anderson—it currently involves minimally the ability to recognize the interests of 535 members of the House and Senate, an acute sensitivity to potential malleability in public opinion, the cultivation of both print and electronic media, the use of sophisticated technologies both to create and to convey an impression of public sentiment, and the marshaling on Capitol Hill and across the country of legions of newly enlisted corporate personnel.

The effort on the part of the business community to shape the legislative debate has taken place on a number of fronts, one of the most important of which has been the politicization of employees and stockholders. Atlantic Richfield (Arco), for example, spends about $1 million annually on a program in which 15,000 employees are members of politically active local committees. In addition, the nearly 80,000 Arco stockholders, suppliers, and distributors are on a mailing list for company newsletters and publications focusing on political and public policy issues. W. Dean Cannon, Jr., executive vice-president of the California Savings and Loan League, suggested in 1978 to savings and loan firms that they give employees "specific assignments to work in politics" and that an employee's raises "might well be tied directly to his involvement in the political assignment you have given him." During the debate over the 1978 tax bill, officials of a single, mid-sized firm, the Barry Wright Corporation in Watertown, Mass, generated 3,800 letters from its stockholders to members of Congress in favor of a reduction in capital gains taxation.

The politicization of management-level employees is a critical element in achieving effective grass-roots lobbying: an employee who sees a direct economic interest in the outcome of legislative battles will be a far more effective and persistent advocate than an employee who is acting in response only to orders or implied orders from superiors. Stockholders, in turn, represent an ideal target for political mobilization. Only 15 percent of American citizens hold stock, according to liberal estimates by the Securities Industry Association, and those who do are, on average, in the upper-income brackets. They have little or no direct interest in the expansion or maintenance of domestic spending programs, although they have considerable interest in lowering tax rates. In this sense, the economic interests of afflu-ent individuals and of corporations are sharply intertwined. Both stockholders and corporations, for example, share a direct interest in either lowering the capi-tal gains rate or shortening the minimum holding period to qualify for the more favorable capital gains rate....

An equally, if not more, effective use of business money in altering the terms of the policy debate has been in the total or partial financing of such private institutions engaged in research and scholarship as the American Enterprise Institute; the Heritage Foundation; the Hoover Institution on War, Revolution and Peace; the National Bureau of Eco-nomic Research; the Center for the Study of American Business at Washington University in St. Louis, and the Ameri-can Council for Capital Formation. In a decade during which economic stagna-tion contributed to the undermining of the intellectual basis of traditional Demo-cratic economic and political strategies, these organizations, among others, have functioned to lay the scholarly and the-oretical groundwork for a major shift in public policy favoring business and the higher-bracket taxpayers....

BUSINESS AND ECONOMIC POLICY

The rising political power of business has been associated with the general increase in the number of political ac-tion committees [PACs] and with the growing volume of money channeled through them. This line of thinking, in turn, has given rise to charges that Congress, overwhelmed by the flow of cash from the PACs, has become the puppet of special interests, a forum in which every organized group, from doctors to dairymen, can, in return for campaign contributions, receive special antitrust exemption from competition or from taxpayer-financed price supports, or special insulation from the federal regulatory process. The most vocal critic of the system has been Common Cause, the principal reform lobby. "Our system of representative government is under siege because of the destructive role that political action committees or PACs are now playing in our political process," Fred Wertheimer, president of Common Cause, declared in 1983....

These analyses, while both accurate and timely, fail to take into account a number of less frequently reported factors adding to the complexity and subtlety of the current political situa-tion on Capitol Hill. For one, Common Cause and the press have become in-creasingly effective watchdogs over the legislative process, preventing many of the attempts by special-interest groups to slip through favorable legislation. More important, however, while these analyses, particularly [New Yorker cor-respondent Elizabeth] Drew's detailed description of the overwhelming concern with fundraising in Congress, accurately portray an essential element of the po-litical process, neither recognizes what has been a major ideological shift in Congress. Business has played a key role in this shift, using not just PAC contri-butions but increasingly sophisticated grass-roots lobbying mechanisms, the financing of a sympathetic intellectual community, and the expenditure of some-where in the neighborhood of $1 billion annually on institutional advertising.

This ideological shift in the nation's capital has been pervasive, alerting ba-sic tax, spending, and regulatory policies and moving both political parties well to the right over the past decade. Of the various elites that have gained strength in recent years, business has been among the most effective. Not only has it gained from highly favorable tax treatment and from a major reduction in regulation, but government action has increased the bargaining leverage of management in its relations with organized labor. This increased leverage grows out of reductions in unemployment compensation and out of the elimination of the public service job programs, and through the appointment of promanagement officials at such key agencies as the Occupational Safety and Health Administration and at the National Labor Relations Board. The end result is a labor movement that has lost much of its clout at the negotiating table and in the polling booth. . . .

THE WAGES OF INEQUALITY

In the late 1970s, a set of political and intellectual forces began to converge and to gain momentum, joining together in a direction that substantially altered economic policy in the United States. While the forces involved were by no means in agreement as to the specific goals to be achieved, they shared an interest in seeking to change the basic assumptions that have dominated taxation and spending policies in the United States. For nearly fifty years, since the administration of Franklin Delano Roosevelt, two dominant themes of taxation and spending policy have been equity and the moderate redistribution of income. The forces gaining ascendancy in the late 1970s sought to replace such liberal goals with a drive to slow the rate of growth in federal spending in order to increase the availability of money for private capital formation; with a reduction of corporate

and individual tax rates, particularly of those rates in the top brackets, in order to provide predicted incentives for work, savings, and investment; and with the paring down of government regulation to facilitate a more productive marketplace. In short, the goal became to influence government policy so as to supplant, in an economic sense, equity with efficiency.

The inherent contradictions between equity, efficiency, redistribution, and investment go to the heart of the conflict in developing economic policy in advanced capitalist democracies. The political resolution of such contradictions determines the balance between competing claims on government: that is, whether government is granted the authority to intervene in the private marketplace in order to correct or to modify inequities inherent in the market system, through a progressive tax rate schedule and through the payment of benefits to the poor; whether it is the role of government to subsidize, encourage, and direct marketplace forces with tax incentives and loan subsidies targeted toward specific industries; or whether government should reduce to a minimum its role in the economy, remaining as remote from and as disengaged as possible from the private sector.

The period from 1977 through the first months of 1982, however, marked a rare moment in American history, when the disparate forces supporting the conservative coalition on these basic economic questions all simultaneously became politically ascendant. Forces coalescing on the political right included a politically revitalized business community; increasing sophistication and centrality among leaders of the ideological new right; the sudden explosion of wealth in the domestic oil community following the 1973 OPEC embargo; the emergence within the academic community and within the major economic research institutions of proponents of tax cuts and of sharp reductions in the tax rate on capital income; a Republican party whose financial resources were exponentially increased by computerized direct-mail and other new political technologies, providing often decisive access to television, to polling, and to highly sophisticated voter targeting tactics; and the rise of politically conservative evangelical Christian organizations. The emergence of these forces coincided with a series of developments and trends giving conservatism new strength. The business and the new, or ideological, right-wing communities developed a shared interest in the candidates of the Republican party, as such organizations as the Chamber of Commerce and the National Conservative Political Action Committee became de facto arms of the GOP. Voting patterns increased the class bias of voter turnout, as the affluent became a stronger force both within the electorate as a whole and within the Republican party.

Conversely, the forces making up the liberal coalition, represented in large part by major segments of the Democratic party—organized labor, civil rights and civil liberties organizations, political reformers, environmental groups, and feminists—were experiencing increasing disunity. The power of organized labor, essential to any coalition of the left, had been steadily declining. Even more damaging was the emergence of growing inflation and unemployment, a continued decline in the rate of productivity growth, and a drop in the take-home pay of the average worker. This economic deterioration not only splintered the fragile coalition of Democrats that had supported policies of equity and redistribution over the previous forty years but created a growing belief that the nation was caught in an economic crisis that the Democratic party could not resolve, a belief compounded by Democratic disarray.

It was this combination of trends, all favoring the right, that provided the opportunity for a major alteration in public policy. The election in 1980 of Ronald Reagan to the presidency and the takeover of the Senate by the Republican party created the political opportunity for this fundamental realignment, but the groundwork had already been carefully laid. This groundwork included an increasingly sophisticated political strategy capitalizing on the conflicts within the fragile Democratic majority, the careful nurturing and financing of intellectual support both in academia and within a growing network of think tanks financed by corporations and conservative foundations, and the advance preparation of specific legislative proposals, particularly of tax legislation....

The power shift that produced the fundamental policy realignment of the past decade did not result from a conservative or Republican realignment of the voters; nor did it produce such a realignment after the tax and spending legislation of 1981 was enacted. Rather, these policy changes have grown out of pervasive distortions in this country's democratic political process. These distortions have created a system of political decision making in which fundamental issues— the distribution of the tax burden, the degree to which the government sanctions the accumulation of wealth, the role of federal regulation, the level of publicly tolerated poverty, and the relative strength of labor and management—are resolved by an increasingly unrepresentative economic elite. To a large extent, these changes have turned the Republican party, in terms of the public policies it advocates, into a party of the elite. For the Democratic party, the political changes of the past decade have distorted the distribution of power and weakened the capacity of the party to represent the interests of its numerous less affluent constituents.... As long as the balance of political power remains so heavily weighted toward those with economic power, national economic policy will remain distorted, regardless of which party is in control of the federal government.

NO

Jeffrey M. Berry

CITIZEN GROUPS AND THE CHANGING NATURE OF INTEREST GROUP POLITICS IN AMERICA

ABSTRACT: The rise of liberal citizen groups that began in the 1960s has had a strong impact on the evolution of interest group advocacy. The success of these liberal organizations was critical in catalyzing the broader explosion in the numbers of interest groups and in causing the collapse of many subgovernments. New means of resolving policy conflicts had to be established to allow for the participation of broader, more diverse policy communities. Citizen groups have been particularly important in pushing policymakers to create new means of structuring negotiations between large numbers of interest group actors. The greater participation of citizen groups, the increased numbers of all kinds of interest groups, and change in the way policy is made may be making the policymaking process more democratic.

Many protest movements have arisen in the course of American history, each affecting the political system in its own way. The social movements that took hold in the 1960s had their own unique set of roots but seemed to follow a conventional life span. The civil rights and antiwar groups that arose to protest the injustices they saw were classic social movements. Their views were eventually absorbed by one of the political parties, and, after achieving their immediate goals, their vitality was sapped. The antiwar movement disappeared, and black civil rights organizations declined in power. The most enduring and vital citizen groups born in this era of protest were never protest oriented. Consumer groups, environmental groups, and many other kinds of citizen lobbies have enjoyed unprecedented prosperity in the last 25 years. Never before have citizen groups been so prevalent in American politics, and never before have they been so firmly institutionalized into the policymaking process.

The rise of citizen groups has not only empowered many important constituencies, but it has altered the policymaking process as well. This article focuses on how citizen groups have affected interest group politics in general and how these organizations have contributed to the changing nature of

From Jeffrey M. Berry, "Citizen Groups and the Changing Nature of Interest Group Politics in America," *The Annals of the American Academy of Political and Social Science*, vol. 528 (July 1993). Copyright © 1993 by The American Academy of Political and Social Science. Reprinted by permission of Sage Publications, Inc. Notes omitted.

public policymaking. A first step is to examine the initial success of liberal advocacy organizations as well as the conservative response to this challenge. Next, I will look at the impact of this growth of citizen group politics on the policymaking process. Then I will turn to how Congress and the executive branch have tried to cope with a dense population of citizen groups and the complex policymaking environment that now envelops government.

Finally, I will speculate as to how all of this has affected policymaking in terms of how democratic it is. The popular perception is that the rise of interest groups along with the decline of political parties has had a very negative impact on American politics. Analysis of the decline of parties will be left to others, but a central point here is that the growth in the numbers of citizen groups and of other lobbying organizations has not endangered the political system. There are some unfortunate developments, such as the increasing role of political action committees in campaign financing, but the rise of citizen groups in particular has had a beneficial impact on the way policy is formulated. The overall argument may be stated succinctly: the rise of liberal citizen groups was largely responsible for catalyzing an explosion in the growth of all types of interest groups. Efforts to limit the impact of liberal citizen groups failed, and the policymaking process became more open and more participatory. Expanded access and the growth in the numbers of competing interest groups created the potential for gridlock, if not chaos. The government responded, in turn, with institutional changes that have helped to rationalize policymaking in environments with a large number of independent actors.

THE RISE OF CITIZEN GROUPS

The lobbying organizations that emerged out of the era of protest in the 1960s are tied to the civil rights and antiwar movements in two basic ways. First, activism was stimulated by the same broad ideological dissatisfaction with government and the two-party system. There was the same feeling that government was unresponsive, that it was unconcerned about important issues, and that business was far too dominant a force in policymaking. Second, the rise of liberal citizen groups was facilitated by success of the civil rights and antiwar movements. More specifically, future organizers learned from these social movements. They learned that aggressive behavior could get results, and they saw that government could be influenced by liberal advocacy organizations. Some activists who later led Washington-based citizen lobbies cut their teeth as volunteers in these earlier movements.

For liberal consumer and environmental groups, an important lesson of this era was that they should not follow the protest-oriented behavior of the civil rights and antiwar movements. There was a collective realization that lasting influence would come from more conventional lobbying inside the political system. For consumer and environmental organizers, "power to the people" was rejected in favor of staff-run organizations that placed little emphasis on participatory democracy. This is not to say that these new organizations were simply copies of business lobbies; leaders of these groups like Ralph Nader and John Gardner placed themselves above politics-as-usual with their moralistic rhetoric and their attacks against the established political order.

While there was significant support for these groups from middle-class liberals, a major impetus behind their success was financial backing from large philanthropic foundations. The foundations wanted to support social change during a time of political upheaval, but at the same time they wanted responsible activism. This early support, most notably from the Ford Foundation's program in public interest law, was largely directed at supporting groups relying on litigation and administrative lobbying. The seed money for these organizations enabled them to flourish and provided them with time to establish a track record so that they could appeal to individual donors when the foundation money ran out. Other groups emerged without the help of foundations, drawing on a combination of large donors, dues-paying memberships, and government grants. Citizen lobbies proved remarkably effective at raising money and at shifting funding strategies as the times warranted.

Citizen groups emerged in a variety of areas. In addition to consumer and environmental groups, there were organizations interested in hunger and poverty, governmental reform, corporate responsibility, and many other issues. A number of new women's organizations soon followed in the wake of the success of the first wave of citizen groups, and new civil rights groups arose to defend other groups such as Hispanics and gays. As has been well documented, the rise of citizen groups was the beginning of an era of explosive growth in interest groups in national politics. No precise baseline exists, so exact measurement of this growth is impossible. Yet the mobilization of interests is unmistakable. One analysis of organizations represented in Washington in 1980 found that 40 percent of the groups had been started since 1960, and 25 percent had begun after 1970.

The liberal citizen groups that were established in the 1960s and 1970s were not simply the first ripples of a new wave of interest groups; rather, they played a primary role in catalyzing the formation of many of the groups that followed. New business groups, which were by far the most numerous of all the groups started since 1960, were directly stimulated to organize by the success of consumer and environmental groups. There were other reasons why business mobilized, but much of their hostility toward the expanded regulatory state was directed at agencies strongly supported by liberal citizen groups. These organizations had seemingly seized control of the political agenda, and the new social regulation demanded increased business mobilization. New conservative citizen lobbies, many focusing on family issues such as abortion and the Equal Rights Amendment, were also begun to counter the perceived success of the liberal groups.

The swing of the ideological pendulum that led to a conservative takeover of the White House in 1980 led subsequently to efforts to limit the impact of liberal citizen groups. The Reagan administration believed that the election of 1980 was a mandate to eliminate impediments to economic growth. Environmental and consumer groups were seen as organizations that cared little about the faltering American economy; President Reagan referred to liberal public interest lawyers as "a bunch of ideological ambulance chasers." Wherever possible, liberal citizen groups were to be removed from the governmental process....

The Reagan administration certainly succeeded in reducing the liberal groups' access to the executive branch. On a broader level, however, the conservative counterattack against the liberal groups was a failure. The reasons go far beyond the more accommodating stance of the Bush administration or the attitude of any conservative administrations that may follow. These organizations have proved to be remarkably resilient, and they are a strong and stable force in American politics. Most fundamentally, though, the Reagan attempt failed because the transformation of interest group politics led to large-scale structural changes in the public policymaking process.

CONSEQUENCES

The rise of citizen groups and the rapid expansion of interest group advocacy in general have had many important long-term consequences for the way policy is formulated by the national government. Most important, policymaking moved away from closed subgovernments, each involving a relatively stable and restricted group of lobbyists and key government officials, to much broader policymaking communities. Policymaking in earlier years is typically described as the product of consensual negotiations between a small number of back-scratching participants.

Policymaking is now best described as taking place within issue networks rather than in subgovernments. An issue network is a set of organizations that share expertise in a policy area and interact with each other over time as relevant issues are debated. As sociologist Barry Wellman states, "The world is composed of networks, not groups." This is certainly descriptive of Washington policymaking. Policy formulation cannot be portrayed in terms of what a particular group wanted and how officials responded to those demands. The coalitions within networks, often involving scores of groups, define the divisions over issues and drive the policymaking process forward. Alliances are composed of both old friends and strange bedfellows; relationships are built on immediate need as well as on familiarity and trust. Organizations that do not normally work in a particular issue network can easily move into a policymaking community to work on a single issue. The only thing constant in issue networks is the changing nature of the coalitions.

The result of issue network politics is that policymaking has become more open, more conflictual, and more broadly participatory. What is crucial about the role of citizen groups is that they were instrumental in breaking down the barriers to participation in subgovernments. Building upon their own constituency support and working with allies in Congress, citizen groups made themselves players. They have not been outsiders, left to protest policies and a system that excluded them. Rather, they built opposition right into the policymaking communities that had previously operated with some commonality of interest. Even conservative administrators who would prefer to exclude these liberal advocacy groups have recognized that they have to deal with their opponents in one arena or another. The Nuclear Regulatory Commission, the epitome of an agency hostile to liberal advocacy groups, cannot get away with ignoring groups like the Union of Concerned Scientists. The consensus over nuclear power has long been broken. Critics and advocacy groups like the Union of Concerned Scientists have the technical expertise to involve themselves in agency proceedings, and they have the political know-how to get themselves heard on Capitol Hill and in the news media.

Issue networks are not simply divided between citizen groups on one side and business groups on another. Organizations representing business usually encompass a variety of interests, many of which are opposed to each other. As various business markets have undergone rapid change and become increasingly competitive, issue networks have found themselves divided by efforts of one sector of groups to use the policymaking process to try to gain market share from another sector of the network. Citizen groups, rather than simply being the enemy of business, are potential coalition partners for different business sectors. A characteristic of the culture of interest group politics in Washington is that there are no permanent allies and no permanent enemies.

Citizen groups are especially attractive as coalition partners because they have such a high level of credibility with the public and the news media. All groups claim to represent the public interest because they sincerely believe that the course of action they are advocating would be the most beneficial to the country. Since they do not represent any vocational or business interest, citizen groups may be perceived by some to be less biased—though certainly not unbiased—in their approach to public policy problems. This credibility is also built around the high-quality research that many citizen groups produce and distribute to journalists and policymakers in Washington. Reports from advocacy organizations such as Citizens for Tax Justice or the Center for Budget and Policy Priorities are quickly picked up by the media and disseminated across the country. Most business groups would love to have the respect that these citizen groups command in the press. For all the financial strength at the disposal of oil lobbyists, no representative of the oil industry has as much credibility with the public as a lobbyist for the Natural Resources Defense Council.

Despite the growth and stability of citizen groups in national politics, their reach does not extend into every significant policymaking domain. In the broad area of financial services, for example, citizen groups have played a minor role at best. There are some consumer groups that have been marginally active when specific issues involving banks, insurance companies, and securities firms arise, but they have demonstrated little influence or staying power. There is, however, a vital consumer interest at stake as public policymakers grapple with the crumbling walls that have traditionally divided different segments of the financial services market. Defense policy is another area where citizen groups have been relatively minor actors. But if citizen groups are conspicuous by their absence in some important areas, their overall reach is surprisingly broad. They have become major actors in policy areas where they previously had no presence at all. In negotiations over a free trade agreement with Mexico, for example, environmental groups became central players in the bargaining. These groups were concerned that increased U.S. investment in Mexico would result in increased pollution there from unregulated manufacturing, depleted groundwater supplies, and other forms of environmental degradation. To its dismay, the Bush White House found that the only practical course was to negotiate with the groups.

The increasing prominence of citizen groups and the expanding size of issue networks change our conception of the policymaking process. The basic structural attribute of a subgovernment was that it was relatively bounded with a stable set of participants. Even if there was some conflict in that subgovernment, there were predictable divisions and relatively clear expectations of what kind of conciliation between interest groups was possible. In contrast, issue networks seem like free-for-alls. In the health care field alone, 741 organizations have offices in Washington or employ a representative there. Where subgovernments suggested control over public policy by a limited number of participants, issue networks suggest no control whatsoever. Citizen groups make policymaking all the more difficult because they frequently sharpen the ideological debate; they have different organizational incentive systems from those of the corporations and trade groups with which they are often in conflict; and they place little emphasis on the need for economic growth, an assumption shared by most other actors.

This picture of contemporary interest group politics may make it seem impossible to accomplish anything in Washington. Indeed, it is a popular perception that Congress has become unproductive and that we are subject to some sort of national gridlock. Yet the policymaking system is adaptable, and the relationship between citizen groups and other actors in issue networks suggests that there are a number of productive paths for resolving complicated policy issues.

COMPLEX POLICYMAKING

The growth of issue networks is not, of course, the only reason why the policymaking process has become more complex. The increasingly technical nature of policy problems has obviously put an ever higher premium on expertise. Structural changes are critical, too. The decentralization of the House of Representatives that took place in the mid-1970s dispersed power and reduced the autonomy of leaders. Today, in the House, jurisdictions between committees frequently overlap and multiple referrals of bills are common. When an omnibus trade bill passed by both houses in 1987 was sent to conference, the House and the Senate appointed 200 conferees, who broke up into 17 subconferences. The growth of the executive branch has produced a similar problem of overlapping jurisdictions. In recent deliberations on proposed changes in wetlands policy, executive branch participants included the Soil Conservation Service in the Agriculture Department, the Fish and Wildlife Service in Interior, the Army Corps of Engineers, the Environmental Protection Agency (EPA), the Office of Management and Budget, the Council on Competitiveness, and the President's Domestic Policy Council.

Nevertheless, even though the roots of complex policymaking are multifaceted, the rise of citizen groups has been a critical factor in forcing the Congress and the executive branch to focus more closely on developing procedures to negotiate settlements of policy disputes. The quiet bargaining of traditional subgovernment politics was not an adequate mechanism for handling negotiations between scores of interest groups, congressional committees, and executive branch agencies.

Citizen groups have been particularly important in prompting more structured negotiations for a number of reasons. First, in many policy areas, citizen groups upset long-standing working arrangements between policymakers and other interest groups. Citizen groups were often the reason subgovernments crumbled; under pressure from congressional allies and public opinion, they were included in the bargaining and negotiating at some stage in the policymaking process.

Second, citizen groups could not be easily accommodated in basic negotiating patterns. It was not a matter of simply placing a few more chairs at the table. These groups' entrance into a policymaking community usually created a new dividing line between participants. The basic ideological cleavage that exists between consumer and environmental interests and business is not easy to bridge, and, consequently, considerable effort has been expended to devise ways of getting mutual antagonists to negotiate over an extended period. As argued above, once accepted at the bargaining table, citizen groups could be attractive coalition partners for business organizations.

Third, ... citizen groups typically have a great deal of credibility with the press. Thus, in negotiating, they often have had more to gain by going public to gain leverage with other bargainers. This adds increased uncertainty and instability to the structure of negotiations.

Fourth, citizen groups are often more unified than their business adversaries. The business interests in an issue network may consist of large producers, small producers, foreign producers, and companies from other industries trying to expand into new markets. All these business interests may be fiercely divided as each tries to defend or encroach upon established market patterns. The environmentalists in the same network, while each may have its own niche in terms of issue specialization, are likely to present a united front on major policy disputes. In a perverse way, then, the position of citizen groups has been aided by the proliferation of business groups. (Even without the intrusion of citizen lobbies, this sharp rise in the number of business groups would have irretrievably changed the nature of subgovernments.) ...

CONCLUSION

Citizen groups have changed the policymaking process in valuable an enduring ways. Most important, they have broadened representation in our political system. Many previously unrepresented or underrepresented constituencies now have a powerful voice in Washington politics. The expanding numbers of liberal citizen groups and their apparent success helped to stimulate a broad mobilization on the part of business. The skyrocketing increase in the numbers of interest groups worked to break down subgovernments and led to the rise of issue networks.

Issue networks are more fragmented, less predictable policymaking environments. Both Congress and the executive branch have taken steps to bring about greater centralized control and coherence to policymaking. Some of these institutional changes seem aimed directly at citizen groups. Negotiated regulations, for example, are seen as a way of getting around the impasse that often develops between liberal citizen groups and business organizations. Centralized regulatory review has been used by Republican administrations as a means of ensuring that business interests are given primacy; regulators are seen as too sympathetic to the citizen groups that are clients of their agencies.

Although government has established these and other institutional mechanisms for coping with complex policymaking environments, the American public does not seem to feel that the government copes very well at all. Congress has been portrayed as unproductive and spineless, unwilling to tackle the tough problems that require discipline or sacrifice. At the core of this criticism is that interest groups are the culprit. Washington lobbies, representing every conceivable interest and showering legislators with the political action committee donations they crave, are said to be responsible for this country's inability to solve its problems.

Although it is counterintuitive, it may be that the increasing number of interest groups coupled with the rise of citizen groups has actually improved the policymaking system in some important ways. More specifically, our policymaking process may be more democratic today because of these developments. Expanded interest group participation has helped to make the policymaking process more open and visible. The closed nature of subgovernment politics meant not only that participation was restricted but that public scrutiny was minimal. The proliferation of interest groups, Washington media that are more aggressive, and the willingness and ability of citizen groups in particular to go public as part of their advocacy strategy have worked to open up policymaking to the public eye.

The end result of expanded citizen group advocacy is policy communities that are highly participatory and more broadly representative of the public. One can argue that this more democratic policymaking process is also one that is less capable of concerted action; yet there is no reliable evidence that American government is any more or less responsive to pressing policy problems than it has ever been. There are, of course, difficult problems that remain unresolved, but that is surely true of every era. Democracy requires adequate representation of interests as well as institutions capable of addressing difficult policy problems. For policymakers who must balance the demand for representation with the need for results, the key is thinking creatively about how to build coalitions and structure negotiations between large groups of actors.

POSTSCRIPT

Is Government Dominated by Big Business?

One of the problems for any pluralist is the danger that many people may not be properly represented. Suppose, for example, that business and environmental groups in Washington compromise their differences by supporting environmental legislation but passing the costs along to consumers. The legislation may be good, even necessary, but has the consumer's interests been taken into account? There are, of course, self-styled consumer groups, but it is hard to determine whether or not they really speak for the average consumer. The same is true of other activist organizations that claim to represent different groups in our society. The challenge for pluralists is to make their system as inclusive as possible.

Social science literature contains a number of works discussing the issues of pluralism and corporate power. Political scientist Charles E. Lindblom supported pluralism in the 1950s, but he later changed his mind and concluded that big business dominates American policy making. Lindblom takes the pluralist perspective in his early book *Politics, Economics, and Welfare* (Harper, 1953), written with political scientist Robert A. Dahl. His repudiation of pluralism was complete by the time he published *Politics and Markets: The World's Political-Economic Systems* (Basic Books, 1977). Lindblom may have been influenced by some of the critiques of pluralism that appeared in the 1960s, including Peter Bachrach, *The Theory of Democratic Elitism* (Little, Brown, 1976), and Theodore Lowi, *The End of Liberalism* (W. W. Norton, 1969). Two of the more recent works arguing that corporate elites possess inordinate power in American society are Michael Schwartz, ed., *The Structure of Power in America* (Holmes & Meier, 1987), and G. William Domhoff, *The Power Elite and the State* (Aldine de Gruyter, 1990). Dan Clawson et al., in *Money Talks: Corporate PACs and Political Influence* (Basic Books, 1992), examine the influence of corporate PACs and argue that "business exercises power on many fronts, [and] that power must be opposed on every front."

Other important studies of corporate elite dominance include Domhoff's earlier *Who Rules America Now?* (Prentice Hall, 1983); Michael Useem, *The Inner Circle* (Oxford University Press, 1984); Beth Mintz and Michael Schwartz, *The Power Structure of American Business* (University of Chicago Press, 1985); and Robert R. Alford and Roger Friedland, *Powers of Theory: Capitalism, the State, and Democracy* (Cambridge University Press, 1985). For two different kinds of pluralist argument, see Andrew M. Greeley, *Building Coalitions* (Franklin Watts, 1974), and David Vogel, *Fluctuating Fortunes: The Political Power of Business in America* (Basic Books, 1989).

ISSUE 13

Should Government Intervene in a Capitalist Economy?

YES: Ernest Erber, from "Virtues and Vices of the Market: Balanced Correctives to a Current Craze," *Dissent* (Summer 1990)

NO: Milton and Rose Friedman, from *Free to Choose: A Personal Statement* (Harcourt Brace Jovanovich, 1980)

ISSUE SUMMARY

YES: Author Ernest Erber argues that capitalism creates serious social problems that need to be redressed by an activist government.

NO: Economists Milton and Rose Friedman maintain that market competition, when permitted to work unimpeded, protects citizens better than government regulations intended to correct for failures of the market.

The expression "That government is best which governs least" sums up a deeply rooted attitude of many Americans. From early presidents Jefferson and Jackson to America's most recent leaders, Reagan, Bush, and Clinton, American politicians have often echoed the popular view that there are certain areas of life best left to the private actions of citizens.

One such area is the economic sphere, where people make their living by buying and selling goods and services. The tendency of most Americans is to regard direct government involvement in the economic sphere as both unnecessary and dangerous. The purest expression of this view is the economic theory of *laissez-faire*, a French term meaning "let be" or "let alone." The seminal formulation of *laissez-faire* theory was the work of eighteenth-century Scottish philosopher Adam Smith, whose treatise *The Wealth of Nations* appeared in 1776. Smith's thesis was that each individual, pursuing his or her own selfish interests in a competitive market, will be "led by an invisible hand to promote an end which was no part of his intention." In other words, when people single-mindedly seek profit, they actually serve the community because sellers must keep prices down and quality up if they are to meet the competition of other sellers.

Laissez-faire economics was much honored (in theory, if not always in practice) during the nineteenth and early twentieth centuries. But as the nineteenth century drew to a close, the Populist Party sprang up. The Populists denounced eastern bankers, Wall Street stock manipulators, and rich "moneyed interests," and they called for government ownership of railroads, a progressive income tax, and other forms of state intervention. The Populist Party died out early in the twentieth century, but the Populist message was not forgotten. In fact, it was given new life after 1929, when the stock market collapsed and the United States was plunged into the worst economic depression in its history.

By 1932, a quarter of the nation's workforce was unemployed, and most Americans were finding it hard to believe that the "invisible hand" would set things right. Some Americans totally repudiated the idea of a free market and embraced socialism, the belief that the state (or "the community") should run all major industries. Most stopped short of supporting socialism, but they were now prepared to welcome some forms of state intervention in the economy. President Franklin D. Roosevelt, elected in 1932, spoke to this mood when he pledged a "New Deal" to the American people. "New Deal" has come to stand for a variety of programs that were enacted during the first eight years of Roosevelt's presidency, including business and banking regulations, government pension programs, federal aid to the disabled, unemployment compensation, and government-sponsored work programs. Side by side with the "invisible hand" of the marketplace was now the very visible hand of an activist government.

Government intervention in the economic sphere increased during World War II as the government fixed prices, rationed goods, and put millions to work in government-subsidized war industries. Activist government continued during the 1950s, but the biggest leap forward occurred during the late 1960s and early 1970s, when the federal government launched a variety of new welfare and regulatory programs: the multibillion-dollar War on Poverty, new civil rights and affirmative action mandates, and new laws protecting consumers, workers, disabled people, and the environment. These, in turn, led to a proliferation of new government agencies and bureaus, as well as shelves and shelves of published regulations. Proponents of the new activism conceded that it was expensive, but they insisted that activist government was necessary to protect Americans against pollution, unjust discrimination, dangerous products, and other effects of the modern marketplace. Critics of government involvement called attention not only to its direct costs but also to its effect on business activity and individual freedom.

In the following selections, Ernest Erber argues that although competitive markets are very productive, they produce a variety of negative consequences, and he concludes that business regulation and other forms of government intervention are necessary to counter some of the harmful effects of the marketplace. Milton and Rose Friedman argue that the "invisible hand" of the market will work effectively if it is allowed to do so without government interference.

YES

VIRTUES AND VICES OF THE MARKET: BALANCED CORRECTIVES TO A CURRENT CRAZE

Not since they encountered it in nursery rhymes have references to the market so intruded into the consciousness of Americans as in recent months. There is now a virtual consensus that the market is the natural state of economic affairs, and its creation in nations not yet blessed with it is the prescription for every economic ailment. This makes vague good sense to most Americans, for whom the market has pleasant associations. Not surprisingly, for the market has long since come to determine their tastes and values, their very lives....

This worldwide consensus would not exist if it did not reflect a body of evidence that links the market with economic growth, increased productivity, and improved living standards. That this historical progress has been facilitated by the market's competitive and entrepreneurial incentives cannot be contested. Neither can the beliefs that the market's function as a pricing mechanism has historically contributed to economic stability conducive to growth, even if plagued by a persistent tendency toward inflation in recent years, nor that the market's negative, even self-destructive, side effects have been largely diminished by state intervention through regulation, credit-budget-tax policies, price supports, and social welfare programs....

NATURE OF THE MARKET

... The market as we know it today is the historically specific product of industrial capitalism and can only be understood if perceived as such....

The Market is, essentially, an economic decision-making process that determines the allocation of society's resources by deciding what and how much is produced and how and to whom it is distributed. Those who participate in this process are buyers and sellers who "meet" in the "marketplace," though they are not only individuals, since buyers and sellers also include businesses of all sizes, farmers and professionals as groups, governments at all levels.

As an alternative to the Market, society's resources can also be directly allocated by political decisions of government (that is, by "command"). Government can also act deliberately to influence indirectly how the Market functions indirectly. Those who determine a government's economic role are citizens, governing officials, and administrators (including, sometimes, planners, though every governmental impact upon the economy should not be called "planning" and, in the United States, it almost never is that). Within capitalist economies, the purpose of governmental intervention in the Market is twofold: (1) to facilitate the functioning of the Market by protecting it from its shortcomings, including tendencies toward self-destructiveness; (2) to supplement the Market by providing those goods and services that the Market has no incentive to supply because they do not entail a profit (public schools, social welfare, low-cost housing, infrastructure, and so on).

The extent to which government should influence the economy is an issue that has been fought over for a very long time. Charles E. Lindblom begins his definitive *Politics and Markets* by observing that "the greatest distinction between one government and another is in the degree to which market replaces government or government replaces market. Both Adam Smith and Karl Marx knew this."

* * *

The word "degree" is used by Lindblom deliberately, for neither the market nor government replaces the other completely. Thus all economies are a mix of the Market and political decision making. Even the totally mad Stalinist effort to eliminate the Market in Soviet-type societies fell short of complete success, for these societies had to tolerate market operations in corners of the economy, ei-

ther by compromise, as in permitted sales from garden plots of collective farmers and *kolkhoz* "surplus" production, or through black market sales of scarce commodities, tolerated because they were considered helpful to the economy.

Another variant of madness, though largely rhetorical, is the Thatcherite and Reaganite pronouncements about getting government out of the economy and "letting the market decide." After a decade of such huffing and puffing, the role of government vis-à-vis the economy, both in Great Britain and in the United States, remains essentially unchanged, some privatizations notwithstanding....

* * *

A final aspect of the Market's historical context is the largely forgotten role played by the state in getting market-based economies off the ground in various parts of the world. Japan, Prussia, and Czarist Russia are outstanding examples of the state's role in "jump starting" both capitalist production and market relations through generous credit, subsidies, enactment of special rights, licenses, and so on. Government construction of infrastructure often played a key role.

What we can conclude is that the prevailing view that attributes the material progress of human societies during the last century or two *solely* to the Market is fallacious, because the Market's contribution cannot be sufficiently separated from that of the Industrial Revolution, the capitalist mode of production, or the nourishing role of the state. To the extent that references to the Market are euphemistic in order to advocate capitalism under another name, there is an implied admission that the market cannot be separated from capitalism, that is, private property in the means of production, labor as a commodity, unearned income, accumulation, and so forth. But insofar as there now exists an effort to utilize the Market's virtues, while straining out its vices, in order to serve the common welfare, an assessment of its feasibility cannot be made until we have clearer insights into how it would resolve a number of contradictions that seem to make this objective unworkable.

THE MARKET'S SIDE EFFECTS AND POLITICAL REMEDIES

The following descriptions of the Market's side effects are valid, on the whole, though in some cases not entirely separable from other causes. The rationale of the Market is competition—for survival and gain. It pits each against all in social Darwinian "survival of the fittest": worker against worker and entrepreneur against entrepreneur, capital against labor and producer against consumer. The weak are eliminated and the strong survive, resulting in the trend toward concentration and monopolies. Businesses live by the "bottom line," with an incentive toward price gouging, adulteration, misrepresentation, environmental degradation. Product or service promotion caters to every human weakness. Advertising seduces consumers to develop endless wants. The central effect is to subvert human solidarity and civic responsibility.

The multitudinous buy/sell decisions that drive the market process are made in total ignorance of their collective impact, as expressed in Adam Smith's now hoary "unseen hand." Its social impact causes society to "fly blind," as when millions of individually bought automobiles collectively spell traffic gridlock and death-dealing air pollution. Government seeks to overcome these destructive results by regulating the manufacture of automobiles and gasoline. If this fails, as is likely, government will have to turn to long-range planning of alternate transportation, replacing private automobile trips with public conveyances. This will be a political decision to allocate resources from the private sector's automobile solution to the public sector's rail and bus solution. This is only one example of the choices between decisions by the Market and by the political process (made with or without planning).

The nineteenth-century laissez-faire market process, almost total economic determination by consumer demand, eventually proved unworkable. This was capitalism as Karl Marx knew it, and unworkable as he had predicted. During the course of the twentieth century, laissez-faire gave way to large-scale political intervention, resulting in state-guided and, increasingly, state-managed capitalism, with the state's control of money flow through central banks (Federal Reserve in the United States), credit control, tariffs and quotas, subsidies, tax policy, industrial and agricultural loans, price supports, wages policy, loan guarantees, savings incentives, marketing assistance, stockpiling, and various regulatory controls. This continuing transformation of market-based economies, which has come to be known as the Keynesian Revolution, is likely to be viewed by historians as of greater significance than the Soviet Revolution.

* * *

The proportions of market vs. political decision making in economic affairs does not necessarily reflect the proportions of private vs. state ownership of the economy. State-owned industries in countries such as Austria, Italy, and France, where they form a high proportion of the economy, are largely indistinguishable from the private sector in operating by the rules of the Market to produce in response to consumer demand. On the other hand, despite a relatively small nationalized sector, the state in Sweden is omnipresent in managing economic affairs. *The current widespread tilt toward privatization does not, therefore, diminish the trend toward an increased role of the state in economic affairs.*

The Market process demands that those who wish to participate pay admission. Those who cannot afford to get in—or who drop out—fall through the cracks; if lucky, into a social safety net. As the burden increased beyond private charities' resources, government was forced to assume it and the twentieth century's "welfare state" emerged. Its "transfer" programs of public goods and services exist outside the Market for those who cannot make it within.

The insecurity of various categories of entrepreneurs (such as farmers, oil drillers, ship owners, owners of small businesses, bank depositors), caused by the instability and unpredictability of the market process, led these entrepreneurs to use their political power to seek public assistance through subsidies, loans, insurance, "bailouts," and so forth, eventually becoming entitlements. The latter, together with welfare state transfer payments, proliferated and grew enormously, in part because they reflected the universal transition within affluent societies from satisfying needs to meeting wants. Adding these to the cost of traditional categories of public goods and services (such as national defense, public schools, parks, libraries, streets and roads) resulted in ballooning governmental budgets and the diversion

through taxation of increasing proportions of the GNPs of industrial nations to their public sectors.

This had the effect of cutting into the availability of accumulated capital for investment in direct wealth-producing enterprise. Government response differed sharply, depending upon whether it followed a national economic policy or relied upon the Market. Sweden, an example of the former, tapped its Supplementary Pension Program to create the so-called fourth fund for targeted industrial investment, creating and sustaining employment that yielded a flow of payroll deductions back into the fund. The United States, on the other hand, permitted Market forces to drive up interest rates, bringing an inflow of foreign capital and an outflow of dividends and interest.

But, regardless of how the problem is managed, there are political limits to the diversion of funds from the private sector to the public sector via taxation. This can be seen in the "tax revolts" in Europe and the United States in the last two decades, which also had repercussions in the Scandinavian countries, including Sweden. This diversion also triggered the resurgence of laissez-faire ideology and right-wing politics.

Even for those countries in which the Market successfully accumulates the "wealth of nations," there results a lopsided inequality of distribution within the population, resulting in recurring economic instability and social confrontation. (Brazil, a country with the eighth largest Market-based economy in the world, leads all others in polarization between rich and poor.) The Market process generates cyclical and chronic unemployment, bankruptcies, mass layoffs, over- and underproduction, strikes and lockouts, and many other kinds of economic warfare and social tension. There is good reason to believe that the sharp shift in income from earned to unearned during the 1980s will be reflected in rising class conflict in the 1990s.

The Market is not a surefire prescription for the "wealth of nations" because its acclaimed incentives, acting as a spur to economic development, are also historically specific. Just because eighteenth-century England used the Market process to turn itself into a "nation of shopkeepers" and nineteenth-century England used it to lead the way in the Industrial Revolution to become the "world's workshop," is no assurance that, at any other time in history, people of any other culture and level of development can similarly use the Market to the same end—notwithstanding the examples of Western Europe, the United States, Canada, and Japan. (South Korea and Taiwan, judged by their per capita incomes, have not yet made it.)

Internationally, the Market has resulted in hierarchical ranking of nations by wealth, grouping a fortunate few as the rich nations and the rest as relatively or absolutely poor. Market-process relations between the industrially developed nations and the rest take the form of the developed responding to the consumer-driven demands of the underdeveloped for investments, loans, goods, and services, thereby aggravating their dependency, and frustrating their ability to accumulate enough capital to significantly improve their productivity (Argentina, Brazil, Mexico, Egypt, India, to name some).

* * *

In summarizing the Market's negative side effects we have noted that it flies blindly; that its growth becomes destructive of communitarian values and institutions and of the natural environment; that its "work ethic" becomes exploitation, even of children (child labor is again on the rise in the United States according to the Department of Labor); that it reduces the cost of production but also triggers inflation; that it produces a cornucopia of goods but also mountains of waste; that its pharmaceutical research lengthens lifespans, but its chemicals (pesticides and herbicides) shorten them; that it makes feverish use of humankind's growing power over nature, born of scientific and technological progress, but puts profits above ecology and market share above the need to conserve natural resources; that it provides conveniences, comforts, and luxuries for an increasing number but shows no ability to close the widening gap between haves and have nots, neither within nor between nations. But, above all, the Market, despite Keynesianism, operates in cycles of boom and bust, victimizing businesses, large and small, farmers, professionals, and wage workers. Left to its own devices, the Market is inherently self-destructive.

Though the Market's negative side effects can be countered through government intervention and largely have been, such countering tends to be ameliorative rather than curative, and often raises new problems requiring additional intervention, thus reinforcing the overall tendency for the state to backstop the Market. But, despite this, Market economies still move blindly, though increasingly within broad channels marked out by government. The Market economy still overheats and runs out of fuel, but government now acts to cool it and then to fuel it (and even attempts to "fine tune" it). Will it prove a viable arrangement in the long term for government to treat the Market as if it were an elemental force of nature?

The people seem to want the benefits of the Market, but look to government to minimize the dreadful side effects that come with it. But one person's "dreadful side effects" are another person's sweet accumulation of capital. Translated into social relations, this conflict of interests expresses itself as interest-group confrontations and social-class struggles. And as decision making in economic affairs continues to shift from the Market to the political process, an ever fiercer political resistance is mounted by the interest groups and classes whose power is far greater and more direct in the Market than in the political arena—for instance, the resurgence of the new right in waging ideological and political warfare on behalf of laissez-faire policies.

THE MARKET'S THRUST VS. SOCIETAL GUIDANCE

Understanding the direction in which the Market is likely to move in the next few decades is critically important to an assessment of its capacity to accommodate solutions for outstanding problems. In the past, especially since World War II, the Market's contribution to easing the great problems of civilization has been in the form of economic growth. The nature of the problems that now loom, however, makes them less subject to solution through economic growth. The rising tide that once raised all boats now leaves many stuck on muddy bottoms.

Market-based growth has not demonstrated an ability to reduce the glaring inequality in living standards and in educational/cultural levels within and between nations. In the United States

during the last decade the gap between the bottom and the top of the income quintiles has widened. And growth solutions now generate new problems: the degradation of the natural environment on earth and in space; the exhaustion of natural resources; the emergence of *social* limits to growth, caused by the level at which acquisition of goods, services, and facilities by enough people spoils the advantages of possessing them; the puzzle of insatiable wants after basic needs have been satisfied (when is enough enough?). There are also the growth of private affluence and public squalor; an individualistic society's reluctance to resort to collective solutions (national health care) before first going through the agony of postponing the inevitable, and other looming problems sensed but seemingly too elusively complex to articulate. These problems join a long list of old problems that go unsolved to become a leaden weight on progress.

* * *

Is there reason to believe that the Market's failure to cope with these problems will (or can) be remedied in the future? Is there anything in the nature and function of the Market that is likely to redirect its performance to be able to solve these problems? Are any of its negative side effects going to be eliminated, except insofar as governmentally applied correctives can curb them without altering the overall thrust of the Market? Left to its own devices, the Market's current trends are likely to expand and exacerbate problems. Are any countervailing forces in view? Yes.

One is the sharpening competition in the world market. The latter is being badly misread. True, a coded message on a computer or fax machine can transfer billions of dollars overseas at the end of the business day and retrieve it first thing in the morning—with earnings added. True, multinationals no longer fly a single flag. But national interests are as sharply defined as ever. And waging war with economic weapons has not reduced competitiveness and aggressiveness. The competitors are dividing into several major blocs: North America (the United States plus Canada and Mexico), Japan (plus the Asian rim countries) and a united Europe. The goal: market share. As Japan has shown (and also Europe to a lesser extent), this warfare requires maximum mobilization of economic resources: capital, management, knowledge-industry, and labor. Japan has shown that the way to bring these together is by making them all part of the corporate state. The power of Japan, Inc. is recognized in all American boardrooms, though a much smaller nation, Sweden, has also used the corporate strategy brilliantly. The striking similarity of Japanese and Swedish economic strategies, though for different social ends, is largely overlooked because the former is dominated by corporations and the latter by organized labor acting through the Social Democratic party.

The corporate state strategy has anti-market overtones. Rather than letting the market decide, it operates through strategic planning and a national industrial (investment) policy. If global market share is the goal, the nation's consumers had better not be permitted to decide on the allocation of resources. Laissez-faire America illustrates why not. The consumers opt for second homes, third cars, snowmobiles, Jacuzzis, and Torneau watches, thereby short-changing education at all levels, skill retraining of the labor force, housing, and health care—all essential ingredients in mobilizing resources to fight for market share.

The last thing any nation needs or will ever want after the debacle of the Stalinist model is an administrative-command economy (misnamed "planning"). Let the Market process determine the number, style, size, and color of shoes. And similarly for other basic needs and reasonable wants. But the nation also has collective needs, and the polity should determine the allocation of resources to supply them. Because this cannot be determined by the blind outcomes of the Market, the latter must be subordinated to strategically planned priorities designed to serve an overriding common purpose.

If coping with the major problems facing humankind in both its social and natural environments requires societal guidance, it necessitates setting goals and choosing strategies to achieve them; in short, strategic planning. This calls for conscious, deliberate, and coordinated measures to mobilize a nation's resources. The American people with its Market-instilled value system is decidedly averse to this (except in time of war, when by political decision a goal-oriented government controlled wages, employment, prices, profits, manufacturing, and construction).

The twenty-first is not likely to be an American Century. Clinging to the Market, the negation of societal guidance, we might not even come in second. More likely we will be third, after a united Europe and an Asian-rim dominant Japan operating with strategic planning. Americans are more likely to be content with nursery reveries of

To market, to market, to buy a fat pig,
Home again, home again, to dance a fast jig.

NO
Milton and Rose Friedman

FREE TO CHOOSE

THE POWER OF THE MARKET

The Role of Prices

The key insight of Adam Smith's *Wealth of Nations* is misleadingly simple: if an exchange between two parties is voluntary, it will not take place unless both believe they will benefit from it. Most economic fallacies derive from the neglect of this simple insight, from the tendency to assume that there is a fixed pie, that one party can gain only at the expense of another.

This key insight is obvious for a simple exchange between two individuals. It is far more difficult to understand how it can enable people living all over the world to cooperate to promote their separate interests.

The price system is the mechanism that performs this task without central direction, without requiring people to speak to one another or to like one another. When you buy your pencil or your daily bread, you don't know whether the pencil was made or the wheat was grown by a white man or a black man, by a Chinese or an Indian. As a result, the price system enables people to cooperate peacefully in one phase of their life while each one goes about his own business in respect of everything else.

Adam Smith's flash of genius was his recognition that the prices that emerged from voluntary transactions between buyers and sellers—for short, in a free market—could coordinate the activity of millions of people, each seeking his own interest, in such a way as to make everyone better off. It was a startling idea then, and it remains one today, that economic order can emerge as the unintended consequence of the actions of many people, each seeking his own interest.

The price system works so well, so efficiently, that we are not aware of it most of the time. We never realize how well it functions until it is prevented from functioning, and even then we seldom recognize the source of the trouble.

The long gasoline lines that suddenly emerged in 1974 after the OPEC oil embargo, and again in the spring and summer of 1979 after the revolution

From Milton and Rose Friedman, *Free to Choose: A Personal Statement* (Harcourt Brace Jovanovich, 1980). Copyright © 1979, 1980 by Milton Friedman and Rose D. Friedman. Reprinted by permission of Harcourt Brace and Company. Notes omitted.

in Iran, are a striking recent example. On both occasions there was a sharp disturbance in the supply of crude oil from abroad. But that did not lead to gasoline lines in Germany or Japan, which are wholly dependent on imported oil. It led to long gasoline lines in the United States, even though we produce much of our own oil, for one reason and one reason only: because legislation, administered by a government agency, did not permit the price system to function. Prices in some areas were kept by command below the level that would have equated the amount of gasoline available at the gas stations to the amount consumers wanted to buy at that price. Supplies were allocated to different areas of the country by command, rather than in response to the pressures of demand as reflected in price. The result was surpluses in some areas and shortages plus long gasoline lines in others. The smooth operation of the price system—which for many decades had assured every consumer that he could buy gasoline at any of a large number of service stations at his convenience and with a minimal wait—was replaced by bureaucratic improvisation....

The Role of Government

Where does government enter into the picture?...

[W]hat role should be assigned to government?

It is not easy to improve on the answer that Adam Smith gave to this question two hundred years ago:

> ... According to the system of natural liberty, the sovereign has only three duties to attend to; three duties of great importance, indeed, but plain and intelligible to common understandings: first, the duty of protecting the society from the violence

and invasion of other independent societies; secondly, the duty of protecting, as far as possible, every member of the society from the injustice or oppression of every other member of it, or the duty of establishing an exact administration of justice; and thirdly, the duty of erecting and maintaining certain public works and certain public institutions, which it can never be for the interest of any individual, or small number of individuals, to erect and maintain; because the profit could never repay the expence to any individual or small number of individuals, though it may frequently do much more than repay it to a great society.

... A fourth duty of government that Adam Smith did not explicitly mention is the duty to protect members of the community who cannot be regarded as "responsible" individuals. Like Adam Smith's third duty, this one, too, is susceptible of great abuse. Yet it cannot be avoided....

Adam Smith's three duties, or our four duties of government, are indeed "of great importance," but they are far less "plain and intelligible to common understandings" than he supposed. Though we cannot decide the desirability or undesirability of any actual or proposed government intervention by mechanical reference to one or another of them, they provide a set of principles that we can use in casting up a balance sheet of pros and cons. Even on the loosest interpretation, they rule out much existing government intervention—all those "systems either of preference or of restraint" that Adam Smith fought against, that were subsequently destroyed, but have since reappeared in the form of today's tariffs, governmentally fixed prices and wages, restrictions on entry into various occupations, and numerous other departures from his "simple system of natural liberty." ...

CRADLE TO GRAVE

... At the end of the war [World War II] it looked as if central economic planning was the wave of the future. That outcome was passionately welcomed by some who saw it as the dawn of a world of plenty shared equally. It was just as passionately feared by others, including us, who saw it as a turn to tyranny and misery. So far, neither the hopes of the one nor the fears of the other have been realized.

Government has expanded greatly. However, that expansion has not taken the form of detailed central economic planning accompanied by ever widening nationalization of industry, finance, and commerce, as so many of us feared it would. Experience put an end to detailed economic planning, partly because it was not successful in achieving the announced objectives, but also because it conflicted with freedom....

The failure of planning and nationalization has not eliminated pressure for an ever bigger government. It has simply altered its direction. The expansion of government now takes the form of welfare programs and of regulatory activities. As W. Allen Wallis put it in a somewhat different context, socialism, "intellectually bankrupt after more than a century of seeing one after another of its arguments for socializing the *means* of production demolished—now seeks to socialize the *results* of production."

In the welfare area the change of direction has led to an explosion in recent decades, especially after President Lyndon Johnson declared a "War on Poverty" in 1964. New Deal programs of Social Security, unemployment insurance, and direct relief were all expanded to cover new groups; payments were increased; and Medicare, Medicaid, food stamps, and numerous other programs were added. Public housing and urban renewal programs were enlarged. By now there are literally hundreds of government welfare and income transfer programs. The Department of Health, Education and Welfare, established in 1953 to consolidate the scattered welfare programs, began with a budget of $2 billion, less than 5 percent of expenditures on national defense. Twenty-five years later, in 1978, its budget was $160 billion, one and a half times as much as total spending on the army, the navy, and the air force. It had the third largest budget in the world, exceeded only by the entire budget of the U.S. government and of the Soviet Union....

No one can dispute two superficially contradictory phenomena: widespread dissatisfaction with the results of this explosion in welfare activities; continued pressure for further expansion.

The objectives have all been noble; the results, disappointing. Social Security expenditures have skyrocketed, and the system is in deep financial trouble. Public housing and urban renewal programs have subtracted from rather than added to the housing available to the poor. Public assistance rolls mount despite growing employment. By general agreement, the welfare program is a "mess" saturated with fraud and corruption. As government has paid a larger share of the nation's medical bills, both patients and physicians complain of rocketing costs and of the increasing impersonality of medicine. In education, student performance has dropped as federal intervention has expanded....

The repeated failure of well-intentioned programs is not an accident. It is not simply the result of mistakes of execution. The failure is deeply rooted in the use of bad means to achieve good objectives.

Despite the failure of these programs, the pressure to expand them grows. Failures are attributed to the miserliness of Congress in appropriating funds, and so are met with a cry for still bigger programs. Special interests that benefit from specific programs press for their expansion—foremost among them the massive bureaucracy spawned by the programs....

CREATED EQUAL

Capitalism and Equality
Everywhere in the world there are gross inequities of income and wealth. They offend most of us. Few can fail to be moved by the contrast between the luxury enjoyed by some and the grinding poverty suffered by others.

In the past century a myth has grown up that free market capitalism—equality of opportunity as we have interpreted that term—increases such inequalities, that it is a system under which the rich exploit the poor.

Nothing could be further from the truth. Wherever the free market has been permitted to operate, wherever anything approaching equality of opportunity has existed, the ordinary man has been able to attain levels of living never dreamed of before. Nowhere is the gap between rich and poor wider, nowhere are the rich richer and the poor poorer, than in those societies that do not permit the free market to operate. That is true of feudal societies like medieval Europe, India before independence, and much of modern South America, where inherited status determines position. It is equally true of centrally planned societies, like Russia or China or India since independence, where access to government determines position. It is true even where central planning was introduced, as in all three of these countries, in the name of equality....

WHO PROTECTS THE CONSUMER?

... The pace of intervention quickened greatly after the New Deal—half of the thirty-two agencies in existence in 1966 were created after FDR's election in 1932. Yet intervention remained fairly moderate and continued in the single-industry mold. The *Federal Register*, established in 1936 to record all the regulations, hearings, and other matters connected with the regulatory agencies, grew, at first rather slowly, then more rapidly. Three volumes, containing 2,599 pages and taking six inches of shelf space, sufficed for 1936; twelve volumes, containing 10,528 pages and taking twenty-six inches of shelf space, for 1956; and thirteen volumes, containing 16,850 pages and taking thirty-six inches of shelf space, for 1966.

Then a veritable explosion in government regulatory activity occurred. No fewer than twenty-one new agencies were established in the next decade. Instead of being concerned with specific industries, they covered the waterfront: the environment, the production and distribution of energy, product safety, occupational safety, and so on. In addition to concern with the consumer's pocketbook, with protecting him from exploitation by sellers, recent agencies are primarily concerned with things like the consumer's safety and well-being, with protecting him not only from sellers but also from himself.

Government expenditures on both older and newer agencies skyrocketed—from less than $1 billion in 1970 to roughly $5 billion estimated for 1979. Prices in general roughly doubled, but these expenditures more than quintupled. The number of government bureaucrats employed in regulatory activities tripled, going from 28,000 in 1970 to 81,000 in 1979; the number of pages in the *Federal Register*, from 17,660 in 1970 to 36,487 in 1978, taking 127 inches of shelf space—a veritable ten-foot shelf....

This revolution in the role of government has been accompanied, and largely produced, by an achievement in public persuasion that must have few rivals. Ask yourself what products are currently least satisfactory and have shown the least improvement over time. Postal service, elementary and secondary schooling, railroad passenger transport would surely be high on the list. Ask yourself which products are most satisfactory and have improved the most. Household appliances, television and radio sets, hi-fi equipment, computers, and, we would add, supermarkets and shopping centers would surely come high on that list.

The shoddy products are all produced by government or government-regulated industries. The outstanding products are all produced by private enterprise with little or no government involvement. Yet the public—or a large part of it—has been persuaded that private enterprises produce shoddy products, that we need ever vigilant government employees to keep business from foisting off unsafe, meretricious products at outrageous prices on ignorant, unsuspecting, vulnerable customers. That public relations campaign has succeeded so well that we are in the process of turning over to the kind of people who bring us our postal service the far more critical task of producing and distributing energy....

Government intervention in the marketplace is subject to laws of its own, not legislated laws, but scientific laws. It obeys forces and goes in directions that may have little relationship to the intentions or desires of its initiators or supporters. We have already examined this process in connection with welfare activity. It is present equally when government intervenes in the marketplace, whether to protect consumers against high prices or shoddy goods, to promote their safety, or to preserve the environment. Every act of intervention establishes positions of power. How that power will be used and for what purposes depends far more on the people who are in the best position to get control of that power and what their purposes are than on the aims and objectives of the initial sponsors of the intervention....

Environment

The environmental movement is responsible for one of the most rapidly growing areas of federal intervention. The Environmental Protection Agency, established in 1970 "to protect and enhance the physical environment," has been granted increasing power and authority. Its budget has multiplied sevenfold from 1970 to 1978 and is now more than half a billion dollars. It has a staff of about 7,000. It has imposed costs on industry and local and state governments to meet its standards that total in the tens of billions of dollars a year. Something between a tenth and a quarter of total net investment in new capital equipment by business now goes for antipollution purposes. And this does not count the costs of requirements imposed by other agencies, such as those designed to control emissions of motor vehicles, or the costs of land-use planning or wilderness preservation or a host of other federal, state, and local government activities undertaken in the name of protecting the environment.

The preservation of the environment and the avoidance of undue pollution are real problems and they are problems concerning which the government has an important role to play. When all the costs and benefits of any action, and the people hurt or benefited, are readily identifiable, the market provides an excellent means for assuring that only those actions are undertaken for which the benefits exceed the costs for all participants. But when the costs and benefits or the people affected cannot be identified, there is a market failure. . . .

Government is one means through which we can try to compensate for "market failure," try to use our resources more effectively to produce the amount of clean air, water, and land that we are willing to pay for. Unfortunately, the very factors that produce the market failure also make it difficult for government to achieve a satisfactory solution. Generally, it is no easier for government to identify the specific persons who are hurt and benefited than for market participants, no easier for government to assess the amount of harm or benefit to each. Attempts to use government to correct market failure have often simply substituted government failure for market failure.

Public discussion of the environmental issue is frequently characterized more by emotion than reason. Much of it proceeds as if the issue is pollution versus no pollution, as if it were desirable and possible to have a world without pollution. That is clearly nonsense. No one who contemplates the problem seriously will regard zero pollution as either a desirable or a possible state of affairs. We could have zero pollution from automobiles, for example, by simply abolishing all automobiles. That would also make the kind of agricultural and industrial productivity we now enjoy impossible, and so condemn most of us to a drastically lower standard of living, perhaps many even to death. One source of atmospheric pollution is the carbon dioxide that we all exhale. We could stop that very simply. But the cost would clearly exceed the gain.

It costs something to have clean air, just as it costs something to have other good things we want. Our resources are limited and we must weigh the gains from reducing pollution against the costs. Moreover, "pollution" is not an objective phenomenon. One person's pollution may be another's pleasure. To some of us rock music is noise pollution; to others of us it is pleasure.

The real problem is not "eliminating pollution," but trying to establish arrangements that will yield the "right" amount of pollution: an amount such that the gain from reducing pollution a bit more just balances the sacrifice of the other good things—houses, shoes, coats, and so on—that would have to be given up in order to reduce the pollution. If we go farther than that, we sacrifice more than we gain. . . .

The Market
Perfection is not of this world. There will always be shoddy products, quacks, con

artists. But on the whole, market competition, when it is permitted to work, protects the consumer better than do the alternative government mechanisms that have been increasingly superimposed on the market.

As Adam Smith said..., competition does not protect the consumer because businessmen are more soft-hearted than the bureaucrats or because they are more altruistic or generous, or even because they are more competent, but only because it is in the self-interest of the businessman to serve the consumer.

If one storekeeper offers you goods of lower quality or of higher price than another, you're not going to continue to patronize his store. If he buys goods to sell that don't serve your needs, you're not going to buy them. The merchants therefore search out all over the world the products that might meet your needs and might appeal to you. And they stand back of them because if they don't, they're going to go out of business. When you enter a store, no one forces you to buy. You are free to do so or go elsewhere. That is the basic difference between the market and a political agency. You are free to choose. There is no policeman to take the money out of your pocket to pay for something you do not want or to make you do something you do not want to do.

But, the advocate of government regulation will say, suppose the FDA weren't there, what would prevent business from distributing adulterated or dangerous products? It would be a very expensive thing to do.... It is very poor business practice—not a way to develop a loyal and faithful clientele. Of course, mistakes and accidents occur—but... government regulation doesn't prevent them. The difference is that a private firm that makes a serious blunder may go out of business.

A government agency is likely to get a bigger budget.

Cases will arise where adverse effects develop that could not have been foreseen—but government has no better means of predicting such developments than private enterprise. The only way to prevent all such developments would be to stop progress, which would also eliminate the possibility of unforeseen favorable developments....

What about the danger of monopoly that led to the antitrust laws? That is a real danger. The most effective way to counter it is not through a bigger antitrust division at the Department of Justice or a larger budget for the Federal Trade Commission, but through removing existing barriers to international trade. That would permit competition from all over the world to be even more effective than it is now in undermining monopoly at home. Freddie Laker of Britain needed no help from the Department of Justice to crack the airline cartel. Japanese and German automobile manufacturers forced American manufacturers to introduce smaller cars.

The great danger to the consumer is monopoly—whether private or governmental. His most effective protection is free competition at home and free trade throughout the world. The consumer is protected from being exploited by one seller by the existence of another seller from whom he can buy and who is eager to sell to him. Alternative sources of supply protect the consumer far more effectively than all the Ralph Naders of the world.

Conclusion

... [T]he reaction of the public to the more extreme attempts to control our behavior—to the requirement of an interlock system on automobiles or the proposed ban of saccharin—is ample evidence that we want no part of it. Insofar as the government has information not generally available about the merits or demerits of the items we ingest or the activities we engage in, let it give us the information. But let it leave us free to choose what chances we want to take with our own lives.

POSTSCRIPT

Should Government Intervene in a Capitalist Economy?

Erber concedes that the market should not be abolished. He writes that a "body of evidence... links the market with economic growth, increased productivity, and improved living standards," and that this linkage "cannot be contested." Nevertheless, he calls for an activist government to subordinate the market to "planned priorities designed to serve an overriding common purpose." The Friedmans believe that such subordination can only destroy the market. The question, then, is whether or not we can successfully graft the market's "invisible hand" to the arm of the state. Would the graft take? Has the experiment perhaps already proven successful in post–New Deal America? Or is the American government in the process of destroying what gave the nation its growth, prosperity, and living standards? It is possible that in a few years these questions will no longer be debatable.

Erber calls the market a "blind" force. The Friedmans seem to agree that the market in itself is amoral, though they feel that it produces good results. But philosopher Michael Novak goes further, contending that the ethic of capitalism transcends mere money-making and is (or can be made) compatible with Judeo-Christian morality. See *The Spirit of Democratic Capitalism* (Madison Books, 1991) and *The Catholic Ethic and the Spirit of Capitalism* (Free Press, 1993). No such claim is made by the Friedmans in *Free to Choose* or in Milton Friedman's earlier *Capitalism and Freedom* (University of Chicago Press, 1962), which portrays capitalism as supportive of democracy and freedom. Another broad-based defense of capitalism is Peter L. Berger's *The Capitalist Revolution: Fifty Propositions About Prosperity, Equality and Liberty* (Basic Books, 1988). For an attack on capitalism, see Victor Perlo, *Superprofits and Crisis: Modern U.S. Capitalism* (International Publishers, 1988). For a mixed view of capitalism, see Charles Wolf, Jr., *Markets or Governments: Choosing Between Imperfect Alternatives* (MIT Press, 1993). Andrew Shonfield's *In Defense of the Mixed Economy* (Oxford University Press, 1984) takes a similar position to Erber and commends Japan for steering the right course between *laissez-faire* and socialism. According to Shonfield, the latter system still has its proponents. J. Philip Wogaman argues that socialism is still applicable today, in "Socialism's Obituary Is Premature," *The Christian Century* (May 30–June 6, 1990), as does Socialist Party co-chair David McReynolds in the April 1993 issue of *The Progressive*. This view is contested by L. A. Kauffman in the same issue.

ISSUE 14

Does Welfare Do More Harm Than Good?

YES: Murray Weidenbaum, from "Beyond Handouts," *Across the Board* (April 1991)

NO: Theodore R. Marmor, Jerry L. Mashaw, and Philip L. Harvey, from *America's Misunderstood Welfare State: Persistent Myths, Enduring Realities* (Basic Books, 1990)

ISSUE SUMMARY

YES: Economist Murray Weidenbaum argues that the extensive system of welfare set up during the 1960s and early 1970s has mired the poor in dependency, making their condition worse, not better.

NO: Social analysts Theodore R. Marmor, Jerry L. Mashaw, and Philip L. Harvey contend that the American welfare state has been widely misunderstood by its critics and that conservative "reforms" will only increase the misery of the poor.

Long before Ronald Reagan's campaign for the presidency in 1980, the welfare problem had become a national issue. As far back as the Nixon administration, plans had been made to reform the system by various means, including the institution of modest cash payments based upon a negative income tax in place of the crazy quilt pattern of services, commodities, checks, and in-kind payments provided by the existing welfare system. The Carter administration also tried to interest Congress in a reform plan that would simplify, though probably not reduce, welfare.

Currently, there is a backlash against welfare recipients, often voiced in mean-spirited jibes such as "Make the loafers work" and "I'm tired of paying them to breed." Such slogans ignore the fact that most people on welfare are not professional loafers but women with dependent children or old or disabled persons. Petty fraud may be common, but "welfare queens" who cheat the system for spectacular sums are extremely rare. The overwhelming majority of people on welfare are those whose condition would become desperate if payments were cut off. Finally, to reassure those who worry that women on welfare commonly bear children in order to increase their benefits, there is no conclusive evidence that child support payments have anything to do with conception; the costs of raising children far exceed the payments.

This does not mean that all objections to welfare can be dismissed. There does seem to be evidence that welfare in some cases reduces work incentives and increases the likelihood of family breakups. Concern about the problem of incentives is being addressed by recent proposed changes in welfare programs that limit the amount of time one can be on welfare, provide training, or require welfare recipients to work. As a result, the issue of incentives might be less of a problem in the future.

What should be done about welfare? Broadly speaking, the suggestions fall into three categories: (1) Some say to *trim* the program. (2) Others advocate *monitoring* it carefully to make sure that the truly needy are receiving a fair share of it and that work incentives are not lost. (3) Others favor outright *abolition* of welfare, except for the aged and the physically handicapped.

The *trim* approach was a central tenet in the philosophy of the Reagan administration. When Reagan first campaigned for the presidency in 1980, he promised to "get government off our backs." His contention was that government welfare programs tend to stifle initiative, depress the economy, and do the poor more harm than good. After eight years in office, Reagan's conservative critics claimed that he had not really fulfilled his promises to trim welfare; his liberal critics claimed that he had indeed carried out his promises, albeit with disastrous results.

The radical approach of abolishing welfare is advocated by writer Charles Murray in his 1984 book *Losing Ground,* which was extremely influential. Conservatives hailed it as a masterful critique, and even writers on the Left paid it a kind of backhanded homage by refuting it at length. In the following selections, Murray Weidenbaum takes Murray's side in denouncing the welfare state. He argues that it has failed to achieve its promised results, that it reduces people's willingness to work, that it encourages irresponsible behavior regarding pregnancy and abandoning children, and that it hinders the poor from taking the steps—mainly getting training, education, and work—to pull themselves out of poverty. Theodore R. Marmor, Jerry L. Mashaw, and Philip L. Harvey counter common criticisms of welfare, particularly Murray's, and they argue that there is no relation between welfare and illegitimacy or labor force participation. They maintain that we should be proud of welfare's achievements.

YES

Murray Weidenbaum

BEYOND HANDOUTS

In 1935, President Franklin D. Roosevelt declared: "I can now see the end of public assistance in America." FDR's forecast did not come true despite the expenditure of what were then unparalleled amounts of Federal funds for a variety of programs to benefit the poor. The Administrations of Harry S. Truman and John F. Kennedy experienced the same frustration.

In 1964, President Lyndon B. Johnson announced: "The days of the dole in our country are numbered." Both the number of Americans in poverty and the size of the anti-poverty efforts expanded under the four Administrations that followed. Federal spending designed to achieve the Roosevelt-Johnson goal has totaled hundreds of billions of dollars during this period. Over the past 25 years, Federal spending for income support to individuals multiplied more than five times in constant dollars. Any way you measure it, the outlay of public funds to end poverty has been expanding faster than inflation and population combined or the number of poor people.

It is inaccurate for Americans to castigate themselves as a heartless society. In recent Presidential Administrations—whether that of Jimmy Carter or Ronald Reagan—a far larger share of the nation's resources has been devoted to social welfare programs than during the years when Roosevelt or Johnson served in the Oval Office. The problem is that these expensive efforts, while producing some gains, did not bring about the promised results.

There is virtually universal agreement in the United States that those who are physically or mentally unable to support themselves should be helped by society, and that such assistance should be provided in adequate amounts and with a minimum of hassle.

But over the years, a subtle yet profound broadening has occurred in the qualification for such aid. Low or no income has become the only basis necessary to qualify for the receipt of welfare, food stamps, and many other types of assistance. The governmental fiscal payments that the public earlier had referred to as "handouts," "charity," or the "dole" have become transformed into "transfer payments" and, more recently, "entitlements."

And what has been the effect of these entitlements? According to economic researchers, they reduce people's willingness to work. If that sounds too jarring, let me resort to economic jargon. Researchers support "significant net negative impacts on labor supply." As would be expected, different researchers report different numerical results, but the overall negative impact of welfare on work effort is clear.

The realization is growing that many long-term welfare "clients" are families or individuals beset by a multiplicity of personal and social problems that are deeply rooted and that do not yield to simple economic approaches such as payment of cash. You needn't be a right-wing zealot to conclude that there is a powerful connection between the health of the family as an institution and the depth and pervasiveness of the poverty problem: Less than one out of every 10 married-couple families is poor. Men living alone consistently have unemployment rates that are more than double those of family men. Nine out of every 10 families on welfare are headed by women.

* * *

Without judging the moral bases of alternative life styles, it is apparent that there are very substantial economic consequences of such actions as having a child out of wedlock, getting divorced, or living with a partner without getting married. Much of the cost of such actions is not borne by the individuals making these decisions, but by society as a whole.

A persuasive argument can be made that in the case of poverty—and in many other areas of human conduct—individuals no longer bear the full consequences of their own actions or inactions. In olden times "a man who deserted his children pretty much insured that they would starve, or near to it, if he was not brought back, and that he

would be horse-whipped if he were," said Senator Daniel Patrick Moynihan nearly two decades ago. "The poor in the United States today enjoy a quite unprecedented de facto freedom to abandon their children in the certain knowledge that society will care for them and, what is more, in a state such as New York, to care for them by quite decent standards."

The freedom Moynihan speaks about is in large part a result of a number of Supreme Court decisions that have invalidated efforts to focus welfare benefits on the family:

• In the Court's 1968 ruling on King v. Smith, an Alabama law denying welfare to households that have "substitute fathers" (adult males unrelated to the mother by blood or marriage) was struck down. The decision, in effect, made cohabitation profitable in most states.

• In its 1972 decision of Weber v. Aetna Casualty and Surety Company, the Court ruled that worker's compensation benefits cannot be limited to legitimate children.

• In New Jersey Welfare Rights Organization v. Cahill, the Court's 1973 decision forbid state government preference for marriage over cohabitation in welfare programs.

• In 1973 the Court ruling on USDA v. Moreno invalidated a provision of the food stamp program basing household eligibility on ties of blood, marriage, or adoption.

In dealing with the problem of poverty, we need to recognize that it is not primarily a matter of how much money the government should spend on poor people. The basic issue is how to deal with poverty's root causes. To begin with, we must recognize that growth of the nation's economy is a necessary but by no means sufficient condition for eliminating poverty. An expanding economy creates new employment opportunities and makes it politically feasible to fund anti-poverty programs. But economic growth alone cannot cure the problem of chronic poverty. Many of the long-term poor have developed attitudes toward work that make it difficult for them to escape poverty.

As *The New Consensus on Family and Welfare*, a recent report issued by a panel of both liberal and conservative analysts, concluded, climbing out of poverty is not something that government can do for an individual. Rather, eliminating poverty is something that the individual must undertake, albeit with some help from society. More often than not it takes just three things for a person to move out of poverty: completing high school; getting and staying married, even if not on the first try; and staying employed, even if at modest wages, such as the statutory minimum wage.

Very few Americans, of any race, who are heads of households are even near poverty—if they have a high school education. In 1986, less than 5 percent of black males and less than 10 percent of black females who met this requirement were in poverty. Of adult black males who were high school graduates in 1986, 86 percent had family incomes more than twice the poverty level.

Welfare (technically aid for dependent children) has come a long way from the original justification—to help widows or divorced women make the difficult transition to a new status. In 1937–38, the father had died or was incapacitated in 71 percent of the welfare cases. Since then, public assistance has in large measure become a program that finances out-of-wedlock births. In 1983, 46 percent of the children receiving welfare benefits were born out of wedlock.

Not only does welfare finance illegitimate births, it also seems to promote them. A *Los Angeles Times* poll in 1985 reported that 70 percent of poor women say it is "almost always" or "often" true that "poor young women have babies so they can collect welfare." Two thirds say that welfare "almost always" or "often" encourages fathers to avoid family responsibilities.

Several specific ways have been suggested to reinforce the responsibility of parents for the support of their children. They include allowing lawyers to accept child-support cases on a contingency fee basis, instituting mandatory paternity findings to identify fathers of out-of-wedlock children receiving welfare, holding all fathers accountable for meeting child-support obligations and making strong efforts to collect from them, requiring young mothers on welfare to complete high school and then seek work, and not paying welfare benefits to mothers under 18 who are living in "independent households."

The third key to solving the poverty problem is work experience itself. It is counterproductive to advise people on welfare to hold out for "good" jobs rather than to leave welfare status for "dead-end" work. It seems obvious that if you stay on welfare, you'll never get any work experience.

Often negative attitudes rather than insufficient work opportunities keep people unemployed. Studies show that poor people do not keep the jobs that they find simply because they cannot get to work on time, will not work a full work schedule, and will not pay attention on the job. When out of work, the typical inner-city youngster is more likely to spend his time "hanging out or watching TV" than engaging in activities likely to help in getting a job, says Richard Freeman, the Harvard economist.

It is becoming apparent that much of what used to be the conventional wisdom about a sound public-assistance program is no longer widely endorsed; particularly unpopular is the keeping of able-bodied people on welfare rolls for long periods of time. A new consensus is emerging in favor of encouraging welfare recipients to get steady work.

* * *

The Working Seminar on Family and American Welfare Policy, which brought together researchers from a variety of policy institutes such as Brookings Institution and the Heritage Foundation, concludes that it is essential that all able recipients of welfare either be working or be enrolled—for just a limited period of time, they stress—in education and training programs. Furthermore, the seminar members urge that "the over-riding emphasis" be placed on personal responsibility for finding jobs in the private sector rather than on government job-placement efforts. Work is seen as more than a way to cut welfare costs and promote self-sufficiency. It confers emotional and psychological benefits on the recipients and is an opportunity for them to join the nation's mainstream.

Many proponents of making welfare recipients work want *all* recipients to hold a job—even those with young children. This does not seem unreasonable. In 1986, 61 percent of all mothers worked (including 53 percent of mothers with children under the age of six), but only 9 percent of mothers on welfare.

When a woman on welfare takes a full-time job, the odds are overwhelming that she is lifting herself out of poverty. In every state, a woman holding a full-time job at the minimum wage—plus the remaining welfare benefits that she is still eligible for—provides enough income to lift the average welfare family (one mother and two children) above the poverty level. And few women working steadily earn only the minimum wage, even without a high school degree.

Most states have not given work requirements a high priority. Saying you tried to get a job by registering with the employment service is usually sufficient to meet the regulatory requirements. West Virginia is an exception. Here, workfare (jobs provided by the state government) is seen as a way of providing public services that the state government cannot otherwise afford. Surveys of work-site supervision indicate that people taking part in the workfare program are, on average, about as productive as regular employees.

Some scholars, such as the sociologists Francis Fox Piven and Barbara Ehrenreich, have criticized the workfare approach as a new form of "mass peonage," contending that forcing millions of poor Americans into an already overcrowded, underpaid labor force will not cure their poverty. These scholars' answer is to raise welfare benefits "at least to the poverty level."

Many researchers, however, assert that trying to increase government transfer payments to the poor sufficiently to eliminate poverty would place in jeopardy the willingness of many other workers to take a host of low and moderately paid jobs. In addition, there is solid evidence to support the widely held belief that welfare recipients migrate to states where they receive the best benefits package.

The new consensus among researchers on welfare policy is that it has been a mistake to offer welfare benefits without imposing on the recipients the same obligations that are assumed by other citizens—to try to become self-sufficient through education, responsible family behavior, and work.

It is unlikely, though, that wholesale changes in life styles, attitudes, and other characteristics of large numbers of low-income individuals can be achieved quickly. The uneven experience with work requirements and other efforts to reform welfare suggest that changes should not be introduced on a massive scale or designed for swift results, but should be made in the spirit of experimentation. It is probable that the financial burden of maintaining large social welfare programs will continue to take a major share of the Federal budget. Any improvements are likely to occur at the margins, but they surely are a worthwhile undertaking.

NO

Theodore R. Marmor,
Jerry L. Mashaw, and
Philip L. Harvey

AMERICA'S MISUNDERSTOOD WELFARE STATE

We believe that claims of social, political, and economic crisis attributable to the welfare state are either demonstrably false or wildly exaggerated....

A... positive view of our social welfare efforts is justified. The public has shown that it supports the programs constituting the American welfare state. It deserves to feel better about that support. There is no dearth of problems in the administration of individual programs; obvious gaps exist in the protection they afford; and practical achievements fall short of our aspirations. Still, claims that these programs actually harm the economy do not withstand close scrutiny. Nagging concerns that the welfare state may be responsible for sluggish economic growth, that it is unaffordable, and that its growth is beyond our control deserve to be dismissed.

THE (ECONOMICALLY) UNDESIRABLE WELFARE STATE

Before we begin, we want to make it clear that we are not here discussing the morally most controversial elements of the American welfare state, in particular, cash assistance to the able-bodied poor. "Welfare" is a perennial topic of controversy, but it is of very little significance to the fiscal difficulties of the modern welfare state. Because cash assistance programs for the able-bodied poor are so small, whatever "perverse incentives" they provide, they can have no significant impact on general economic productivity. We will document and elaborate these points [later]. For now, we only want to avoid confusing the "crisis of the welfare state" with the "problems of welfare." The vast majority of welfare state expenditures are for social insurance programs that provide cash and in-kind assistance to persons who are not expected to work and who have earned their entitlement to welfare state support through prior contributions to social insurance. It is these large, politically popular social insurance programs that are at issue in debates over the economic effects of the welfare state....

[I]t is easy to think of [social welfare spending] as a drain on the economy's output, a wasteful reallocation of productive capacity from other uses. Viewed in this way, social welfare spending looks like it is absorbing a larger and larger share of total output, analogous to the allocation of a growing share of GNP [gross national product] to education, health care, or the production of armaments. It is therefore imagined that the money we spend providing social welfare benefits is unavailable for investment, and the large amounts involved seem like an enormous drag on our opportunities for economic growth.

What this view of social welfare spending misses is that such spending consists, for the most part, of transfer payments rather than direct purchases of the economy's output. When the government provides educational services or purchases military hardware, it does effectively commandeer productive resources that cannot then be used for other purposes (such as the accumulation of more physical capital). When the government issues a Social Security benefit check, however, it does not commandeer any productive resources. It merely transfers purchasing power from currently employed workers to Social Security beneficiaries. Transfer payments redistribute claims on the economy's output, but they do not directly determine how productive resources will be used. The public has the same aggregate purchasing power after the transfer is made as it did before. What is different is the relative size of individual claims on total output. The public as a whole is free to consume (or invest) just as much of GNP after the transfer as it was before.

Thus, the allegedly negative effect of social welfare spending on economic growth rates cannot stem from a direct withdrawal of productive resources from growth-inducing uses....

THE UNAFFORDABLE WELFARE STATE

... [the claim that social welfare expenditures are unaffordable probably means] that there are not sufficient tax revenues to finance current expenditures for social welfare programs and that the public is unwilling to pay sufficient taxes for their current support or for the debt retirement necessary to bring these accounts back into balance. As such, the claim is transparently false. The major American programs of social insurance are in current balance—indeed headed toward mammoth surpluses—and the public reports itself willing to pay more to maintain them at current levels. There is no deficit here of either fiscal capacity or fiscal will. Public willingness to support the smaller, noninsurance portions of the welfare state is not as strong as the support for social insurance, and its continued support is, therefore, not so certain should the economy worsen. But if we declared AFDC [Aid to Families with Dependent Children] and Food Stamps "unaffordable" tomorrow and reduced their expenditures to zero, we would have erased only 10 percent of the overall [annual] budget deficit. These programs are simply too small to have much bearing on the affordability of the welfare state....

There is no reason to believe that the current size or character of the American welfare state is a serious impediment to economic growth, threatens us with imminent public bankruptcy, or makes adjustment and "steering" of social policy and expenditure impossible. For all the talk of "crisis" in the welfare state, there is precious little evidence to bolster that claim. The institutions of the welfare state have not reflected—either in their programmatic actions or by their inability to adjust—the sense of critical disjuncture that hostile intellectuals have managed, with the help of some politicians, to popularize....

[T]here exists something like a set of standard beliefs among well-educated adults concerning welfare, poverty, and the welfare state.

The standard belief goes something like this: First, by "welfare," most people mean cash assistance for needy families provided by the Aid to Families with Dependent Children program (AFDC). Second, "welfare," so defined, is viewed as a substantial and growing component of American social welfare expenditures. Third, AFDC in particular, and means-tested programs in general, are viewed as the government's primary weapons in combating poverty. Finally, there is, if not a conviction, at least a concern that these massive expenditures have failed to turn the tide in the war against poverty. Many people adopt the even more pessimistic view that welfare actually has contributed to the incidence of poverty. "Welfare," in short, is seen as having failed in its essential goals....

There is a straightforward problem with these standard beliefs concerning welfare's place in the American welfare state. Many, indeed most, of them are false. The consequences of this misunderstanding, moreover, are not benign. Not only do we risk misapprehending what we should want to do about our welfare programs, but we simultaneously deny ourselves the possibility of recognizing our past successes and of developing sensible expectations about the likely prospects of programmatic reforms....

THE SIZE, GROWTH, AND CHARACTER OF "WELFARE"

... [T]he belief that the American welfare state has grown dramatically over the past two decades is surely correct. Total federal spending has risen spectacularly since the 1960s, whether measured in terms of total dollars spent or as a percentage of either total federal spending or gross national product. But "welfare" is not "the welfare state." Indeed, once we begin to dig into the numbers, we discover that social welfare spending and welfare spending have followed radically different paths.

First, take a look at spending for AFDC, the program that most people equate with welfare.... The facts are startling, given the common view that welfare expenditures constitute a substantial and growing component of the American welfare state. In real terms, AFDC spending was lower in 1987 than it was in 1971. As a percentage of total federal social welfare expenditures, of total federal outlays, and of GNP, it has also shrunk. Nor is this shrinkage trivial. In relation to total spending by the federal government, AFDC has been cut to less than a third of its former relative size. At less than 4 percent of total federal social welfare spending, AFDC is fiscally an insubstantial part of the American welfare state. At less than two-fifths of one percent of GNP, this program's contribution, if any, to our current fiscal strain is vanishingly small.

Why are popular impressions of the size of welfare programs so wide of the mark? There are several answers to this question, and all are important for understanding the American welfare state and the quite different public assistance system for low-income persons that we actually have constructed. There is a tendency to equate "welfare" with AFDC, to equate both with the "welfare state," and to regard the latter as synonymous with "antipoverty" programs. As a comparison of the welfare state's growth with AFDC's relative decline makes clear, some of these equivalencies are wildly wrong-headed. Welfare is a minuscule fraction of the American welfare state....

A Brief Recapitulation. We now know a fair amount about the state of welfare and poverty in the American welfare state. Cash assistance to the poor has never been a large part of our welfare state and is literally dwarfed by social insurance expenditures. This pattern of expenditure fits our preferences for pooling common risks and the creation of opportunity as the primary functions of the welfare state. The American public may care about the elimination of poverty, but it is not keen on addressing income poverty through the simple expedient of cash transfers to the poor. Fortunately, however, our large and growing welfare state, particularly its social insurance component, does prevent much poverty. As the American welfare state has grown over the last three decades, the rate of poverty has declined by nearly 40 percent....

WELFARE AND DEPENDENCY

Why did progress against poverty stagnate in the early 1970s? Why did the incidence of poverty actually grow in the early 1980s? Why did both of these results occur while overall welfare state expenditures were steadily increasing? Charles Murray provided a widely pub-licized answer to these questions that captured the imaginations of many in his 1984 book, appropriately entitled, *Losing Ground.* The welfare state must spend more and more to do less and less, said Murray, because it actually aggravates the problem it is ostensibly designed to solve. Welfare generates rather than reduces dependency.

The World According to Murray. From this perspective the substantial success story we have been telling is instead a story of failure. We should be looking not at how many are poor *after* welfare state transfers, but how many are poor *before* those payments are made. The welfare state should be viewed as a success only if the pretransfer or "latent" poor are declining. The numbers show that this is not the case. The latent poor are in fact increasing. Why? Murray claims that it is because the welfare state encourages dependency. It gives people money and other support for taking up positions in society for which transfers are available. We are now simply spending more and more to support the dependents that we have created and continue to create. The only solution is to stop making the payments....

A basic failing in Murray's argument is one we have already encountered. His approach is enormously overgeneral. Does he really mean that income transfers and other supports are causing people to get old, to become blind or disabled, to need medical care? Not really. In fact, of the welfare state's major support programs, Murray is really only concerned with "welfare," principally AFDC. And since we know that the major growth areas of the welfare state have been elsewhere, the image that Murray conjures up of massive expenditures on antipoverty efforts to no, or to detrimental, effect is just that—image, not reality....

What then is Murray really concerned about? The answer is straightforward: young, unemployed males and young, unmarried females with illegitimate children, especially among blacks. Now let us get one thing straight at the outset. We agree with Murray that these are people who deserve our concern. Youth unemployment, illegitimacy, and the formation of female-headed households are indeed serious problems. They are highly associated with poverty, and they are particularly concentrated in poor black communities. The question, however, is what the relationship is between these problems and welfare....

If Murray is correct about incentive effects, we should expect to find that the illegitimacy rates in states with very high AFDC payments would be greater than the illegitimacy rates in states with lower payments. But careful research fails to reveal any significant effect of AFDC levels on illegitimacy.

Perhaps Murray's thesis is not that absolute levels of AFDC benefits control illegitimacy rates, but that the rate of change in those benefits is determinative. If so, the data again fail to support his position. In the period 1960 to 1970, there is no consistent relationship between the rate of change in AFDC payments nationwide and the rate of change in illegitimacy.

In short, researchers have not been able to find any substantial evidence to support Murray's thesis that links increased illegitimacy to welfare changes. But what about unemployment or labor force participation? According to Murray's thesis, as the real value of AFDC benefits rises, more Harolds live off of more Phyllises' AFDC checks and become unemployed

or drop out of the labor force. The reverse should also be the case—as AFDC benefits go down in real terms, the number of unemployed Harolds should decrease as well. [In *Losing Ground*, Murray examines the question of the relationship between youth unemployment, illegitimacy, and the formation of female-headed households in terms of a hypothetical couple named Harold and Phyllis. They represent young, poorly educated, unmarried, prospective parents considering the benefits and disadvantages of getting married and getting jobs—Eds.]

Testing this thesis is not as easy as one might think. The unemployment figures do not identify which of the unemployed are Harolds with a Phyllis to support them and which are the Homers who haven't a romantic prospect in sight. About the best that can be done is to look at the unemployment rates for young black men. Because black women receive about one-half of all AFDC payments, we are here in something like the right ballpark. But as the charts and tables in Murray's own book attest, the numbers moved in exactly the opposite direction from the one he would have predicted. As AFDC benefits went up in the late 1960s, the unemployment of young black men fell. As the real value of AFDC benefits declined over the whole of the 1970s, the unemployment rates for young black men rose....

Our point is that Murray's story of the dynamics of welfare and dependency is wildly exaggerated. The change in economic incentives produced by the welfare "reforms" of the 1960s were quite modest, and the effects of those incentives on behavior were so small that serious social scientists have been unable to detect them after assiduous effort.

But if Murray is right that the latent poverty rate was going up during the 1970s and 1980s, and if we are right that this increase in "dependency" cannot be ascribed to American welfare policy, then what was happening? The answer is quite straightforward. First, pretransfer poverty is highly sensitive to the unemployment rate.... The poverty rate for most periods parallels the unemployment rate. Indeed, serious attempts to estimate the impact of unemployment on poverty rates find that an increase in the unemployment rate of 1 percent increases pretransfer poverty by 0.7 percent.

Second, demographic trends also affect the poverty rate. Certain groups—the aged, children, female-headed households, and nonwhites—have always been at greater risk of poverty in the United States. If the percentage of residents having these characteristics was increasing over the period from the mid-1960s to the mid-1980s, one would expect the poverty rate before transfers to be increasing as well. This has indeed been the case. When the poverty rate for all persons is adjusted for changes in demographics, it falls nearly $1\frac{1}{2}$ percentage points below the official poverty rate reported by the Census Bureau.

Finally, a trend toward increasing inequality in earned income has been at work in the United States for the past several decades. Through the mid-1970s this trend was counterbalanced by the equalizing effect of rapidly rising income transfer benefits. But as the growth in social welfare spending slowed, the underlying tendency toward increasing inequality began to predominate. The causes of this trend are not well-understood, but it has been very broad-based, affecting virtually all population groups, occupations, and industries. It has not been limited to the poor but instead appears to reflect a trend towards inequality in the distribution of market income generally.

These three factors—rising average unemployment rates, an increase in the percentage of the population in high-risk groups, and a long-term trend toward inequality in the distribution of market income—explain virtually all of the change in pretransfer poverty rates which has occurred in the United States from the beginning of the War on Poverty to the publication of *Losing Ground.* There is little cause for comfort in the identification of these trends. They pose a series of daunting challenges to policymakers. But we can at least feel confident that our efforts to relieve poverty have not been causing it to grow.

Welfare is not causing poverty, illegitimacy, and a flight from work. But overall poverty rates are as high now as they were in the late 1960s; illegitimacy is increasing; and the employment rates of some subgroups, particularly of young black men, lag far behind the general population....

Unemployment and Poverty. The principal determinant of poverty is unemployment, and of long-term poverty, long-term unemployment. This is true not only in the United States; it is what our Western European allies have found as well. Most of the developed Western nations have seen their levels of poverty creep up over the last decade along with their levels of unemployment. In the United Kingdom, France, Germany, and elsewhere, there is increasing talk of a permanent class of persons left out of the labor market. Many factors contribute to this emerging problem, but in every case analysts have found high unemployment rates to be the principal cause....

Illegitimacy and Poverty. To the extent that child poverty is the product of illegitimacy and the single-parent family, it is far beyond the power of the Family Support Act to control. One could describe the statute as telling Harold he will not get away with abandoning his illegitimate kids and Phyllis that she cannot expect to be a single parent "at leisure." Indeed, symbolically it does so. But it would be wrong to expect the Family Support Act to reshape the trend away from marriage and toward illegitimacy and single-parenting. These trends have been evident in the United States and in most European countries across all population groups and income levels since the early 1950s.

Indeed, because these trends have been developing for several decades in countries having very different policies for the redistribution of income, it seems highly unlikely that marginal changes in one of our income transfer programs will have any significant impact. The population at risk is likely to continue to grow for the foreseeable future. It is almost impossible to identify or predict, much less to control, the cultural shifts or other changes that might alter this forecast. Meanwhile, we can make both welfare benefits and eligibility conditions more generous, reducing somewhat the post-transfer poverty of single-parent families. With a tight labor market, generous child allowances, health care, day care, and job training, we, like the Swedes, might control the incidence of child poverty and put virtually all parents to work. But the notion that the welfare reforms of 1988 are going to force Harold and Phyllis to the altar or make most families headed by Phyllises both fully self-supporting and free of poverty is a flight of fancy....

Much of this... has been about misinformation. A quite remarkable proportion of what is written and spoken about social welfare policy in the United States is, to put it charitably, mistaken. These mistakes are repeated by popular media addicted to the current and the quotable. Misconceptions thus insinuate themselves into the national consciousness; they can easily become the conventional wisdom....

Economists have become the policy gurus of the late twentieth century. We turn to them, or their methods, to predict the likely outcome of most changes in social welfare policy. Their stock in trade is a simple story. People behave rationally. If you increase or decrease the economic rewards of particular activities, you will get more or less of those activities, *unless*, of course, something else happens simultaneously to alter behavior in a different direction. Although simple, this story is also powerful. It makes perfect sense in terms of much of our ordinary experience....

Consider a few of the examples that we have encountered in the preceding pages. First, remember Harold and Phyllis. Charles Murray told a simple and superficially convincing story. Welfare did seem to be changing in a direction that provided greater incentives for avoiding marriage and for having illegitimate children. And we were, for a time, experiencing declining marriage rates, rising illegitimacy rates, and rising AFDC rates. It was easy to conclude that the changes in economic incentives—AFDC benefits—were driving the behavioral changes—illegitimacy and welfare dependency. But a careful look at the periods involved, as well as at the differential rates of change in different localities, revealed the hypothesis to be false. Incentives did not translate directly into behaviors—indeed, could not be shown to be affecting behavior at all.

The reason for the lack of correlation seems apparent. Decisions about childbearing, marriage, and living arrangements are very complex. They surely are not unaffected by economic incentives, but they are affected by a host of other factors as well. If those other factors—for example, the general societal perception of out-of-wedlock births or of single parenting—are also shifting, they may dwarf the effects of the economic incentives. And, even if they are not, there may be very few people for whom small changes in economic well-being would make a difference sufficient for them to change their sexual behavior or basic living arrangements. Reducing the economic price of illegitimacy has a much less predictable effect on behavior than reducing the price of bananas.

In addition, the economic incentives relevant to the issues addressed by Murray are themselves both more varied and more complex than his simple story suggests. It is the strength but also the vice of economic analysis to focus on isolated, easily measured economic variables. In the real world, the multiple pressures and diffuse expectations created by economic forces are much harder to sort out. Whatever effect changes in AFDC eligibility and benefit formulas have had on the behavior of the poor, a host of other economic factors—especially labor market conditions—have probably played a more important role.

POSTSCRIPT

Does Welfare Do More Harm Than Good?

Welfare is an ambiguous term. In the popular sense it usually means "aid to the poor," which would include programs like Aid to Families with Dependent Children (AFDC) and food stamps. But these programs constitute a small percentage of "welfare" in the broadest sense of "government assistance to individuals." In that sense, some would argue, the largest welfare program is Social Security, which dispenses almost $300 billion annually (compared to $25 billion for AFDC), much of it to people who are not poor. It could also be argued that there are other forms of middle- and upper-class "welfare," including farm subsidies and homeowners' tax breaks.

But the complaint of Weidenbaum in the narrow sense of "aid to the poor" is not just that it costs a lot but that it hurts its own intended beneficiaries by contributing to the breakup of the family and reducing individuals' incentive to become responsible wage earners. Marmor, Mashaw, and Harvey deny that any relationship exists between welfare and work incentives. Note that both sides draw on studies to support their views. For an extensive review of the literature on this point, see Robert Moffitt, "Incentive Effects of the U.S. Welfare System: A Review," *Journal of Economic Literature* (vol. 30), pp. 1–60. One thing is clear: payments to families with dependent children have eroded considerably relative to the cost of living over the last two decades, so the incentive to get off welfare has increased.

Sar A. Levitan and Clifford M. Johnson conclude that the current welfare system is a rational and necessary response to emerging societal needs in *Beyond the Safety Net: Reviving the Promise of Opportunity in America* (Ballinger, 1984). Michael B. Katz, in *The Undeserving Poor: From the War on Poverty to the War on Welfare* (Pantheon Books, 1989), traces the evolution of welfare policies in the United States from the 1960s through the 1980s. Michael K. Brown, ed., *Remaking the Welfare State: Retrenchment and Social Policy in America and Europe* (Temple University Press, 1988), is a collection of 14 essays pondering the present and future of the welfare state. Writers who criticize the welfare program for going too far include Lawrence M. Mead, *The New Politics of Poverty* (Basic Books, 1992), and Jack D. Douglas, *The Myth of the Welfare State* (Transaction, 1989). Fred Block and his colleagues respond to attacks on welfare in *The Mean Season: The Attack on the Welfare State* (Pantheon Books, 1987). A work that should be examined to understand the psychology of the recipients of welfare is Leonard Goodwin's *Causes and Cures of Welfare: New Evidence on the Social Psychology of the Poor* (Lexington Books, 1983).

ISSUE 15

Are Central Cities Becoming Obsolete?

YES: Robert Fishman, from "Megalopolis Unbound," *The Wilson Quarterly* (Winter 1990)

NO: Ruth Messinger and Andrew Breslau, from "I Am City, Hear Me Roar," *Social Policy* (Spring 1993)

ISSUE SUMMARY

YES: Associate professor of history Robert Fishman argues that centralizing forces built the great cities but that decentralizing forces are now building the suburban rings that are taking over the roles of the central cities.

NO: Ruth Messinger, New York City's Manhattan Borough President, and her press secretary, Andrew Breslau, maintain that edge cities can be no greater than the central city of which they are satellites and that central cities are still centers for business and culture.

Historically, cities have been closely linked to technology, culture, and power. Cities were not even possible until the technology for settled agriculture that could produce surpluses of food to supply the cities was developed. Large cities also depended on the development of technologies for long-haul transportation systems. Although technology created the potential for cities, that potential could only be realized through political and economic domination of the surrounding countryside and, for large cities, the domination of vast territories. The largest ancient city was Rome, which ruled the Mediterranean world for centuries but never had a population that exceeded 350,000—less than half the size of the metropolitan area of contemporary Tulsa, Oklahoma. Nevertheless, Rome sustained a remarkable culture and created one of the great civilizations of the ancient world.

After the empire broke up, the populations of European cities seldom exceeded 50,000 people for over 1,000 years. Life in these cities was rather miserable for most residents. Most cities, for example, lacked sanitation facilities, so wastes were dumped into open sewers. Not surprisingly, death rates were higher in cities than in rural areas, and epidemics would occasionally wipe out a quarter or even half of their population. During this period, societies were largely rural.

It was not until new technologies spawned the Industrial Revolution and greatly improved living conditions in the cities that they grew greatly in size and number. Today the industrial world is predominantly urban, and until recently the pattern of land use was fairly predictable: The central city would have a downtown central business district with skyscrapers and very dense land use. This would be surrounded by a less dense zone of factories, commercial buildings, and nearby, crowded working-class housing. Next would be a ring of middle-class suburban homes, and, finally, some less expensive homes would sit out on the periphery. Often, there would also be some special corridors that would move out through the rings, such as a string of upper-class residences on one side of town or along a river.

The above pattern is changing because of new technologies and new patterns of domination. Widespread automobile ownership meant that factories no longer had to be in the central city to get the workers they needed, so they moved out of the high-rent central cities to rural areas and commercial corridors in the suburbs. More recent technologies and a world economy are leading to massive relocations of economic activities: low-skill manufacturing has moved abroad in the past decade; routine clerical work has moved abroad more recently; and information/knowledge jobs will probably move to high quality-of-life locations, such as waterfront communities, in the future.

As new technologies remake the economic landscape again and again, what will happen to cities? The world is expected to be over 50 percent urban by the year 2000. What will this urban world be like? Some predict the decline of central cities in the United States. Demographic data seem to support this view, as the suburbs are growing much faster than central cities in both population and jobs. As shopping centers and office buildings follow manufacturing out of the central city to the suburbs, the suburbs seem to be growing into "edge cities" and weakening the centrality of the city. As urban problems of violence, crime, drugs, and squalor reach epidemic proportions, central cities are repelling rather than attracting people and businesses.

In the readings that follow, Robert Fishman describes trends suggesting that central cities are in decline. He argues that government housing, defense, transportation, and annexation policies that favor suburbs over cities have contributed to the ascendancy of the suburbs. Ruth Messinger and Andrew Breslau, however, argue that the destiny of the suburban ring depends entirely on the condition of the central city and that the advantages of cities will increase rather than decrease in the future.

YES

Robert Fishman

MEGALOPOLIS UNBOUND

Jim and Delores Bach live in a redwood contemporary in West Nyack, N.Y., about 25 miles north of Manhattan. Twenty years ago, their cul de sac was an apple orchard, and today two gnarled old trees on the front lawn still hold up their fruit to the early autumn sun.

This morning, two of the Bach children will board buses to school and Delores will drive young Alex to a day-care center in nearby Nanuet. Then she will drive 20 minutes down the Garden State Parkway to her job at a medical laboratory in Montvale, N.J. Her husband, meanwhile, will be on the New York State Thruway, headed east over the Hudson River on the Tappan Zee Bridge to his job with IBM in Westchester County.

A decade ago, Delores Bach could not have imagined finding such a good job so close to home. She stayed home with the children and Jim commuted to midtown Manhattan. But since the 1970s, northern New Jersey and New York's Westchester County—the very county whose genteel "bedroom communities" the writer John Cheever lived in and wrote about for the *New Yorker*—have become carpeted with office complexes and stores. West Nyack and other towns in Rockland County have filled up with families who can't afford Westchester's stratospheric home prices. Others are moving even farther to the northwest, to Orange County. Now, the Tappan Zee, built as part of the interstate highway system 35 years ago to link New York City with Albany and other distant upstate areas, is jammed every rush hour. In fact, Jim Bach's trip will take about an hour, longer than his old 50-minute commute by express bus to Manhattan.

The Bachs still make it a point to get to Manhattan once every six months or so for a day at the museum with the kids or a night out at the theater. They still subscribe to the *New York Times*. But they have friends who have not been to "the City," as it is called, in 10 years. Why bother? They can get good jobs nearby, buy anything they could possibly desire at one of a dozen convenient malls, attend a college, get fine medical care or legal advice—virtually anything they could want is within a one-hour radius. All they have to do is get in the car and drive.

The Bachs are fictional, but West Nyack is a real place—one of literally hundreds of former suburbs around the nation which, without anybody quite realizing it, have detached themselves from the big city and coalesced into "new cities." They lack skyscrapers, subways, and other symbolic structures of the central city, but they have acquired almost all of its functions.

Wright's Prophecy

"The big city," Frank Lloyd Wright announced prophetically in 1923, "is no longer modern." Although his forecast of a new age of urban decentralization was ignored by his contemporaries, we can now see that Wright and a few other thinkers of his day understood the fragility of the great behemoth—the centralized industrial metropolis—which then seemed to embody and define the modernity of the 20th century.

These capital cities of America's industrial revolution, with New York and Chicago at their head, were built to last. Their very form, as captured during the 1920s in the famous diagrams by Robert E. Park and Ernest W. Burgess of the Chicago School of sociology, seemed to possess a logic that was permanent. At the core was the "central business district," with its skyscraper symbols of local wealth, power, and sophistication; surrounding the core was the factory zone, the dense region of reinforced concrete factories and crowded workers' housing; and finally, a small ring of affluent middle-class suburbs occupied the outskirts. These were the triumphant American cities, electric with opportunity and excitement, and as late as the 1920s they were steadily draining the countryside of its population.

But modernism is a process of constant upheaval and self-destruction. Just when the centralized metropolis was at its zenith, powerful social and economic forces were combining to create an irresistible movement toward decentralization, tearing asunder the logic that had sustained the big city and distributing its prized functions over whole regions. The urban history of the last half-century is a record of this process.

Misleading Name

Superficially, the process might be called "the rise of the suburb." The term "suburb," however, inevitably suggests the affluent and restricted "bedroom communities" that first took shape around the turn of the century in New York's Scarsdale, the North Shore of Chicago, and other locales on the edge of the 19th-century metropolis. These genteel retreats from urban life established the model of the single-family house on its own landscaped grounds as the ideal middle-class residence, just as they established the roles of commuter and housewife as social models for upper-middle-class men and women. But Scarsdale and its kind were limited zones of privilege that strictly banned almost all industry and commerce and excluded not only the working class but even the majority of the less-affluent middle class. The traditional suburb therefore remained an elite enclave, completely dependent on the central city for jobs and essential services.

Since 1945, however, the relationship between the urban core and the suburban periphery has undergone a startling transformation—especially during the past two decades. Where suburbia was once an exclusive refuge for a small elite, U.S. Census figures show that 45 percent of the American population is now "suburban," up from only 23 percent in 1950. Allowing for anomalies in the Census Bureau's methods, it is almost certain that a majority of Americans live in the suburbs. About one third remain in the central cities. Even more dramatic has been the exodus of commerce and industry from the cities. By 1980, 38 percent of the nation's workers commuted to their jobs from suburb-to-suburb, while only half as many made the stereotypical suburb-to-city trek.

Manufacturing has led the charge from the cities; the industrial park, as it is so bucolically dubbed, has displaced the old urban factory district as the headquarters of American manufacturing. Commerce has also joined the exodus. Where suburbanites once had little choice but to travel to downtown stores for most of their clothing and household goods, suburban shopping malls and stores now ring up the majority of the nation's retail sales.

During the last two decades, the urban peripheries have even outpaced the cores in that last bastion of downtown economic clout, office employment. More than 57 percent of the nation's office space is now located outside the central cities. And the landscaped office parks and research centers that dot the outlying highways and interstates have become the home of the most advanced high-technology laboratories and factories, the national centers of business creativity and growth. *Inc.* magazine, which tracks the nation's emerging industries, reported in a survey earlier this year that "growth is in the 'edge cities.' " Topping its list of "hot spots" were such unlikely locales as Manchester-Nashua, New Hampshire; West Palm Beach, Florida; and Raleigh-Durham, North Carolina.

The complex economy of the former suburbs has now reached a critical mass, as specialized service enterprises of every kind, from hospitals equipped with the latest CAT scanners to gourmet restaurants to corporate law firms, have established themselves on the fringes. In all of these ways, the peripheries have replaced the urban cores as the heartlands of our civilization. These multi-functional late-20th century "suburbs" can no longer be comprehended in the terms of the old bedroom communities. They have become a new kind of city.

THE FEATURES OF THE NEW CITY

Familiar as we all are with the features of the new city, most of us do not recognize how radically it departs from the cities of old. The most obvious difference is scale. The basic unit of the new city is not the street measured in blocks but the "growth corridor" stretching 50 to 100 miles. Where the leading metropolises of the early 20th century—New York, London, or Berlin—covered perhaps 100 square miles, the new city routinely encompasses two to three *thousand* square miles. Within such "urban regions," each element is correspondingly enlarged. "Planned unit developments" of cluster-housing are as large as townships; office parks are set amid hundreds of acres of landscaped grounds; and malls dwarf some of the downtowns they have replaced.

These massive units, moreover, are arrayed along the beltways and "growth corridors" in seemingly random order, without the strict distinctions between residential, commercial, and industrial zones that shaped the old city. A subdivision of $300,000 single-family houses outside Denver may sit next to a telecom- munications research-and-production complex, and a new mall filled with boutiques once found only on the great shopping streets of Europe may—and indeed *does*—rise amid Midwestern corn fields.

The new city, furthermore, lacks what gave shape and meaning to every urban form of the past: a dominant single core and definable boundaries. At most, it contains a multitude of partial centers, or "edge cities," more-or-less unified clusters of malls, office developments, and entertainment complexes that rise where major highways cross or converge. As *Washington Post* writer Joel Garreau has observed, Tysons Corner, perhaps the largest American edge city, boasts more office space than downtown Miami, yet it remains only one of 13 edge cities— including Rockville-Gaithersburg, Maryland, and Rosslyn-Ballston, Virginia—in the Washington, D.C., region.

Rapid Growth

Even some old downtowns have been reduced to "first among equals" among the edge cities of their regions. Atlanta has one of the most rapidly growing downtowns in the country. Yet between 1978 and 1983—the years of its accelerated growth—the downtown's share of regional office space shrank from 34 percent to 26 percent. Midtown Manhattan is the greatest of all American downtowns, but northern New Jersey now has more office space.

If no one can find the center of the new city, its borders are even more elusive.

Low-density development tends to gain an inevitable momentum, as each extension of a region's housing and economy into previously rural areas becomes the base for further expansion. When one successful area begins to fill up, land values and taxes rise explosively, pushing the less affluent even farther out. During the past two decades, as Manhattan's "back offices" moved 30 miles west into northern New Jersey along interstates 78 and 80, new subdivisions and townhouse communities began sprouting 40 miles farther west along these growth corridors in the Pocono Mountains of eastern Pennsylvania. "By the time we left [New Jersey]," one new resident of eastern Pennsylvania told the *New York Times,* "there were handyman specials for $150,000 you wouldn't put your dog in." Now such formerly depressed and relatively inexpensive areas as Pennsylvania's Lehigh Valley are gaining population, attracting high-tech industries and office employment, and thus stimulating further dispersion.

Baltimore and Washington, D.C., once separated by mile after mile of farms and forests, are now joined by an agglomeration of office parks, shopping strips, and housing. Census Bureau officials have given up attempting to draw a statistical boundary between the two metropolitan areas and have proposed combining them into a single consolidated region for statistical purposes. Indeed, as the automobile gives rise to a complex pattern of multi-directional travel that largely by-passes the old central cities, the very concept of "center" and "periphery" becomes obsolete.

Sprawl

Although a few prophets like Wright foresaw the downfall of the old city, no one imagined the form of the new. Instead, it was built up piecemeal, as a result of millions of uncoordinated decisions made by housing developers, shopping-mall operators, corporate executives, highway engineers and, not least, the millions of Americans who saved and sacrificed to buy single-family homes in the expanding suburbs. The new city's construction has been so rapid and so unforeseen that we lack even a commonly-accepted name for what we have created. Or, rather, we have too many names: ex-urb, spread city, urban village, megalopolis, outtown, sprawl, slurb, the burbs, nonplace urban field, polynucleated city, and (my own coinage) technoburb.

Not urban, not rural, not suburban, but possessing elements of all three, the new city eludes all the conventional terminology of the urban planner and the historian. Yet it is too important to be left in conceptual limbo. The success or failure of the new city will affect the quality of life of the majority of Americans well into the 21st century. In a few scattered locales today, one can discern the promise of a decentralized city that fulfills its residents' basic hopes for comfortable homes in sylvan settings with easy access to good schools, good jobs, and recreational facilities of many kinds. More ambitiously, one might hope for a decentralized civilization that finally overcomes the old antithesis of city and countryside, that fulfills in daily life the profound cultural need for an environment that combines the machine and nature in a new unity.

But the dangers of the new city are perhaps more obvious than the promise. The immense speed and scale of development across the nation threaten to annihilate the natural environment of entire regions, leaving the tranquility and natural beauty that Americans seek in the new city perpetually retreating another 10 exits down the interstate. The movement of urban functions to an environment never designed for them has produced the anomaly of urban-style crowding and congestion in a decentralized setting. Through greed and ignorance we could destroy the very things that inspired the new city and build instead a degenerate urban form that is too congested to be efficient, too chaotic to be beautiful, and too dispersed to possess the diversity and vitality of a great city.

The new city is still under construction. Like all new urban types, its early form is necessarily raw and chaotic. The real test of the new city as a carrier of civilization will come when the first flush of hectic building slows down and efforts to redesign and reconstruct begin, as they have in the old downtowns today. But before we can improve the new urban world we are building we need to understand it.

Encouraging Expansion

In Europe, governments fearful of losing precious farm land to the encroaching cities have severely restricted decentralization wherever they could. As early as 1938 the British government prohibited London and the other large British cities from expanding beyond their existing boundaries. A decade later it created permanent "greenbelts" of farm and park land around the cities, including an impressive five-mile wide Metropolitan Greenbelt which still rings London. (Paris, on the other hand, is ringed by a Red Belt, so called because its working-class residents consistently vote Communist. This reflects another unique quality of European development: The affluent middle-class generally prefers urban to suburban living.) In the United States, however, Washington, as well as state and local governments, indefatigably promoted expansion. Government "planning" was largely unconscious and unintended, but that did not lessen its effects. Between 1930 and 1960, state intervention in four different arenas profoundly affected the shape of the nation's cities:

- *Housing.* Although the American preference for single-family suburban houses was well-established by the 1920s, it took the New Deal's Federal Housing Administration (1934) to reform the nation's rickety system of mortgage finance and, ultimately, put the American dream house within reach of millions of citizens. As historian Kenneth Jackson has shown, FHA regulations also funneled mortgage money to newly built suburbs, considered good credit risks, while virtually starving the cities of residential construction loans.

- *Defense Industries.* During World War II, the new factories built to manufacture synthetics, alloys, aircraft, and other products under the auspices of the Defense Plants Corporation were rarely located in the central cities. For example, Nassau County, Long Island, future site of the archetypal postwar suburb of Levittown, became the East Coast's center for aircraft production during the war, as Grumman, Republic, and other manufacturers opened plants there. Unlike the old urban factories, they were built on a single level on great tracts of land, in accordance with new ideas of industrial efficiency. Almost overnight these new factories gave the metropolitan peripheries and decentralized sunbelt cities a substantial industrial base on which they could build during the postwar period.

- *Highway Construction.* From the beginning, highways were regarded as a public responsibility, entitled to subsidies with tax dollars, while the rail system was not. Rail freight (and often mass transit as well) remained under the control of private corporations. After 1920, the owners were increasingly unable or unwilling to improve their services to attract customers. Highway engineers presided over one of the most massive construction efforts in history, culminating after 1958 in the 44,000 miles of the federal interstate highway system built at a cost of $108 billion. While these Main Streets of the emerging new cities flourished, the rail lines that served the downtowns stagnated or declined.

- *Local Government.* After the turn of the century, city after city failed to annex its suburbs because of suburban resistance. As a result, cities lost the tax base of the most prosperous and rapidly expanding areas of the region. And since zoning in the American system is essentially a matter of local control, the power to regulate new development passed to the hundreds of suburban governments, which had little interest in restraining growth to create a balanced metropolitan region. Developers learned they could play one small local planning board off another, escaping all control. As the developer Sam Lefrak observed, "There is no zoning: only deals."

Relieved of the task of delivering the full range of services required by a great city, suburbs could tailor public spending to the specific needs of their constituents. With surprising speed, suburban public school systems developed into formidable enterprises, soon rivaling and then surpassing the once-dominant big-city schools.

Without anybody intending for it to happen, all of these seemingly unrelated forces converged to generate enormous momentum behind the great tide of decentralization that washed over the

American metropolis after 1945. The tide has continued relentlessly, through booms and recessions, under Democratic and Republican administrations, until the old industrial city became, if not an extinct species, at least a highly endangered one.

The first significant sign was a drop in population. Between 1950 and 1960, all of the large, established cities lost people. Boston, the worst case, shrank by 13 percent, while its suburbs gained 17 percent. New York and Chicago lost less than two percent each, but their suburbs gained over 70 percent. To these blows were added shrinkage of the industrial base. Between 1947 and 1967, the 16 largest and oldest central cities lost an average of 34,000 manufacturing jobs each, while their suburbs gained an average of 87,000. This trend continued through the 1970s, as the cities suffered the elimination of from 25 percent (Minneapolis) to 40 percent (Philadelphia) of the manufacturing jobs that remained.

ARE THESE "REAL" CITIES?

Building on their growing base of population and jobs, suburban entrepreneurs during the 1950s and 1960s began transforming the new city into a self-sufficient world. "We don't go downtown anymore," became the new city's motto. Shopping centers displaced downtown department stores; small merchants and repairmen deserted Main Street for stores "along the highway" or folded up shop under the competitive pressure of the growing national chain stores. Even cardiologists and corporate lawyers moved their offices closer to their customers.

By the 1970s and 1980s, the new city found itself at the top of a whole range of national and even international trends.

The movement from snowbelt to sunbelt meant a shift toward urban areas that had been "born decentralized" and organized on new-city principles. The new city, moreover, moved quickly to dominance in the most rapidly expanding sections of the industrial economy—electronics, chemicals, pharmaceuticals, and aircraft—leaving the old city with such sunset industries as textiles, iron and steel, and automobiles.

Finally, during the 1970s, the new city successfully challenged the old downtowns in the last area of their supremacy, office employment. The "office park" became the locale of choice for many businesses, new and old. Jaded New Yorkers looked on in stunned disbelief as one major corporation after another pulled up stakes and departed for former commuter towns like Stamford, Connecticut, or more distant sunbelt locations. By the 1980s, even social scientists could not ignore the fact that the whole terminology of "suburb" and "central city," deriving from the era of the industrial metropolis, had become obsolete. As Mumford had predicted, the single center had lost its dominance.

But are the sprawling regions *cities*? Judged by the standards of the centralized metropolis, the answer is no. As I have suggested, this "city" lacks any definable borders, a center or a periphery, or a clear distinction between residential, industrial, and commercial zones. Instead, shopping malls, research and production facilities, and corporate headquarters all seem scattered amid a chaos of subdivisions, apartment complexes, and condominiums. It is easy to understand why urban planners and social scientists trained in the clear functional logic of the centralized metropolis can see only disorder in these "nonplace urban fields," or why ordinary people use the word "sprawl" to describe their own neighborhoods.

Nevertheless, I believe that the new city has a characteristic structure—one that departs radically not only from the old metropolis but from all cities of the past.

To grasp this structure we must return to the prophetic insights of Frank Lloyd Wright. From the 1920s until his death in 1959, Wright was preoccupied with his plan for an ideal decentralized American city which he called Broadacres. Although many elements of the plan were openly utopian—he wished, for example, to ensure that every American would have access to at least an acre of land so that all could reap the economic and psychological benefits that he associated with part-time farming—Wright also had a remarkable insight into the highway-based world that was developing around him. Above all he understood the consequences of a city based on a grid of highways rather than the hub-and-spokes of the older city. Instead of a single privileged center, there would be a multitude of crossings, no one of which could assume priority. And the grid would be boundless by its very nature, capable of unlimited extension in all directions.

Such a grid, as it indeed developed, did not allow for the emergence of an "imperial" metropolis to monopolize the life of a region. For Wright, this meant that the family home would be freed from its fealty to the city and allowed to emerge as the real center of American life. As he put it, "The true center, (the only centralization allowable) in Usonian democracy, is the individual Usonian house." (Usonia was Wright's name for the United States.)

In the plans for Broadacres—a city he said would be "everywhere or nowhere"—Wright foresaw what I believe to be the essential element in the structure of the new city: a megalopolis based on *time* rather than space.

A CITY OF TIME INSTEAD OF SPACE

Even the largest of the old "big cities" had a firm identity in space. The big city had a center as its basic point of orientation—the Loop, Times Square—and also a boundary. Starting from the center, sooner or later one reached the edge of the city.

In the new city, however, there is no single center. Instead, as Wright suggested, each family home has become the central point for its members. Families create their own "cities" out of the destinations they can reach (usually travelling by car) in a reasonable length of time. Indeed, distance in the new cities is generally measured in terms of time rather than blocks or miles. The supermarket is 10 minutes away. The nearest shopping mall is 30 minutes in another direction, and one's job 40 minutes away by yet another route. *The pattern formed by these destinations represents "the city" for that particular family or individual.* The more varied one's destinations, the richer and more diverse is one's personal "city." The new city is a city à la carte.

It can be seen as composed of three overlapping networks, representing the three basic categories of destinations that define each person's city. These are the household network; the network of consumption; and the network of production.

Networks
The household network is composed of places that are part of family and personal life. For a typical household

of two parents and two children, this network is necessarily oriented around childrearing—and it keeps parents scurrying frantically in station wagons and minivans from one place to another. Its set of destinations include the homes of the children's playmates (which may be down the street or scattered around a county), the daycare center, the schools, a church or synagogue, community centers, and the homes of the parents' friends. Although this network is generally more localized than the other two, it is almost always wider than the traditional urban neighborhood.

The two-parent family with children is the archetypical new-city household, but, especially since 1970, the new city has made a place for others. For single or divorced people, single parents, young childless couples or older "empty nest" couples, widows and widowers, the new city offers a measure of familiarity and security that many find lacking in the central city. Its housing is increasingly diverse. No longer confined to single-family homes, it now includes apartment towers, town homes and condominiums, and various kinds of retirement housing, from golf-oriented communities to nursing homes. There are more places to socialize. The same mall that caters essentially to families on weekends and evenings may also serve as an informal community center for older people in the morning, while its bars and restaurants play host to a lively singles scene after the stores close.

The network of consumption—Mallopolis, in economist James Millar's phrase—comprises essentially the shopping centers and malls which, as Wright predicted, have located themselves at the strategic crossroads of the highway system. It also includes movie theaters, restaurants, health clubs, playing fields and other recreational facilities, and perhaps a second home 30 to 100 miles away.

Although this network serves much the same function as the old downtown, it is scattered, and each consumer is free to work out his particular set of preferences from the vast menu of offerings presented by Mallopolis.

Finally, there is the network of production. It includes the place of employment of one or both spouses. It also includes the suppliers—from computer-chip manufacturers to janitorial services—which these enterprises rely upon. Information comes instantaneously from around the world while raw materials, spare parts, and other necessities are trucked in from the firms that cluster along nearby highways.

Convenience

This network minimizes the traditional distinction between the white-collar world of administration and the blue-collar world of production. Both functions co-exist in virtually every "executive office park." Its most successful enterprises are those where research and development and specialized techniques of production are intimately intertwined: pharmaceuticals, for example, or electronics. Conversely, its most routinized labor can be found in the so-called "back-offices," data-processing centers that perform tasks once done at a downtown corporate headquarters.

Each of these networks has its own spatial logic. For example, primary schools are distributed around the region in response to the school-age population; shopping malls reflect population density, wealth, and the road system; large firms locate where their workers and their suppliers can easily reach them. But because the networks overlap, the pattern on the ground is one of juxtaposition and interpenetration. Instead of the logical division of functions of the old metropolis, one finds a post-modern, post-urban collage.

In some places, a particularly active locale like Tysons Corner, in Fairfax County, Virginia, may draw together elements from different networks—shopping malls and offices—to form an approximation of an old downtown. But the logic of the new city generally confounds that kind of concentration. Such areas immediately become points of especially bad traffic congestion, denying the ready access that is a hallmark of the new city. (It may be poetic justice that the leaders of the American Automobile Association, patron saint of the suburban motorist, have become so frustrated by the bumper-to-bumper traffic in the area around Tysons Corner that they have decided to move AAA headquarters to the relatively open roads of Orlando, Florida.) Tysons Corner is an exception. In general, the new city allows and requires each citizen to make connections among the three networks—to make a city—on his own. The new city has no center or boundary because it does not need them.

Women

Women have been a not-so-hidden force behind the new city's economic success. Since 1957, the proportion of married women aged 27 to 54 with jobs has grown from 33 percent to 68 percent. More than half of all women with children aged three years or younger are now employed outside the home. Much of the economic life of the new city, especially with its concentration on retail

trade and back-office data processing, would be impossible without these new workers. Indeed, the presence of employment opportunities so close to home—convenient, with decent pay and flexible schedules—is surely responsible for part of the remarkable influx of married women into the work force (although the plentiful supply of workers could just as easily be said to have attracted employers). The outcome is more than a little ironic, considering the fact that the bedroom suburb had originally been designed to separate women from the corruptions of the world of work.

The new city thus decisively breaks with the older suburban pattern that restricted married middle-class women with children to a life of neighborhood-oriented domesticity. Women still work closer to home than men do, and they still bear most of the responsibility for childcare and housekeeping, but, in contrast to the old metropolis, the economic and spatial structure of the new city tends to equalize gender roles....

THE CONDITION OF
THE OLD CITY

When Frank Lloyd Wright envisioned Broadacre City, he failed to consider the role of the old centralized industrial cities in the new world of the future. He simply assumed that the old cities would disappear once the conditions that had created them were gone. The reality has not been so simple. Just as the industrial metropolis grew up around the older mercantile city, so the new city of our time has surrounded the old metropolis. What was once the sole center is now one point of concentration among many.

In general, the skyscraper cores of the central cities have adapted to this change and prospered. Even a decentralized region needs a "headquarters," a place of high status and high rents where the movers-and-shakers can rub shoulders and meet for power lunches. By contrast, the old factory zones have not found a function in the new environment. As a result, the central city has reverted to what it was before industrialization: a site for high-level administration and luxury consumption, where some of the wealthiest members of society live in close proximity to many of the poorest.

"Renaissance"

The recent boom in downtown office construction should not conceal the fact that downtown prosperity rests on a much narrower base than it did in its heyday during the 1920s. Most of the retail trade has fled to the malls; the grand old movie palaces and many of the nightspots are gone. Only the expansion of corporate headquarters, law firms, banks and investment houses, advertising agencies, and other corporate and governmental services has kept the downtown towers filled, and even in these fields there have been major leakages of back-office employment to the new city. Nevertheless, this employment base has enabled most core areas to retain an array of specialized shops, restaurants, and cultural activities unequalled in their region. This in turn encourages both the gentrification of surrounding residential neighborhoods and the "renaissance" of the core as a tourist and convention center.

Yet only blocks away from a thriving core like Baltimore's Inner Harbor one can usually find extensive poverty, decay, de-industrialization, and abandonment that stretches out to encompass the old factory zone. The factory zones have found no new role. Their working-class populations have largely followed the factories to the new city, leaving a supply of cheap, old housing which has attracted poor black, Hispanic, and other minority migrants with no other place to go. If the industrial city in its prime brought people together with jobs, cheap housing in the inner city now lures the jobless to those areas where employment prospects are dimmest. The old factory zone is thus doubly disadvantaged: The jobless have moved in, the jobs out.

Public transportation retains its traditional focus on the core, but the inner-city population generally lacks the education to compete for the high-level jobs that are available there. By contrast, the new city usually has an abundance of entry-level jobs, many of them already going begging as the supply of women and students seeking jobs diminishes. Unfortunately, residents of the new city have generally resisted attempts to build low-income housing in middle-class areas and have discouraged public transportation links. They want to keep the new city's expanding tax base for themselves and to avoid any direct fiscal responsibility for the urban poor. The new city has thus walled itself off from the problems of the inner city in a way that the Social Darwinists of the 19th century could only envy.

NO

**Ruth Messinger and
Andrew Breslau**

I AM CITY, HEAR ME ROAR

As President Clinton contemplates a new approach to urban policy, he does so amid a noisy chorus of anti-urban sentiment. Both the Republican and Democratic parties held their conventions in major urban centers last year; yet if one listened closely to the weavers of conventional wisdom, both parties' political goals might have been better served if they had held their assemblies in the beating heart of the "new" American suburbia—someplace like Tysons Corner, VA, or Irvine, CA. As anyone who has even a moderate addiction to political punditry knows by now, "for the first time, the majority of voters live in suburbia." This purportedly epochal demographic shift is broadly interpreted as the death knell of the power and relevance of urbanism in America. "The Suburban Century Begins," proclaimed William Schneider, in *The Atlantic,* in the heat of the presidential race.

It's about time these unchallenged assertions get addressed. The fact is, far from atrophying and despite more than a decade of malignant federal neglect, America's cities are alive and well, if not quite kicking. Their contribution to the country's economy and culture remains the fulcrum around which the rest of the country revolves. If the nation continues to neglect them, and if we are further distracted from the task of healing urban woes by fashionable theory, we do so at our nation's peril.

ADJUSTING THE PICTURE

The current intense allergy to all things urban is entirely out of proportion to the fuzzy picture painted by the data, and it suggests that something different from dispassionate analysis is afoot. Hysteria about urbanity is a recurring event in American political discourse. While Bill Schneider and others in the anti-urban choir may think they're singing a new tune, the truth is, it's a melody as old as the hills.

Before we start shoveling the dirt on our cities' graves, we need to look not only at whether or not cities are truly on the wane but also ask ourselves whether or not there is an identifiable, static collection of interests we can call suburban.

Here's the supposedly damning "epochal" demography. In 1960 American cities comprised 32.3 percent of the nation's population, in 1990 31.3 percent. It is this 1 percent decline relative to the rest of the nation's population on which this recent wave of hand-wringing and prognostication rests. In fact, the urban population of America has remained stable as a percentage of the whole, ranging since 1930 between a low of 30.8 percent and a high of 32.5 percent. According to the recent US census, metropolitan areas of almost all American cities' over a million—including such benighted cities as Oakland and Philadelphia—have actually expanded. Only five of the top forty metropolitan areas have actually lost population.

But this type of number crunching can only take us so far. What constitutes each measured metropolitan region is determined by the federal Office of Management and Budget, and is a factor of a multiplicity of variables, many of which have changed over the years for political or other reasons. In some cases the definition of metropolitan area has included only the "city proper"; in others it includes immediately adjacent suburbs; in still others outlying communities across state borders are included. Still, in the end, a demographic analysis leaves us with one, fairly broad historical constancy: the ratio of what has been measured as the "metropolitan" to the "other" has been remarkably even.

A different interpretation of the statistics is given by Joel Garreau, a skilled journalist and author of the influential book *Edge City*. Garreau, a frequently cited advocate of the new suburban epoch, is more thoughtful than his popular appropriators, but his essential arguments remain off-base. He contends that metropolitan growth is almost entirely charged by the novel phenomenon he titles his book after, and he argues that while surrounding suburban communities have expanded into entities that are not "sub-anything," many of America's central cities are outmoded behemoths that have fallen into an irreversible period of decline.

Garreau has been quoted as saying "Babylon fell, what's so special about Detroit?" He heralds the coming of a new era and a new model of social organization. Central to his argument of urban decline and the arrival of something "new" is the notion that what has changed is not only that people have moved outside downtown areas, but for the first time they have taken their economies with them.

THE DOUGHNUT THEORY

The problem is that Garreau and other naysayers can't see the forest for the trees. Their notion of economic life is what Mitchell Moss, director of New York University's Urban Research Center, and others have called the "doughnut theory." Explaining what's wrong with the concept, Moss argues that people do not live, nor do economies function, in a doughnut environment—"surrounding suburbs with a hole in the middle." Proving the point, the National League of Cities reported in its outstanding study, "Metropolitan Disparities and Economic Growth," a clear relationship between inner-city and suburban income. The smaller the disparity between city per capita income and suburban per capita income, the higher the rate of employment growth throughout the region. Conversely, large disparities are shown to produce negative economic growth.

As these disparities increase, rates of population growth also decline. In other words, the edge only thrives when the center is strong.

And, as is pointed out in the Economic Policy Institute's study of American cities, jobs in the central cities of large metropolitan areas garner 37.7 percent of nationwide earnings. These are higher paying jobs than those available in outlying areas, and they attract a constant influx of new talent from around the world. America's history of economic regeneration is directly tied to the renewal offered by our immigrant tradition. In the city of New York, immigrants from nearly 100 countries entered our boroughs and our workforce this past year. Our center cities are also our centers of media, tourism and the arts. These industries will remain a constant source of economic growth for our downtowns.

To be successful, suburban communities must work in concert with a regional center, typically the much maligned inner city. A study by Arthur Goldberg, of the City University of New York, shows that the 22 percent of Americans living outside our 100 largest cities but within 20 miles of them have nearly half of their households containing a family member working in the city. Fully 67 percent of them depend on the city for major medical care, and 43 percent have family members attending, or planning to attend, city-based educational institutions.

WE'RE NOT DEAD YET

Metropolitan regions are interactive, synergistic wholes. The "in-between triumphant" Garreau declares is not only an impossibility, it is a prescription for economic decapitation.

One of the great assumptions now infecting the debate over urban economic decline is the idea that the increasing prevalence of information technologies and advanced telecommunications systems will have a profound decentralizing effect. Reminiscent of earlier and equally misguided urban doomsday forecasts that surrounded the advent of the telegraph, telephone and federal highway systems, this "chipping away" forecast is significantly flawed.

What we tend to see in our outlying communities are specialized, back office or other space-driven corporate functions. These, for the most part, still remain anchored to downtown institutions. Many manufacturers and Fortune 500 headquarters remain ensconced in our cities not out of nostalgia, but because their economic interests are best served by the creative dynamism, the access to markets, and the close proximity to sub-contractors that are uniquely available in urban settings.

Since 1990 only two big companies' headquarters have left New York City— W. R. Grace and American Home Products—one to a competing downtown, the other to the Jersey suburbs. In that same time period, the German media giant Bertelsmann bought a piece of Times Square for its US headquarters, and SONY completed an enormous leasing deal for 620,000 square feet of New York. As the CEO of a major publishing firm recently put it, "Our success is in large part a function of the quality of the editorial staff. I believe these people thrive on the arts.... If we moved to Wichita, we would lose our editorial staff and much of what makes this place tick."

The commonly accepted thesis that increases in computer efficiency breed a collapse of labor demand, supposedly most keenly felt by our cities, isn't borne out by the facts. In addition to the high-technology jobs accruing to cities by virtue of their market size, technology itself sometimes facilitates employment growth. A recent Bureau of Labor Statistics study forecast the impact of technological change on some 378 industries and 562 occupations in 1995. Almost all of the 350 occupations with more than 25,000 workers, a high concentration of which are in cities, showed employment growth. This study points to the almost heretical idea that faster work often turns out to mean more work.

Finally, the dominant national impulse remains toward both growth and efficiency. This combination is best provided through the density of our cities. One of the defining elements of suburban identity is its relationship to the automobile. In the age of limited fossil fuel, a culture or economy dependent on cars is monstrously inefficient. In the New York region alone, public transportation cuts fuel consumption by 1.33 billion gallons annually. Two rail tracks have the capacity to carry as many people in one hour as 16 lanes of highway. The economic efficiency of an entire region is enhanced through the reduction of personal vehicular traffic. Reduction through the expanded use of mass transit not only drastically improves environmental air quality, it makes the vital commercial use of our roadways less costly and more productive. Such advantages only become possible if tight knit metropolitan communities revolve around an urban anchored mass-transit system.

The challenge for cities, and for national policy makers, is to remain focused on the vocational, educational and quality-of-life needs of our urban workforce, and to nurture workers'

adaptability to new industries. What we don't need to do is cower in the face of the future. Cities are where the workers are, and where the work will be done. Industry recognizes this. Recently, in New York, long-term agreements to retain the Commodities Exchanges and Prudential Securities have included training-to-employment programs for inner-city youth. In Boston around The Boston Compact, and in Minneapolis around The Youth Trust, consortiums of local business and manufacturing leaders have joined with government to establish a comprehensive set of agreements with local schools, vocational centers and the like to provide targeted job opportunities.

A CHANGING URBAN LANDSCAPE

That the fates of city dweller and nation are intimately linked should be a surprise to anyone is what is most surprising about the state of the current debate. What's surprising as well is that the ebb and flow of urban centers is seen as so portentous by many of today's critics. It isn't anything new or particularly fatal. American cities have constantly gone through periods of adaptation, change, decline and renewal.

The marines say only the few and the proud qualify. We might add that among cities, the few, the proud, and those with locational advantages and sound economic planning survive and thrive. In the early part of this century, Buffalo, New York, was bigger than Detroit, and Allegheny, Pennsylvania, was larger than Atlanta. In the last 25 years, Dallas, San Jose and Phoenix have become major metropolitan centers. Some will have what it takes to survive as large cities for the next 75 years, others may not.

The logic of concentration, that which earmarks what we traditionally call a city, asserts itself over time. If Phoenix or any other new American metropolis has what it takes, the signifiers of urbanity will mark them over time. Concentration is more than an anachronistic architectural fashion. Technology or terrain may well determine the initial figure of association, but it is the timeless logic of human need and commerce that will draw the whole picture....

WELL, WHAT ABOUT DETROIT?

What, then, can be said about Detroit? The city, at first glance, does seem to be suffering the death of a thousand cuts. It is the current poster child of the anti-urban movement. It is one of the metro regions losing population. It struggles with an all-too-high crime rate, rampant unemployment, a thriving drug trade, AIDS, high infant-mortality rates, low life expectancies, and whatever other urban horror story you can imagine.

Given its abundant problems, many are assuming that Detroit will soon die. But the fact is, Rasputin-like, the city has so far refused to succumb to various attacks on its life. Unlike the mad monk, however, it may well have the stamina ultimately to survive and once again prosper. The anti-urbanist critics may have chosen the wrong city to pick on.

How can one possibly construct a rosy future for a city as besieged as Detroit? Those qualities that allowed the city to take root and flourish for 75 years or so speak well to its capacity to come back. Detroit possesses incredible, irreducible assets: its port on Lake Huron, its role as a major center of national trucking, its fiber optics network—the second largest in the Northeast. The recent, controver-sial free-trade agreement may prove to be a significant asset to Detroit as well. The city already exports some $1.2 billion worth of goods a year to Canada, making it the most active trading zone in the United States. In addition, while the US auto industry is beset with problems, if it ever is to resuscitate itself, Detroit will clearly be a major beneficiary.

Unlike Babylon, which was conquered by the expansionist Cyrus of Persia, or unlike Scranton, which succumbed to an overreliance on one industry, Detroit may very well have exactly the breadth of resources it needs to adapt and thrive in the 21st century.

CITY PROBLEMS DON'T STAY DOWNTOWN

Whether or not Detroit survives, however, the problems of cities should not be minimized. Nonetheless, our sense of horror about them is, and must be, informed by the knowledge that they are problems that belong to all of us: the problems of our cities have never remained downtown. The American city has always been our hothouse of struggle. It is the place we have always begun to confront our national demons. There never were "good old days" for urban America. One look at the photos of Jacob Riis or a quick flip through any history of metropolitanism shows us that our cities always struggled with violent crime, extreme class and ethnic divisions; they always were on the front line of health crises, always wrapped in a scary drama of survival.

Today, L.A.'s Bloods and Crips or New York's Born to Kill Gang are symbols of our inner cities out of control and out of reach. They are seen to be an indication that crime is dominating our city life to some unprecedented degree. Yet—while the addition of semiautomatic weapons to the mix is hardly salutary—vicious, bullying gangs fueled by illegal markets are hardly a new problem. The afterglow of yesteryear seems to have addled our collective memory. Our streets have never been exactly safe. We have forgotten the mayhem and murder perpetrated by the Dead Rabbit Gang, the Whyos or the Pug Uglies. These infamous New York gangs of the late 19th and early 20th centuries were so brazen and violent they used to roam the streets of Gotham passing out rate sheets to advertise their services: $10 for nose and jaw broke, $15 for an ear chewed off, $50 for poisoning a team of horses or $100 and up for the "big job." In 1909, a bloody Tong war broke out in New York's Chinatown that cost some 350 residents their lives.

In our fondly remembered "golden age" of cities, instead of AIDS, urban centers were racked by deadly outbreaks influenza, yellow fever, small pox, polio or TB. In years past, Irish, German and Italian immigrants fought each other for turf and a place in the social pecking order. Today, West Indian, Vietnamese and Dominican immigrants fight the same fights. Through crisis, clash and creativity, this is how we have always manufactured the new America.

IT'S AS OLD AS THE REPUBLIC

Why do so many people now seem to be so pessimistic about cities? Why aren't we viewing the current situation as a signal of the growth of urbanism or of the possibilities of reconstitution and renewal? The recent spark of anti-urbanism represents a pattern of political parrying as old as the nation. "Our cities," said one American politician, are "more pestilential than yellow fever to the morals, the health and the liberties of man." Another prominent American and influential thinker said, "the life of the city was artificial and curtailed"; it destroyed solitude, poetry and philosophy. Still another American whose vision shapes our notions of home, city and place said, "the death of the city is to be the greatest service the machine will ultimately render the human being." The quotations are from Thomas Jefferson, Ralph Waldo Emerson and Frank Lloyd Wright.

High-pitched political, and even moral, argument about the significance of urban areas is as American as apple pie and as old as the republic. Yet today, the battle over cities has enormous stakes. Disputes between and among the Democrats and Republicans, the searching for new constituencies and the stretch for new paradigms of urban policy are not merely about intellectual or partisan differences, but about whose location, whose way of living, whose home is determined strategically important to the nation's future.

In any era of dwindling resources, this determination is particularly fraught. It is additionally charged by the issues of race and class. Who populates our inner cities? The poor, the young, people of color, and the rainbow of immigrants still teeming to our shores make up a significant part of our urban population. This past election was choked with code words and subtle pandering to majority fears. Despite civil unrest in Los Angeles and many other cities in the election year, the contest was marked by the avoidance of the cities as an important issue. Precious little was said about our urban challenges, but gallons of ink were spilled in rationalizing that avoidance. It's time to get out of denial.

WISHING CITIES AWAY

While we believe cities have history on their side, what they don't have is the Republicans. Although the Democratic party hasn't exactly beaten down the barricades with an eagerness to confront urban woes, at least urban policy is part of its platform. For twelve years Republican urban policy was a perverse twist on the theme of "Field of Dreams." In that film, Kevin Costner was told by unseen voices to "build it and they will come"; the Republican approach to cities seems to be "ignore them and they will go away.

Under the Republican stewardship, the share of federal revenues going to cities was reduced by a devastating amount. Over the last decade, federal funds as a percentage of city budgets have been cut by over 64 percent. Last year New York City struggled with a $3 billion dollar budget shortfall, exactly the size of its reduced federal contribution. In the course of the 1980s, cities lost 50 percent of their adjusted share of mass-transit revenues, 55 percent of employment and training monies and 54 percent of Community Development Block Grant funding. Helpful, community-building initiatives like Urban Development Action Grants and General Revenue Sharing were wiped out.

Such mindless hacking away at the economic future of our cities hurt no one but ourselves. No other country in the industrial world neglects its cities as we do. Japan is in the midst of an $8 trillion investment in its urban infrastructure; Paris, London, Bonn and Rome all enjoy levels of national support that—if

they were offered here—would make the nation's mayors weep with joy. By ignoring our cities' needs, we are jeopardizing our future competitiveness in the world economy.

H. L. Mencken, Baltimore's prophet of rage, once said that "for every complex, difficult problem, there is a simple, easy solution... and it is wrong." There are no quick fixes or dazzling new policy options for the problems that beleaguer America's cities. America must commit itself to the slow, frequently unsatisfying progress that a commitment to long-term planning brings. Investments in mass transit, job training, preventive health care, and a wide variety of educational and criminal justice initiatives will all aid cities in their renewal. Over time these investments will more than pay for themselves—healthy cities translate into a healthy nation.

Of course, America is changing. We are no longer predominately a nation of villages and farms. But we must realize that what hasn't changed is the relationship of the center to what surrounds it, be it the various manifestations of suburbia, incipient cities, agribusiness or rural community. Urban centers remain remarkably constant in their historical position of strength in our country. Despite the steady diet of images we are fed, American cities are more than a bundle of urban problems: they are the source of our nation's solutions. Bill Clinton and Henry Cisneros must recognize this and reverse the course of the last 12 years or our nation's ideal of a vibrant pluralism will be degraded to a dangerous and surely tragic extent.

Perhaps as a nation we've grown tired, immune to the magic of the urban project. But when you walk down Orchard Street in New York City, you can't help but feel and see its spirit. The web of affirmation, conflict, chaos, assimilation and empowerment that is our cities remains breathtaking. The vitality it confers is infectious. This past weekend on Orchard Street a Sikh was arguing on a corner with a Puerto Rican restaurateur, an elderly Chinese man and a Hasidic Jew shared a joke, a group of young African-American women bargained over the price of a leather coat with a Russian emigré, and a young Italian man stared fiercely over a chess board at a Filipino opponent. These tableaux aren't some sanitized, Norman Rockwell picture of our experience, they are the faces of the American city.

With all their problems, cities are still the place where America reimagines itself. The American "task," its agenda, is forged in its cities. Cities are the engine of learning, of culture, and the economy. They are the factories of national socialization. They are where we grapple with the unique project of managing difference. There is no substitute.

POSTSCRIPT

Are Central Cities Becoming Obsolete?

Fishman maintains that the population figures indicate that the suburbs are surging ahead of central cities. He also sees stores and jobs following the residential trail. Messinger and Breslau, however, look at where the decisions are made that govern the world economy and national politics and find that they are still made in the cities. There seems to be two forces operating here: power and coordination are concentrating in cities, while population is moving out to the suburbs. Messinger and Breslau are not complacent about the health of cities but are disturbed by the national mood, which is too ready to abandon the policies that benefit cities. Since "cities are where the workers are, and where the work will be done," they argue, national policy should focus on the training and education of these workers. In contrast, Fishman has recommended elsewhere that policymakers should concentrate on planning in the suburbs so that the pursuit of quality life by suburbanites is not frustrated by unplanned, pell-mell growth.

The classic work on cities is Lewis Mumford's *The City in History* (Harcourt Brace Jovanovich, 1961), which provides a fascinating account of the rise of cities and the key role that they played in history. On the issue of suburban dominance, three key articles are: Peter O. Muller, "Are Cities Obsolete?" *The Sciences* (March/April 1986); William Schneider, "The Suburban Century Begins," *The Atlantic Monthly* (July 1992); and Peter D. Salins, "Cities, Suburbs, and the Urban Cities," *The Public Interest* (Fall 1993). Also see the book *Edge City* (Doubleday, 1991), by Joel Garreau.

Sociologists have for a long time focused on the characteristics of city life that either attract people to or repel people from the city. A classic analysis of the nature of city life is found in Louis Wirth, "Urbanism as a Way of Life," *American Journal of Sociology* (vol. 44, 1938), pp. 8–20. A more recent description of urban life is Claude S. Fischer, *The Urban Experience*, 2d ed. (Harcourt Brace Jovanovich, 1984). A key feature of city life is its scale. Kirkpatrick Sale explores the impact of this factor on social life in *Human Scale* (Coward, McCann, & Geohegan, 1980). William H. Whyte tries to correct many misunderstandings concerning city life and to put cities in a more favorable light in *City: Rediscovering the Center* (Doubleday, 1988). On the negative side, Wesley G. Skogan, in *Disorder and Decline: Crime and the Spiral of Decay in American Neighborhoods* (Free Press, 1990), demonstrates how crime produces disorder in city neighborhoods and how this disorder produces more crime. A profound analysis of the interests and the processes that are behind the urban and suburban policies toward economic growth is presented by John R. Logan and Harvey L. Molotch in *Urban Fortunes* (University of California Press, 1987).

PART 5

Crime and Social Control

All societies label certain hurtful actions as crimes and punish those who commit the crimes. Other harmful actions, however, are not defined as crimes, and the perpetrators are not punished. Today the definition of crime and the appropriate treatment of criminals is widely debated. Some of the major questions are: Does street crime pose more of a threat to the public's well-being than white-collar crime? Billions of dollars have been spent on the "war on drugs," but who is winning? Would legalizing some drugs free up money that could be directed to other types of social welfare programs, such as the rehabilitation of addicts? And is imprisonment an effective means of reducing crime by removing criminals from the streets, or is it, in the long run, costly and inhumane?

- Is Street Crime More Harmful Than White-Collar Crime?

- Should Drugs Be Legalized?

- Is Incapacitation the Answer to the Crime Problem?

ISSUE 16

Is Street Crime More Harmful Than White-Collar Crime?

YES: John J. DiIulio, Jr., from "The Impact of Inner-City Crime," *The Public Interest* (Summer 1989)

NO: Jeffrey Reiman, from *The Rich Get Richer and the Poor Get Prison: Ideology, Class, and Criminal Justice*, 3rd ed. (Macmillan, 1990)

ISSUE SUMMARY

YES: John J. DiIulio, Jr., an associate professor of politics and public affairs, analyzes the enormous harm done—especially to the urban poor and, by extension, to all of society—by street criminals and their activities.

NO: Professor of philosophy Jeffrey Reiman argues that the dangers posed by negligent corporations and white-collar criminals are a greater menace to society than are the activities of typical street criminals.

The word *crime* entered the English language (from the Old French) around A.D. 1250, when it was identified with "sinfulness." Later, the meaning of the word was modified: crime became the kind of sinfulness that was rightly punishable by law. Even medieval writers, who did not distinguish very sharply between church and state, recognized that there were some sins for which punishment was best left to God; the laws should punish only those that cause harm to the community. Of course, their concept of harm was a very broad one, embracing such offenses as witchcraft and blasphemy. Modern jurists, even those who deplore such practices, would say that the state has no business punishing the perpetrators of these types of offenses.

What, then, should the laws punish? The answer depends in part on our notion of harm. We usually limit the term to the kind of harm that is tangible and obvious: taking a life, causing bodily injury or psychological trauma, and destroying property. For most Americans today, particularly those who live in cities, the word *crime* is practically synonymous with street crime. Anyone who has ever been robbed or beaten by street criminals will never forget the experience. The harm that these criminals cause is tangible, and the connection between the harm and the perpetrator is very direct.

But suppose the connection is not so direct. Suppose, for example, that A hires B to shoot C. Is that any less a crime? B is the actual shooter, but is A any less guilty? Of course not, we say; he may even be more guilty, since he is the ultimate mover behind the crime. A would be guilty even if the chain of command were much longer, involving A's orders to B, and B's to C, then on to D, E, and F to kill G. Organized crime kingpins go to jail even when they are far removed from the people who carry out their orders. High officials of the Nixon administration, even though they were not directly involved in the burglary attempt at the Democratic National Committee headquarters at the Watergate Hotel complex in 1972, were imprisoned.

This brings us to the topic of white-collar crime. The burglars at the Watergate Hotel were acting on orders that trickled down from the highest reaches of political power in the United States. Other white-collar criminals are as varied as the occupations from which they come. They include stockbrokers who make millions through insider trading, as Ivan Boesky did; members of Congress who take payoffs; and people who cheat on their income taxes, like hotel owner and billionaire Leona Helmsley. Some, like Helmsley, get stiff prison sentences when convicted, though many others (like most of the officials in the Watergate scandal) do little or no time in prison. Do they deserve stiffer punishment, or are their crimes less harmful than the crimes of street criminals?

Although white-collar criminals do not directly cause physical harm or relieve people of their wallets, they can still end up doing considerable harm. The harm done by Nixon's aides threatened the integrity of the U.S. electoral system. Every embezzler, corrupt politician, and tax cheat exacts a toll on our society. Individuals can be hurt in more tangible ways by decisions made in corporate boardrooms: Auto executives, for example, have approved design features that have caused fatalities. Managers of chemical companies have allowed practices that have polluted the environment with cancer-causing agents. And heads of corporations have presided over industries wherein workers have been needlessly killed or maimed.

Whether or not these decisions should be considered crimes is debatable. A crime must always involve "malicious intent," or what the legal system calls *mens rea*. This certainly applies to street crime—the mugger obviously has sinister designs—but does it apply to every decision made in a boardroom that ends up causing harm? And does that harm match or exceed the harm caused by street criminals? In the following selections, John J. DiIulio, Jr., focuses on the enormous harm done—especially to the poor—by street criminals. Not only does street crime cause loss, injury, terror, and death for individuals, he argues, but it also causes neighborhood decline, community disintegration, loss of pride, business decline and failure, hampered schools, and middle-class flight to the suburbs. According to Jeffrey Reiman, white-collar crime also does more harm than is commonly recognized. By his count, white-collar crime causes far more deaths, injuries, illnesses, and financial loss than street crime. In light of this, he argues, we must redefine our ideas about what crime is and who the criminals are.

YES

John J. DiIulio, Jr.

THE IMPACT OF INNER-CITY CRIME

My grandmother, an Italian immigrant, lived in the same Philadelphia row house from 1921 till her death in 1986. When she moved there, and for the four decades thereafter, most of her neighbors were Irish and Italian. When she died, virtually all of her neighbors were black. Like the whites who fled, the first blacks who moved in were mostly working-class people living just above the poverty level.

Until around 1970, the neighborhood changed little. The houses were well-maintained. The children played in the streets and were polite. The teenagers hung out on the street corners in the evenings, sometimes doing mischief, but rarely—if ever—doing anything worse. The local grocers and other small businesspeople (both blacks and the few remaining whites) stayed open well past dark. Day or night, my grandmother journeyed the streets just as she had during the days of the Great Depression, taking the bus to visit her friends and relatives, going shopping, attending church, and so on.

She was a conspicuous and popular figure in this black community. She was conspicuous for her race, accent, and advanced age; she was popular for the homespun advice (and home-baked goods) she dispensed freely to the teenagers hanging out on the corners, to the youngsters playing ball in the street in front of her house, and to their parents (many of them mothers living without a husband).

Like the generations of ethnics who had lived there before them, these people were near the bottom of the socioeconomic ladder. I often heard my grandmother say that her new neighbors were "just like us," by which she meant that they were honest, decent, law-abiding people working hard to advance themselves and to make a better life for their children.

But in the early 1970s, the neighborhood began to change. Some, though by no means all, of the black families my grandmother had come to know moved out of the neighborhood. The new neighbors kept to themselves. The exteriors of the houses started to look ratty. The streets grew dirty. The grocery and variety stores closed or did business only during daylight hours. The children played in the schoolyard but not in front of their homes. The teenagers on the corners were replaced by adult drug dealers and their "runners." Vandalism

Excerpted from John J. DiIulio, Jr., "The Impact of Inner-City Crime," *The Public Interest*, no. 96 (Summer 1989), pp. 28–46. Copyright © 1989 by National Affairs, Inc. Reprinted by permission of *The Public Interest* and the author.

and graffiti became commonplace. My grandmother was mugged twice, both times by black teenagers; once she was severely beaten in broad daylight.

In the few years before she died at age eighty-four, and after years of pleading by her children and dozens of grandchildren, she stopped going out and kept her doors and windows locked at all times. On drives to visit her, when I got within four blocks of her home, I instinctively checked to make sure that my car doors were locked. Her house, where I myself had been raised, was in a "bad neighborhood," and it did not make sense to take any chances. I have not returned to the area since the day of her funeral.

My old ethnic and ghetto neighborhood had become an underclass neighborhood. Why is it that most readers of this article avoid, and advise their friends and relatives to avoid, walking or driving through such neighborhoods? Obviously we are not worried about being infected somehow by the extremely high levels of poverty, joblessness, illiteracy, welfare dependency, or drug abuse that characterize these places. Instead we shun these places because we suppose them to contain exceedingly high numbers of predatory street criminals, who hit, rape, rob, deal drugs, burglarize, and murder.

This supposition is absolutely correct. The underclass problem, contrary to the leading academic and journalistic understandings, is mainly a crime problem. It is a crime problem, moreover, that can be reduced dramatically (although not eliminated) with the human and financial resources already at hand.

Only two things are required: common sense and compassion. Once we understand the underclass problem as a crime problem, neither of those two qualities should be scarce. Until we understand the underclass problem as a crime problem, policymakers and others will continue to fiddle while the underclass ghettos of Philadelphia, Newark, Chicago, Los Angeles, Miami, Washington, D.C., and other cities burn....

THE TRULY DEVIANT

Liberals... have understood the worsening of ghetto conditions mainly as the byproduct of a complex process of economic and social change. One of the latest and most influential statements of this view is William Julius Wilson's *The Truly Disadvantaged: The Inner City, the Underclass, and Public Policy* (1987).

Wilson argues that over the last two decades a new and socially destructive class structure has emerged in the ghetto. As he sees it, the main culprit is deindustrialization. As plants have closed, urban areas, especially black urban areas, have lost entry-level jobs. To survive economically, or to enjoy their material success, ghetto residents in a position to do so have moved out, leaving behind them an immobilized "underclass."...

Wilson has focused our attention on the socioeconomic straits of the truly disadvantaged with an elegance and rhetorical force that is truly admirable.[1] But despite its many strengths, his often subtle analysis of the underclass problem wrongly deemphasizes one obvious possibility: "The truly disadvantaged" exist mainly because of the activities of "the truly deviant"—the large numbers of chronic and predatory street criminals—in their midst. One in every nine adult black males in this country is under some form of correctional supervision (prison, jail, probation, or parole).[2] Criminals come disproportionately from underclass neighborhoods. They victimize their neighbors directly through crime, and indirectly by creating or worsening the multiple social and economic ills that define the sad lot of today's ghetto dwellers.

PREDATORY GHETTO CRIMINALS

I propose [another] way of thinking about the underclass problem. The members of the underclass are, overwhelmingly, decent and law-abiding residents of America's most distressed inner cities. Fundamentally, what makes them different from the rest of us is not only their higher than normal levels of welfare dependency and the like, but their far higher than normal levels of victimization by predatory criminals.

This victimization by criminals takes several forms. There is *direct victimization*—being mugged, raped, or murdered; being threatened and extorted; living in fear about whether you can send your children to school or let them go out and play without their being bothered by dope dealers, pressured by gang members, or even struck by a stray bullet. And there is *indirect victimization*—dampened neighborhood economic development, loss of a sizable fraction of the neighborhood's male population to prison or jail, the undue influence on young people exercised by criminal "role models" like the cash-rich drug lords who rule the streets, and so on.

Baldly stated, my hypothesis is that this victimization causes and perpetuates the other ills of our underclass neighborhoods. Schools in these neighborhoods are unable to function effectively because of their disorderly atmosphere and because of the violent behavior of the criminals (especially gang members) who hang around their classrooms. The truly deviant are responsible for a high percentage of teen pregnancies, rapes, and sexual assaults. Similarly, many of the chronically welfare-dependent, female-headed households in these neighborhoods owe their plights to the fact that the men involved are either unable (because they are under some form of correctional supervision) or unwilling (because it does not jibe well with their criminal lifestyles) to seek and secure gainful employment and live with their families. And much of the poverty and joblessness in these neighborhoods can be laid at the door of criminals whose presence deters local business activity, including the development of residential real estate.

Blacks are victims of violent crimes at much higher rates than whites. Most lone-offender crime against blacks is committed by blacks, while most such crimes against whites are committed by whites; in 1986, for instance, 83.5 percent of violent crimes against blacks were committed by blacks, while 80.3 percent of violent crimes against whites were committed by whites. This monochrome picture of victim-offender relationships also holds for multiple-offender crimes. In 1986, for example, 79.6 percent of multiple-offender violent crimes against blacks were committed by blacks; the "white-on-white" figure was 59.4 percent.

Criminals are most likely to commit crimes against people of their own race. The main reason is presumably their physical proximity to potential victims. If so, then it is not hard to understand why underclass neighborhoods, which have more than their share of would-be criminals, have more than their share of crime.

Prison is the most costly form of correctional supervision, and it is normally reserved for the most dangerous felons—violent or repeat offenders. Most of my readers do not personally know anyone in prison; most ghetto dwellers of a decade or two ago probably would not have known anyone in prison either. But most of today's underclass citizens do; the convicted felons were their relatives and neighbors—and often their victimizers.

For example, in 1980 Newark was the street-crime capital of New Jersey. In the Newark area, there were more than 920 violent crimes (murders, non-negligent manslaughters, forcible rapes, robberies, and aggravated assaults) per 100,000 residents; in the rest of the state the figure was under 500, and in affluent towns like Princeton it was virtually nil. In the same year, New Jersey prisons held 5,866 criminals, 2,697 of them from the Newark area.[3] In virtually all of the most distressed parts of this distressed city, at least one of every two hundred residents was an imprisoned felon.[4] The same basic picture holds for other big cities.[5]

Correlation, however, is not causation, and we could extend and refine this sort of crude, exploratory analysis of the relationship between crime rates, concentrations of correctional supervisees, and the underclass neighborhoods from which they disproportionately come. But except to satisfy curiosity, I see no commanding need for such studies. For much the same picture emerges from the anecdotal accounts of people who have actually spent years wrestling with—as opposed to merely researching—the problem.

For example, in 1988 the nation's capital became its murder capital. Washington, D.C., had 372 killings, 82 percent of them committed on the streets by young black males against other young black males. The city vied with Detroit for the highest juvenile homicide rate in America. Here is part of the eloquent testimony on this development given by Isaac Fulwood, a native Washingtonian and the city's police-chief designate:

> The murder statistics don't capture what these people are doing. We've had in excess of 1,260 drug-related shootings.... People are scared of these kids. Someone can get shot in broad daylight, and nobody saw anything.... Nobody talks. And that's so different from the way it was in my childhood.

The same thing can be said about the underclass neighborhoods of other major cities. In Detroit, for instance, most of the hundreds of ghetto residents murdered over the last six years were killed within blocks of their homes by their truly deviant neighbors.

To devise meaningful law-enforcement and correctional responses to the underclass problem, we need to understand why concentrations of crime and criminals are so high in these neighborhoods, and to change our government's criminal-justice policies and practices accordingly.

UNDERSTANDING THE PROBLEM

We begin with a chicken-and-egg question: Does urban decay cause crime, or does crime cause urban decay?

In conventional criminology, which derives mainly from sociology, ghettos are portrayed as "breeding grounds" for predatory street crime. Poverty, joblessness, broken homes, single-parent families, and similar factors are identified as the "underlying causes" of crime.[6] These conditions cause crime, the argument goes; as they worsen—as the ghetto community becomes the underclass neighborhood—crime worsens. This remains the dominant academic perspective on the subject, one that is shared implicitly by most public officials who are close to the problem.

Beginning in the mid-1970s, however, a number of influential studies appeared that challenged this conventional criminological wisdom.[7] Almost without exception, these studies have cast grave doubts on the classic sociological explanation of crime, suggesting that the actual relationships between such variables as poverty, illiteracy, and unemployment, on the one hand, and criminality, on the other, are far more ambiguous than most analysts freely assumed only a decade or so ago....

LOCKS, COPS, AND STUDIES

Camden, New Jersey, is directly across the bridge from Philadelphia. Once-decent areas have become just like my grandmother's old neighborhood: isolated, crime-torn urban war zones. In February 1989 a priest doing social work in Camden was ordered off the streets by drug dealers and threatened with death if he did not obey. The police chief of Camden sent some extra men into the area, but the violent drug dealers remained the real rulers of the city's streets.

The month before the incident in Camden, the Rockefeller Foundation announced that it was going to devote some of its annual budget (which exceeds $100 million) to researching the underclass problem. Other foundations, big and small, have already spent (or misspent) much money on the problem.

But Rockefeller's president was quoted as follows: "Nobody knows who they are, what they do.... The underclass is not a topic to pursue from the library. You get out and look for them."

His statement was heartening, but it revealed a deep misunderstanding of the problem. Rather than intimating that the underclass was somehow hard to locate, he would have done better to declare that his charity would purchase deadbolt locks for the homes of ghetto dwellers in New York City who lacked them, and subsidize policing and private-security services in the easily identifiable neighborhoods where these poor people are concentrated.

More street-level research would be nice, especially for the networks of policy intellectuals (liberal and conservative) who benefit directly from such endeavors. But more locks, cops, and corrections officers would make a more positive, tangible, and lasting difference in the lives of today's ghetto dwellers.

NOTES

1. In addition, he has canvassed competing academic perspectives on the underclass; see William Julius Wilson, ed., "The Ghetto Underclass: Social Science Perspectives," *Annals of the American Academy of Political and Social Science* (January 1989). It should also be noted that he is directing a $2.7 million research project on poverty in Chicago that promises to be the most comprehensive study of its kind yet undertaken.

2. According to the Bureau of Justice Statistics, in 1986 there were 234,430 adult black males in prison, 101,000 in jail, an estimated 512,000 on probation, and 133,300 on parole. There were 8,985,000 adult black males in the national residential population. I am grateful to Larry Greenfeld for his assistance in compiling these figures.

3. I am grateful to Hank Pierre, Stan Repko, and Commissioner William H. Fauver of the New Jersey Department of Corrections for granting me access to these figures and to related data on density of prisoner residence; to Andy Ripps for his heroic efforts in organizing them; and to my Princeton colleague

Mark Alan Hughes for his expert help in analyzing the data.

4. Ten of the thirteen most distressed Newark census tracts were places where the density of prisoner residence was that high. In other words, 76.9 percent of the worst underclass areas of Newark had such extremely high concentrations of hardcore offenders. In most of the rest of Newark, and throughout the rest of the state, such concentrations were virtually nonexistent.

5. In 1980 in the Chicago area, for example, in 182 of the 1,521 census tracts at least one of every two hundred residents was an imprisoned felon. Fully twenty of the thirty-five worst underclass tracts had such extraordinary concentrations of serious criminals; in several of them, more than one of every hundred residents was behind prison bars. I am grateful to Wayne Carroll and Commissioner Michael Lane of the Illinois Department of Corrections for helping me with these data.

6. For example, see the classic statement by Edwin H. Sutherland and Donald R. Cressey, *Principles of Criminology,* 7th rev. ed. (Philadelphia: J. P. Lippincott, 1966).

7. See, for example, James Q. Wilson, *Thinking About Crime* (New York: Basic Books, 1975), especially the third chapter.

NO

Jeffrey Reiman

A CRIME BY ANY OTHER NAME

If one individual inflicts a bodily injury upon another which leads to the death of the person attacked we call it manslaughter; on the other hand, if the attacker knows beforehand that the blow will be fatal we call it murder. Murder has also been committed if society places hundreds of workers in such a position that they inevitably come to premature and unnatural ends. Their death is as violent as if they had been stabbed or shot. . . . Murder has been committed if society knows perfectly well that thousands of workers cannot avoid being sacrificed so long as these conditions are allowed to continue. Murder of this sort is just as culpable as the murder committed by an individual.

Frederick Engels
The Condition of the Working Class in England

WHAT'S IN A NAME?

If it takes you an hour to read this chapter, by the time you reach the last page, two of your fellow citizens will have been murdered. *During that same time, at least four Americans will die as a result of unhealthy or unsafe conditions in the workplace!* Although these work-related deaths could have been prevented, they are not called murders. Why not? Doesn't a crime by any other name still cause misery and suffering? What's in a name?

The fact is that the label "crime" is not used in America to name all or the worst of the actions that cause misery and suffering to Americans. It is primarily reserved for the dangerous actions of the poor.

In the March 14, 1976 edition of the *Washington Star*, a front-page article appeared with the headline: "Mine Is Closed 26 Deaths Late." The article read in part:

> *Why, the relatives [of the twenty-six dead miners] ask, did the mine ventilation fail and allow pockets of volatile methane gas to build up in a shaft 2,300 feet below the surface?*
>
> *Why wasn't the mine cleared as soon as supervisors spotted evidence of methane gas near where miners were driving huge machines into the 61-foot-high coal seam? . . .*
>
> *[I]nvestigators of the Senate Labor and Welfare Committee . . . found that there have been 1,250 safety violations at the 13-year-old mine since 1970. Fifty-seven of those violations were serious enough for federal inspectors to order the mine closed and 21 of*

those were in cases where federal inspectors felt there was imminent danger to the lives of the miners working there. . . .

Federal inspectors said the most recent violations found at the mine were three found in the ventilation system on Monday—the day before 15 miners were killed.

Next to the continuation of this story was another, headlined: "Mass Murder Claims Six in Pennsylvania." It described the shooting death of a husband and wife, their three children, and a friend in a Philadelphia suburb. This was murder, maybe even mass murder. My only question is, "Why wasn't the death of the miners also murder?"

Why do twenty-six dead miners amount to a "disaster" and six dead suburbanites a "mass murder"? "Murder" suggests a murderer, whereas "disaster" suggests the work of impersonal forces. If more than 1,000 safety violations had been found in the mine—three the day before the first explosion—was no one responsible for failing to eliminate the hazards? Was no one responsible for *preventing* the hazards? If someone could have prevented the hazards and did not, does that person not bear responsibility for the deaths of twenty-six men? Is he less evil because he did not want them to die although he chose to leave them in jeopardy? Is he not a murderer, perhaps even a *mass* murderer?

These questions are at this point rhetorical. My aim is not to discuss this case but rather to point to the blinders we wear when we look at such a "disaster." Perhaps there will be an investigation. Perhaps someone will be held responsible. Perhaps he will be fined. But will he be tried for *murder?* Will anyone think of him as a murderer? *And if not, why not?* Would the miners not be safer if such people were treated as murderers? Might they

not still be alive? . . . Didn't those miners have a right to protection from the violence that took their lives? *And if not, why not?*

Once we are ready to ask this question seriously, we are in a position to see that the reality of crime—that is, the acts we label crime, the acts we think of as crime, the actors and actions we treat as criminal—is *created:* It is an image shaped by decisions as to *what* will be called crime and *who* will be treated as a criminal.

THE CARNIVAL MIRROR

. . . The American criminal justice system is a mirror that shows a distorted image of the dangers that threaten us—an image created more by the shape of the mirror than by the reality reflected. What do we see when we look in the criminal justice mirror?

On the morning of September 16, 1975, the *Washington Post* carried an article in its local news section headlined "Arrest Data Reveal Profile of a Suspect." The article reported the results of a study of crime in Prince George's County, a suburb of Washington, D.C. It read in part that

The typical suspect in serious crime in Prince George's County is a black male, aged 14 to 19. . . .

This is the Typical Criminal feared by most law-abiding Americans. His crime, according to former Attorney General John Mitchell (who was by no means a typical criminal), is forcing us "to change the fabric of our society, . . . forcing us, a free people, to alter our pattern of life, . . . to withdraw from our neighbors, to fear all strangers and to limit our activities to 'safe' areas." These poor, young, urban (disproportionately) black males comprise the core of the enemy forces in the war against crime. They are the heart of a vicious, unorganized guerrilla army, threatening the lives, limbs, and possessions of the law-abiding members of society—necessitating recourse to the ultimate weapons of force and detention in our common defense. They are the "career criminals" President Reagan had in mind when he told the International Association of Chiefs of Police, assuring them of the tough stance that the federal government would take in the fight against crime, that "a small number of criminals are responsible for an enormous amount of the crime in American society."

... The acts of the Typical Criminal are not the only acts that endanger us, nor are they the acts that endanger us the most. We have a greater chance... of being killed or disabled, for example, by an occupational injury or disease, by unnecessary surgery, or by shoddy emergency medical services than by aggravated assault or even homicide! Yet even though these threats to our well-being are graver than that posed by our poor, young, urban, black males, they do not show up in the FBI's Index of serious crimes. The individuals who are responsible for them do not turn up in arrest records or prison statistics. *They never become part of the reality reflected in the criminal justice mirror, although the danger they pose is at least as great and often greater than those who do!*

Similarly, the general public loses more money *by far*... from price-fixing and monopolistic practices and from consumer deception and embezzlement than from all the property crimes in the FBI's Index combined. Yet these far more costly acts are either not criminal, or if technically criminal, not prosecuted, or if prosecuted,

not punished, or if punished, only mildly. In any event, although the individuals responsible for these acts take more money out of the ordinary citizen's pocket than our Typical Criminal, they rarely show up in arrest statistics and almost never in prison populations. *Their faces rarely appear in the criminal justice mirror, although the danger they pose is at least as great and often greater than those who do.*

The inescapable conclusion is that the criminal justice system does not simply *reflect* the reality of crime; it has a hand in *creating* the reality we see.

The criminal justice system is like a mirror in which society can see the face of the evil in its midst. Because the system deals with some evil and not with others, because it treats some evils as the gravest and treats some of the gravest evils as minor, the image it throws back is distorted like the image in a carnival mirror. Thus, the image cast back is false, not because it is invented out of thin air, but because the proportions of the real are distorted: Large becomes small and small large; grave becomes minor and minor grave. Like a carnival mirror, although nothing is reflected that does not exist in the world, the image is more a creation of the mirror than a picture of the world....

This is my point. Because we accept the belief... that the model for crime is one person specifically intending to harm another, we accept a legal system that leaves us unprotected against much greater dangers to our lives and well-being than those threatened by the Typical Criminal....

Work May Be Dangerous to Your Health

Since the publication of *The President's Report on Occupational Safety and Health* in 1972, numerous studies have documented both the astounding incidence of disease, injury, and death due to hazards in the workplace *and* the fact that much or most of this carnage is the consequence of the refusal of management to pay for safety measures and of government to enforce safety standards.

In that 1972 report, the government estimated the number of job-related illnesses at 390,000 per year and the number of annual deaths from industrial disease at 100,000. For 1986, the Bureau of Labor Statistics [BLS] of the U.S. Department of Labor estimates 136,800 job-related illnesses and 3,610 work-related deaths. Note that the latter figure applies only to private-sector work environments with eleven or more employees. It is not limited to death from occupational disease but includes all work-related deaths, including those resulting from accidents on the job.

Before considering the significance of these figures, it should be pointed out that there is wide agreement that occupational diseases are seriously underreported. *The Report of the President to the Congress on Occupational Safety and Health for 1980* stated that

recording and reporting of illnesses continue to present measurement problems, since employers (and doctors) are often unable to recognize some illnesses as work-related. The annual survey includes data only on the visible illnesses of workers. To the extent that occupational illnesses are unrecognized and, therefore, not recorded or reported, the illness survey estimates may understate their occurrence.

... For these reasons, plus the fact that BLS's figures on work-related deaths are only for private workplaces with eleven or more employees, we must supplement the BLS figures with other estimates. In 1982, then U.S. Secretary of Health and Human Services Richard Schweiker stated that "current estimates for overall workplace-associated cancer mortality vary within a range of five to fifteen percent." With annual cancer deaths currently running more than 460,000, that translates into between 23,000 and 69,000 job-related cancer deaths per year. In testimony before the Senate Committee on Labor and Human Resources, Dr. Philip Landrigan, director of the Division of Environmental and Occupational Medicine at the Mount Sinai School of Medicine in New York City, stated that

Recent data indicate that occupationally related exposures are responsible each year in New York State for 5,000 to 7,000 deaths and for 35,000 new cases of illness (not including work-related injuries). These deaths due to occupational disease include 3,700 deaths from cancer....

Crude national estimates of the burden of occupational disease in the United States may be developed by multiplying the New York State data by a factor of 10. New York State contains slightly less than 10 percent of the nation's workforce, and it includes a broad mix of employment in the manufacturing, service and agricultural sectors. Thus, it may be calculated that occupational disease is responsible each year in the United States for 50,000 to 70,000 deaths, and for approximately 350,000 new cases of illness.

It is some confirmation of Dr. Landrigan's estimates that they imply work-related cancer deaths of approximately 37,000 a year—a figure that is squarely in the middle of the range implied in Secretary Schweiker's statement on this issue. Thus, even if we discount OSHA's [Occupational Safety and Health Administration's] 1972 estimate of 100,000 deaths a year due to occupational disease or Dr. Landrigan's estimate of between 50,000 to 70,000, we would surely be erring in the other direction to accept the BLS figure of 3,610. We can hardly be overestimating the actual toll if we set it at 25,000 deaths a year resulting from occupational disease.

As for the BLS estimate of 136,800 job-related illnesses, here, too, there is reason to assume that the figure considerably understates the real situation. Dr. Landrigan's estimates suggest that the BLS figure represents less than half of the actual number. However, the BLS figure is less accurate than its figure for job-related deaths for at least two reasons: It is not limited to firms with eleven or more employees and symptoms of illness generally can be expected to appear sooner after contracting an illness than does death. To stay on the conservative side, then, I shall assume that there are annually in the United States approximately 150,000 job-related illnesses and 25,000 deaths from occupational diseases. How does this compare to the threat posed by crime? Before jumping to any conclusions, note that the risk of occupational disease and death falls only on members of the labor force, whereas the risk of crime falls on the whole population, from infants to the elderly. Because the labor force is less than half the total population (110,000,000 in 1986, out of a total population of 241,000,000), to get a true picture of the *relative* threat posed by occupational diseases compared to that posed by crime we should *halve* the crime statistics when comparing them to the figures for industrial disease and death. Using the 1986 statistics, this means that the *comparable* figures would be:

	Occupational Disease	Crime (halved)
Death	25,000	10,000
Other physical harm	150,000	400,000

... It should be noted further that the statistics given so far are *only* for occupational *diseases* and deaths from those diseases. They do not include death and disability from work-related injuries. Here, too, the statistics are gruesome. The National Safety Council reported that in 1986, work-related accidents caused 10,700 deaths and 1.8 million disabling work injuries, at a total cost to the economy of $34.8 billion. This brings the number of occupation-related deaths to 36,700 a year. If, on the basis of these additional figures, we recalculated our chart comparing occupational to criminal dangers, it would look like this:

	Occupational Hazard	Crime (halved)
Death	36,700	10,000
Other physical harm	1,950,000	400,000

Can there be any doubt that workers are more likely to stay alive and healthy in the face of the danger from the underworld than in the face of what their employers have in store for them on the job?...

[T]he vast majority of occupational deaths result from disease, not accident, and disease is generally a function of conditions outside a worker's control. Examples of such conditions are the level of coal dust in the air (about 10 percent of all active coal miners have black lung disease) or textile dust (some 85,000 American cotton textile workers presently suffer breathing impairments caused by acute byssinosis or brown lung, and another 35,000 former mill workers are totally disabled with chronic brown lung) or asbestos fibers (a study of 632 asbestos-insulation workers between 1943 and 1971 indicates that 11 percent have died of asbestosis and 38 percent of cancer; two doctors who have studied asbestos workers conclude "we can anticipate three thousand excess respiratory, cardiopulmonary deaths and cancers of the lung—three thousand excess deaths *annually* for the next twenty or thirty years"), or coal tars ("workers who had been employed five or more years in the coke ovens died of lung cancer at a rate three and a half times that for all steelworkers"; coke oven workers also develop cancer of the scrotum at a rate five times that of the general population). Also, some 800,000 people suffer from occupationally related skin disease each year (according to a 1968 estimate by the U.S. surgeon general), and "the number of American workers experiencing noise conditions that may damage their hearing is estimated [in a 1969 Public Health Service publication of the Department of Health, Education and Welfare] to be in excess of 6 million, and may even reach 16 million."

To blame the workers for occupational disease and deaths is simply to ignore the history of governmental attempts to compel industrial firms to meet safety standards that would keep dangers (such as chemicals or fibers or dust particles in the air) that are outside of the worker's control down to a safe level. This has been a continual struggle, with firms using everything from their own "independent" research institutes to more direct and often questionable forms of political pressure to influence government in the direction of loose standards and lax enforcement. So far, industry has been winning because OSHA has been given neither the personnel nor the mandate to fulfill its purpose....

When inspectors do find violations, the penalties they can assess are severely limited by the OSHA law that Congress has not updated since it established the agency. The maximum penalty for a serious OSHA violation is $1,000; an employer who acts willfully can be fined up to $10,000 for each incident....

Even when the agency hits employers hard, however, the sting does not often last very long. The big proposed fines that grab headlines are seldom paid in full. The two record-breaking citations of last year, against Union Carbide Corporation for $1.37 million and Chrysler for $910,000, were each settled this year for less than a third of the original amounts.

According to *Occupational Hazards,*

... NIOSH's [National Institute for Occupational Safety and Health's] budget, rather than being increased, had continued to be cut—by as much as 47 percent since 1980, when adjusted for inflation. And that while nations such as Finland spend approximately $2 per worker each year on occupational disease surveillance, the United States spends about 2¢ per worker.

... Is a person who kills another in a bar brawl a greater threat to society than a business executive who refuses to cut into his profits in order to make his plant a safe place to work? By any measure of death and suffering the latter is by far a greater danger than the former. Because he wishes his workers no harm, because he is only indirectly responsible for death and disability, while pursuing legitimate economic goals, his acts are not called "crimes." Once we free our imagination from the irrational shackle of the one-on-one model of crime, can there

Table 1

How Americans Are Murdered

Total	Firearms	Knife or Other Cutting Instrument	Other Weapon: Club, Arson, Poison, Strangulation, etc.	Personal Weapon: Hands, Fists, etc.
19,257[a]	11,381	3,957	2,609	1,310

[a] Note that this figure diverges somewhat from the figure of 20,613 murders and nonnegligent manslaughters used elsewhere in the FBI *Uniform Crime Reports*, 1987; see for example, p. 7.

Source: FBI *Uniform Crime Reports*, 1987: "Murder Victims: Weapons Used, 1986."

be any doubt that the criminal justice system does *not* protect us from the gravest threats to life and limb? It seeks to protect us when danger comes from a young, lower-class male in the inner city. When a threat comes from an upper-class business executive in an office, the criminal justice system looks the other way. This is in the face of growing evidence that for every American citizen murdered by some thug, two American workers are killed by their bosses.

Health Care May Be Dangerous to Your Health

... On July 15, 1975, Dr. Sidney Wolfe of Ralph Nader's Public Interest Health Research Group testified before the House Commerce Oversight and Investigations Subcommittee that there "were 3.2 million cases of unnecessary surgery performed each year in the United States." These unneeded operations, Dr. Wolfe added, "cost close to $5 billion a year and kill as many as 16,000 Americans." Wolfe's estimates of unnecessary surgery were based on studies comparing the operations performed and surgery recommended by doctors who are paid for the operations they do with those performed and recommended by salaried

doctors who receive no extra income from surgery.

... In an article on an experimental program by Blue Cross and Blue Shield aimed at curbing unnecessary surgery, *Newsweek* reports that

a Congressional committee earlier this year [1976] estimated that more than 2 million of the elective operations performed in 1974 were not only unnecessary—but also killed about 12,000 patients and cost nearly $4 billion.

... In fact, if someone had the temerity to publish a *Uniform Crime Reports* that really portrayed the way Americans are murdered, the FBI's statistics on the *type of weapon used* in murder would have to be changed for 1986, from those shown in Table 1 to something like those shown in Table 2.

The figures shown in Table 2 would give American citizens a much more honest picture of what threatens them. We are not likely to see it broadcast by the criminal justice system, however, because it would also give American citizens a more honest picture of *who* threatens them.

We should not leave this topic without noting that, aside from the other losses it imposes, unnecessary surgery was estimated to have cost between $4 and

Table 2

How Americans Are (Really) Murdered

Total	Occupational Hazard & Disease	Inadequate Emergency Medical Care	Knife or Other Cutting Instrument Including Scalpel	Firearms	Other Weapon: Club, Poison, Hypodermic, Prescription Drug	Personal Weapon: Hands, Fists, etc.
114,957	61,700	20,000	15,957[a]	11,381	4,609[a]	1,310

[a]These figures represent the relevant figures in Table 1 plus the most conservative figures for the relevant categories discussed in the text.

$5 billion in 1974. The price of medical care has nearly tripled between 1974 and 1986. Thus, assuming that the same number of unneeded operations were performed in 1986, the cost of unnecessary surgery would be between $12 and $15 billion. To this we should add the unnecessary 22 percent of the 6 billion administered doses of medication. Even at the extremely conservative estimate of $3 a dose, this adds about $4 billion. In short, assuming that earlier trends have continued, there is reason to believe that unnecessary surgery and medication cost the public between $16 and $19 billion annually—far outstripping the $11.6 billion taken by thieves that concern the FBI. This give us yet another way in which we are robbed of more money by practices that are not treated as criminal than by practices that are.

Waging Chemical Warfare Against America

... "A 1978 report issued by the President's Council on Environmental Quality (CEQ) unequivocally states that 'most researchers agree that 70 to 90 percent of cancers are caused by environmental influences and are hence theoretically preventable.'" This means that a con-

certed national effort could result in saving 300,000 or more lives a year and reducing each individual's chances of getting cancer in his or her lifetime from one in four to one in twelve or less....

The simple truth is that the government that strove so mightily to protect us against a guerrilla war 10,000 miles from home [the Vietnam War, in which the United States spent around $165 billion] is doing next to nothing to protect us against the chemical war in our midst. This war is being waged against us on three fronts:

- Air pollution
- Cigarette smoking
- Food additives

Not only are we losing on all three fronts, but it looks like we do not even have the will to fight....

In 1970, Lester B. Lave and Eugene P. Seskin reviewed more than fifty scientific studies of the relationship between air pollution and morbidity and mortality rates for lung cancer, nonrespiratory tract cancers, cardiovascular disease, bronchitis, and other respiratory diseases. They found in every instance a *positive quantifiable relationship*. Using sophisticated statistical techniques, they concluded that a

50 percent reduction in air pollution in major urban areas would result in:

- A 25 percent reduction in mortality from lung cancer (using 1974 mortality rates, this represents a potential saving of 19,500 lives per year)
- A 25 percent reduction in morbidity and mortality due to respiratory disease (a potential saving of 27,000 lives per year)
- A 20 percent reduction in morbidity and mortality due to cardiovascular disease (a potential saving of 52,000 lives per year)....

A more recent study, done in 1978 by Robert Mendelsohn of the University of Washington and Guy Orcutt of Yale University, estimates that air pollution causes a total of 142,000 deaths a year....

Based on the knowledge we have, there can be no doubt that air pollution, tobacco, and food additives amount to a chemical war that makes the crime wave look like a football scrimmage. Quite conservatively, I think we can estimate the death toll in this war as at least a quarter of a million lives a year—*more than ten times the number killed by criminal homicide!*...

Summary

Once again, our investigations lead to the same result. The criminal justice system does not protect us against the gravest threats to life, limb, or possessions. Its definitions of crime are not simply a reflection of the objective dangers that threaten us. The workplace, the medical profession, [and] the air we breathe... lead to far more human suffering, far more death and disability, and take far more dollars from our pockets than the murders, aggravated assaults, and thefts reported annually by the FBI. What is more, this human suffering is preventable. A government really intent on protecting our well-being could enforce work safety regulations, police the medical profession, [and] require that clean air standards be met,... but it does not. Instead we hear a lot of cant about law and order and a lot of rant about crime in the streets. It is as if our leaders were not only refusing to protect us from the major threats to our well-being but trying to cover up this refusal by diverting our attention to crime—as if this were the only real threat. As we have seen, the criminal justice system is a carnival mirror that presents a distorted image of what threatens us.... All the mechanisms by which the criminal justice system comes down more frequently and more harshly on the poor criminal than on the well-off criminal take place *after* most of the dangerous acts of the well-to-do have been excluded from the definition of crime itself.

POSTSCRIPT

Is Street Crime More Harmful Than White-Collar Crime?

DiIulio implies that much of the social misery of America, including the persistence of poverty, can be traced to the "truly depraved" street criminals in our central cities. Is this focus too narrow? Surely there are many other sources of the social crisis that afflicts our central cities. Reiman's focus, on the other hand, may be overly broad. He claims that more people are killed and injured by "occupational injury or disease, by unnecessary surgery, and by shoddy emergency medical services than by aggravated assault or even homicide!" Can shoddy medical services be categorized as a crime? And could the residents of city ghettos, where most of the violent crime occurs, ever be convinced that they face a greater risk from occupational injury or disease than from street criminals? In the end, the questions remain: What is a crime? Who are the criminals?

A set of readings that support Reiman's viewpoint is *Corporate Violence: Injury and Death for Profit*, edited by Stuart L. Hills (Rowman & Littlefield, 1987). Further support is provided by Marshall B. Clinard, *Corporate Corruption: The Abuse of Power* (Praeger, 1990). *White-Collar Crime*, edited by Gilbert Geis and Robert F. Meier (Free Press, 1977), is a useful compilation of essays on corporate and political crime, as is Gary Green's *Occupational Crime* (Nelson-Hall, 1990). Four other books that focus on crime in high places are J. Douglas and J. M. Johnson, *Official Deviance* (J. B. Lippincott, 1977); J. Anthony Lukas, *Nightmare: The Underside of the Nixon Years* (Viking Press, 1976); Marshall B. Clinard, *Corporate Elites and Crime* (Sage Publications, 1983); and David R. Simon and Stanley Eitzen, *Elite Deviance* (Allyn & Bacon, 1982). A work that deals with the prevalence and fear of street crime is Elliott Currie, *Confronting Crime: An American Challenge* (Pantheon Books, 1985). Two works on gangs, which are often connected with violent street crime, are Martin Sanchez Jankowski, *Islands in the Street: Gangs and American Urban Society* (University of California Press, 1991), and Felix M. Padilla, *The Gang as an American Enterprise* (Rutgers University Press, 1992). One interesting aspect of many corporate or white-collar crimes is that they involve crimes of obedience, as discussed in Herman C. Kelman and V. Lee Hamilton, *Crimes of Obedience: Toward a Social Psychology of Authority and Responsibility* (Yale University Press, 1989).

ISSUE 17

Should Drugs Be Legalized?

YES: Ethan A. Nadelmann, from "Should We Legalize Drugs? Yes," *American Heritage* (February/March 1993)

NO: David T. Courtwright, from "Should We Legalize Drugs? No," *American Heritage* (February/March 1993)

ISSUE SUMMARY

YES: Ethan A. Nadelmann, an assistant professor of politics and public affairs, argues that history shows that not only is drug prohibition costly but that it also exacerbates the drug problem. He maintains that controlled legalization would reduce the drug problem in the United States.

NO: Professor of history David T. Courtwright argues that legalizing drugs would not eliminate drug-related criminal activity and that it would increase drug use. Therefore, the government should continue the war against drugs.

A century ago, drugs of every kind were freely available to Americans. Laudanum, a mixture of opium and alcohol, was popularly used as a painkiller. One drug company even claimed that it was a very useful substance for calming hyperactive children, and the company called it Mother's Helper. Morphine came into common use during the Civil War. Heroin, developed as a supposedly less addictive substitute for morphine, began to be marketed at the end of the nineteenth century. By that time, drug paraphernalia could be ordered through Sears and Roebuck catalogues, and Coca-Cola, which contained small quantities of cocaine, had become a popular drink.

Public concerns about addiction and dangerous patent medicines, and an active campaign for drug laws waged by Dr. Harvey Wiley, a chemist in the U.S. Department of Agriculture, led Congress to pass the first national drug regulation act in 1906. The Pure Food and Drug Act required that medicines containing certain drugs, such as opium, must say so on their labels. The Harrison Narcotic Act of 1914 went much further and cut off completely the supply of legal opiates to addicts. Since then, ever stricter drug laws have been passed by Congress and by state legislatures.

Drug abuse in America again came to the forefront of public discourse during the 1960s, when heroin addiction started growing rapidly in inner-city neighborhoods. Also, by the end of the decade, drug experimentation had spread to the middle-class, affluent baby boomers who were then attending college. Indeed, certain types of drugs began to be celebrated by some of the leaders of the counterculture. Heroin was still taboo, but other drugs, notably marijuana and LSD (a psychedelic drug), were regarded as harmless and even spiritually transforming. At music festivals like Woodstock in 1969, marijuana and LSD were used openly and associated with love, peace, and heightened sensitivity. Much of this enthusiasm cooled over the next 20 years as baby boomers entered the workforce full-time and began their careers. But even among the careerists, certain types of drugs enjoyed high status. Cocaine, noted for its highly stimulating effects, became the drug of choice for many hard-driving young lawyers, television writers, and Wall Street bond traders.

The high price of cocaine put it out of reach for many people, but in the early 1980s, cheap substitutes began to appear on the streets and to overtake poor urban communities. Crack cocaine, a potent, highly addictive, smokable form of cocaine, came into widespread use. By the end of the 1980s, the drug known as "ice," or as it is called on the West Coast, "L.A. glass," a smokable form of amphetamine, had hit the streets. These stimulants tend to produce very violent, disorderly behavior. Moreover, the street gangs who sell them are frequently at war with one another and are well armed. Not only gang members but also many innocent people have become victims of contract killings, street battles, and drive-by shootings.

This new drug epidemic prompted President Bush to declare a "war on drugs," and in 1989 he asked Congress to appropriate $10.6 billion for the fight. Although most Americans support such measures against illegal drugs, some say that in the years since Bush made his declaration, the drug situation has not showed any signs of improvement. Some believe that legalization would be the best way to fight the drug problem.

The drug legalization issue is especially interesting to sociologists because it raises basic questions about what should be socially sanctioned or approved, what is illegal or legal, and what is immoral or moral. An aspect of the basic value system of America is under review. The process of value change may be taking place in front of our eyes. As part of this debate, Ethan A. Nadelmann argues that the present policy does not work and is counterproductive. Legalization, he contends, would stop much of the violence and crime associated with illegal drugs. Although Nadelmann concedes that it may increase the use of lower-potency drugs, he believes that legalization would reduce the use of the worst drugs. David T. Courtwright agrees that the current policy is not solving the problem, but he argues that drug use and addiction would surge disastrously with legalization. He also believes that drug-related crime would persist and drug rings would continue operating under a policy of controlled legalization.

YES

Ethan A. Nadelmann

SHOULD WE LEGALIZE DRUGS?

Most opponents of "drug legalization" assume that it would involve making cocaine and heroin available the way alcohol and tobacco are today. But most legalization supporters favor nothing of the kind; in fact, we disagree widely as to which drugs should be legalized, how they should be controlled, and what the consequences are likely to be. Where drug-policy reformers do agree is in our critique of the drug-prohibition system that has evolved in the United States—a system, we contend, that has proved ineffective, costly, counterproductive, and immoral.

Efforts to reverse drug prohibition face formidable obstacles. Americans have grown accustomed to the status quo. Alcohol prohibition was overturned before most citizens had forgotten what a legal alcohol policy was like, but who today can recall a time before drug prohibition? Moreover, the United States has succeeded in promoting its drug-prohibition system throughout the world. Opponents of alcohol prohibition could look to successful foreign alcohol-control systems, in Canada and much of Europe, but contemporary drug anti-prohibitionists must look further—to history.

The principal evidence, not surprisingly, is Prohibition. The dry years offer many useful analogies, but their most important lesson is the need to distinguish between the harms that stem from drugs and the harms that arise from outlawing them. The Americans who voted in 1933 to repeal Prohibition differed greatly in their reasons for overturning the system. They almost all agreed, however, that the evils of alcohol consumption had been surpassed by those of trying to suppress it.

Some pointed to Al Capone and rising crime, violence, and corruption; others to the overflowing courts, jails, and prisons, the labeling of tens of millions of Americans as criminals and the consequent broadening disrespect for the law, the dangerous expansions of federal police powers and encroachments on individual liberties, the hundreds of thousands of Americans blinded, paralyzed, and killed by poisonous moonshine and industrial alcohol, and the increasing government expenditure devoted to enforcing the Prohibition laws and the billions in forgone tax revenues. Supporters of Prohibition blamed the consumers, and some went so far as to argue that those who violated the laws deserved whatever ills befell them. But by 1933 most Americans blamed Prohibition.

From Ethan A. Nadelmann, "Should We Legalize Drugs? Yes," *American Heritage*, vol. 44, no. 1 (February/March 1993). Copyright © 1993 by Forbes, Inc. Reprinted by permission of American Heritage, a division of Forbes, Inc.

If there is a single message that contemporary anti-prohibitionists seek to drive home, it is that drug prohibition is responsible for much of what Americans identify today as the "drug problem." It is not merely a matter of the direct costs—twenty billion dollars spent this year on arresting, prosecuting, and incarcerating drug-law violators. Choked courts and prisons, an incarceration rate higher than that of any other nation in the world, tax dollars diverted from education and health care, law-enforcement resources diverted from investigating everything from auto theft to savings-and-loan scams—all these are just a few of the costs our current prohibition imposes.

* * *

Consider also Capone's successors—the drug kingpins of Asia, Latin America, and the United States. Consider as well all the murders and assaults perpetrated by young drug dealers not just against one another but against police, witnesses, and bystanders. Consider the tremendous economic and social incentives generated by the illegality of the drug market—temptations so overwhelming that even "good kids" cannot resist them. Consider the violent drug dealers becoming the heroes of boys and young men, from Harlem to Medellín. And consider tens of millions of Americans being labeled criminals for doing nothing more than smoking a marijuana cigarette. In all these respects the consequences of drug prohibition imitate—and often exceed—those of alcohol prohibition.

Prohibition reminds us, too, of the health costs of drug prohibition. Sixty years ago some fifty thousand Americans were paralyzed after consuming an adulterated Jamaica ginger extract known as "jake." Today we have marijuana made more dangerous by government-sprayed paraquat and the chemicals added by drug dealers, heroin adulterated with poisonous powders, and assorted pills and capsules containing everything from antihistamines to strychnine. Indeed, virtually every illicit drug purchased at the retail level contains adulterants, at least some of which are far more dangerous than the drug itself. And restrictions on the sale of drug paraphernalia has, by encouraging intravenous drug addicts to share their equipment, severely handicapped efforts to stem the transmission of AIDS. As during Prohibition, many Americans view these ills as necessary and even desirable, but others, like their forebears sixty years ago, reject as perverse a system that degrades and destroys the very people it was designed to protect.

Prohibition's lessons extend in other directions as well. The current revisionist twist on that "Great Experiment" now claims that "Prohibition worked," by reducing alcohol consumption and alcohol-related ills ranging from cirrhosis to public drunkenness and employee absenteeism. There is some truth to this claim. But in fact, the most dramatic decline in American alcohol consumption occurred not between 1920 and 1933, while the Eighteenth Amendment was in effect, but rather between 1916 and 1922. During those years the temperance movement was highly active and successful in publicizing the dangers of alcohol. The First World War's spirit of self-sacrifice extended to temperance as a means of grain conservation, and there arose, as the historian David Kyvig puts it, "an atmosphere of hostility toward all things German, not the least of which was beer." In short, a great variety of factors coalesced in this brief time to substantially reduce alcohol consumption and its ills.

The very evidence on which pro-prohibition historians rely provides further proof of the importance of factors other than prohibition laws. One of these historians, John Burnham, has noted that the admission rate for alcohol psychoses to New York hospitals shrank from 10 percent between 1909 and 1912 to 1.9 percent in 1920—a decline that occurred largely before national prohibition and in a state that had not enacted its own prohibition law.

At best one can argue that Prohibition was most effective in its first years, when temperance norms remained strong and illicit sources of production had yet to be firmly established. By all accounts, alcohol consumption rose after those first years—despite increased resources devoted to enforcement. The pre-Prohibition decline in consumption, like the recent decline in cigarette consumption, had less to do with laws than with changing norms and the imposition of non-criminal-justice measures.

Perhaps the most telling indictment of Prohibition is provided by the British experience with alcohol control during a similar period. In the United States the death rate from cirrhosis of the liver dropped from as high as 15 per 100,000 population between 1910 and 1914 to 7 during the twenties only to climb back to pre-1910 levels by the 1960s, while in Britain the death rate from cirrhosis dropped from 10 in 1914 to 5 in 1920 and then gradually declined to a low of 2 in the 1940s before rising by a mere point by 1963. Other indicators of alcohol consumption and misuse dropped by similar magnitudes, even though the United Kingdom never enacted prohibition. Instead wartime Britain restricted the amount of alcohol available, taxed it, and drastically reduced the hours of sale. At war's end the government dropped restrictions on quantity but made taxes even higher and set hours of sale at only half the pre-war norm.

*   *   *

Britain thus not only reduced the negative consequences of alcohol consumption more effectively than did the United States, but did so in a manner that raised substantial government revenues. The British experience—as well as Australia's and most of continental Europe's—strongly suggests not only that our Prohibition was unsuccessful but that more effective post-Repeal controls might have prevented the return to high consumption levels.

But no matter how powerful the analogies between alcohol prohibition and contemporary drug prohibition, most Americans still balk at drawing the parallels. Alcohol, they insist, is fundamentally different from everything else. They are right, of course, insofar as their claims rest not on health or scientific grounds but are limited to political and cultural arguments. By most measures, alcohol is more dangerous to human health than any of the drugs now prohibited by law. No drug is as associated with violence in American culture—and even in illicit-drug-using subcultures—as is alcohol. One would be hard pressed to argue that its role in many Native American and other aboriginal communities has been any less destructive than that of illicit drugs in America's ghettos.

The dangers of all drugs vary greatly, of course, depending not just on their pharmacological properties and how they are consumed but also on the attitudes and beliefs of their users and the settings in which they use them. Alcohol by and large plays a benign role in Jewish and Asian-American cultures but a devastating one in some Native American societies, and by the same token the impact of cocaine among Yuppies during the early 1980s was relatively benign compared with its impact a few years later in impoverished ghettos.

* * *

The culture helps determine the setting of drug use, but so do the laws. Prohibitions enhance the dangers not just of drugs but of the settings in which they are used. The relationship between prohibition and dangerous adulterations is clear. So too is its impact on the potency and forms of drugs. For instance, Prohibition caused a striking drop in the production and sale of beer, while that of hard liquor increased as bootleggers from Al Capone on down sought to maximize their profits and minimize the risks of detection. Similarly, following the Second World War, the enactment of anti-opium laws in many parts of Asia in which opium use was traditional—India, Hong Kong, Thailand, Laos, Iran— effectively suppressed the availability of opium at the cost of stimulating the creation of domestic heroin industries and substantial increases in heroin use. The same transition had occurred in the United States following Congress's ban on opium imports in 1909. And when during the 1980s the U.S. government's domestic drug-enforcement efforts significantly reduced the availability and raised the price of marijuana, they provided decisive incentives to producers, distributors, and consumers to switch to cocaine. In each case, prohibition forced switches from drugs that were bulky and relatively benign to drugs that were more compact, more lucrative, more potent, and more dangerous.

In the 1980s the retail purity of heroin and cocaine increased, and highly potent crack became cheaply available in American cities. At the same time, the average potency of most legal psychoactive substances declined: Americans began switching from hard liquor to beer and wine, from high-tar-and-nicotine to lower-tar-and-nicotine cigarettes, and even from caffeinated to decaffeinated coffee and soda. The relationship between prohibition and drug potency was, if not indisputable, still readily apparent.

In turn-of-the-century America, opium, morphine, heroin, cocaine, and marijuana were subject to few restrictions. Popular tonics such as Vin Mariani and Coca-Cola and its competitors were laced with cocaine, and hundreds of medicines—Mrs. Winslow's Soothing Syrup may have been the most famous— contained psychoactive drugs. Millions, perhaps tens of millions of Americans, took opiates and cocaine. David Courtwright estimates that during the 1890s as many as one-third of a million Americans were opiate addicts, but most of them were ordinary people who would today be described as occasional users.

Careful analysis of that era—when the very drugs that we most fear were widely and cheaply available throughout the country—provides a telling antidote to our nightmare legalization scenarios. For one thing, despite the virtual absence of any controls on availability, the proportion of Americans addicted to opiates was only two or three times greater than today. For another, the typical addict was not a young black ghetto resident but a middle-aged white Southern woman or a West Coast Chinese immigrant. The violence, death, disease, and crime that we today associate with drug use barely existed, and many medical authorities regarded opiate addiction as far less destructive than alcoholism (some doctors even prescribed the former as treatment for the latter). Many opiate addicts, perhaps most, managed to lead relatively normal lives and kept their addictions secret even from close friends and relatives. That they were able to do so was largely a function of the legal status of their drug use.

But even more reassuring is the fact that the major causes of opiate addiction then simply do not exist now. Late-nineteenth-century Americans became addicts principally at the hands of physicians who lacked modern medicines and were unaware of the addictive potential of the drugs they prescribed. Doctors in the 1860s and 1870s saw morphine injections as a virtual panacea, and many Americans turned to opiates to alleviate their aches and pains without going through doctors at all. But as medicine advanced, the levels of both doctor- and self-induced addiction declined markedly.

In 1906 the first Federal Pure Food and Drug Act required over-the-counter drug producers to disclose whether their products contained any opiates, cocaine, cannabis, alcohol, or other psychoactive ingredients. Sales of patent medicines containing opiates and cocaine decreased significantly thereafter—in good part because fewer Americans were interested in purchasing products that they now knew to contain those drugs.

Consider the lesson here. Ethical debates aside, the principal objection to all drug legalization proposals is that they invite higher levels of drug use and misuse by making drugs not just legal but more available and less ex-

pensive. Yet the late-nineteenth-century experience suggests the opposite: that in a legal market most consumers will prefer lower-potency coca and opiate products to the far more powerful concoctions that have virtually monopolized the market under prohibition. This reminds us that opiate addiction per se was not necessarily a serious problem so long as addicts had ready access to modestly priced opiates of reliable quality—indeed, that the opiate addicts of late-nineteenth-century America differed in no significant respects from the cigarette-addicted consumers of today. And it reassures us that the principal cause of addiction to opiates was not the desire to get high but rather ignorance—ignorance of their addictive qualities, ignorance of the alternative analgesics, and ignorance of what exactly patent medicines contained. The antidote to addiction in late-nineteenth-century America, the historical record shows, consisted primarily of education and regulation—not prohibition, drug wars, and jail.

Why, then, was drug prohibition instituted? And why did it quickly evolve into a fierce and highly punitive set of policies rather than follow the more modest and humane path pursued by the British? In part, the passage of the federal Harrison Narcotic Act, in 1914, and of state and local bans before and after that, reflected a belated response to the recognition that people could easily become addicted to opiates and cocaine. But it also was closely intertwined with the increasingly vigorous efforts of doctors and pharmacists to professionalize their disciplines and to monopolize the public's access to medicinal drugs. Most of all, though, the institution of drug prohibition reflected the changing nature of the opiate- and cocaine-using population. By 1914 the number of middle-class Americans blithely consuming narcotics had fallen sharply. At the same time, however, opiate and cocaine use had become increasingly popular among the lower classes and racial minorities. The total number of consumers did not approach that of earlier decades, but where popular opinion had once shied from the notion of criminalizing the habits of elderly white women, few such inhibitions impeded it where urban gamblers, prostitutes, and delinquents were concerned.

The first anti-opium laws were passed in California in the 1870s and directed at the Chinese immigrants and their opium dens, in which, it was feared, young white women were being seduced. A generation later reports of rising cocaine use among young black men in the South—who were said to rape white women while under the influence—prompted similar legislation. During the 1930s marijuana prohibitions were directed in good part at Mexican and Chicano workers who had lost their jobs in the Depression. And fifty years later draconian penalties were imposed for the possession of tiny amounts of crack cocaine—a drug associated principally with young Latinos and African-Americans.

But more than racist fears was at work during the early years of drug prohibition. In the aftermath of World War I, many Americans, stunned by the triumph of Bolshevism in Russia and fearful of domestic subversion, turned their backs on the liberalizing reforms of the preceding era. In such an atmosphere the very notion of tolerating drug use or maintaining addicts in the clinics that had arisen after 1914 struck most citizens as both immoral and unpatriotic. In 1919 the mayor of New York created the Committee on Public Safety to investigate two ostensibly related problems: revolutionary bombings and heroin use among youth. And in Washington that same year, the Supreme Court effectively foreclosed any possibility of a more humane policy toward drug addicts when it held, in *Webb et al.* v. *U.S.*, that doctors could not legally prescribe maintenance supplies of narcotics to addicts.

* * *

But perhaps most important, the imposition of drug prohibition cannot be understood without recalling that it occurred almost simultaneously with the advent of alcohol prohibition. Contemporary Americans tend to regard Prohibition as a strange quirk in American history—and drug prohibition as entirely natural and beneficial. Yet the prohibition against alcohol, like that against other drugs, was motivated in no small part by its association with feared and despised ethnic minorities, especially the masses of Eastern and Southern European immigrants.

Why was Prohibition repealed after just thirteen years while drug prohibition has lasted for more than seventy-five? Look at whom each disadvantaged. Alcohol prohibition struck directly at tens of millions of Americans of all ages, including many of society's most powerful members. Drug prohibition threatened far fewer Americans, and they had relatively little influence in the halls of power. Only the prohibition of marijuana, which some sixty million Americans have violated since 1965, has come close to approximating the Prohibition experience, but marijuana smokers consist mostly of young and relatively powerless Americans. In the final analysis alcohol prohibition was repealed, and opiate, cocaine, and marijuana prohibition retained, not because scientists had concluded that alcohol was the least dangerous of the various psychoactive drugs but because of the prejudices and preferences of most Americans.

There was, of course, one other important reason why Prohibition was repealed when it was. With the country four years into the Depression, Prohibition increasingly appeared not just foolish but costly. Fewer and fewer Americans were keen on paying the rising costs of enforcing its laws, and more and more recalled the substantial tax revenues that the legal alcohol business had generated. The potential analogy to the current recession is unfortunate but apt. During the late 1980s the cost of building and maintaining prisons emerged as the fastest-growing item in many state budgets, while other costs of the war on drugs also rose dramatically. One cannot help wondering how much longer Americans will be eager to foot the bills for all this.

Throughout history the legal and moral status of psychoactive drugs has kept changing. During the seventeenth century the sale and consumption of tobacco were punished by as much as death in much of Europe, Russia, China, and Japan. For centuries many of the same Muslim domains that forbade the sale and consumption of alcohol simultaneously tolerated and even regulated the sale of opium and cannabis.

Drug-related moralities have always been malleable, and their evolution can in no way be described as moral progress. Just as our moral perceptions of particular drugs have changed in the past, so will they in the future, and people will continue to circumvent the

legal and moral barriers that remain. My confidence in this prediction stems from one other lesson of civilized human history. From the dawn of time humans have nearly universally shown a desire to alter their states of consciousness with psychoactive substances, and it is this fact that gives the lie to the declared objective of creating a "drug-free society" in the United States.

Another thing common to all societies, as the social theorist Thomas Szasz argued some years ago, is that they require scapegoats to embody their fears and take blame for whatever ails them. Today the role of bogeyman is applied to drug producers, dealers, and users. Just as anti-Communist propagandists once feared Moscow far beyond its actual influence and appeal, so today anti-drug proselytizers indict marijuana, cocaine, heroin, and assorted hallucinogens far beyond their actual psychoactive effects and psychological appeal. Never mind that the vast majority of Americans have expressed—in one public-opinion poll after another—little interest in trying these substances, even if they were legal, and never mind that most of those who have tried them have suffered few, if any, ill effects. The evidence of history and of science is drowned out by today's bogeymen. No rhetoric is too harsh, no penalty too severe.

* * *

Lest I be accused of exaggerating, consider the following. On June 27, 1991, the Supreme Court upheld, by a vote of five to four, a Michigan statute that imposed a mandatory sentence of life without possibility of parole for anyone convicted of possession of more than 650 grams (about 1.5 pounds) of cocaine. In other words, an activity that was entirely legal at the turn of the century, and that poses a danger to society roughly comparable to that posed by the sale of alcohol and tobacco, is today treated the same as first-degree murder.

The cumulative result of our prohibitionist war is that roughly 20 to 25 percent of the more than one million Americans now incarcerated in federal and state prisons and local jails, and almost half of those in federal penitentiaries, are serving time for having engaged in an activity that their great-grandparents could have pursued entirely legally.

Examples of less striking, but sometimes more deadly, penalties also abound. In many states anyone convicted of possession of a single marijuana joint can have his or her driver's license revoked for six months and be required to participate in a drug-treatment program. In many states anyone caught cultivating a marijuana plant may find all his or her property forfeited to the local police department. And in all but a few cities needle-exchange programs to reduce the transmission of AIDS among drug addicts have been rejected because they would "send the wrong message"—as if the more moral message is that such addicts are better off contracting the deadly virus and spreading it.

Precedents for each of these penalties scarcely exist in American history. The restoration of criminal forfeiture of property—rejected by the Founding Fathers because of its association with the evils of English rule—could not have found its way back into American law but for the popular desire to give substance to the rhetorical war on drugs.

Of course, changes in current policy that make legally available to adult Americans many of the now prohibited psychoactive substances are bound to entail a litany of administrative problems and certain other risks.

* * *

During the last years of the Volstead Act, the Rockefeller Foundation commissioned a study by the leading police scholar in the United States, Raymond Fosdick, to evaluate the various alternatives to Prohibition. Its analyses and recommendations ultimately played an important role in constructing post-Prohibition regulatory policies. A comparable study is currently under way at Princeton University, where the Smart Family Foundation has funded a working group of scholars from diverse disciplines to evaluate and recommend alternative drug-control policies. Its report will be completed late in 1993.

History holds one final lesson for those who cannot imagine any future beyond drug prohibition. Until well into the 1920s most Americans regarded Prohibition as a permanent fact of life. As late as 1930 Sen. Morris Shepard of Texas, who had coauthored the Prohibition Amendment, confidently asserted: "There is as much chance of repealing the Eighteenth Amendment as there is for a humming-bird to fly to the planet Mars with the Washington Monument tied to its tail."

History reminds us that things can and do change, that what seems inconceivable today can seem entirely normal, and even inevitable, a few years hence. So it was with Prohibition, and so it is—and will be—both with drug prohibition and the ever-changing nature of drug use in America.

NO

David T. Courtwright

SHOULD WE LEGALIZE DRUGS?

One thing that all parties in the American drug-policy debate agree on is that they want to eliminate the traffic in illicit drugs and the criminal syndicates that control it. There are two divergent strategies for achieving this end: the drug war and drug legalization, or, more precisely, controlled legalization, since few people want the government to simply abandon drug control and proclaim laissez faire.

The drug war was launched during the Reagan administration. It is actually the fourth such campaign, there having been sustained legislative and governmental efforts against drug abuse between 1909 and 1923, 1951 and 1956, and 1971 and 1973. What distinguishes the current war is that it is more concerned with stimulants like cocaine than with opiates, it is larger, and—no surprise in our age of many zeros—it is much more expensive.

The war against drugs has included the treatment of addicts and educational programs designed to discourage new users, but the emphasis has been on law enforcement, with interdiction, prosecution, imprisonment, and the seizure of assets at the heart of the campaign. The news from the front has been mixed. Price and purity levels, treatment and emergency-room admissions, urinalyses, and most other indices of drug availability showed a worsening of the problem during the 1980s, with some improvement in 1989 and 1990. The number of casual cocaine users has recently declined, but cocaine addiction remains widespread, affecting anywhere from about 650,000 to 2.4 million compulsive users, depending on whose definitions and estimates one chooses to accept. There has been some success in stopping marijuana imports—shipments of the drug are relatively bulky and thus easier to detect—but this has been offset by the increased domestic cultivation of high-quality marijuana, which has more than doubled since 1985. Heroin likewise has become both more available and more potent than it was in the late 1970s.

But cocaine has been the drug of greatest concern. Just how severe the crisis has become may be gauged by federal cocaine seizures. Fifty years ago the annual haul for the entire nation was 1 or 2 pounds, an amount that could easily be contained in the glove compartment of a car. As late as 1970 the total was under 500 pounds, which would fit in the car's trunk. In fiscal year

From David T. Courtwright, "Should We Legalize Drugs? No," *American Heritage*, vol. 44, no. 1 (February/March 1993). Copyright © 1993 by Forbes, Inc. Reprinted by permission of American Heritage, a division of Forbes, Inc.

1990 it was 235,000 pounds—about the weight of 60 mid-size cars. And this represented a fraction, no more than 10 percent, of what went into the nostrils and lungs and veins of the approximately seven million Americans who used cocaine during 1990. Worse may be in store. Worldwide production of coca surged during 1989 to a level of 225,000 metric tons, despite U.S. efforts to eradicate cultivation. Global production of opium, marijuana, and hashish has likewise increased since President Reagan formally declared war on drugs in 1986.

* * *

The greatest obstacle to the supply-reduction strategy is the enormous amount of money generated by the illicit traffic. Drug profits have been used to buy off foreign and domestic officials and to secure protection for the most vulnerable stages of the drug-cultivation, -manufacturing, and -distribution process. These profits also hire various specialists, from assassins to money launderers to lawyers, needed to cope with interlopers; they pay for technological devices ranging from cellular phones to jet planes; and they ensure that should a trafficker die or land in jail, there will be no shortage of replacements.

It is hardly surprising that these stubborn economic realities, together with the drug war's uneven and often disappointing results, have led several commentators to question the wisdom of what they call the prohibition policy. What is unprecedented is that these disenchanted critics include mayors, prominent lawyers, federal judges, nationally syndicated columnists, a congressman, a Princeton professor, and a Nobel laureate in economics. They espouse variations of a position that is often called controlled legalization, meaning that the sale of narcotics should be permitted under conditions that restrict and limit consumption, such as no sales to minors, no advertising, and substantial taxation. They cite the numerous advantages of this approach: several billion dollars per year would be realized from tax revenues and savings on law enforcement; crime would diminish because addicts would not have to hustle to keep themselves supplied with drugs; the murders associated with big-city drug trafficking would abate as lower-cost, legal drugs drive the traffickers out of business. Because these drugs would be of known quality and potency, and because they would not have to be injected with shared needles, the risk of overdose and infection would drop. The issue of foreign complicity in the drug traffic, which has complicated American diplomatic relations with many countries, would disappear. Under a policy of controlled legalization, it would be no more criminal or controversial to import coca from Colombia than to import coffee.

The more candid of the legalization proponents concede that these advantages would be purchased at the cost of increased drug abuse. Widespread availability, lower prices, and the elimination of the criminal sanction would result in more users, some of whom would inevitably become addicts. But how many more? Herbert Kleber, a treatment specialist and former deputy director of the Office of National Drug Control Policy, has argued that there would be between twelve and fifty-five million addicted users if cocaine and heroin were legally available. While it is impossible to anticipate the exact magnitude of the increase, history does support Kleber's argument. In countries like Iran or Thailand, where narcotics have long been cheap, potent, and readily available, the prevalence of addiction has been and continues to be quite high. Large quantities of opium sold by British and American merchants created a social disaster in nineteenth-century China; that Chinese sailors and immigrants subsequently introduced opium smoking to Britain and America is a kind of ironic justice. Doctors, who constantly work with and around narcotics, have historically had a very serious addiction problem: estimates of the extent of morphine addiction among American physicians at the turn of the century ran from 6 percent to an astonishing 23 percent. In a word, exposure matters.

Kleber has also attacked the crime-reduction rationale by pointing out that addicts will generally use much more of an illicit substance if the cost is low. They would spend most of their time using drugs and little of it working, thus continuing to resort to crime to acquire money. If the total number of addicts rose sharply as availability increased, total crime would also increase. There would be less crime committed by any single addict but more crime in the aggregate.

The debate over decriminalization is, in essence, an argument about a high-stakes gamble, and so far the opponents represent the majority view. At the close of the 1980s, four out of every five Americans were against the legalization of marijuana, let alone cocaine. But if the drug war produces another decade of indifferent results, growing disillusionment could conceivably prompt experiments in controlled legalization.

* * *

The controlled-legalization argument rests on the assumption that legal sales would largely eliminate the illicit traffic and its attendant evils. The history of drug use, regulation, and taxation in the United States suggests otherwise. The very phrase *controlled legalization* implies denying certain groups access to drugs. Minors are the most obvious example. No one advocates supplying narcotics to children, so presumably selling drugs to anyone under twenty-one would remain a criminal offense, since that is the cut-off point for sales of beverage alcohol. Unfortunately, illicit drug abuse in this century has become concentrated among the young—that is, among the very ones most likely to be made exceptions to the rule of legal sales.

Until about 1900 the most common pattern of drug dependence in the United States was opium or morphine addiction, brought about by the treatment of chronic diseases and painful symptoms. Addicts were mainly female, middle-class, and middle-aged or older; Eugene O'Neill's mother, fictionalized as Mary Tyrone in *Long Day's Journey into Night*, was one. Habitual users of morphine, laudanum, and other medicinal opiates in their adolescence were extremely rare, even in big cities like Chicago.

Another pattern of drug use was nonmedical and had its roots in marginal, deviant, and criminal subcultures. The "pleasure users," as they were sometimes called, smoked opium, sniffed cocaine, injected morphine and cocaine in combination, or, after 1910, sniffed or injected heroin. Nonmedical addicts began much younger than their medical counterparts. The average age of addiction (not first use, which would have been lower still) for urban heroin addicts studied in the 1910s was only nineteen or twenty years. They were also more likely to be male than those whose addiction was of medical origin, and more likely to have been involved in crime.

Initially the pleasure users were the smaller group, but during the first two decades of this century—the same period when the police approach to national drug control was formulated—the number of older, docile medical addicts steadily diminished. There were several reasons: doctors became better educated and more conservative in their use of narcotics; the population grew healthier; patent-medicine manufacturers were forced to reveal the contents of their products; and the numerous morphine addicts who had been created in the nineteenth century began to age and die off. Drug use and addiction became increasingly concentrated among young men in their teens and twenties, a pattern that continues to this day.

In 1980, 44 percent of drug arrests nationwide were of persons under the age of twenty-one. There were more arrests among teen-agers than among the entire population over the age of twenty-five; eighteen-year-olds had the highest arrest rate of any age group. By 1987 the proportion of those arrested under twenty-one had declined to 25 percent. This was partly due to the aging of the population and to the effects of drug education on students. But when large numbers of "echo boomers"—the children of the baby boomers—become adolescents during the 1990s, the percentage of under-twenty-one drug arrests will likely increase.

So, depending on timing and demographic circumstances, at least a quarter and perhaps more than a third of all drug buyers would be underage, and there would be a great deal of money to be made by selling to them. The primary source of supply would likely be diversion—adults legally purchasing drugs and selling them to customers below the legal age. The sellers (or middlemen who collected and then resold the legal purchases) would make a profit through marking up or adulterating the drugs, and there might well be turf disputes and hence violence. Some of the dealers and their underage purchasers would be caught, prosecuted, and jailed, and the criminal-justice system would still be burdened with drug arrests. The black market would be altered and diminished, but it would scarcely disappear.

* * *

Potential for illegal sales and use extends far beyond minors. Pilots, police officers, fire fighters, drivers of buses, trains, taxis, and ambulances, surgeons, active-duty military personnel, and others whose drug use would jeopardize public safety would be denied access to at least some drugs, and those of them who did take narcotics would be liable to criminal prosecution, as would their suppliers. Pregnant women would also pose a problem. Drugs transmitted to fetuses can cause irreversible and enormously costly harm. Federal and local governments may soon be spending billions of dollars a year just to prepare the impaired children of addicts for kindergarten. Society has the right and the obligation to stop this neurological carnage, both because it cruelly handicaps innocents and because it harms everyone else through higher taxes and health-insurance premiums. Paradoxically, the arguments for controlled legalization might lead to denying alcohol and tobacco to pregnant women along with narcotics. Alcohol and tobacco can also harm fetal development, and several legalization proponents have observed that it is both inconsistent and unwise to treat them as if they were not dangerous because they are legal. If cocaine is denied to pregnant women, why not alcohol too? The point here is simply that every time one makes an exception for good and compelling reasons—every time one accents the "controlled" as opposed to the "legalization"—one creates the likelihood of continued illicit sales and use.

The supposition that this illegal market would be fueled by diversion is well founded historically. There has always been an undercurrent of diversion, especially in the late 1910s and 1920s, when black-market operators like Legs Diamond got their supplies not so much by smuggling as by purchases from legitimate drug companies. One possible solution is to require of all legal purchasers that which is required of newly enrolled methadone patients: consumption of the drug on the premises. Unfortunately, unlike methadone, heroin and cocaine are short-acting, and compulsive users must administer them every few hours or less. The dayrooms of drug-treatment clinics set up in Britain after 1968 to provide heroin maintenance were often clogged with whining addicts. Frustrated and angry, the clinic staffs largely abandoned heroin during the 1970s, switching instead to methadone, which, having the advantages of oral administration and twenty-four-hour duration, is far more suitable for clinic-based distribution. Confining the use of heroin or cocaine or other street drugs to clinics would be a logistical nightmare. But the alternative, take-home supplies, invites illegal sales to excluded groups.

Another historical pattern of black-market activity has been the smuggling of drugs to prisoners. Contraband was one of the reasons the government built specialized narcotic hospitals in Lexington, Kentucky, and Fort Worth, Texas, in the 1930s. Federal wardens wanted to get addicts out of their prisons because they were constantly conniving to obtain smuggled drugs. But when drug-related arrests multiplied after 1965 and the Lexington and Fort Worth facilities were closed, the prisons again filled with inmates eager to obtain drugs. Birch Bayh, chairing a Senate investigation of the matter in 1975, observed that in some institutions young offenders had a more plentiful supply of drugs than they did on the outside.

Since then more jails have been crammed with more prisoners, and these prisoners are more likely than ever to have had a history of drug use. In 1989, 60 to 80 percent of male arrestees in twelve large American cities tested positive for drugs. It is hard to imagine a controlled-legalization system that would permit sales to prisoners. Alcohol, although a legal drug, is not sold licitly in prisons, and for good reason, as more than 40 percent of prisoners were under its influence when they committed their crimes. If drugs are similarly denied to inmates, then the contraband problem will persist. If, moreover, we insist that our nearly three million parolees and probationers remain clean on the theory that drug use aggravates recidivism, the market for illegal sales would be so much the larger.

By now the problem should be clear. If drugs are legalized, but not for those under twenty-one, or for public-safety officers, or transport workers, or military personnel, or pregnant women, or prisoners, or probationers, or parolees, or psychotics, or any of several other special groups one could plausibly name, then just exactly who is going to buy them? Noncriminal adults, whose drug use is comparatively low to begin with? Controlled legalization entails a dilemma. To the extent that its controls are enforced, some form of black-market activity will persist. If, on the other hand, its controls are not enforced and drugs are easily diverted to those who are underage or otherwise ineligible, then it is a disguised form of wholesale legalization and as such morally, politically, and economically unacceptable.

One of the selling points of controlled legalization was also one of the decisive arguments for the repeal of Prohibition: taxation. Instead of spending billions to suppress the illicit traffic, the government would reap billions by imposing duties on legitimate imports and taxes on domestically manufactured drugs. Not only could these revenues be earmarked for drug treatment and education programs, but they would also increase the prices paid by the consumer, thus discouraging consumption, especially among adolescents.

The United States government has had extensive historical experience with the taxation of legal narcotics. In the nineteenth and early twentieth centuries, opium was imported and subject to customs duties. The imports were assigned to one of three categories. The first was crude opium, used mainly for medicinal purposes and for the domestic manufacture of morphine. Foreign-manufactured morphine, codeine, and heroin made up the second class of imports, while the third was smoking opium, most of it prepared in Hong Kong and shipped to San Francisco.

* * *

The imposts [taxes] on these imported drugs fluctuated over the years, but they were generally quite stiff. From 1866 to 1914 the average ad valorem duty [calculated according to value] on crude opium was 33 percent; for morphine or its salts, 48 percent. From 1866 to 1908 the average duty on smoking opium was an extraordinarily high 97 percent. This last was in the nature of a sin tax; congressmen identified opium smoking with Chinese coolies, gamblers, pimps, and prostitutes and wished to discourage its importation and use.

These customs duties produced revenue; they also produced widespread smuggling, much of it organized by violent criminal societies like the Chinese tongs. The smugglers were as ingenious as their latter-day Mafia counterparts. They hid their shipments in everything from hollowed-out lumber to snake cages. Avoiding the customs collectors, they saved as much as three dollars a pound on crude opium, three dollars an ounce on morphine, and twelve dollars a pound on smoking opium. Twelve dollars seems a trifling sum by modern standards, hardly worth the risk of arrest, but in the nineteenth century it was more than most workers earned in a week. Someone who smuggled in fifty pounds of smoking opium in 1895 had gained the equivalent of a year's wages. One knowledgeable authority estimated that when the duty on smoking opium was near its peak, the amount smuggled into the United States was nearly twice that legally imported and taxed. Something similar happened with eighteenth-century tobacco imports to the British Isles. More than a third of the tobacco consumed in England and Scotland circa 1750 had been clandestinely imported in order to avoid a duty of more than five pence per pound. The principle is the same for domestically produced drugs: if taxes are sufficiently onerous, an illegal supply system will spring up. Moonshining existed before and after, as well as during, Prohibition.

The obvious solution is to set taxes at a sufficiently low level to discourage smuggling and illegal manufacturing. But again there is a dilemma. The most important illicit drugs are processed agricultural products that can be grown in several parts of the world by peasant labor. They are not, in other words, intrinsically expensive. Unless they are heavily taxed, legal consumers will be able to acquire them at little cost, less than ten dollars for a gram of cocaine. If drugs are that cheap, to say nothing of being 100 percent pure, the likelihood of a postlegalization epidemic of addiction will be substantially increased. But if taxes are given a stiff boost to enhance revenues and limit consumption, black marketeers will reenter the picture in numbers proportionate to the severity of the tax.

Tax revenues, like drugs themselves, can be addictive. In the twelve years after the repeal of Prohibition, federal liquor tax revenues ballooned from 259 million to 2.3 billion dollars. The government's dependence on this money was one important reason anti-liquor forces made so little progress in their attempts to restrict alcohol consumption during World War II. Controlled drug legalization would also bring about a windfall in tax dollars, which in an era of chronic deficits would surely be welcomed and quickly spent. Should addiction rates become too high, a conflict between public health and revenue concerns would inevitably ensue.

When both proponents and opponents of controlled legalization talk about drug taxes, they generally assume a single level of taxation. The assumption is wrong. The nature of the federal system permits state and local governments to levy their own taxes on drugs in addition to the uniform federal customs and excise taxes. This means that total drug taxes, and hence the prices paid by consumers, will vary from place to place. Variation invites interstate smuggling, and if the variation is large enough, the smuggling can be extensive and involve organized crime.

The history of cigarette taxation serves to illustrate this principle. In 1960 state taxes on cigarettes were low, between zero and eight cents per pack, but after 1965 a growing number of states sharply increased cigarette taxes in response to health concerns and as a politically painless way of increasing revenue. Some states, mainly in the Northeast, were considerably more aggressive than others in raising taxes. By 1975 North Carolina purchasers were paying thirty-six cents per pack while New Yorkers paid fifty-four cents. The price was higher still in New York City because of a local levy that reached eight cents per pack (as much as the entire federal tax) at the beginning of 1976.

Thus was born an opportunity to buy cheap and sell dear. Those who bought in volume at North Carolina prices and sold at New York (or Connecticut, or Massachusetts) prices realized a substantial profit, and by the mid-1970s net revenue losses stood at well over three hundred million dollars a year. Much of this went to organized crime, which at one point was bootlegging 25 percent of the cigarettes sold in New York State and *half* of those sold in New York

City. The pioneer of the illegal traffic, Anthony Granata, established a trucking company with thirty employees operating vehicles on a six-days-a-week basis. Granata's methods—concealed cargoes, dummy corporations, forged documents, fortresslike warehouses, bribery, hijacking, assault, and homicide—were strikingly similar to those used by illicit drug traffickers and Prohibition bootleggers.

* * *

Although high-tax states like Florida or Illinois still lose millions annually to cigarette bootleggers, the 1978 federal Contraband Cigarette Act and stricter law enforcement and accounting procedures have had some success in reducing over-the-road smuggling. But it is relatively easy to detect illegal shipments of cigarettes, which must be smuggled by the truckload to make a substantial amount of money. Cocaine and heroin are more compact, more profitable, and very easy to conceal. Smuggling these drugs to take advantage of state tax differentials would consequently be much more difficult to detect and deter. If, for example, taxed cocaine retailed in Vermont for ten dollars a gram and in New York for twelve dollars a gram, anyone who bought just five kilograms at Vermont prices, transported them, and sold them at New York prices would realize a profit of ten thousand dollars. Five kilograms of cocaine can be concealed in an attaché case.

* * *

Of course, if all states legalized drugs and taxed them at the same rate, this sort of illegal activity would not exist, but it is constitutionally and politically unfeasible to ensure uniform rates of state taxation. And federalism poses other challenges. Laws against drug use and trafficking have been enacted at the local, state, and federal levels. It is probable that if Congress repeals or modifies the national drug laws, some states will go along with controlled legalization while others will not. Nevada, long in the legalizing habit, might jettison its drug laws, but conservative Mormon-populated Utah might not. Alternately, governments could experiment with varying degrees of legalization. Congress might decide that anything was better than the current mayhem in the capital and legislate a broad legalization program for the District of Columbia. At the same time, Virginia and Maryland might experiment with the decriminalization of marijuana, the least risky legalization option, but retain prohibition of the nonmedical use of other drugs. The result would again be smuggling, whether from Nevada to Utah or, save for marijuana, from the District of Columbia to the surrounding states. It is hard to see how any state that chose to retain laws against drugs could possibly stanch the influx of prohibited drugs from adjacent states that did not. New York City's futile attempts to enforce its strict gun-control laws show how difficult it is to restrict locally that which is elsewhere freely available.

I referred earlier to the legalization debate as an argument about a colossal gamble, whether society should risk an unknown increase in drug abuse and addiction to eliminate the harms of drug prohibition, most of which stem from illicit trafficking. "Take the crime out of it" is the rallying cry of the legalization advocates. After reviewing the larger history of narcotic, alcohol, and tobacco use and regulation, it appears that this debate should be recast. It would be more accurate to ask whether society should risk an unknown but possibly substantial increase in drug abuse and addiction in order to bring about an unknown *reduction* in illicit trafficking and other costs of drug prohibition. Controlled legalization would take some, but by no means all, of the crime out of it. Just how much and what sort of crime would be eliminated would depend upon which groups were to be denied which drugs, the overall level of taxation, and differences in state tax and legalization policies. If the excluded groups were few *and* all states legalized all drugs *and* all governments taxed at uniformly low levels, then the black market would be largely eliminated. But these are precisely the conditions that would be most likely to bring about an unacceptably high level of drug abuse. The same variables that would determine how successful the controlled-legalization policy would be in eliminating the black market would also largely determine how unsuccessful it was in containing drug addiction.

POSTSCRIPT

Should Drugs Be Legalized?

The analogy often cited by proponents of drug legalization is the ill-fated attempt to ban the sale of liquor in the United States, which lasted from 1919 to 1933. Prohibition has been called "an experiment noble in purpose," but it was an experiment that greatly contributed to the rise of organized crime. The repeal of Prohibition brought about an increase in liquor consumption and alcoholism, but it also deprived organized crime of an important source of income. Would drug decriminalization similarly strike a blow at the drug dealers? Possibly, and such a prospect is obviously appealing. But would drug decriminalization also exacerbate some of the ills associated with drugs? Would there be more violence, more severe addiction, and more crack babies born to addicted mothers?

There are a variety of publications and theories pertaining to drug use and society. Ronald L. Akers, in *Drugs, Alcohol, and Society* (Wadsworth, 1992), relates drug patterns to social structure. For a comprehensive overview of the history, effects, and prevention of drug use, see Weldon L. Witters, Peter J. Venturelli, and Glen R. Hanson, *Drugs and Society*, 3rd ed. (Jones & Bartlett, 1992). Terry Williams presents a field study of a teenage drug ring in *The Cocaine Kids* (Addison Wesley, 1989) and describes the goings-on in a crackhouse in *Crackhouse: Notes from the End of the Zone* (Addison Wesley, 1992). Erich Goode, in *Drugs in American Society* (McGraw-Hill, 1988), provides a sociological perspective on drugs. Larry Sloman's *Reefer Madness: The History of Marijuana in America* (Grove Press, 1983) describes changing attitudes and laws regarding marijuana, while Lester Brinspoon and James B. Bakalar do the same for cocaine in *Cocaine: A Drug and Its Social Evolution* (Basic Books, 1985). James A. Inciardi, in *The War on Drugs: Heroin, Cocaine, Crime and Public Policy* (Mayfield, 1986), takes a close-up look at the cocaine and crime scene. For a relatively balanced yet innovative set of drug policies, see Elliott Carrie, *Reckoning: Drugs, the Cities, and the American Future* (Hill & Wang, 1993). Franklin E. Zimring and Gordon Hawkins, in *The Search for Rational Drug Control* (Cambridge University Press, 1992), and Thomas S. Szasz, in *Ceremonial Chemistry: The Ritual Persecution of Drugs, Addicts, and Pushers* (Learning Publications, 1985), criticize the current antidrug crusades. William O. Walker III, ed., *Drug Control Policy* (Pennsylvania State University Press, 1992), critically evaluates drug policies from historical and comparative perspectives. The connection between drugs and crime is explored in *Drugs and Crime*, edited by Michael Toney and James Q. Wilson (University of Chicago Press, 1990). A work on the legalization debate, biased toward the legalization side, is *The Drug Legalization Debate*, edited by James A. Inciardi (Sage Publications, 1991).

ISSUE 18

Is Incapacitation the Answer to the Crime Problem?

YES: Morgan O. Reynolds, from "Crime Pays, But So Does Imprisonment," *Journal of Social, Political, and Economic Studies* (Fall 1990)

NO: David L. Bazelon, from "Solving the Nightmare of Street Crime," *USA Today Magazine,* a publication of the Society for the Advancement of Education (January 1982)

ISSUE SUMMARY

YES: Professor of economics Morgan O. Reynolds argues that the decline in the cost of crime for criminals has contributed greatly to the increase in crime and that catching, convicting, and imprisoning more criminals would greatly reduce the crime rate.

NO: Judge David L. Bazelon discusses the moral and financial costs of the incapacitation approach and argues that society must attack the brutal social and economic conditions that are the root causes of street crime.

Not a day passes in America without reports of murders, rapes, or other violent crimes. As crime has increasingly captured the headlines, public indignation has intensified—particularly when spectacular cases have been brought to light about paroled convicts committing new felonies, light sentences being handed down for serious crimes, and cases being thrown out of court on legal technicalities. The perception that Michael Dukakis was soft on criminals seriously hurt his bid for the presidency in 1988. (As governor of Massachusetts, Dukakis approved a prison furlough program that released a convict named Willie Horton, who subsequently went on to commit a widely publicized, horribly violent crime in another state.) Over the past three decades, there has been a dramatic increase in the number of Americans who think that the authorities should be tougher on criminals. To take one prominent example: while a majority of Americans in the 1960s favored the abolition of the death penalty, today more than 70 percent favor its use for certain crimes.

Even in the intellectual community, there has been a turnaround. When the Southern Democrat and presidential candidate George Wallace and other politicians raised the issue of "law and order" at the end of the 1960s, the term was called "a code word for racism" in academic and literary circles.

This is understandable because Wallace *had* previously identified himself with white racism. The attitude toward crime that was popular in academic circles during the 1960s might be briefly summarized under two headings: the prevention of crime and the treatment of criminals.

To prevent crime, some academics argued, government must do more than rely upon police, courts, and jails. It must do something about the underlying social roots of crime, especially poverty and racism. It was assumed that, once these roots were severed, crime would begin to fade away or at least cease to be a major social problem.

The prescription for treating criminals followed much the same logic. The word *punishment* was avoided in favor of *treatment* or *rehabilitation*, for the purpose was not to inflict pain or to "pay back" the criminal but to bring about a change in his behavior. If that could be done by lenient treatment—short prison terms, education, counseling, and above all by understanding—then so much the better.

By the late 1970s, the intellectual community itself showed signs that it was reassessing its outlook toward crime. Criminologist and sociologist James Q. Wilson's views on crime became widely respected in universities and in the mass media. He argued that society's attempts to change social conditions had met with little success and that locking up criminals remained the best way to deal with the crime problem in the short term. Wilson's view is carried forward by Morgan O. Reynolds, who, after examining data collected on crimes and time in prison, has found that "crime pays" because most crimes do not result in significant jail time for the criminal. From 1950 to 1974, in fact, expected time in prison for serious crimes dropped from 24 days to 5.5 days. Seeking to reverse the trend, Reynolds discusses a number of ways to reduce the costs of punishing criminals that might slow down the revolving doors of prisons.

David L. Bazelon admits that incapacitation is a short-term solution to street crime that delivers some results. He points out, however, that it has high financial and moral costs and that the United States already imprisons a larger proportion of its citizens than do all other developed nations. A threefold increase in the prison population will not make a significant dent in the rate of serious crimes, maintains Bazelon, and the new prisons needed to house those increased numbers will cost many billions of dollars. More importantly, he says, the incapacitation approach assumes that convicted offenders will continue to commit crimes and in effect punishes them for future misdeeds. Bazelon asserts that the only satisfactory answer is to attack the social and economic conditions that are the root causes of street crime.

YES   Morgan O. Reynolds

CRIME PAYS, BUT SO DOES IMPRISONMENT

America is burdened by an appalling amount of crime. Even though the crime rate is not soaring as it did during the 1960s and 1970s, we still have more crimes per capita than any other developed country.

- Every year nearly 6 million people are victims of violent crimes—murder, rape, robbery or assault.
- Another 29 million Americans each year are victims of property crimes—arson, burglary and larceny-theft.
- There is a murder every 25 minutes, a rape every six minutes, a robbery every minute and an aggravated assault every 35 seconds.
- There is a motor vehicle theft every 22 seconds, a burglary every ten seconds, and a larceny-theft every four seconds.

Although the number of crimes reported to the police each year has leveled off somewhat in the 1980s, our crime rate today is still enormously high—411 percent higher, for example, than it was in 1960.

Why is there so much crime?

THE EXPECTED PUNISHMENT FOR COMMITTING A CRIME

The economic theory of crime is a relatively new field of social science. According to this theory, most crimes are not irrational acts. Instead, crimes are freely committed by people who compare the expected benefits of crime with the expected costs. The reason we have so much crime is that, for many people, the benefits outweigh the costs. For some people, a criminal career is more attractive than their other career options. Put another way, the reason we have so much crime is that crime pays.

Because criminals and potential criminals rarely have accurate information about the probabilities of arrest, conviction and imprisonment, a great deal of uncertainty is involved in the personal assessment of the expected punishment from committing crimes. Individuals differ in skill and intellect.

From Morgan O. Reynolds, "Crime Pays, But So Does Imprisonment," *Journal of Social, Political, and Economic Studies* (Fall 1990). Copyright © 1990 by The Council for Social and Economic Studies, P.O. Box 35070, NW Washington, DC 20043. Reprinted by permission. Notes omitted.

The more skillful and more intelligent criminals have better odds of committing successful crimes. Some people overestimate their probability of success, while others underestimate theirs.

Despite the element of subjectivity, the economic theory of crime makes one clear prediction: Crime will increase if the expected cost of crime to criminals declines. This is true for "crimes of passion" as well as economic crimes such as burglary or auto theft. The less costly crime becomes, the more often people fail to control their passions.

The economic theory of crime is consistent with public opinion, and with the perceptions of potential criminals. It is supported by considerable statistical research. According to the theory, the amount of crime is inversely related to expected punishment. What follows is a brief summary of the punishment criminals can expect.

EXPECTED TIME IN PRISON

What is the expected punishment for committing major types of serious crime in the United States today?... [T]he expected punishment is shockingly low.

• Even for committing the most serious crime—murder—an individual can expect to spend only 2.3 years in prison.

• On the average, an individual who commits an act of burglary can expect to spend only 7.1 days in prison.

• Someone considering an auto theft can expect to spend only 6.3 days in prison.

Crime and Punishment

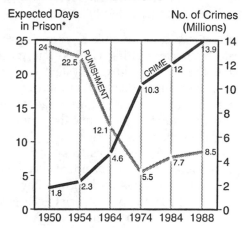

Expected Days in Prison*

No. of Crimes (Millions)

* Median prison sentence for all serious crimes, weighted by probabilities of arrest, prosecution, conviction, and imprisonment.

THE DECLINE IN EXPECTED IMPRISONMENT AND THE RISE IN CRIME

... On the average, those crimes with the longest expected prison terms (murder, rape, robbery and assault) are the crimes least frequently committed, comprising only about 10 percent of all serious crime. The remaining 90 percent carry an expected prison term of only a few days. When expected punishment is weighted by the frequency of types of crimes, the picture is even more shocking: On the average, a perpetrator of a serious crime in the United States can expect to spend about eight days in prison.... [T]his overall expectation has changed over time.

• Since the early 1950s, the expected punishment for committing a serious crime in the United States (measured in terms of expected time in prison) has been reduced by two-thirds.

• Over the same period, the total number of serious crimes committed has increased sevenfold.

THE "PRICES" WE CHARGE FOR CRIME

It is virtually impossible to prevent people from committing crimes. The most that the criminal justice system can do is impose punishment after the crime has been committed. People are largely free to commit almost any crime they choose. What the criminal justice system does is construct a list of prices (expected punishments) for various criminal acts. People commit crimes so long as they are willing to pay the prices society charges, just as many of us might risk parking or speeding tickets.

Viewed in this way, the expected prison sentences . . . are the prices we charge for various crimes. Thus, the price of murder is about 2.3 years in prison; the price of burglary is 7.7 days; the price for stealing a car is 4.2 days. Since these prices are so low, it is small wonder so many people are willing to pay them.

CALCULATING THE EXPECTED PUNISHMENT FOR CRIME

Five adverse events must occur before a criminal actually ends up in prison. The criminal must be arrested, indicted, prosecuted, convicted and sent to prison. As a result, the expected punishment for crime depends upon a number of probabilities: The probability of being arrested, given that a crime is committed; the probability of being prosecuted, given an arrest; the probability of conviction, given prosecution; and the probability of being sent to prison, given a conviction. As Table 1 shows, the overall probability of being punished is the result of multiplying four probabilities.

Even if each of the separate probabilities is reasonably high, their product can be quite low. For example, suppose that each of these probabilities were 0.5. That is, one-half of crimes result in an arrest, one-half of arrests lead to prosecution, one-half of prosecutions lead to a conviction, and one-half of convictions lead to a prison term. In this case, the overall probability that a criminal will spend time in prison is only 6.25 percent.

Table 1 also depicts recent probabilities in the case of burglary. Note that burglars who are sent to prison stay there for about 17 months, on the average. . . . But someone considering an act of burglary will surely be influenced by the fact that the probability of being arrested is only 14 percent. Although the probabilities of prosecution and conviction following an arrest are high, the criminal's probability of going to prison is less than one in three after being convicted. When all factors are taken into account (including the probability that the crime will never be reported), the overall probability that a burglar will end up in prison is less than one percent. The expected punishment prior to committing the crime is only 7.1 days.

PROBABILITY OF ARREST

. . . The striking fact . . . is the degree to which arrest rates have declined over the past 40 years, even for the most serious crimes. For example:

• Since 1950, the probability of being arrested after committing a murder has fallen by 25 percent.

• The probability of arrest for rapists has fallen 35 percent, for robbers 42 percent and for burglars 53 percent.

On the average, during the 1980s, only about 21 percent of all crimes in the United States were cleared by arrest. In Japan, by contrast, the clearance-by-

Table 1

Calculating the Expected Punishment for Potential Criminals

Expected Time in Prison	=	Probability of arrest	×	Probability of prosecution, given arrest
	×	Probability of conviction, given prosecution	×	Probability of imprisonment, given conviction
	×	median sentence		

Example: Expected punishment for burglary

Expected Time in Prison	=	14% (Probability of arrest)	×	88% (Probability of prosecution, given arrest)
	×	81% (Probability of conviction, given prosecution)	×	28% (Probability of imprisonment, given conviction)
	×	1/2 (Adjustment for unreported crimes)*	×	17 months (median sentence)
	=	7.1 days		

* Approximately one-half of all burglaries are not reported to the police. Law enforcement agencies "clear" (or solve) an offense when at least one person is arrested, charged with the offense, and turned over for prosecution.

---

arrest rate is 50 percent. Moreover, Japan with a population of 122 million has fewer murders each year than New York City with a population of seven million.

PROBABILITY OF PROSECUTION, CONVICTION AND IMPRISONMENT

Although there are 13 million arrests each year in the United States, including 2.8 million for serious (Index) crimes, annual admissions to prison only topped 200,000 in 1986. In other words, only eight of every 100 arrests for Index crimes results in imprisonment after defense attorneys, prosecutors and courts complete their work.

OVERALL PROBABILITY OF GOING TO PRISON

A criminal's overall probability of imprisonment has fallen dramatically since 1950...:

• Since 1950, the percent of crimes resulting in a prison sentence has declined by at least 60 percent for every major category of crime.

• This includes a 60 percent drop for murder, a 79 percent decrease for rape, an 83 percent reduction for robbery and a 94 percent plunge for auto theft.

UNREPORTED CRIMES

Based on the number of crimes reported to the police, 1.66 percent of all serious crimes are punished by imprisonment; therefore 98.34 percent of serious crimes are not. According to the National Crime Survey, however, only 37 percent of serious crimes are actually reported. If there are two unreported crimes for every one reported, then the overall probability of going to prison for the commission of a serious crime falls to about 0.61 percent (.37 × 1.66%). This amounts to one prison term for every 164 felonies committed.

A POSSIBLE EXPLANATION: THE ROLE OF THE WARREN COURT

The main factor in the decline in expected punishment over the last three decades was a virtual collapse in the probability of imprisonment. Why? We cannot point to a shrinkage in law enforcement personnel as an explanation.... [T]he number of full-time police employees has risen steadily over the past three decades. Further, total employment in the criminal justice sector increased from 600,000 in 1965 to nearly 1.5 million in 1986. Government spending on the criminal justice sector doubled as a share of GNP, rising from less than 0.6 percent to nearly 1.2 percent. During the same period, private employment in detective and protection services grew rapidly, reaching half a million persons by the end of 1989. Apparently, more people now produce less justice.

The 1960s was a turbulent decade—the Vietnam War, the counterculture, urban riots. But one policy change that lasted well into the 1970s and 1980s was the change in the criminal justice system caused by the Supreme Court. Influenced by sociologists and other intellectuals, there was a growing reluctance to apprehend and punish criminals during the 1960s. In particular, 1961 brought the first landmark decision of the U.S. Supreme Court expanding the rights of criminal defendants and making it more costly for police and prosecutors to obtain criminal convictions.

Mapp v. Ohio (1961) declared that illegally obtained evidence could not be admitted in any state criminal prosecution, imposing the so-called "exclusionary rule" on all state judicial systems. A series of related decisions followed: *Gideon v. Wainwright* (1963) required taxpayer-funded counsel for defendants; *Escobedo v. Illinois* (1964) and *Malloy v. Hogan* (1964) expanded privileges against self-incrimination, thereby impeding interrogation by the police; and *Miranda v. Arizona* (1966) went further and made confessions, even if voluntary, inadmissible as evidence unless the suspect had been advised of certain rights.

The enforcement system was transformed by these decisions. Under the exclusionary rule, according to Justice Cardozo, "The criminal is to go free because the constable has blundered." Justice White, dissenting in the *Miranda* case, warned that the decision would have "a corrosive effect on the criminal laws as an effective device to prevent crime." It appears that the "pursuit of perfect justice," as Judge Macklin put it, changed the rules and increased the time and effort required to apprehend, convict and punish the guilty....

THE COST OF CRIME DETERRENCE

If America is to succeed in lowering the crime rate to, say, the level that prevailed in the 1950s, we must create at least as much crime deterrence as existed in the 1950s. For example, [there are] three ways of raising the expected prison sentence for burglary to its 1950 level. Since the probabilities of prosecution and conviction, given an arrest, are already high, the options are:

• Increase the proportion of burglaries cleared by arrest from 14 to 42 percent; or

• Increase the percent of convicted burglars sent to prison from 28 to 84 percent; or

• Increase the median prison sentence for burglars from 17 to 51 months.

All three alternatives are expensive. A higher arrest rate requires that more money be spent on criminal investigation. A higher sentencing rate requires more court and litigation costs. All three alternatives require more prison space. Unless prison space can be expanded, little else in the way of deterrence will be of much value.

America is in the midst of the biggest prison building boom in its history. On December 30, 1989, prisons held 673,565 convicts, up from 438,830 prisoners at the beginning of 1984 and at 110 percent of design capacity. In 1988 the system added 42,967 inmates, or enough to fill 86 new 500-bed prisons.

• Today, one out of every 364 Americans is in prison—not jail, probation or parole but in prison.

• With an additional 296,000 in local jails, 362,000 on parole and 2.4 million on probation, one out of every 69 Americans is under the supervision of the corrections establishment, or one of every 52 adults.

At an annual cost exceeding $20,000 per prisoner, the total prison tab is more than $15 billion a year. That cost will surely rise. Thirty-five states are under court orders to relieve prison overcrowding and others face litigation. To increase capacity, more than 100 new state and federal prisons currently are under construction around the country. California alone is spending $3.5 billion on new prison beds and has added 21,000 beds since 1984. State governments spent some $9 billion in 1989 on new prisons. In most cases, the construction cost per prison bed exceeds $50,000.

HOW TO REDUCE PRISON COSTS

Much could be done to reduce the high costs of constructing and operating prisons. The most promising ways to reduce taxpayer costs exploit private sector competition and efficiency in constructing and operating prisons and employing prisoners. Contracting out construction and remodeling is a proven economizer. Short of full privatization, government-operated correctional facilities should be corporatized and required to operate like private businesses, with profit and loss statements. Even within the existing system, economies are possible. What follows is a brief summary of ways to economize.

OPPORTUNITIES FOR REDUCING COSTS WITHIN THE PUBLIC SECTOR

Better Management Practices. Although entrepreneurship in the public sector is rare, opportunities for innovation in prison construction abound. For example:

• Florida expanded an existing facility by 336 beds for only $16,000 per cell.

• South Carolina used inmate labor to reduce construction costs by an estimated 50 percent with no quality loss and some delay.

• New York City has begun using renovated troop barges and a ferry boat for detention facilities.

Early Release of Elderly Prisoners. Although the recidivism rate is about 22 percent for prisoners age 18 to 24, among prisoners over 45 years old the recidivism rate is only 2.1 percent. Nationwide, there are at least 20,000 inmates over the age of 55. Moreover, the average maintenance cost of an elderly prisoner is about $69,000—three times the cost of a younger prisoner. Early release of elderly prisoners to make room for younger criminals makes sense and would improve crime deterrence.

Boot Camp Therapy for Young Prisoners. Called "shock incarceration" by federal drug Czar William Bennett, boot camp therapy as an alternative to prison for youngsters (not yet hardened criminals) is being used in Georgia, Alabama, Florida, Louisiana, Mississippi, New York, Oklahoma, South Carolina and Texas. Costs are lower, although the recidivism rate is about the same as for the prison system as a whole.

Electronic Ankle Bracelets. The cost of punishment would be greatly reduced if ways were found of punishing criminals without imprisonment. Few people would deny that imprisonment is necessary and desirable for violent crimes such as homicide, rape, robbery and assault. But less than half of U.S. prisoners have been incarcerated for such crimes. A mid-1980s survey found that:

• One-third of the prisoners were imprisoned for property offenses and another 20 percent for crimes against public order (including drug offenses).

• In Arkansas, nonviolent offenders outnumbered violent ones by a ratio of three to one.

• In Mississippi, Kentucky, Missouri and Wyoming the ratio was two to one.

A recent alternative to imprisonment is the electronic monitoring device that is worn by parolees. Judges can impose conditions of parole, including restrictions on the range and timing of activities, and they can be enforced by monitoring companies....

PRODUCTIVE WORK FOR PRISONERS

A recent survey commissioned by the National Institute of Justice identified more than 70 companies which employ inmates in 16 states in manufacturing, service and light assembly operations. Prisoners work as reservations clerks for TWA and Best Western, sew leisure wear, manufacture water-bed mattresses, and assemble electronic components. PRIDE, a state-sponsored private corporation that runs Florida's 46 prison industries from furniture-making to optical glass grinding, made a $4 million profit in 1987. This work benefits nearly everyone. It enables prisoners to earn wages, acquire skills, and subtly learn individual responsibility and the value of productive labor. It also insures that they can contribute to victim compensation, and to their own and their families' support....

THE COST OF NOT BUILDING PRISONS

Although the cost of building and maintaining prisons is high, the cost of not creating more prisons appears to be much higher. A study by the National Institute of Justice concluded that the "typical" offender let loose in society will engage in a one-man crime wave, creating damage to society more than 17 times as costly than imprisonment. Specifically:

- Sending someone to prison for one year costs the government about $25,000.
- A Rand Corporation survey of 2190 professional criminals found that the average criminal committed 187 to 287 crimes a year, at an average cost per crime of $2,300.
- On the average, then, a professional criminal out of prison costs society $430,000 per year, or $405,000 more than the cost of a year in prison.

The failure to keep offenders in prison once they are there is also a hazard of too little prison space, and early release often leads to much more crime. A Rand Corporation survey of former inmates found that:

- In California, 76 percent were arrested within three years of their release and 60 percent were convicted of new crimes.
- In Texas, 60 percent of former inmates were arrested within three years and 40 percent were reconvicted.
- A survey of 11 states showed that 62.5 percent of all released prisoners were arrested within 3 years, 46.8 percent were reconvicted and 41.1 percent were reincarcerated.

In California, a comparison between ex-convicts and criminals who received probation rather than a prison sentence showed a disheartening rate of failure for both. Each ex-convict committed an estimated 20 crimes. Each probationer committed 25 crimes.

A Bureau of Justice Statistics study of 22 states found that 69 percent of young adults (ages 17 to 22) released from prison in 1978 were arrested within six years—each committing an average of 13 new crimes.

CONCLUSION

While crime continues on the high plateau, there are grounds for optimism. The number of young males began to decline in the 1980s and will continue to do so through the 1990s. Further, the odds of imprisonment for a serious offense increased in the 1980s as legislators responded to the public's "get tough" attitude. Yet we remained plagued with crime rates (per capita) triple those of the 1950s.

What can be done to build on this relatively promising recent trend? At a minimum the analysis in this report suggests three things. First, the U.S. Supreme Court should continue to reestablish the rule of law by restricting application of the exclusionary rule and other expansions of criminal privileges inherited from the Warren Court. Second, the public sector must continue raising the odds of imprisonment toward those of the 1950s in order to improve personal security. Deterrence of criminals implies building prisons and reducing prison costs by privatization. Third, the laws hampering productive employment of prisoners must be relaxed to take full advantage of the benefits of privatization.

ACKNOWLEDGMENT

My thanks to Dr. John Goodman, President, National Center for Policy Analysis, Dallas, Texas, for his help on this paper and his permission to reprint material from NCPA Report No. 149. Author.

NO

David L. Bazelon

SOLVING THE NIGHTMARE
OF STREET CRIME

The nightmare of street crime is slowly paralyzing American society. Across the nation, terrified people have altered their lifestyles, purchasing guns and doubling locks to protect their families against the rampant violence outside their doors. After seething for years, public anxiety is now boiling over in a desperate search for answers. Our leaders are reacting to these public demands. In New York, Gov. Hugh Carey proposed the hiring of more police officers and prosecutors; in California, Attorney General Deukmejian has asked the legislature for immediate adoption of a package of new law enforcement bills.

A recent address by the Chief Justice of the United States has helped to place this crisis high on the public agenda. Speaking before the American Bar Association in February, Chief Justice Warren Burger described ours as an "impotent society," suffering a "reign of terror" in its streets and homes. The time has come, he declared, to commit vast social resources to the attack on crime—a priority comparable to the national defense.

Some have questioned whether a sitting Chief Justice should advocate sweeping changes in the criminal justice system and others have challenged his particular prescriptions, but I believe the prestige of his office has focused the nation's attention on issues critical to our future. We should welcome this opportunity to begin a thoughtful and constructive debate about our national nightmare.

In this debate, public concern is sure to generate facile sloganeering by politicians and professionals alike. It would be easy to convert this new urgency into a mandate for a "quick fix." The far-harder task is to marshall that energy toward examining the painful realities and agonizing choices we face. Criminologists can help make our choices the product of an informed, rational, and morally sensitive strategy. As citizens and as human beings, they have a special responsibility to contribute their skills, experience, and knowledge to keep the debate about crime as free of polemics and unexamined assumptions as possible.

I would like to outline some avenues of inquiry worthy of exploration. I offer no programs, no answers. After 31 years on the bench, I can say with

From David L. Bazelon, "Solving the Nightmare of Street Crime," *USA Today Magazine* (January 1982). Copyright © 1982 by The Society for the Advancement of Education. Reprinted by permission.

confidence that we can never deal intelligently and humanely with crime until we face the realities behind it. First, we must carefully identify the problem that so terrorizes America. Second, we should seek to understand the conditions that breed those crimes of violence. Finally, we should take a close look at both the short- and long-term alternatives for dealing with the problem.

TYPES OF CRIMES AND WHO COMMITS THEM

A reasoned analysis must begin by asking: What is it that has our society in such a state of fear? Politicians, journalists, and criminal justice professionals who should know better speak rather generally about "crime in America" without specifying exactly what they mean. There are, in fact, several distinct types of crimes and people who commit them.

Consider white-collar crime. This category embraces activities ranging from shoplifting to tax fraud to political corruption. It is undoubtedly a phenomenon of the gravest concern, costing society untold billions of dollars—far more than street crime. To the extent that such crimes appear to go unpunished, they breed disrespect for law and cynicism about our criminal justice institutions. Yet, as costly and corrosive as such crimes are, they do not instill the kind of fear reflected in the recent explosion of public concern. White-collar crimes, after all, are committed by the middle and upper classes, by "[p]eople who look like one's next-door neighbor," as sociologist Charles Silberman puts it. These people do not, by and large, threaten our physical safety or the sanctity of our homes.

Nor do the perpetrators of organized crime. After all, hired guns largely kill each other. The average citizen need not lock his doors in fear that he may be the object of gang warfare. Organized crime unquestionably does contribute to street crime—the most obvious connection is drugs—but organized crime has certainly not produced the recent hysteria.

Nor do crimes of passion cause us to bolt our doors so firmly at night. That would be like locking the fox *inside* the chicken coop. Clearly, it is the random assault of *street* crime—the muggings, rapes, purse snatchings, and knifings that plague city life—which puts us all in such mortal fear for our property and lives.

Once we focus on the kind of crime we fear, the second step in a constructive analysis is to identify those people who commit it. This is no pleasant task. The real roots of crime are associated with a constellation of suffering so hideous that, as a society, we can not bear to look it in the face. Yet, we can never hope to understand street crime unless we summon the courage to look at the ugly realities behind it. Nobody questions that street criminals typically come from the bottom of the socioeconomic ladder—from among the ignorant, the ill-educated, and the unemployed, and the unemployable. A recent National Institute of Justice study confirms that our prison population is disproportionately black and young. The offenders that give city dwellers nightmares come from an underclass of brutal social and economic deprivation. Urban League president Vernon Jordan calls them America's "boat people without boats."

It is no great mystery why some of these people turn to crime. They are born into families struggling to survive, if they have families at all. They are raised in deteriorating, overcrowded housing. They lack adequate nutrition and health care. They are subjected to prejudice and educated in unresponsive schools. They are denied the sense of order, purpose, and self-esteem that makes law-abiding citizens. With nothing to preserve and nothing to lose, they turn to crime for economic survival, a sense of excitement and accomplishment, and an outlet for frustration, desperation, and rage.

Listen to the words of a 15-year-old ghetto youth:

> In Brooklyn you fall into one of two categories when you start growing up.... First, there's the minority of the minority, the "ducks" or suckers. These are the kids who go to school every day. They even want to go to college. Imagine that! School after high school! ... They're wasting their lives waiting for a dream that won't come true.
>
> The ducks are usually the ones getting beat up on by the majority group—the "hard rocks." If you're a real hard rock you have no worries, no cares. Getting high is as easy as breathing. You just rip off some duck. You don't bother going to school, it's not necessary. You just live with your mom until you get a job—that should be any time a job comes looking for you. Why should you bother to go looking for it? Even your parents can't find work.
>
> Hard rocks do what they want to do when they want to do it. When a hard rock goes to prison it builds up his reputation. He develops a bravado that's like a long sad joke. But it's all lies and excuses. It's a hustle to keep ahead of the fact that he's going nowhere....

This, then, is the face behind the mask we call "the crime problem."

Having identified the kind of crime that causes public anxiety and the kind of people who commit it, we can now consider some alternative responses. For purpose of analysis, we can divide the alternatives into two types. The first set, which enjoys the greatest currency in the political arena today, consists of short-term proposals. They proceed from our universally acknowledged need to protect ourselves *immediately* from the menace of crime. These kinds of prescriptions are endorsed by many good people in high places, including the Chief Justice of the United States and the Mayor of New York. The short-term proposals rely principally on deterrence and incapacitation as means of controlling the symptoms of our national disease. The second, more long-term proposals seek to attack the root causes of crime. Both of these approaches have great costs as well as benefits that must be carefully understood and weighed before we set our course.

DETERRENCE

Let us first examine the short-run proposals. Deterrence has always been intuitively attractive. The recent spate of prescriptions underscores the popularity of this theory and has taken many forms. The Chief Justice says we must provide "swift and certain consequences" for criminal behavior. The California Attorney General advocates mandatory prison terms for certain kinds of crimes. New York Mayor Edward Koch favors harsher sentences including the death penalty. Former U.S. Attorney Whitney North Seymour, Jr., contends that tougher prosecution is necessary. Each of these proposals is premised on Harvard University Prof. James Q. Wilson's theory that, "if the expected cost of crime goes up without a corresponding increase in the expected benefits, then the would-be criminal—unless he or she is among that small fraction of criminals who are utterly irrational—engages in less crime." To the same effect, Wayne State Prof. Ralph Slovenko wrote in a letter to the editor of *The New York Times* that, since "[p]rofits are tax-free and penalties are minimal," those who violate the law are "criminals by choice."

This "rational man" theory of crime is quite plausible with respect to certain kinds of criminals. I can believe that those who have alternatives to crime can indeed be dissuaded from choosing the lawless path if the price is made high enough. If the Abscam episode accomplished nothing else, it induced some potentially corrupt politicians to forbear from taking bribes—at least where there might be cameras around. In fact, white-collar offenders may be so susceptible to deterrence that punishment is superfluous. The fellow country-club members of a corporate embezzler whose life is ruined in a storm of publicity may not need to actually see him go to jail in order to be deterred.

However, the white-collar criminal is *not* the object of these deterrence proposals. Seymour says his proposals are aimed at "the hoodlums and ruffians who are making life in our cit[ies] a nightmare for many citizens"; in other words, at the "hard rocks." Can *these* kinds of criminals be effectively deterred? Diana Gordon, Executive Vice Pres. of the National Council on Crime and Delinquency, points out that the threat of prison may be a meaningless deterrent to one whose urban environment is itself a prison; and as our 15-year-old ghetto resident informs us, "[w]hen a hard rock goes to prison it builds up his reputation."

Common sense is confirmed by experience. New York's highly touted Rockefeller drug law did not produce a decrease in heroin use. In fact, it was actually followed by an increase in property crimes associated with heroin users. Nor is the New York situation unique. Since 1965, the average time served in Federal prison has *risen* from 18 to 30 months. Yet, crime continues to rise unabated.

Even the high priest of deterrence, Prof. Wilson, recognizes the limits of this theory. Although many bandy about his name in support of get-tough proposals, Wilson suggests that the *severity* of punishment has little deterrent effect. Indeed, "the more severe the penalty, the more unlikely that it will be imposed." The benefits of deterrence, according to Wilson, lie only in *certainty* of punishment.

How can we increase that certainty? The *Miranda* rule, the right to seek collateral review, and even the time to prepare for trial have all come under attack in the name of "swift and certain" punishment. These trial and appellate safeguards reflect our fundamental commitment to the presumption of innocence. Before we trade them away, we must know what we are getting in return. From an exhaustive review of the evidence, Silberman concluded that "criminal courts generally *do* an effective job of separating the innocent from the guilty; most of those who should be convicted are convicted, and most of those who should be punished are punished." Today, we prosecute, convict, and incarcerate a larger proportion of those arrested for felonies than we did 50 years ago; yet, the crime rate continues to rise. Clearly, the uncertainty about punishment derives from the great unlikelihood of *arrest.* For every 100 crimes committed, only six persons will be arrested. Thus, sacrificing the constitutional protections of those charged with crime will do little to deter the "hard rocks."

What must we do to achieve certainty of arrest sufficient to have an impact on crime? I asked my good friend, Maurice Cullinane, the former Chief of Police of the District of Columbia, about this. He presided over a force with far more policemen per capita than any other in the country, and that is aside from the several thousand park, Capitol, and other Federal police visible all over Washington. Chief Cullinane told me that, in order to deter street crime to any significant degree, he would have to amass an enormous concentration of patrolmen in one particular area. Only then might the physical presence of a policeman on virtually every block possibly keep crime under control. Of course, crime suppressed in one neighborhood would burgeon in other, unguarded parts of the city. Before we can endorse certainty of arrest as an effective deterrent, we must consider whether we could tolerate the kind of police state it might require.

We need to know much more about the precise costs of an effective program of deterrence before we can dismiss the recent proposals. At the present time, however, the case for deterrence has not been convincingly made. After a comprehensive review of the literature, a panel of the National Academy of Sciences concluded:

> Despite the intensity of the research effort, the empirical evidence is still not sufficient for providing a rigorous confirmation of the existence of a deterrent effect.... Policy makers in the criminal justice system are done a disservice if they are left with the impression that the empirical evidence, which they

themselves are frequently unable to evaluate, strongly supports the deterrence hypothesis.

INCAPACITATION

A more realistic rationale put forth for short-term proposals, in my opinion, is incapacitation. This politely named theory has become the new aim of corrections. No one who has been in an American prison can seriously adhere to the ideal of rehabilitation, and more and more of us have come to suspect the futility of deterrence. The new theory of incapacitation essentially translates as lock the bastards up. At least then they will pose no threat to us while incarcerated. Incapacitation takes many forms: preventive detention, isolation of "career criminals," and stricter parole release requirements.

This notion has something to be said for it. We *must* do something to protect ourselves immediately so that we may "live to fight another day." Thus, the swift and tough route is appealing—get the attackers off the street forthwith; put them away fast and long so that the threat they pose to our daily lives can be neutralized.

A thorough commitment to this policy might indeed make our streets somewhat safer, but at what price? Consider first the cost in dollars. Today, even without an avowed commitment to incapacitation, we already imprison a larger proportion of our citizens than any other industrialized nation in the world, except Russia and South Africa. This dubious honor has cost us dearly. A soon-to-be published survey by the Department of Justice's National Institute of Justice reports that the 1972-78 period saw a 54 percent increase in the population of state prisons. The survey predicts that demand for prison space will continue to outstrip capacity. It has been conservatively estimated that we need $8–10,000,000,000 immediately for construction just to close the gap that exists *now.*

Embarking on a national policy of incapacitation would require much more than closing the gap. One study has estimated that, in New York, a 264 percent increase in state imprisonment would be required to reduce serious crime by only 10 percent! Diana Gordon has worked out the financial requirements for this kind of incapacitation program. In New York alone, it would cost about $3,000,000,000 just to construct the additional cells necessary and probably another $1,000,000,000 each year to operate them. The public must be made aware of the extraordinary financial costs of a genuine incapacitation policy.

In addition, there are significant nonmonetary costs. Incapacitation rests on the assumption that convicted offenders would continue to commit crimes if not kept in prison, but can we determine in advance which offenders would in fact repeat and which would not? We simply do not know enough about the "hard rocks" to decide who to warehouse, and for how long. It has been estimated that, to be sure of identifying one potential criminal, we would have to include as many as eight people who would not offend. Thus, to obtain the benefits of incapacitation, we might have to incarcerate a substantial number of people who would have led a blameless life if released. A policy of sentencing individuals based on crimes not yet committed would therefore raise serious doubts about our dedication to the presumption of innocence. The thought of having to choose between immediate safety and sacred constitutional values is frightening.

Nor can there be any comfort that the grave moral and financial costs of incapacitation will only be temporary. Even as we put one generation of offenders behind bars, another set of "hard rocks" will emerge from the hopeless subculture of our ghettos, ready to follow the model set by their fathers and brothers. Unless we intend to keep every criminal and potential criminal in prison *forever*, we must acknowledge the futility of expecting them to behave when they get out. As journalist Tom Wicker recently observed, "to send them to the overcrowded, underfunded, inadequately staffed and policed prisons of America would negate [the] purpose; because more, and more frightening, criminals come out of these schools of crime and violence than go into them." Merely providing inmates with educational and counseling services would do little good "when they return to a society largely unwilling to hire them." We should not fool ourselves that the "hard rocks" will emerge from the cesspools of American prisons willing or able to conduct law-abiding lives.

Incapacitation, then, must be recognized as an extraordinarily costly and risky policy. To meaningfully affect crime, it might require a garrison state. This is not to deny that our "clear and present danger" must be addressed immediately. Still, reason and good faith require us to consider alternatives to a program of endlessly warehousing succeeding generations of human beings.

ATTACKING THE ROOT CAUSES OF CRIME

A more long-term response to crime is to attack its root causes. This approach also offers no decisive balance of costs and benefits. The unique advantage of a successful attack on the roots of crime would be the promise of *enduring* social tranquility. If we can first break the cycle of suffering which breeds crime, we could turn it to our advantage. We would achieve more than "damage control." Our nation could begin to tap the resources of those we now fear. Instead of a police or garrison state, ours would then be a social order rooted in the will and hearts of our people. We would achieve criminal justice by pursuing social justice.

However, like the short-term solutions, this path would involve substantial risks and uncertainties. The root causes of crime are, of course, far more complex and insidious than simple poverty. After all, the vast majority of the poor commit no crime. Our existing knowledge suggests that the roots of street crime lie in poverty *plus*—plus prejudice, plus poor housing, plus inadequate education, plus insufficient food and medical care, and, perhaps most importantly, plus a bad family environment or no family at all.

Accepting the full implications of what we know about street crime might require us to provide every family with the means to create the kind of home all human beings need. It might require us to afford the job opportunities that pose for some the only meaningful alternatives to violence. It would assure all children a constructive education, a decent place to live, and proper pre- and post-natal nutrition. It would seek to provide those children of inadequate family environments with proper day care or foster care. More fundamentally, it would seek to eradicate racism and prejudice.

Such an attack on the roots of crime would obviously be an extremely long and expensive process. Before we can determine which programs offer the greatest promise, we must face what we know about crime and build on previous efforts to attack its root causes.

More importantly, a genuine commitment to attacking the roots of crime might force us to reconsider our entire social and economic structure. Like the short-term approach, this might conflict with other deeply held values. Can we break the cycle at crime's roots without invading the social sphere of the ghetto? Would this require the state to impose its values on the young? If we really want a lasting solution to crime, can we afford not to?

In short, any approach we take to crime presents attractive benefits and frightening risks. None of our choices offers a cheap or easy solution. Analysis takes us this far. As I have repeatedly emphasized, we can not choose which difficult path to take without facing the realities of street crime. Obviously, we can not deter those whom we do not understand. Nor can we make a rational assessment of incapacitation without knowing how many we will have to incapacitate and for how long. Finally, of course, we can not evaluate the long-term approach without some idea of its specific strategies and their various costs.

A constructive and fruitful debate about the best means of solving the nightmare of street crime is long overdue. The public's fear of crime cries out for a response and our leaders have made it a national priority, but we can never hope to achieve a just and lasting solution to crime without first facing the realities that underlie it. Emerson said, "God offers to every mind its choice between truth and repose." Truth will not come easy. It will take patience and the strength to put aside emotional reactions. If we do not strive for truth, this nation and all it stands for is bound to enjoy only a brief, false, and dangerous repose.

POSTSCRIPT

Is Incapacitation the Answer to the Crime Problem?

If realism is the criterion for choosing policy options, then Reynolds's case is the stronger. Bazelon himself allows that incapacitation is a realistic short-term solution, though he argues that it is too costly and that it produces unsatisfactory long-term results. Bazelon's major argument is a moral one. He criticizes the incapacitation approach as inhumane, dangerous to civil liberties, and hypocritical. The rehabilitation of criminals—not their punishment—should be our goal, even if its accomplishment is very difficult, maintains Bazelon, adding that the incapacitation approach also threatens the civil liberties upon which this society stands. However, do criminals deserve to retain their civil liberties? Are these rights something that cannot be taken away, even from a rapist or a murderer?

Reynolds seems to feel that criminals create enough damage to society to warrant their detention. He also feels that incapacitation is a deterrent to crime and that increasing the amount of time a criminal can expect to spend in prison will reduce the crime rate. However, if the legal system cannot ensure longer prison sentences for convicted criminals, then the threat of punishment (the deterrent) is minimal.

In *Crime in America* (Simon & Schuster, 1971), former attorney general Ramsey Clark takes a position that is in many ways similar to Bazelon's. Hans Zeisel, in *The Limits of Law Enforcement* (University of Chicago Press, 1983), argues that the criminal justice system can do little to effectively reduce crime. He emphasizes increasing protection from crime and attacking its root causes in the conditions of poverty. On the other side, Andrew Von Hirsch's *Doing Justice* (Hill & Wang, 1976) is critical of Bazelon's philosophy.

The issue of deterrence is hotly debated by Ernest van den Haag and John P. Conrad in their book on the ultimate in deterrence punishment, *The Death Penalty: A Debate* (Plenum Press, 1983). Graeme Newman presents an extreme position on punishment in advocating electric shocks and whippings in *Just and Painful: A Case for the Corporal Punishment of Criminals* (Macmillan, 1983). A history of punishment choices other than prison is presented in *Alternatives to Prison: Punishment, Custody and the Community* (Sage Publications, 1990). Wilbert Rideau and Ron Wikberg's *Life Sentences: Rage and Survival Behind Bars* (Random House, 1992) presents a sympathetic insider's view of prison life that might soften the tough sentencing view of many.

PART 6

The Future: Population/ Environment/Society

Can a world with limited resources support an unlimited population? This question has taken on new dimensions as we approach the start of a new century. Technology has increased enormously in the last 100 years, as have worldwide population growth and new forms of pollution that threaten to undermine the world's fragile ecological support system. Will technology itself be the key to controlling or accommodating an increased population growth along with the resulting increase in waste production? All nations have a stake in the health of the planet and the world economy. Is America in a political and economic position to meet these global challenges?

- Does Population Growth Threaten Humanity?

- Is America Declining?

ISSUE 19

Does Population Growth Threaten Humanity?

YES: Lester R. Brown, from "The New World Order," in Lester R. Brown et al., *State of the World 1991* (W. W. Norton, 1991)

NO: Julian L. Simon, from "More People, Greater Wealth, More Resources, Healthier Environment," University of Maryland, College Park, MD (1994)

ISSUE SUMMARY

YES: Lester R. Brown, president of the Worldwatch Institute, describes the major ways in which the environment is deteriorating due to economic and population growth.

NO: Professor of economics and business administration Julian L. Simon maintains that the negative effects of population growth that are cited by environmentalists are factually incorrect.

Much of the literature on socioeconomic development in the 1960s was premised on the assumption of inevitable material progress for all. It largely ignored the impacts of development on the environment and presumed that the availability of raw materials would not be a problem. The belief was that all societies would get richer because all societies were investing in new equipment and technologies that would increase productivity and wealth. Theorists recognized that some poor countries were having trouble developing but blamed those problems on the deficiencies of their values and attitudes and on inefficient organizations. Nevertheless, progress was thought possible even in the least developed countries. If certain social and psychological defects could be overcome by a modernizing elite, and if 10 percent of the gross national product could be devoted to capital formation for at least three decades, then poor countries would take off into self-sustained growth, just as industrial societies had done decades earlier. See Walt W. Rostow, *The Stages of Economic Growth* (Cambridge University Press, 1960), for a review of this. After take-off, growth would be self-sustaining and would continue for the foreseeable future.

In the late 1960s and early 1970s an intellectual revolution occurred. Environmentalists had criticized the growth paradigm throughout the 1960s, but they were not taken very seriously at first. By the end of the 1960s, however, marine scientist Rachel Carson's book *Silent Spring* (Alfred A. Knopf, 1962) had worked its way into the public's consciousness. Carson's book traced the noticeable loss of birds to the use of pesticides. Her book made the middle and upper classes in the United States realize that pollution affected complex ecological systems in ways that put even the wealthy at risk.

In 1968 Paul Ehrlich, a professor of population studies, published *The Population Bomb* (Ballantine Books), which stated that overpopulation was the major problem facing mankind and that population had to be controlled or the human race might cause the collapse of the global ecosystem and its own destruction. Ehrlich explained why he thought the death of the world was imminent:

> Because the human population of the planet is about five times too large, and we're managing to support all these people—at today's level of misery—only by spending our capital, burning our fossil fuels, dispersing our mineral resources and turning our fresh water into salt water. We have not only overpopulated but overstretched our environment. We are poisoning the ecological systems of the earth—systems upon which we are ultimately dependent for all of our food, for all of our oxygen and for all of our waste disposal.

In 1973 *The Limits to Growth* (Universe), by Donella H. Meadows et al., was published, and it presented a dynamic systems computer model for world economic, demographic, and environmental trends. When the computer model projected trends into the future, it predicted that the world would experience ecological collapse and population die-off unless population growth and economic activity were greatly reduced. This study was both attacked and defended, and the debate about the health of the world has been heated ever since.

Let us review the population growth rates past, present, and future. At about A.D. 0, the world had about one-quarter billion people. It took about 1,650 years to double this number to one-half billion and 200 years to double the world population again to 1 billion by 1850. The next doubling took only about 80 years, and the last doubling time took about 45 years (from 2 billion in 1930 to about 4 billion in 1975). The world population may double again to 8 billion sometime between 2010 and 2020. Is population growth and the increased economic activity that it requires diminishing the carrying capacity of the planet and jeopardizing the prospects for future generations?

In the following selections, Lester R. Brown answers this question affirmatively and argues for the need to control population growth and to quickly reverse the dangerous deterioration of the environment that is occurring throughout the world. Julian L. Simon, currently the major proponent of the optimistic view of further economic development without serious environmental consequences, argues that the environment is becoming more beneficent for human beings because pollution is decreasing, resources are becoming more available and inexpensive, people are living longer, and population growth has largely positive economic and social impacts.

YES

Lester R. Brown

THE NEW WORLD ORDER

As the nineties begin, the world is on the edge of a new age. The cold war that dominated international affairs for four decades and led to an unprecedented militarization of the world economy is over. With its end comes an end to the world order it spawned.

The East-West ideological conflict was so intense that it dictated the shape of the world order for more than a generation. It provided a clear organizing principle for the foreign policies of the two superpowers and, to a lesser degree, of other governments as well. But with old priorities and military alliances becoming irrelevant, we are now at one of those rare points in history—a time of great change, a time when change is as unpredictable as it is inevitable.

No one can say with certainty what the new order will look like. But if we are to fashion a promising future for the next generation, then the enormous effort required to reverse the environmental degradation of the planet will dominate world affairs for decades to come. In effect, the battle to save the planet will replace the battle over ideology as the organizing theme of the new world order.

As the dust from the cold war settles, both the extent of the environmental damage to the planet and the inadequacy of efforts to cope with it are becoming all too apparent. During the 20 years since the first Earth Day, in 1970, the world lost nearly 200 million hectares of tree cover, an area roughly the size of the United States east of the Mississippi River. Deserts expanded by some 120 million hectares, claiming more land than is currently planted to crops in China. Thousands of plant and animal species with which we shared the planet in 1970 no longer exist. Over two decades, some 1.6 billion people were added to the world's population—more than inhabited the planet in 1900. And the world's farmers lost an estimated 480 billion tons of topsoil, roughly equivalent to the amount on India's cropland.

This planetary degradation proceeded despite the environmental protection efforts of national governments over the past 20 years. During this time nearly all countries created environmental agencies. National legislatures passed thousands of laws to protect the environment. Tens of thousands of

From Lester R. Brown, "The New World Order," in Lester R. Brown et al., *State of the World 1991* (W. W. Norton, 1991). Copyright © 1991 by The Worldwatch Institute. Reprinted by permission. Notes omitted.

grassroots environmental groups sprung up in response to locally destructive activities. Membership in national environmental organizations soared. But as Earth Day 1990 chairman Denis Hayes asks, "How could we have fought so hard, and won so many battles, only to find ourselves now on the verge of losing the war?"

One reason for this failure is that although governments have professed concern with environmental deterioration, few have been willing to make the basic changes needed to reverse it. Stabilizing climate, for example, depends on restructuring national energy economies. Getting the brakes on population growth requires massive changes in human reproductive behavior. But public understanding of the consequences of continuously rising global temperatures or rapid population growth is not yet sufficient to support effective policy responses.

The battle to save the earth's environmental support systems will differ from the battle for ideological supremacy in some important ways. The cold war was largely an abstraction, a campaign waged by strategic planners. Except for bearing the economic costs, which were very real, most people in the United States and the Soviet Union did not directly take part. In the new struggle, however, people everywhere will need to be involved: individuals trying to recycle their garbage, couples trying to decide whether to have a second child, and energy ministers trying to fashion an environmentally sustainable energy system. The goal of the cold war was to get others to change their values and behavior, but winning the battle to save the planet depends on changing our own values and behavior....

TWO VIEWS OF THE WORLD

Anyone who regularly reads the financial papers or business weeklies would conclude that the world is in reasonably good shape and that long-term economic trends are promising. Obviously there are still problems—the U.S. budget deficit, Third World debt, and the unsettling effect of rising oil prices—but to an economist, things appear manageable. Even those predicting a severe global recession in 1991 are bullish about the longer term economic prospects for the nineties.

Yet on the environmental front, the situation could hardly be worse. Anyone who regularly reads scientific journals has to be concerned with the earth's changing physical condition. Every major indicator shows a deterioration in natural systems: forests are shrinking, deserts are expanding, croplands are losing topsoil, the stratospheric ozone layer continues to thin, greenhouse gases are accumulating, the number of plant and animal species is diminishing, air pollution has reached health-threatening levels in hundreds of cities, and damage from acid rain can be seen on every continent.

These contrasting views of the state of the world have their roots in economics and ecology—two disciplines with intellectual frameworks so different that their practitioners often have difficulty talking to each other. Economists interpret and analyze trends in terms of savings, investment, and growth. They are guided largely by economic theory and indicators, seeing the future more or less as an extrapolation of the recent past. From their vantage point, there is little reason to worry about natural constraints on human economic activity;

rare is the economic text that mentions the carrying capacity principle that is so fundamental to ecology. Advancing technology, economists believe, can push back any limits. Their view prevails in the worlds of industry and finance, and in national governments and international development agencies.

In contrast, ecologists study the relationship of living things with each other and their environments. They see growth in terms of S-shaped curves, a concept commonly illustrated in high school biology classes by introducing a few algae into a petri dish. Carefully cultured at optimum temperature and with unlimited supplies of food, the algae multiply slowly at first, and then more rapidly, until growth eventually slows and then stops, usually because of waste accumulation. Charting this process over time yields the familiar S-shaped curve to which all biological growth processes in a finite environment conform.

Ecologists think in terms of closed cycles—the hydrological cycle, the carbon cycle, and the nitrogen cycle, to name a few. For them, all growth processes are limited, confined within the natural parameters of the earth's ecosystem. They see more clearly than others the damage to natural systems and resources from expanding economic activity....

The contrast between... basic global economic indicators and those measuring the earth's environmental health could not be greater. While... economic measurements are overwhelmingly positive, all the principal environmental indicators are consistently negative. As the need for cropland led to the clearing of forests, for example, and as the demand for firewood, lumber, and paper soared, deforestation gained momentum. By the end of the decade, the world's forests were shrinking by an estimated 17 million hectares each year. Some countries, such as Mauritania and Ethiopia, have lost nearly all their tree cover.

Closely paralleling this is the loss of topsoil from wind and water erosion, and the associated degradation of land. Deforestation and overgrazing, both widespread throughout the Third World, have also led to wholesale land degradation. Each year, some 6 million hectares of land are so severely degraded that they lose their productive capacity, becoming wasteland.

During the eighties, the amount of carbon pumped into the atmosphere from the burning of fossil fuels climbed to a new high, reaching nearly 6 billion tons in 1990. In a decade in which stock prices climbed to record highs, so too did the mean temperature, making the eighties the warmest decade since recordkeeping began more than a century ago. The temperature rise was most pronounced in western North America and western Siberia. Preliminary climate data for 1990 indicate it will be the hottest year on record, with snow cover in the northern hemisphere the lightest since the satellite record began in 1970.

Air and water pollution also worsened in most of the world during the last 10 years. By 1990, the air in hundreds of cities contained health-threatening levels of pollutants. In large areas of North America, Europe, and Asia, crops were being damaged as well. And despite widespread reduction in water pollution in the United States, the Environmental Protection Agency reported in 1988 that groundwater in 39 states contained pesticides. In Poland, at least half the river water was too polluted even for industrial use.

These changes in the earth's physical condition are having a devastating effect on the biological diversity of the planet. Although no one knows how many plant and animal species were lost during the eighties, leading biologists estimate that one fifth of the species on earth may well disappear during this century's last two decades. What they cannot estimate is how long such a rate of extinction can continue without leading to the wholesale collapse of ecosystems.

How can one set of widely used indicators be so consistently positive and another so consistently negative? One reason the economic measures are so encouraging is that national accounting systems—which produce figures on gross national product—miss entirely the environmental debts the world is incurring. The result is a disguised form of deficit financing. In sector after sector, we are consuming our natural capital at an alarming rate—the opposite of an environmentally sustainable economy, one that satisfies current needs without jeopardizing the prospects of future generations. As economist Herman Daly so aptly puts it, "there is something fundamentally wrong in treating the earth as if it were a business in liquidation."

To extend this analogy, it is as though a vast industrial corporation quietly sold off a few of its factories each year, using an incomplete accounting system that did not reflect these sales. As a result, its cash flow would be strong and profits would rise. Stockholders would be pleased with the annual reports, not realizing that the profits were coming at the expense of the corporation's assets. But once all the factories were sold off, corporate officers would have to inform stockholders that their shares were worthless.

In effect, this is what we are doing with the earth. Relying on a similarly incomplete accounting system, we are depleting our productive assets, satisfying our needs today at the expense of our children....

WHAT FOOD INDICATORS SAY

Of all the sectors in the world economy, it is agriculture where the contrast between the economic and environmental indicators is most obvious. It is in the relentless push to produce more food that several decades of borrowing from the future are beginning to take a toll. In many countries, growth in the farm sector is pressing against the limits of land and water supplies. And in some, the backlog of technology available for farmers to raise food output is shrinking.

By traditional measures, world agriculture appears to be doing well. Western Europe worries about surpluses, particularly of dairy products, and the United States still idles cropland to control production. Grain-exporting countries use subsidies to compete for markets that never seem large enough. For an economist, there may be distribution problems in the world food economy, but not a production problem.

To an ecologist who sees a substantial fraction of current world food output being produced on highly erodible land that will soon be abandoned or by overpumping groundwater, which cannot continue indefinitely, the prospect is far less promising. As world agriculture presses against natural limits imposed by the area of productive land, by the amount of fresh water produced by the hydrological cycle, and by the geophysical processes that produce soil, growth in output is beginning to slow. Modest new additions to the cropland base are offset by the conversion of land to nonfarm uses and by the abandonment of severely degraded land.

The scarcity of fresh water is imposing limits on crop production in many agricultural regions. Competition among countries for the water from internationally shared rivers, such as the Tigris-Euphrates, Jordan, and Nile in the Middle East, is a source of growing political tension. In Soviet central Asia, the Amu Darya, the source of most of the region's irrigation water, now runs dry long before it reaches the Aral Sea. Falling water tables are now commonplace in heavily populated countries such as India and China, which are overpumping aquifers in their effort to satisfy the growing need for irrigation water. Under parts of the North China Plain, water tables are dropping up to a meter per year. And the vast Ogallala aquifer, which supplies irrigation water to U.S. farmers and ranchers from central Nebraska to the Texas panhandle, is gradually being depleted. Cities such as Denver and Phoenix are outbidding farmers in the intensifying competition for water.

In addition to the degradation of land by farming practices, outside forces are also beginning to take a little-acknowledged toll on agriculture. Air pollution is reducing U.S. crop production by an officially estimated 5–10 percent, and is probably having a similar effect in the coal-burning economies of Eastern Europe and China. As deforestation progresses in the mountainous areas of the world, the term "flood-damaged harvests" appears with increasing frequency in world crop reports.

Even as these environmental and resource constraints slow world food output growth, the backlog of unused agricultural technology is diminishing. In Asia, for example, the highest yielding rice varieties available to farmers were released in 1966, a quarter-century ago. The International Rice Research Institute, the world's premier research facility in this field, observed in a strategy paper released for 1990 that "during the past five years, growth in rice yields has virtually ceased."

One way of assessing the technological prospect for boosting food output during the nineties is to look at trends in fertilizer use, since the phenomenal growth in world food output from 1950 to 1984 was due largely to the ninefold growth in fertilizer use. In large measure, other major advances in agriculture, such as the near-tripling of irrigated area and the adoption of ever higher yielding varieties, greatly enhanced the potential to use more fertilizer profitably. But as the nineties begin many countries have reached the point where using additional fertilizer does little to boost food output....

For the world as a whole, the annual growth in grain production from 1984 to 1990 was 1 percent, while that of population was nearly 2. The diminishing crop response to the additional use of fertilizer, the negative effect of environmental degradation on harvests, and the lack of any new technology to replace fertilizer as the engine of agricultural growth are each contributing to a potentially hungry future for much of humanity. In both 1984 and 1990, per hectare yields of the three grains that dominate the world diet—wheat, rice, and corn—set new records, indicating unusually favorable growing conditions in all the major grain-growing regions. If these two years are broadly comparable weatherwise, as they appear to be, then this slower growth in world grain output may indeed be a new trend....

POPULATION:
THE NEGLECTED ISSUE

Nowhere is the conceptual contrast between economists and ecologists more evident than in the way they view population growth. In assessing its effect, economists typically have not seen it as a particularly serious threat. In their view, if a nation's economy is growing at 5 percent per year and its population at 3 percent, this leads to a steady 2-percent gain in living standards. Relying on economic variables alone, this situation seemed to be tenable, one that could be extrapolated indefinitely into the future.

Ecologists looking at biological indicators in the same situation see rising human demand, driven by population growth and rising affluence, surpassing the carrying capacity of local forests, grasslands, and soils in country after country. They see sustainable yield thresholds of the economy's natural support systems being breached throughout the Third World. And as a result, they see the natural resource base diminishing even as population growth is expanding.

Against this backdrop, biologists find recent population trends profoundly disturbing. Accelerating sharply during the recovery period after World War II, the annual growth of world population peaked at about 1.9 percent in 1970. It then slowed gradually, declining to 1.7 percent in the early eighties. But during the late eighties it again began to accelerate, reaching 1.8 percent, largely because of a modest rise of the birth rate in China and a decrease in the death rate in India. With fertility turning upward in the late eighties instead of declining, as some

had expected and many had hoped, the world is projected to add at least 960 million people during this decade, up from 840 million in the eighties and 750 million in the seventies.

Concern with the effects of population growth is not new. Nearly two centuries have passed since [economic theorist Thomas Robert] Malthus published his famous treatise in which he argued that population tends to grow exponentially while food production grows arithmetically. He argued that unless profligate childbearing was checked, preferably through abstinence, famine and hunger would be inevitable. Malthus was wrong in the sense that he did not anticipate the enormous potential of advancing technology to raise land productivity. He was writing before [Austrian botanist Gregor Johann] Mendel formulated the basic principles of genetics and before [Justus] Von Leibeg demonstrated that all the nutrients taken from the soil by plants could be returned in mineral form.

Malthus was correct, however, in anticipating the difficulty of expanding food output as fast as population growth. Today, hundreds of millions of the earth's inhabitants are hungry, partly because of inequitable distribution, but increasingly because of falling per capita food production. And as the nineties begin, the ranks of the hungry are swelling.

Malthus was concerned with the relationship between population growth and the earth's food-producing capacity. We now know that increasing numbers and economic activity affect many other natural capacities, such as the earth's ability to absorb waste. At any given level of per capita pollution, more people means more pollution. As the discharge of various industrial and agricultural wastes overwhelms the waste-absorptive capacity of natural systems, the cumulative effects of toxic materials in the environment begins to affect human health.

Another consequence of continuing population growth in much of the Third World is a shortage of firewood, the primary fuel. As the local demand for firewood for cooking exceeds the sustainable yield of local woodlands, the forests recede from the villages. Women, who gather most of the firewood, often find themselves trekking long distances to find enough to prepare meals. In some situations, families are reduced to only one hot meal a day. Malthus worried about whether there would be enough food, but he never reckoned that finding the fuel to prepare it would become part of the daily struggle for survival.

The record population growth projected for the nineties means the per capita availability of key resources such as land, water, and wood will also shrink at an unprecedented rate. (See Table 1.) Since the total cropland area is not expected to change during the decade, the land available per person to produce our basic staples will shrink by 1.7 percent a year. This means that grainland per person, averaging 0.13 hectares in 1990, will be reduced by one sixth during the nineties. And with a projected growth in overall irrigated land of less than 1 percent per year, the irrigated area per person will decline by nearly a tenth.

Forested area per person, reduced both by the overall loss in forests and by population growth, is likely to decline by one fifth or more during this decade. The 0.61 hectares per person of grazing land, which produces much of our milk, meat, and cheese, is also projected to drop by one fifth by the year 2000 as population grows and desertification spreads. Maintaining an improvement in

Table 1

Availability of Basic Natural Resources Per Person in 1990 and 2000

Resource	1990	2000
	(hectares)	
Grain land	0.13	0.11
Irrigated land	0.045	0.04
Forest land	0.79	0.64
Grazing land	0.61	0.50

Source: Based on U.S. Department of Agriculture, Economic Research Service, *World Grain Database* (unpublished printouts) (Washington, D.C.: 1990); U.N. Food and Agriculture Organization, *Production Yearbook* (Rome: various years); and U.N. Department of International Economic and Social Affairs, *World Population Prospects 1988* (New York: 1989).

living conditions with this reduction in per capita natural resources will not be easy....

A NEW AGENDA, A NEW ORDER

With the end of the ideological conflict that dominated a generation of international affairs, a new world order, shaped by a new agenda, will emerge. If the physical degradation of the planet becomes the principal preoccupation of the global community, then environmental sustainability will become the organizing principle of this new order. (For a discussion of the rough outline of an environmentally sustainable global economy, see Chapter 10 in *State of the World 1990*.) The world's agenda will be more ecological than ideological, dominated less by relationships among nations and more by the relationship between nations and nature. For the first time since the emergence of the nation-state, all countries can unite around a common theme. All societies have an interest in satisfying the needs of the current generation without compromising the ability of future generations to meet their needs. It is in the interest of everyone to protect the earth's life-support systems, for we all have a stake in the future habitability of the planet....

Although it is premature to describe the shape of the post–cold war world order, its determining characteristics can now be identified. A commitment to the long-term improvement in the human condition is contingent on substituting environmental sustainability for growth as the overriding goal of national economic policymaking and international development. Political influence will derive more from environmental and economic strength than from military strength. And in the new order, the political stresses between East and West are likely to be replaced by the economic stresses between North and South, including such issues as the need to reduce Third World debt, access to markets in the industrial North, and how the costs of environmental protection initiatives are allocated between rich and poor....

With time running out in the effort to reverse the environmental destruction of the earth, there is an obvious need for initiatives that will quickly convert our environmentally unsustainable global economy into one that is sustainable. The many means of achieving this transformation range from voluntary life-style changes, such as limiting family size or reducing waste, to regulated changes such as laws boosting the fuel efficiencies of automobiles and household appliances. But the most effective instrument of all promises to be tax policy—specifically, the partial replacement of income taxes with those that discourage environmentally destructive activities. Prominent among the activities to tax are carbon emissions, the use of virgin materials, and the generation of toxic waste.

We can see what environmentally unsustainable growth does to the earth. And we know what the outlines of an environmentally sustainable economy look like. If the move toward the latter is not speeded up, we risk being overwhelmed by the economic and social consequences of planetary degradation. This in turn depends on more of us becoming environmental activists, working on behalf of the future of the planet and our children. Unless we can reverse quickly some of the environmental trends that are undermining our economy, our dream of a better life for our children and grandchildren will remain just that.

NO

Julian L. Simon

MORE PEOPLE, GREATER WEALTH, MORE RESOURCES, HEALTHIER ENVIRONMENT

INTRODUCTION

This is the economic history of humanity in a nutshell: From 2 million or 200,000 or 20,000 or 2,000 years ago until the 18th Century there was slow growth in population, almost no increase in health or decrease in mortality, slow growth in the availability of natural resources (but not increased scarcity), increase in wealth for a few, and mixed effects on the environment. Since then, there has been rapid growth in population due to spectacular decreases in the death rate, rapid growth in resources, widespread increases in wealth, and an unprecedentedly clean and beautiful living environment in many parts of the world, along with a degraded environment in the poor and socialist parts of the world.

That is, more people and more wealth has correlated with more (rather than less) resources and a cleaner environment—just the opposite of what Malthusian theory leads one to believe. The task before us is to make sense of these mind-boggling happy trends.

The current gloom-and-doom about a "crisis" of our environment is all wrong on the scientific facts. Even the U. S. Environmental Protection Agency acknowledges that U.S. air and our water have been getting cleaner rather than dirtier in the past few decades. Every agricultural economist knows that the world's population has been eating ever-better since World War II. Every resource economist knows that all natural resources have been getting more available rather than more scarce, as shown by their falling prices over the decades and centuries. And every demographer knows that the death rate has been falling all over the world—life expectancy almost tripling in the rich countries in the past two centuries, and almost doubling in the poor countries in just the past four decades.

The picture also is now clear that population growth does not hinder economic development. In the 1980s there was a complete reversal in the consensus of thinking of population economists about the effects of more people. In 1986, the National Research Council and the National Academy of Sciences completely overturned its "official" view away from the earlier worried view expressed in 1971. It noted the absence of any statistical evidence of a negative connection between population increase and economic growth. And it said that "The scarcity of exhaustible resources is at most a minor restraint on economic growth."

This U-turn by the scientific consensus of experts on the subject has gone unacknowledged by the press, the antinatalist [anti-birth] environmental organizations, and the agencies that foster population control abroad.

Here is my central assertion: Almost every economic and social change or trend points in a positive direction, as long as we view the matter over a reasonably long period of time.

For proper understanding of the important aspects of an economy we should look at the long-run trends. But the short-run comparisons—between the sexes, age groups, races, political groups, which are usually purely relative—make more news. To repeat, just about every important long-run measure of human welfare shows improvement over the decades and centuries, in the United States as well as in the rest of the world. And there is no persuasive reason to believe that these trends will not continue indefinitely.

Would I bet on it? For sure. I'll bet a week's or month's pay—anything I win goes to pay for more research—that just about any trend pertaining to material human welfare will improve rather than get worse. You pick the comparison and the year.

THE FACTS

Let's quickly review a few data on how human life has been doing, beginning with the all-important issue, life itself.

The Conquest of Too-Early Death

The most important and amazing demographic fact—the greatest human achievement in history, in my view—is the decrease in the world's death rate.... It took thousands of years to increase life expectancy at birth from just over 20 years to the high 20's about 1750. Then, about 1750, life expectancy in the richest countries suddenly took off and tripled in about two centuries. In just the past two centuries the length of life you could expect for your baby or yourself in the advanced countries jumped from less than 30 years to perhaps 75 years. What greater event has humanity witnessed than this conquest of premature death in the rich countries? It is this decrease in the death rate that is the cause of there being a larger world population nowadays than in former times.

Then starting well after World War II, since the 1950s, the length of life you could expect in the poor countries has leaped upwards by perhaps fifteen or even twenty years, caused by advances in agriculture, sanitation, and medicine.

Let's put it differently. In the 19th century the planet Earth could sustain only one billion people. Ten thousand years ago, only 4 million could keep themselves alive. Now, 5 billion people are living longer and more healthily than ever before, on average. The increase in the world's population represents our victory over death.

Here arises a crucial issue of interpretation: One would expect lovers of humanity to jump with joy at this triumph

Figure 1
Copper Prices Indexed by Wages

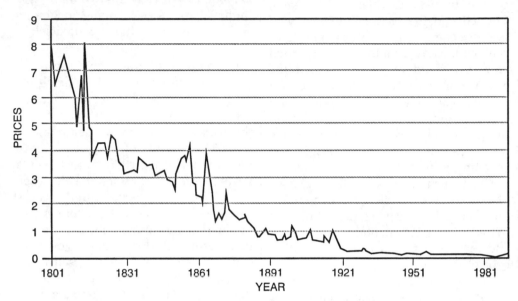

of human mind and organization over the raw killing forces of nature. Instead, many lament that there are so many people alive to enjoy the gift of life.... And it is this worry that leads them to approve the Indonesian, Chinese and other inhumane programs of coercion and denial of personal liberty in one of the most precious choices a family can make—the number of children that it wishes to bear and raise.

The Decreasing Scarcity of Natural Resources

Throughout history, the supply of natural resources always has worried people. Yet the data clearly show that natural resource scarcity—as measured by the economically-meaningful indicator of cost or price—has been decreasing rather than increasing in the long run for all raw materials, with only temporary exceptions from time to time. That is, availability has been increasing. Con-

sider copper, which is representative of all the metals. In Figure 1 we see the price relative to wages since 1801. The cost of a ton is only about a tenth now of what it was two hundred years ago.

This trend of falling prices of copper has been going on for a very long time. In the 18th century B.C.E. [before the Common Era] in Babylonia under Hammurabi—almost 4000 years ago—the price of copper was about a thousand times its price in the United States now relative to wages. At the time of the Roman Empire the price was about a hundred times the present price.

In Figure 2 we see the price of copper relative to the consumer price index. Everything that we buy—pens, shirts, tires—has been getting cheaper over the years because we know how to make them cheaper, especially during the past 200 years. Even so, the extraordinary fact is that natural resources have been

Figure 2
Copper Prices Divided by CPI

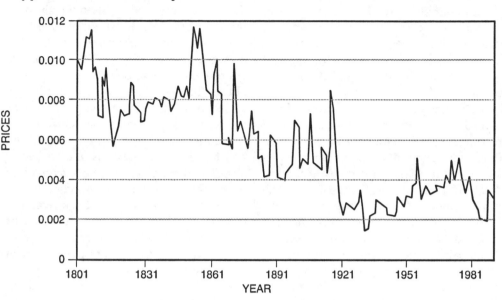

getting cheaper even faster than consumer goods.

So by any measure, natural resources
have been getting more available rather
than more scarce....

Regarding oil, the shocking price
rises during the 1970s and 1980s were
not caused by growing scarcity in the
world supply. And indeed, the price
of petroleum in inflation-adjusted dollars has returned to levels about where
they were before the politically-induced
increases, and the price of gasoline is
about at the historic low and still falling.
Concerning energy in general, there is
no reason to believe that the supply of
energy is finite, or that the price of energy
will not continue its long-run decrease
forever....

Food is an especially important resource. The evidence is particularly
strong for food that we are on a benign

trend despite rising population. The
long-run price of food relative to wages
is now only perhaps a tenth as much as
it was in 1800 in the United States. Even
relative to consumer products the price
of grain is down, due to increased productivity, just as with all other primary
products.

Famine deaths due to insufficient food
supply have decreased even in absolute
terms, let alone relative to population, in
the past century, a matter which pertains
particularly to the poor countries. Per-
person food consumption is up over the
last 30 years. And there are no data showing that the bottom of the income scale is
faring worse, or even has failed to share
in the general improvement, as the average has improved.

Africa's food production per person is
down, but by 1994 almost no one any
longer claims that Africa's suffering re-

sults from a shortage of land or water or sun. The cause of hunger in Africa is a combination of civil wars and collectivization of agriculture, which periodic droughts have made more murderous.

Here let us digress from the general discussion to a resource which has been of special historical interest... in the Netherlands—agricultural land. Let's consider it as an example of all natural resources. Though many people consider land to be a special kind of resource, it is subject to the same processes of human creation as other natural resources. The most important fact about agricultural land is that less and less of it is needed as the decades pass. This idea is utterly counter-intuitive. It seems entirely obvious that a growing world population would need larger amounts of farmland. But the title of a remarkable prescient article in 1951 by Theodore Schultz tells the story: "The Declining Economic Importance of Land."

The increase in actual and potential productivity per unit of land have grown much faster than population, and there is sound reason to expect this trend to continue. Therefore, there is less and less reason to worry about the supply of land. Though the stock of usable land seems fixed at any moment, it is constantly being increased—at a rapid rate in many cases—by the clearing of new land or reclamation of wasteland. Land also is constantly being enhanced by increasing the number of crops grown per year on each unit of land and by increasing the yield per crop with better farming methods and with chemical fertilizer. Last but not least, land is created anew where there was no land.

There is only one important resource which has shown a trend of increasing scarcity rather than increasing abundance. That resource is the most important of all—human beings. Yes, there are more people on earth now than ever before. But if we measure the scarcity of people the same way that we measure the scarcity of other economic goods—by how much we must pay to obtain their services—we see that wages and salaries have been going up all over the world, in poor countries as well as in rich countries. The amount that you must pay to obtain the services of a barber or a cook has risen in India, just as the price of a barber or cook—or economist—has risen in the United States over the decades. This increase in the price of peoples' services is a clear indication that people are becoming more scarce even though there are more of us.

About pollution now: Surveys show that the public believes that our air and water have been getting more polluted in recent years. The evidence with respect to air indicates that pollutants have been declining, especially the main pollutant, particulates. (See Figure 3.) With respect to water, the proportion of monitoring sites in the United States with water of good drinkability has increased since the data began in 1961. (See Figure 4.)

Every forecast of the doomsayers has turned out flat wrong. Metals, foods, and other natural resources have become more available rather than more scarce throughout the centuries. The famous Famine 1975 forecast by the Paddock brothers—that we would see millions of famine deaths in the United States on television in the 1970s—was followed instead by gluts in agricultural markets. Paul Ehrlich's primal scream about "What will we do when the [gasoline] pumps run dry?" was followed by gasoline cheaper than since the 1930s. The Great Lakes are not dead; instead

Figure 3
National Ambient Concentrations of Pollutants

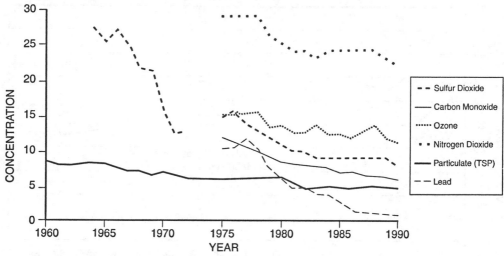

Source: Council on Enviromental Quality, Environmental Quality, 22nd Annual Report, 1992, p. 276
Council on Environmental Quality, Environmental Quality 1981, 12th Annual Report, 1981, p. 243
Sulfur 1964 thru 1972: EPA (1973): 32 stations

they offer better sport fishing than ever. The main pollutants, especially the particulates which have killed people for years, have lessened in our cities. (Socialist countries are a different and tragic environmental story, however!)

... But nothing has reduced the doomsayers' credibility with the press or their command over the funding resources of the federal government....

With respect to population growth: A dozen competent statistical studies, starting in 1967 with an analysis by Nobel prizewinner Simon Kuznets, agree that there is no negative statistical relationship between economic growth and population growth. There is strong reason to believe that more people have a positive effect in the long run.

Population growth does not lower the standard of living—all the evidence agrees. And the evidence supports the view that population growth raises it in the long run.

Incidentally, it was those statistical studies that converted me in about 1968 from working in favor of population control to the point of view that I hold today. I certainly did not come to my current view for any political or religious or ideological reason.

The basic method is to gather data on each country's rate of population growth and its rate of economic growth, and then to examine whether—looking at all the data in the sample together—the countries with high population growth rates have economic growth rates lower than average, and countries with low population growth rates have economic growth rates higher than average. All the studies agree in concluding that this is not so; there is no correlation between economic growth and population growth in the intermediate run.

Figure 4
National Ambient Water Quality in Rivers and Streams, 1973–1990

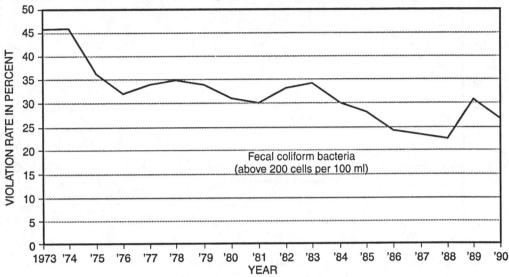

Source: Statistical Abstract of the United States, various issues

Of course one can adduce cases of countries that seemingly are exceptions to the pattern. It is the genius of statistical inference, however, to enable us to draw valid generalizations from samples that contain such wide variations in behavior. The exceptions can be useful in alerting us to possible avenues for further analysis, but as long as they are only exceptions, they do not prove that the generalization is not meaningful or useful.

The research-wise person may wonder whether population density is a more meaningful variable than population growth. And indeed, such studies have been done. And again, the statistical evidence directly contradicts the common-sense conventional wisdom. If you make a chart with population density on the horizontal axis and either the income level or the rate of change of income on the vertical axis, you will see that higher density is associated with better rather than poorer economic results. . . .

The most important benefit of population size and growth is the increase it brings to the stock of useful knowledge. Minds matter economically as much as, or more than, hands or mouths. Progress is limited largely by the availability of trained workers. The more people who enter our population by birth or immigration, the faster will be the rate of progress of our material and cultural civilization.

Here we need a qualification that tends to get overlooked: I do not say that all is well everywhere, and I do not predict that all will be rosy in the future. Children are hungry and sick; people live out lives of physical or intellectual poverty, and lack of opportunity; war or some new pollution may finish us off. What I am saying is that for most relevant economic matters I have checked, the aggregate trends are improving rather than deteriorating.

Also, I don't say that a better future happens automatically or without effort. It will happen because women and men will struggle with problems with muscle and mind, and will probably overcome, as people have overcome in the past— if the social and economic system gives them opportunity to do so.

THE EXPLANATION OF THESE AMAZING TRENDS

Now we need some theory to explain how it can be that economic welfare grows along with population, rather than humanity being reduced to misery and poverty as population grows.

The Malthusian theory of increasing scarcity, based on supposedly-fixed resources—the theory that the doomsayers rely upon—runs exactly contrary to the data over the long sweep of history. Therefore it makes sense to prefer another theory.

The theory that fits the facts very well is this: More people, and increased income, cause problems in the short run. Short-run scarcity raises prices. This presents opportunity, and prompts the search for solutions. In a free society, solutions are eventually found. And in the long run the new developments leave us better off than if the problems had not arisen.

To put it differently, in the short-run, more consumers mean less of the fixed available stock of goods to be divided among more people. And more workers laboring with the same fixed current stock of capital mean that there will be less output per worker. The latter effect, known as "the law of diminishing returns," is the essence of Malthus's theory as he first set it out.

But if the resources with which people work are not fixed over the period be-ing analyzed, then the Malthusian logic of diminishing returns does not apply. And the plain fact is that, given some time to adjust to shortages, the resource base does not remain fixed. People create more resources of all kinds.

When we take a long-run view, the picture is different, and considerably more complex, than the simple short-run view of more people implying lower average income. In the very long run, more people almost surely imply more available resources and a higher income for everyone.

I suggest you test this idea against your own knowledge: Do you think that our standard of living would be as high as it is now if the population had never grown from about four million human beings perhaps ten thousand years ago? I don't think we'd now have electric light or gas heat or autos or penicillin or travel to the moon or our present life expectancy of over seventy years at birth in rich countries, in comparison to the life expectancy of 20 to 25 years at birth in earlier eras, if population had not grown to its present numbers....

THE ROLE OF ECONOMIC FREEDOM

Here we must address another crucial element in the economics of resources and population—the extent to which the political-social-economic system provides personal freedom from government coercion. Skilled persons require an appropriate social and economic framework that provides incentives for working hard and taking risks, enabling their talents to flower and come to fruition. The key elements of such a framework are economic liberty, respect for property, and fair and sensible rules of the market that are enforced equally for all.

The world's problem is not too many people, but lack of political and economic freedom. Powerful evidence comes from an extraordinary natural experiment that occurred starting in the 1940s with three pairs of countries that have the same culture and history, and had much the same standard of living when they split apart after World War II—East and West Germany, North and South Korea, Taiwan and China. In each case the centrally planned communist country began with less population "pressure," as measured by density per square kilometer, than did the market-directed economy. And the communist and non-communist countries also started with much the same birth rates.

The market-directed economies have performed much better economically than the centrally-planned economies. The economic-political system clearly was the dominant force in the results of the three comparisons. This powerful explanation of economic development cuts the ground from under population growth as a likely explanation of the speed of nations' economic development.

THE ASTOUNDING SHIFT IN SCHOLARLY CONSENSUS

So far we've been discussing the factual evidence. But in 1994 there is an important new element not present twenty years ago. The scientific community of scholars who study population economics now agrees with almost all of what is written above. The statements made above do not represent a single lone voice, but rather the current scientific consensus.

The conclusions offered earlier about agriculture and resources and demographic trends have always represented the consensus of economists in those fields. And... the consensus of population economists also is now not far from what is written here.

In 1986, the U.S. National Research Council and the U.S. National Academy of Sciences published a book on population growth and economic development prepared by a prestigious scholarly group. This "official" report reversed almost completely the frightening conclusions of the previous 1971 NAS report. "Population growth [is] at most a minor factor.... The scarcity of exhaustible resources is at most a minor constraint on economic growth," it now says. It found benefits of additional people as well as costs.

A host of review articles by distinguished economic demographers in the past decade have confirmed that this "revisionist" view is indeed consistent with the scientific evidence, though not all the writers would go as far as I do in pointing out the positive long-run effects of population growth. The consensus is more toward a "neutral" judgment. But this is a huge change from the earlier judgment that population growth is economically detrimental.

By 1994, anyone who asserts that population growth damages the economy must either turn a blind eye to the scientific evidence, or be blatantly dishonest intellectually.

SUMMARY AND CONCLUSION

In the short run, all resources are limited. An example of such a finite resource is the amount of time allotted to me to speak. The longer run, however, is a different story. The standard of living has risen along with the size of the world's population since the beginning of recorded time. There is no convincing economic reason why these trends toward a better life should not continue indefinitely.

The key theoretical idea is this: The growth of population and of income create actual and expected shortages, and hence lead to price run-ups. A price increase represents an opportunity that attracts profit-minded entrepreneurs to seek new ways to satisfy the shortages. Some fail, at cost to themselves. A few succeed, and the final result is that we end up better off than if the original shortage problems had never arisen. That is, we need our problems though this does not imply that we should purposely create additional problems for ourselves.

I hope that you will now agree that the long-run outlook is for a more abundant material life rather than for increased scarcity, in the United States and in the world as a whole. Of course such progress does not come about automatically. And my message certainly is not one of complacency. In this I agree with the doomsayers—that our world needs the best efforts of all humanity to improve our lot. I part company with them in that they expect us to come to a bad end despite the efforts we make, whereas I expect a continuation of humanity's history of successful efforts. And I believe that their message is self-fulfilling, because if you expect your efforts to fail because of inexorable natural limits, then you are likely to feel resigned; and therefore to literally resign. But if you recognize the possibility—in fact the probability—of success, you can tap large reservoirs of energy and enthusiasm.

Adding more people causes problems, but people are also the means to solve these problems. The main fuel to speed the world's progress is our stock of knowledge, and the brakes are (a) our lack of imagination and (b) unsound social regulations of these activities. The ultimate resource is people—especially skilled, spirited, and hopeful young people endowed with liberty—who will exert their wills and imaginations for their own benefit, and so inevitably they will benefit not only themselves but the rest of us as well.

REFERENCES

Schultz, Theodore W., "The Declining Economic Importance of Land," *Economic Journal*, LXI, December, 1951, pp. 725–740.

National Research Council, Committee on Population, and Working Group on Population Growth and Economic Development, *Population Growth and Economic Development: Policy Questions* (Washington, D.C.: National Academy Press, 1986).

POSTSCRIPT

Does Population Growth Threaten Humanity?

This debate cannot be resolved because the future is indeterminate. The key issue of the debate is whether or not future technological improvements can continue to overcome the law of diminishing returns on investments and increasing costs for nonrenewable resources and environmentally benign waste disposal. Brown argues that the environment cannot be properly assessed in strictly economic terms. He points out the difference between economics and ecology: economics gives little recognition to limits except as obstacles to overcome, whereas limits and carrying capacity are central concepts of ecology. Furthermore, ecosystems are complex and are tampered with at great risk. Unintended consequences of major developmental activities often cause unintended environmental disasters. Simon points out that the pessimists always underestimate humankind's ability to adapt to environmental problems. Although the pessimists can cite a long list of environmental problems, Simon is confident that they will be taken care of by human effort and inventiveness. He expects necessity to give birth to inventions because technological developments will reap substantial economic rewards as resources become scarce. Simon's thesis is supported by Charles Maurice and Charles W. Smith with 10 major historical examples in *The Doomsday Myth: Ten Thousand Years of Economic Crisis* (Hoover Institution Press, 1985).

Publications by some of the prominent optimists on the issues of the availability of resources and health of the environment include Herman Kahn, *World Economic Development 1979 and Beyond* (Westville Press, 1979); Julian L. Simon, *The Ultimate Resource* (Princeton University Press, 1981); Julian L. Simon and Herman Kahn, eds., *The Resourceful Earth: A Response to Global 2000* (Basil Blackwell, 1984); Dixy Lee Ray and Lou Guzzo, *Environmental Overkill* (Regnery Gateway, 1993); and Ronald Bailey, *Eco-Scam: The False*

Prophets of Ecological Doom (St. Martin's Press, 1993). Publications by some of the prominent pessimists include Ferdinand E. Banks, *Scarcity, Energy, and Economic Progress* (Lexington Books, 1977); *The Global 2000 Report to the President* (Government Printing Office, 1980); William Catton, *Overshoot* (University of Illinois Press, 1980); Kingsley Davis and Mikhail S. Bernstam, eds., *Resources, Environment, and Population* (Oxford University Press, 1991); Paul R. Ehrlich and Anne H. Ehrlich, *Healing the Planet* (Addison Wesley, 1991); Al Gore, *Earth in the Balance* (Houghton Mifflin, 1992); Donella H. Meadows, Dennis L. Meadows, and Jorgen Randers, *Beyond the Limits* (Chelsea Green, 1992); and David W. Orr, *Ecological Literacy* (SUNY Press, 1992).

For a balanced review of both sides of the debate, see Barry B. Hughes, *World Futures: A Critical Analysis of Alternatives* (Johns Hopkins University Press, 1985).

ISSUE 20

Is America Declining?

YES: Edward N. Luttwak, from "Is America on the Way Down? Yes," *Commentary* (March 1992)

NO: Robert L. Bartley, from "Is America on the Way Down? No," *Commentary* (March 1992)

ISSUE SUMMARY

YES: Foreign policy strategist Edward N. Luttwak believes that Japan and Europe will soon be richer than the United States because of the failure of America's economic policies and social programs.

NO: Robert L. Bartley, the editor and vice president of the *Wall Street Journal*, asserts that America is and will remain the wealthiest country in the world and that it will continue to play the role of world leader.

After World War II the United States emerged as the most powerful nation in the world. In part, this was because of the cumulative economic costs of two world wars for Germany, Great Britain, Japan, and the Soviet Union. America escaped the physical devastation that these nations suffered, and its economy boomed during and after the wars. With its unequalled prosperity and power, the United States assumed international leadership in armaments, investments, and aid.

Today that leadership is in question. In the past three decades, Japan, Germany, Taiwan, South Korea, China, and other countries in Europe and Asia have made enormous economic strides. Increasingly, American stores are being flooded with foreign-made goods—from shoes and textiles to cars and television sets. For the past decade, America's trade deficit has been running $100 billion annually. Japan alone sells almost $44 billion more goods to America than it buys from it. American workers have been laid off as industries have downsized or moved part of their operations to Mexico and the Caribbean, where they can operate more cheaply than in the United States. The government, in the meantime, has continued to spend more than it receives in revenue, and America's national debt (the total of its accumulated annual budget deficits) is now more than $4 trillion. Many Americans worry that future generations will be burdened with debts that will drive the nation deeper into economic malaise.

The thesis that America is on the decline seems to be confirmed by some of the grim aspects of daily life in America today, particularly in its urban centers: homeless people sprawled on sidewalks, streets lined with boarded-up buildings, crumbling schools with metal detectors at the doors and peeling paint in the classrooms, bridges with chunks of concrete falling off them, and housing projects taken over by drug dealers. What is going on in America? Is the nation simply undergoing an awkward transition to a new postindustrial era, or has the country somehow lost the spirit and the will that made it the leader of the free world?

It is difficult for Americans to accept the view that the nation's power and influence will not endure. Yet historians frequently note the rise and fall of great powers, as has contemporary historian Paul Kennedy in his widely acclaimed and much debated 1987 book *The Rise and Fall of the Great Powers.* Kennedy summarized his thesis thusly: "The historical record suggests that there is a very clear connection *in the long run* between an individual Great Power's economic rise and fall and its growth and decline as an important military power (or world empire)." Nations must spend to create the armies and navies that protect their wealth and security; but if they spend too much, they weaken their economic competitiveness. *Imperial overstretch* is Kennedy's term for the tendency of great powers to commit too much wealth to overseas commitments and too little to domestic economic growth.

Kennedy identified the loss of power with the decline of economic competitiveness. In his account, the most powerful nations in the last five centuries—successively, Spain, the Netherlands, France, and England—were unable or unwilling to tax themselves sufficiently to pay for their armed forces and empires. The United States now finds itself in a comparable position. The greater the power of a state, the greater the expenditure that must be made to support it.

Ironically, these concerns about America were first being expressed at the very time that the Soviet Union, America's chief adversary in the world until its breakup in late 1991, was on the brink of collapse. Today, America is the world's only military superpower. But if the 70-year history of the Soviet Union demonstrates anything, it is that all the armaments in the world cannot preserve a nation if its economic structure falls into ruin.

In the selections that follow, Edward N. Luttwak argues that Americans are courting disaster because they are failing to save and invest, to modernize the industrial structure, to pressure other countries for more favorable trade concessions, and to provide children with the education and skill necessary to compete economically. Robert L. Bartley argues that America is experiencing "a second industrial revolution," which, like the first, is causing dislocations and discomfort but which is also propelling the nation toward ever-greater living standards and continued world leadership.

YES
Edward N. Luttwak

IS AMERICA ON THE WAY DOWN?

When will the United States become a third-world country? One estimate would place the date as close as the year 2020. A more optimistic projection might add another ten or fifteen years. Either way, if present trends simply continue, all but a small minority of Americans will be impoverished soon enough, left to yearn hopelessly for the lost golden age of American prosperity.

Nor can American decline remain only economic. The arts and sciences cannot flower and grow without the prosperity that pays for universities, research centers, libraries, museums, the theater, orchestras, ballet companies. It was the ample earnings of Italian traders and bankers that fed the scholars, painters, sculptors, architects, and poets who gave us the Renaissance. When Italy was by-passed by the new flows of oceangoing trade, its impoverished merchants and bankrupt financiers could no longer commission artists or keep scholars at their work, so that economic decline was followed in short order by the bleak downfall of Italian art and scholarship.

Finally, democracy too must become fragile once better hopes are worn away by bitter disappointment. What Americans have in common are their shared beliefs, above all in equality of opportunity in the pursuit of affluence. It would be too much to expect that democratic governance would long survive the impoverishment of all Americans except for a small privileged minority of inheritors, agents of foreign interests, and assorted financial manipulators.

When Buenos Aires was still a leading world metropolis, when the people of Argentina still enjoyed their famous steak-at-every-meal abundance that lasted into the 1950's, they would never have believed that their future would be a 40-year slide into poverty. Equally, the citizens of the U.S., still today by far the richest country in the world, steadfastly refuse to recognize what future is in store for them unless they can alter the course they are now on. Yet the simplest numbers confirm the slide, and suggest the chilling forecast.

* * *

In 1970, Americans were two-and-a-half times as productive as the Japanese, and twice as productive as the citizens of the European Community on average. By 1980, the pattern of decline had already set in. The United States was still well ahead of the European Community and Japan, but its edge has been cut in half in a mere ten years, while West Germany had actually overtaken it.

At that point, in 1980, a simple straight-line projection of the sort that professional economists deplore as much too simplistic would have suggested that in one more decade the United States would be overtaken by the richer Europeans and by Japan. And that is exactly what happened.

This being a 20-year trend and not just a brief downturn, it is perfectly reasonable to calculate what the future numbers would be if the United States were to remain on its present path. Already in the year 2000, Japan's gross national product per person would be twice that of America, while the richer European countries would have a 50-percent edge over the United States. Ten years after that, Japan would be more than three times as productive per person as the United States, and the richer European countries would be almost twice as productive per person as the United States.

Finally in 2020, when the children of today's middle-aged Americans will themselves be middle-aged, the richest Europeans would be more than twice as productive, while the gap between Japanese and Americans at 5-to-1 would be just about the same as the 1980 gap between Americans and Brazilians. At that point, the United States would definitely have become a third-world country—at least by Japanese standards. Certainly Americans would no longer be in the same class as West Europeans....

* * *

There is no doubt that to project the future by simply extending the past is a procedure truly simplistic, because unexpected changes can always outweigh continuities. But so far, at least, the path seems straight enough—and straight downhill. It is also true that international comparisons can easily be distorted by abrupt exchange-rate fluctuations: one reason Switzerland reached the astounding gross national product of $30,270 per person in 1989 was that the Swiss franc happened to be very high during that year. Moreover, all fluctuations aside, exchange rates routinely deform comparisons because they reflect only the *international* supply and demand for capital, goods, and services denominated in any particular currency (as well as speculation and central-bank manipulations), and not the much greater amount of purely domestic transactions. Hence currencies can be greatly overvalued or undervalued as compared to their purchasing power at home.

Because the United States has chosen to open its markets to imports to a much greater extent than most other countries, let alone famously import-phobic Japan and Korea, the great outflow of dollars reduces the exchange rate far below the dollar's purchasing power at home. If we rely on a measure based on purchasing-power parities, we find that the United States scores much higher in international comparisons. Yet while purchasing-power values can depict living standards more or less realistically, it is only comparisons based on straight exchange rates that determine the "who-does-what-to-whom" of the international economy—including the little matter of which parties can buy attractive pieces of other (open-door) economies, and which parties can only sell them off. And that, of course, can make the enjoyment of even splendid living standards somewhat ephemeral.

Finally, if we switch to the purchasing-power plus gross-domestic-product criterion, we find that although the United States is still ahead, the trend is just as unfavorable as it is with other measures, and the pattern of relative decline just as evident.

To be sure, both the gross national product and the gross domestic product are indeed gross measures: a car accident increases both of them by the amount of ambulance, hospital, and bodyshop bills, while a healthy drop in cigarette smoking reduces them as sales and excise taxes go down. Nor can any international comparison be free of all sorts of distortions, large and small, no matter what criterion is employed, if only because the different consumption preferences prevalent in different countries are hard to equate. And yet, after all possible objections and all proper reservations are listed, it cannot finally be denied that the totality of all the relevant numbers contains irrefutable evidence that the American economy has long been in severe decline by world standards—and still is.

* * *

Many observers would reach the same verdict without need of any numbers. Follow a traveler from Tokyo to New York—though it would be much the same if he came from Zurich, Amsterdam, or Singapore. After leaving his taxi at Tokyo's downtown City Air Terminal—a perfectly ordinary Tokyo taxi and therefore shiny clean, in perfect condition, its neatly dressed driver in white gloves—our traveler will find himself aboard an equally spotless airport bus in five minutes flat, with his baggage already checked in, boarding card issued, and passport stamped by the seemingly effortless teamwork of quick, careful porters who refuse tips, airline clerks who can actually use computers at computer speed, passport officers who act as if it were their job to expedite travel, and bus crews who sell tickets, load baggage, and courteously help the encumbered while strictly keeping to departure schedules timed to the exact minute.

Then, after an hour's bus ride over the crowded expressway to the gleaming halls of Tokyo's Narita international airport, and after the long trans-Pacific flight, when our traveler finally arrives, he will be confronted by sights and sounds that would not be out of place in Lagos or Bombay. He has landed at New York's John F. Kennedy airport.

Instead of the elegance of Narita, or Frankfurt, or Amsterdam, or Singapore, arriving travelers at one of the several JFK terminals that belong to near-bankrupt airlines will find themselves walking down dingy corridors in need of paint, over frayed carpets, often struggling up and down narrow stairways alongside out-of-order escalators. Those are JFK's substitutes for the constantly updated facilities of first-world airports. The rough, cheap remodeling of sadly outdated buildings with naked plywood and unfinished gypsum board proclaims the shortage of long-term money to build with, of invested capital. Equally, the frayed carpets, those defective escalators, and the pervasive minor dirt reveal how day-to-day money is being saved: by deferred maintenance—the most perfect sign of third-world conditions, the instantly recognizable background of South Asian, African, and Latin American street scenes, with their potholed streets, dilapidated buildings, crudely painted signs, and decrepit buses.

If the sheer lack of capital to provide proper facilities is the first third-world trait, the second is undoubtedly the lack of skill and diligence in the labor force. This phenomenon will be brutally obvious as soon as our traveler arrives in the customs hall, where baggage is contemptuously thrown off the incoming belts in full view of the hapless passengers. By then he will be too exhausted to complain: after a long flight, he is likely to have waited for hours to have his passport examined.

In due course, if our traveler transfers to a domestic flight, he may well encounter airline porters already paid to place suitcases on conveyor belts who nevertheless ask for tips in brusque undertones, just as in Nairobi or Karachi, sometimes hinting that the baggage might not arrive safely if no money changes hands. And he will in all probability then be trapped in slow lines while imminent flight departures are called out, waiting to be checked in by untrained clerks who tap on computer keyboards very slowly, with one finger.

Here, then, is the final trait typical of the third world—the chronic disorganization of perfectly routine procedures.

If our traveler is headed for a Manhattan hotel, he can choose between a dirty, battered, and possibly unsafe bus, or a dirtier and more battered taxi, usually driven by an unkempt lout who resembles his counterparts in Islamabad or Kinshasa rather than in London or Tokyo, where licensing requirements are strict and dress codes are enforced. At that point, a first-time visitor may still believe that both airport and taxi are glaring exceptions to the America he had always imagined—clean, modern, efficient. If so, he will immediately be disillusioned by the jolting drive over potholed highways and crumbling bridges, through miles of slums or miserable public housing.

Not as colorful as in Jakarta or Madras, the passing scene will still amaze those who come from the many European and even Asian cities where slums are now reduced to isolated survivals in remote parts of town (New York tour guides report a growing demand for the thrills of the South Bronx from European tourists quite uninterested in its pleasant greenery or the zoo, but eager to see open-air drug dealing at street corners, and the rows of burned-out buildings). After this unsettling encounter with an America already in full third-world conditions, an affluent tourist will next reach the luxurious glitter of a Manhattan hotel, but even there beggars may be standing near the door, just as in New Delhi or Lima.

* * *

It seems only yesterday that the professional optimists among us were still pointing to the continued American dominance of the world's entertainment, biotechnology, and aviation industries to reassure us that all was well, in spite of the virtual extinction of the U.S. consumer-electronics industry, the steady retreat of the auto industry, the drastic decline of the steel industry, and the widespread collapse of the machine-tool industry, still very much the foundation of all other industries.

Since then, Columbia Pictures has been sold to Sony, which had already purchased CBS Records in a previous transaction; the multimedia industry leader MCA has been sold off to Matsushita; Time-Warner, which includes HBO, has been partly sold to Toshiba and C. Itoh for $1 billion; and other notable names now belong to French and Italian interests. Word has it that it is only a matter of time before the remaining entertainment giants will go on the block in full or in part. Even hugely successful Disney, long the toast of Wall Street, chose to sell off the ownership of the hugely profitable Disneylands in France and Japan to local investors, in a typical exercise of capitalism-without-capital in the New American style.

Thus, Michael Jackson records may still sell by the millions all over the world, and American films may continue to dominate the global market, but the profits and the resulting opportunity for further capital accumulation now accrue to foreign owners.

Then there is the biotechnology industry, the *locus classicus* of the dynamic creativity and bold entrepreneurship that are supposed to compensate for all the other weaknesses of the American economy. The names of both buyers and sellers are far more obscure than in the Hollywood pairings, and the deals are much smaller (e.g., Chugai's $100 million purchase of Gen-Probe), but the great sell-off is under way just the same.

The pattern is by now well established. Americans still do most of the inventing, but because they cannot find capital at home to build the required facilities, they sell out to Japanese and European companies, receiving millions in license fees for products whose sales can eventually earn billions. Unfortunately, it is only those millions—and not the billions that will be earned mainly by foreign companies—that can be taxed to pay for basic research as well as all other government expenditures. As it is, the United States spent $5 billion on biotechnology research in 1990 as compared with only $1.7 billion for Japan, and less for Europe, but it is the Japanese and Europeans who are prospering, in great part by selling products originally developed in the U.S., mostly at the taxpayers' expense....

* * *

When a farmer is reduced to selling off his broad acres rather than only his crops, his ultimate fate is not in doubt. Of course the analogy should be false because instead of a waning stock of acres, there is the unending flow of new technology that comes from the constantly celebrated creativity of our pluralist, multi-ethnic, undisciplined but ever-dynamic society.

Note, however, the small print that accompanied the dramatic announcement of the very latest example of that famous creativity. As soon as the suitably Korean-born chief developer of digital High-Definition (HD) TV revealed that the suitably small company he works for had totally overtaken the Japanese giants and their merely analog HD-TV, the company's owner, General Instrument, let it be known that it would not even try to raise the capital needed to produce and market the new invention, preferring to license production to established TV manufacturers, i.e., the Japanese TV giants.

In a manner literally pathetic, for pathos is the emotion evoked in the spectators to an inevitable downfall, a company spokesman hopefully speculated that if 20 million HD-TV sets were sold annually, its royalties at $10 per set could amount to as much as $200 million a year, a nice bit of change as they say— but truly mere change as compared to the $20–25 *billion* that the actual producers would earn each year, largely, no doubt, by exports to the United States.

But that is by now standard operating procedure, given our bootless capitalism-without-capital. It was Ampex, a U.S. company, which first developed the video-recorder technology that was then licensed for mere change to Matsushita, Sony, and the rest of those vigorous exporters—though of course their VCR export earnings did come back to the United States, through the purchase of CBS Records, Columbia Pictures, and MCA.

It is all very well to speak of the "globalization of industry" and to deride concerns for the nationality of production in an era of "transnational manufacturing," but when Taiwan acquires 40 percent of Douglas, or Japan's consortium has 20 percent of the next Boeing airliner, they assume no such responsibility for funding future U.S. aviation research, or Medicare for that matter—and the future earnings from those efforts will accrue to their balance of payments, and not ours.

* * *

What is happening to the U.S. aviation industry in particular exposes the embarrassingly wide gap between the realities of what I have labeled geoeconomics, and the free-trade-plus-globalization fantasy that remains unchallenged dogma for so many Americans, not least in the Bush White House.

To begin with, the American aviation industry's only significant foreign competitor is the European consortium Airbus Industrie, which has been very successful of late even against Boeing, by selling its government-subsidized aircraft with the aid of government-subsidized loans at low interest. Similarly, Taiwan Aerospace is a government-guaranteed company, no more exposed to the vagaries of the free market than the Vatican; as such, it will always be able to count on government subsidies to underbid Douglas subcontractors, thereby taking over specialized

manufactures conducive to its own planned growth into an independent maker of civilian airliners.

The wider meaning of such narrowly-aimed industrial subsidies and "national technology programs" is plain enough. Just as past generations were put in uniform to be marched off in pursuit of geopolitical schemes of territorial conquest, today's taxpayers in Europe and elsewhere have been persuaded to subsidize geo-economic schemes of industrial conquest. The free-trade true believers smile at such foolish generosity, and invite us to enjoy the resulting subsidy of our own consumption. Thus they safeguard the interests of the citizen-as-consumer, while ignoring the interests of the citizen-as-producer, but of the two roles it is only the latter that comports with the satisfactions of achievement and the dignity of employment. Moreover, the benefits of subsidized consumption that displaces our own production can only last so long as we still have acreage, famous buildings, golf courses, industries, and new technologies to sell off....

* * *

None of this is to say that Japanese corporate expansionism, or foreign interests in general, are responsible for the woes of the American economy....

Certainly neither our European competitors nor the Japanese can be blamed for the long list of self-inflicted wounds that have been engendering the third-worldization of America.

They did not arrange the regulatory and business-culture changes that brought the mores and urgencies of Las Vegas to Wall Street and corporate boardrooms across the land, to subordinate both future growth and current employment to immediate payoffs for well-placed principals.

They had no say in the most original invention of American statecraft: representation without taxation to extract "entitlements" galore, so that savings, already scant, have been absorbed in Treasury paper, instead of modern factories or updated infrastructure.

They did not seize control of our classrooms, to discredit the discipline and absolute standards that are the prerequisites of all education, nor lately appoint the "multiculturalism" inspectors who equate arithmetic with racism, and who annex the study of history to group therapy....

A search for the deeper sources of all the blatantly obvious diseases of American society would take us very far—though it might be said in passing that Anglo-Saxon style individualism could only be successful so long as there was still enough Calvinism to go around. But at least the immediate causes of our third-worldization are simply economic, a matter of capital and labor. And while the inadequate diligence of our labor force obviously has no simple cause, the immediate reason for our disastrous shortage of capital is plain enough. Americans have little to invest because they save so little.

Obviously, it is possible to invest without saving, if others lend the necessary money. And of course the United States has borrowed hugely in recent years, and also absorbed a vast amount of foreign investment. Yet given the size of the American economy, even the huge inflow of money from abroad could not possibly remedy the disastrous difference between our rate of savings and those of our competitors.

* * *

In any case, the relentless erosion of the entire economic base of American society is revealed by undisputed statistics that have none of the flaws of international comparisons. During the last 20 years—half a working lifetime—American "non-farm, non-supervisory" employees actually earned slightly less, year by year. As a matter of fact, by 1990 their real earnings (corrected for inflation) had regressed to the 1965 level. Will they regress further—perhaps to the 1960 level by 1995, and then to the 1955 level by the year 2000? It seems distinctly possible. Given the lack of invested capital, it is only with ever-cheaper labor that we can compete internationally. Therein lies our own path to Bangladesh.

Who are these poor unfortunates whose real earnings have been declining since 1965? Are they perhaps some small and peculiar minority? Not so. In November 1990, the last month for which those statistics are complete, they numbered 74,888,000, or just over 81 percent of all non-farm employees—that is, more than eight out of ten of all Americans who are not self-employed, from corporate executives earning hundreds or even thousands of dollars per hour, to those working at the minimum wage.

Far from being a minority whose fate cannot affect the base of American society, then, they *are* the base of American society, the vast majority of the labor force of manufacturing, mining, construction, transport, utility, wholesale and retail trade, finance, insurance, real estate, all other service enterprises, and government employees.

How can the entire structure of American affluence and advancement from luxurious living to scientific laboratories *not* decline when the vast majority of all working Americans are earning less and less? And how can the U.S. not slide toward third-world conditions if this absolute decline continues while in both Western Europe and East Asia real earnings continue to increase?

Inevitably, the most telling comparison is with Japan. In 1970, Japanese manufacturing employees earned only just over a quarter (or more precisely 27 percent) as much as their American counterparts. In 1988, they earned 7 percent more. If the trend were to continue straight on both sides, in 18 more years American earnings would be reduced to less than a quarter (23 percent) of the Japanese level, almost the same proportion as now obtains between Brazilian and American hourly wages in manufacturing.

It stands to reason that by then the United States would become Japan's Brazil, an amusing, sometimes unsettling country of vast expanses with a cheerful but impoverished third-world population. The casual banter that nowadays greets errors of blatant incompetence in American offices, factories, and shops; the patient silence evoked even by acts of willful negligence and aggressive apathy; the learned ability to ignore unkempt urban vagrants and all their importunings; and generally our increasing acceptance of breakdowns, delays, and all forms of physical decay—all this shows that we are indeed adapting to our fate, by acquiring the necessary third-world traits of fatalistic detachment. But they, of course, ensure that the slide will continue.

NO

Robert L. Bartley

IS AMERICA ON THE WAY DOWN?

To the ordinary, everyday sense of mankind, America has not declined, it has prevailed. Its foe of two generations has collapsed and now even seeks to adopt American institutions of democracy and market economics.

Though to people who use their eyes and ears it is obvious that American influence in the world is on the rise, we have not been able to put the notion of decline behind us. For a segment of American opinion refuses to use its eyes and ears. Instead, proponents of decline confuse themselves with statistics they do not understand, or in some cases willingly distort....

[T]he notion of decline faded as Ronald Reagan filled the military spare-parts bins, frankly labeled the Soviet Union an "evil empire," invaded Grenada, bombed Libya, revived the option of missile defense. The diplomatic turning point was 1983, when the West withstood a determined Soviet campaign, including street demonstrations and the suspension of arms negotiations, to stop the deployment of Pershing missiles in Europe. At the same time, the United States was curbing its inflation with Paul Volcker's monetary policy and reviving economic growth with Ronald Reagan's tax cuts. Seven years of uninterrupted economic expansion did wonders for military preparedness, diplomatic creativity, and public morale. The economic revival that started in the United States and quickly spread to Europe proved the final undoing of the totalitarian challenge.

The containment policy the West had patiently pursued for two generations predicted that under steady pressure the Soviet empire would mellow or crack. Then it happened at a stroke. In 1989 the Berlin Wall was breached, and by 1991 the Communist remnants proved themselves inept even at coup-making. Meanwhile, an American-led attack decimated the world's fourth-largest army in six weeks of combat and at the cost of 148 Americans lost in action. The world's new military balance was clear, leaving only the mysteries of why President Bush stopped short of Baghdad and how the hysterical Cassandras who had predicted a desert debacle managed to retain their *bona fides* as military experts.

Nor is American predominance merely or even primarily a matter of military power. American ideals of democratic pluralism and market economics were spreading not only in the former Soviet Union but throughout South

From Robert L. Bartley, "Is America on the Way Down? No," *Commentary* (March 1992). Copyright © 1992 by The American Jewish Committee. Reprinted by permission of *Commentary* and the author. All rights reserved.

376

America, Eastern Europe, and even Africa. America remains the favored destination of the world's refugees and immigrants. Its university system (despite the political-correctness plague) is unparalleled: it graduates many foreign nationals in science and engineering, of course, but many of them choose to stay in the U.S. For all the accomplishments of the industrious Japanese, America still dominates scientific innovation. Many transnational corporations, even if based in Germany or Switzerland, locate their research divisions in New Jersey or North Carolina. Japanese auto companies open design labs in Los Angeles. Above all, the U.S. utterly dominates the single capstone technology of our era, which in every language is called "software."

* * *

Whatever the momentary economic ups and downs, too, the plain fact is that the United States is the wealthiest society in the history of mankind. Or at least this is plain to the economically literate, who understand that no meaningful comparison can be based on momentary exchange rates among different national currencies. In translating among currencies to make international comparisons, the only meaningful basis is purchasing-power parity (PPP), the exchange rate at which two currencies would each buy the same basket of goods. The Organization for Economic Cooperation and Development spends endless hours of tedious calculation to churn out PPP rates precisely for the purpose of facilitating such comparisons.

Under the current regime of floating exchange rates, currencies can vary widely from their purchasing-power parity. This distorts comparisons and above all trends—for temporary and reversible variations in exchange rates are likely to swamp any changes in underlying fundamentals. As recently as 1985, the dollar was well over its PPP rate, exaggerating the American standard of living. In later years, the dollar has been below PPP, making America look less wealthy than it actually is.

So current comparisons built on current exchange rates show America falling behind, but properly adjusting the comparisons to PPP makes the picture entirely different. *The Economist Book of Vital World Statistics*, for example, found that at 1988 figures and exchange rates, the United States ranked only ninth in the world in gross domestic product per capita—behind Switzerland, Japan, and the Scandinavian countries. But it also reported that at PPP exchange rates, the American standard of living was far above other advanced nations. With the U.S. at 100, Canada rated 92.5 and Switzerland 87.0. Then came the Scandinavian nations and some small countries, including Kuwait. West Germany rated tenth at 78.6, and Japan twelfth at 71.5. Other developed nations trailed.

In short, the American standard of living is substantially above that of Japan and most of Europe.

This is confirmed by physical measures. American automobile ownership, for example, is one car for every 1.8 persons. Iceland has two people for each car, while Canada, New Zealand, and West Germany have 2.2. France has 2.5, the United Kingdom 2.8, and Japan 4.2. Similarly, there are 1.2 Americans per television set, compared to 1.7 Japanese and 2.4 Germans. The United States is also one of the world's great undeveloped countries, with 26.3 persons per square mile, compared to 102.1 in France, 233.8 in the United Kingdom, 246.1 in

West Germany, 324.5 in Japan, and 395.8 in the Netherlands. While I have no figures handy, the American standard of living is most evident of all in housing; the Japanese measure apartment sizes in tatami mats.

As for the recent trends, the American economy led the world out of the economic crisis of the late 1970's by staging so remarkable a boom between 1983 and 1990 that it is now hard to remember such bywords as "stagflation" or "malaise" or "Euro-pessimism." In this expansion, the U.S. economy grew by 31 percent after adjustment for inflation, about equivalent to building 1982 West Germany from scratch. Real disposable income per capita rose by 18 percent. Productivity resumed growth after stagnating in the 1970's, and in fact surged in manufacturing. Manufacturing output grew faster than GNP, and exports leapt by more than 92 percent. More than eighteen million new jobs were created, even while the *Fortune* 500 companies pared their payrolls. Tax revenues kept pace with GNP growth and, since this was supposedly a decade of greed, it should be noted that charitable giving grew at 5.1 percent a year, compared with 3.5 percent a year over the previous 25 years.

Again, a remarkable leap in living standards is confirmed by physical measures. In 1980, hard as it may be to remember, only 1 percent of American households owned a videocassette recorder. By 1989, the figure was more than 58 percent. For all practical purposes, every video rental shop in the nation was started during the seven fat years. In 1980, cable-television systems reached 15 percent of American households, mostly in remote areas with difficult reception. At the end of the decade, half of all homes were wired. In 1981, when the Apple II was a hackers' toy, a little over two million personal computers were in use in the whole country. That year, IBM introduced its first PC, and Apple followed with the Macintosh in 1984. By 1988, the two million PC's had exploded to 45 million. Of this number, roughly half were in homes.

* * *

The most remarkable feature of the 1980's, though, was economic globalization. The 24-hour trading markets were stitched together; dollars circled the world at electronic speed. Rock-and-roll invaded Prague and Moscow, and Japanese auto companies built plants in Tennessee (Nissan), Ohio (Honda), and Kentucky (Toyota). "Interdependence" became the new byword, though one inadequate to describe the evolution of the world economy into an organic whole.

As the U.S. economy led the world out of the doldrums of 1982, the world voted with its money. In 1979, foreigners invested $38.7 billion in the United States; in 1980 this number was $58.1 billion. But investment inflows soared to $83.0 billion in 1981, $93.7 billion in 1982, $130.0 billion in 1985, and $229.8 billion in 1987. With the Volcker monetary policy and the Reagan tax cuts, America was where the world's investors saw the most promising return. And demand in America created the export markets that led Europe out of its pessimism.

A great source of the confusion about the American economy, and a great source of the current poor-mouthing, is that the United States has still not come to terms with its integration into the world economy. Thus America's sages gazed on the developments sketched above and decided the sky was falling. In sending their money here those perfidious foreigners expected to get paid back. Indeed, the whole reason they were sending their money here was that they anticipated a higher return here than they could get at home....

* * *

In the midst of this burgeoning prosperity and creativity, the Left decided that America was declining, and undertook to prove it by peering into the international statistics. While there were earlier precursors, the theme came to its fruition with Paul Kennedy's *The Rise and Fall of the Great Powers*. In 1988, as voters were rewarding a platform of "read my lips" and Willie Horton, book-buyers were handsomely rewarding Professor Kennedy's thesis of "imperial overstretch." In this view, the filling of the spare-parts bins and the reassertion of American military power abroad was not the cure for decline, it was the cause of decline. Indeed, it was decline itself.

... Excessive military spending undermined the economy, the critique went, and the slackening economy could not support the military commitments. To be sure, the U.S. was still only in "relative decline," still first in importance, but its lead was shrinking. For

> the only way the United States can pay its way in the world is by importing ever-larger sums of capital, which has transformed it from being the world's largest creditor to the world's largest debtor nation *in the space of a few years.*

... The liberal declinists, however, did find some allies on the presumed Right—most prominently, the heads of transnational corporations headquartered in the United States, like Chrysler and Motorola, who found that they could not keep up with Toyota and Sony, transnational corporations headquartered in Japan. They were understandably eager to blame their predicament on anything but their own shortcomings. They and their labor-union allies belabored the trade-deficit and debtor-nation themes in their campaign to erect protectionist walls athwart history's march to an integrated world economy.

Then, too, there was a species of financial conservative who found debt worse than taxes. Bond traders and central bankers have a natural tendency to focus on the supply of and demand for credit (to whatever extent they can be measured). And though growing corporations add debt every year as a matter of course, the executives running them were taught in their childhood to judge government finance solely by whether current income matches current outgo. And finally, there is a jingoistic conservatism casting about for a new foe to fight after the decline of Communism; it has settled on the Japanese trading companies.

Given these various roots of support, it is perhaps not surprising that the notion of decline proved so resilient in the face of both self-evident prosperity and intellectual refutation. I thought the matter had been laid to rest in the *Wall Street Journal* by May 1988, when Charles Wolf of the RAND Corporation took his usual beady aim. Yes, said Wolf, the U.S. share of world product had declined from 45 percent in 1950, "a manifestly atypical year." But against the mid-1960's or 1938, the U.S. share remained at 22 percent to 24 percent. "Japan's central-government debt is a larger fraction of its GNP than is that of the U.S., while the foreign indebtedness of the U.S. has been grossly overestimated in the official statistics." Somehow statist politics and economics had spread internationally in the 1960's and 1970's, while market economics and democracy had advanced in the 1980's. "The rhetoric of decline is wrong because it portrays a past that wasn't, a present that isn't, and a future that probably won't be." ...

My *Wall Street Journal* colleague, Karen Elliot House, who spent months interviewing hundreds of leaders around the world, found that *they* did not think America was threatened by decline. Jean-François Poncet, a former Foreign Minister of France, told her: "It's hard to take seriously that a nation has deep problems if they can be fixed with a 50-cent-a-gallon gasoline tax." Seizaburo Sato, a sometime adviser to the Japanese prime minister, recalled Henry Luce. "The 20th century was the American century," he said, "and the 21st century will be the American century."

* * *

At least it ought to be, because far from sinking into decline, America is now at the center of one of the great, exciting moments in mankind's economic history. A second industrial revolution is remaking world society. Not since the industrial revolution itself has technological advance been so breathtaking, or more pregnant with changes in the way mankind lives and thinks of itself.

More breathtaking now, probably, than even then. James Watt's steam engine pales beside what our generation has already seen: the splitting of the atom, the decoding of the gene, and the invention of the transistor and the computers it spawned. These are not only magnificent leaps of the technological imagination, they are potential precursors of currently unimaginable economic advance. Atomic power, unless cold fusion turns out to be real after all, has perhaps not realized what we once thought of as its potential. The first fruits of biotechnology are just now entering the markets. But already the transistor and the rest are changing the world.

Indeed, we live every day with the electronic revolution. As the first industrial revolution changed an agricultural economy into an industrial economy, a second industrial revolution is changing an industrial economy into a service economy. More specifically, into an information economy, in which the predominant activity is collecting, processing, and communicating information. We are headed toward a world in which everyone on the globe is in instant communication with everyone else.

It is this web of instant communication that has stitched the world into increasing interdependence. In fact, throughout this century the world economy has been more interdependent than anyone realized: the Great Depression, for example, was preeminently a world event, and its origins lay in disturbances in the international economy. But with today's 24 hour financial markets and transnational corporations, economic interdependence is hard to miss.

The same web of instant communication is responsible for the political developments that have rocked our age. Orwell, in his *Nineteen Eighty-Four*, saw information technology as an instrument of Big Brother. We are now seeing clearly that it is quite the opposite. The onslaught of the information age played a key role in liberating Eastern Europe and in spreading democratic currents through the Soviet Union and the developing world. The totalitarians have found they cannot control a people in touch with the outside. In Albert Wohlstetter's phrase, *the fax shall make you free.* Big Brother can of course build a society without computers, but that society will not be able to compete in the modern world, as China seems to be learning after Tiananmen Square....

Naturally our time and our nation have their problems. Americans should take education more seriously, instead of subordinating it to goals like racial balance and asbestos removal. Our legal system should let police enforce the law against vagrants, and should stop inflicting a parasitic tort-bar industry upon us. Our political system is so frozen it seems unable to address these everyday problems.

More broadly, there is such a thing as being too liberated, having too many options. We are still learning to live with our new freedoms. The onslaught of modernity has not been good for institutions such as the family. We are overly susceptible to fads—health scares, for example—and for that matter the fad of declinism....

* * *

This is not to say that the short-run problems were imaginary. In the short run, technological advance destroyed agricultural jobs faster than it created manufacturing jobs, especially since guilds and the like created bottlenecks. A type of mass unemployment arose that had been unknown in the Middle Ages, and with it urban slums, gin mills, and great social debates over the Poor Laws. Malthus's pessimism was echoed a few decades later by Dickens. But we now know that during the lives of both men mankind was rapidly building wealth.

If, then, we are currently experiencing a second industrial revolution, it is not surprising to hear such Malthusian themes as overpopulation and the exhaustion of resources echoing through our public discourse. From the primitive technology of a wooden sailing ship, the earth's forces look overwhelming. Now that we have the technological prowess to put men on the moon, the earth looks like a fragile flower, puny beside our own powers.

The rapid change of the second industrial revolution, moreover, upsets established institutions and established elites. As instant information and instant markets erode the power of governments, so too they erode the power of corporate chieftains and labor bosses. We can now all watch the poor chairman of Exxon writhing over an oil spill in Alaska. Many chief executives find themselves displaced, albeit with golden parachutes: half of *Fortune*'s top 500 corporations in 1980 were gone from the list in 1990. Under the force of industrial competition and information on wages and working conditions, labor unions find their private-sector membership declining.

So too with intellectual elites, who find their skills fading in relevance and their positions endangered. Perhaps political correctness in the academy is best seen as a brand of Luddism. And surely much of our articulate class feels threatened in a deeply personal way by the notion that a historic corner was turned under a simple-minded movie actor.

This mixture of neurosis, special pleading, ideological hostility, ignorance, and confusion is obviously a phenomenon to be reckoned with. Indeed, even an unbridled optimist has to admit that there is after all one way America actually could decline. To wit, if this neurotic pessimism becomes a self-realizing prophecy.

* * *

This would be a historic tragedy, for the confluence of the second industrial revolution and the collapse of totalitarianism presents the human race with an unparalleled opportunity. The decade of the 1990's is not a time for pessimism, but a time for large thoughts and large ambitions. The tide in the affairs of men is running, and we must take the current when it serves. The brightest hope for mankind today is that the breaching of the Berlin Wall on November 9, 1989 marked the end of a beastly era that started with the assassination of Archduke Francis Ferdinand in Sarajevo on June 28, 1914.

The consciousness of everyone alive today was forged in an abnormal era, a century of world war, revolution, and totalitarianism. While mankind has always suffered wars and other miseries, our century ranks with the most wretched in history. Technology turned battle from a contest of knights into an assault on whole civilian populations. A Great Depression sank the world economy. With the rise of Hitler and Stalin, the human soul was under siege. World War II dissolved into a worldwide confrontation between the West and Communism.

At issue was the nature of man—a cog in the great dialectical machine of history, or an autonomous individual capable of free will and self-government? If reform succeeds in Russia, or even survives, all this will be history. We will have a new era to define....

[I]nstead of the promise of world cooperation led by the United States, we have the gloomy apostles of decline, alarmed because goods and capital move across lines someone drew on maps, trying to manufacture conflict out of the peaceful and mutually beneficial intercourse among peoples.

The last time the will of the West was tested, it rose to the challenge. In particular, the American electorate understood that the threat was Soviet Communism, not the military-industrial complex. With the more subtle test of a litany of decline coming out of Cambridge, Detroit, and Washington, there will again be confusion and apparent close calls, but in the end the delusion will not sell. Indeed, given any sort of intellectual and political leadership to frame the challenge, the American nation will rise to the rich opportunity before it.

POSTSCRIPT

Is America Declining?

Both Luttwak and Bartley look at some of the same developments in the United States, but they see them with different eyes. For example, Luttwak views foreign investments in America as evidence that American sovereignty is eroding, while Bartley sees it as evidence that other countries find America worth investing in. Bartley also sees the vast increase in consumer spending as a sign that living standards are rising, while Luttwak views such spending as a waste of money that should be saved and invested. Which view is more correct, Bartley's rosy assessment or Luttwak's gloomy one?

In their selections, Bartley and Luttwak look back over the 1980s, the Reagan and Bush years. It was President Reagan's economic and military policies that set the tone of that decade, and Bartley defends those policies. In his book *Seven Fat Years and How to Do It Again* (Free Press, 1992), Bartley discusses Reaganomics (Reagan's economic program), which, he contends, brought prolonged prosperity to America. A very different view of America is presented by Paul Kennedy in *The Rise and Fall of the Great Powers* (Random House, 1987). As noted in the introduction to this issue, this book provided the historical framework for America's current national soul-searching.

What are other nations going to be doing while America is struggling with its economy and infrastructure? Lester C. Thurow, in *Head to Head: The Coming Economic Battle Among Japan, Europe, and America* (William Morrow, 1992), argues that a united Western Europe will abandon traditional free trade for trading blocs and managed trade, while Japan will enjoy the economic advantages of momentum, a high rate of investment, and a cohesive internal culture. Confronted by these challenges, the United States must recognize the need to change from individualistic to communitarian capitalism. Two other works that view American competitiveness negatively are the Office of Technology Assessment, *Competing Economies: America, Europe, and the Pacific Rim* (Government Printing Office, 1992), and *Building a Competitive America* (1992), the first annual report from the Competitive Council. In contrast, John Case praises American competitiveness in *From the Ground Up: The Resurgence of American Entrepreneurship* (Simon & Schuster, 1992).

Kennedy's decline thesis is rejected by Richard McKenzie, in "The Decline of America: Myth or Fate?" *Society* (November/December 1989), and by Owen Harries, in "The Rise of American Decline," *Commentary* (May 1988). For Norman Podhoretz, the issue is not overstretching or overspending but national will. In *The Present Danger* (Simon & Schuster, 1980), he poses the question: "Do we have the will to reverse the decline of American power?"

CONTRIBUTORS
TO THIS VOLUME

EDITORS

KURT FINSTERBUSCH is a professor of sociology at the University of Maryland at College Park. He received a B.A. in history from Princeton University in 1957, a B.D. from Grace Theological Seminary in 1960, and a Ph.D. in sociology from Columbia University in 1969. He is the author of *Understanding Social Impacts* (Sage Publications, 1980), and he is the coauthor, with Annabelle Bender Motz, of *Social Research for Policy Decisions* (Wadsworth, 1980) and, with Jerald Hage, of *Organizational Change as a Development Strategy* (Lynne Rienner, 1987). He has been the editor for the Dushkin Publishing Group's *Annual Editions: Sociology* since 1984, and he recently coedited, with Janet S. Schwartz, *Sources: Notable Selections in Sociology* (The Dushkin Publishing Group, 1993).

GEORGE McKENNA is a professor of political science and the chair of the Department of Political Science at City College, City University of New York, where he has been teaching since 1963. He received a B.A. from the University of Chicago in 1959, an M.A. from the University of Massachusetts in 1962, and a Ph.D. from Fordham University in 1967. He has written articles in the fields of American government and political theory, and his publications include *American Populism* (Putnam, 1974) and *American Politics: Ideals and Realities* (McGraw-Hill, 1976). He is the coeditor, with Stanley Feingold, of the Dushkin Publishing Group's *Taking Sides: Clashing Views on Controversial Political Issues*, now in its eighth edition, and he is the author of the textbook *The Drama of Democracy: American Government and Politics*, 2d ed. (The Dushkin Publishing Group, 1994).

STAFF

Mimi Egan   Publisher
Brenda S. Filley   Production Manager
Libra Ann Cusack   Typesetting Supervisor
Juliana Arbo   Typesetter
Shawn Callahan   Graphics
Diane Barker   Editorial Assistant
David Brackley   Copy Editor
David Dean   Administrative Editor
Richard Tietjen   Systems Manager

AUTHORS

LAWRENCE AUSTER is a writer whose articles have appeared in such publications as *National Review, Academic Questions*, the *New York Newsday*, the *Miami Herald*, and the *Arizona Republic*. He is currently working on a book on immigration and the future of American civilization.

EDWARD BANFIELD is a professor emeritus of urban studies in the Department of Faculty Arts and Sciences at Harvard University. He is the author of a number of articles and books on urban problems, including *The Unheavenly City Revisited: A Revision of the Unheavenly City* (Scott, Foresman, 1974).

JAMES A. BANKS is a professor of education and the director of the Center for Multicultural Education at the University of Washington in Seattle, Washington, and a former president of the National Council for the Social Studies. His publications include *Teaching Strategies for the Social Studies: Inquiry, Valuing, and Decision-Making*, 4th ed. (Longman, 1990).

ROBERT L. BARTLEY, a recipient of the 1980 Pulitzer Prize for editorial writing, is the editor and vice president of the *Wall Street Journal*, with primary responsibility for the editorial page. He is a member of the Council on Foreign Relations and the American Political Science Association, and he holds honorary doctor of laws degrees from Macalester College and Babson College. His publications include *The Seven Fat Years: And How to Do It Again* (Free Press, 1992).

DAVID L. BAZELON is a senior circuit judge of the U.S. Court of Appeals for the District of Columbia circuit and a lecturer of psychiatry at the Johns Hopkins University School of Medicine in Baltimore, Maryland. He is the author of *Questioning Authority: Justice and Criminal Law* (Alfred A. Knopf, 1988).

JEFFREY M. BERRY is a professor of political science at Tufts University in Medford, Massachusetts. He is the author of *Feeding Hungry People* (Rutgers University Press, 1984) and *The Interest Group Society*, 2d ed. (Scott, Foresman, 1989), and he is the coauthor, with Kent E. Portney and Ken Thomson, of *The Rebirth of Urban Democracy* (Brookings Institution, 1993).

ELLEN BRAVO is the executive director of 9to5, the National Association of Working Women in Cleveland, Ohio, which advocates for better pay and advancement opportunities, the elimination of sex and race discrimination, and improved working conditions for women office workers. She has held academic positions at St. Mary's College, San Diego State University, and the University of Wisconsin–Milwaukee, and she has also held several positions with the Wisconsin state government.

ANDREW BRESLAU is the press secretary to Ruth Messinger, New York City's Manhattan Borough President.

LESTER R. BROWN is the founder, president, and senior researcher at the Worldwatch Institute in Washington, D.C., an independent research organization whose mission is to analyze world conditions and problems such as famine, overpopulation, and scarcity of natural resources. His publications include *Build-*

ing a Sustainable Society (W. W. Norton, 1981), and his *State of the World* reports remain his most highly regarded and popular works.

ELLEN CASSEDY is an author who has written on issues of sexual harassment.

DAVID T. COURTWRIGHT is a professor of history and the chair of the Department of History and Philosophy at the University of North Florida in Jacksonville, Florida. A member of the American Historical Association and the Organization of American Historians, his research interests focus on history and on drug abuse and alcoholism. His publications include *Dark Paradise: Opiate Addiction in America Before 1940* (Harvard University Press, 1982) and, coauthored with Herman Joseph and Don Des Jarlais, *Addicts Who Survived: An Oral History of Narcotic Use in America, 1923–1965* (University of Tennessee Press, 1989).

JOHN J. DiIULIO, JR., is an associate professor of politics and public affairs at Princeton University in Princeton, New Jersey. His publications include *No Escape: The Future of American Corrections* (Basic Books, 1991).

DINESH D'SOUZA, a former senior domestic policy analyst for the Reagan administration, is the John M. Olin Research Fellow at the American Enterprise Institute in Washington, D.C., and the editor of *Crisis*, a Catholic monthly magazine of news and opinion. He is the author of *Illiberal Education: The Politics of Race and Sex on Campus* (Vintage Books, 1991).

THOMAS BYRNE EDSALL is a political reporter for the *Washington Post*. He is the author of *Chain Reaction: The Impact of Race, Rights, and Taxes on American Politics* (W. W. Norton, 1991).

ERNEST ERBER is affiliated with the American Planning Association in Washington, D.C., a coalition of public and private planning agency officials, professional planners, planning educators, elected and appointed officials, and other persons involved in urban and rural development.

STANLEY FISH is the chair of the Department of English and a professor in the School of Law at Duke University in Durham, North Carolina. Considered to be a pioneering literary theorist, he is the author of more than 75 publications, including *Doing What Comes Naturally: Change, Rhetoric, and the Practice of Theory in Legal and Literary Studies* (Duke University Press, 1989). He has held academic appointments at the University of California, Berkeley; the University of Southern California, Los Angeles; and Columbia University.

ROBERT FISHMAN is an associate professor of history at Rutgers–The State University in Camden, New Jersey. His research interests focus on the history of urban design and the future of cities, and his publications include *Urban Utopias in the Twentieth Century: Ebenezer Howard, Frank Lloyd Wright, Le Corbusier* (Basic Books, 1977). He received an A.M. in 1969 and a Ph.D. in 1974 from Harvard University, and he has held academic appointments at the University of Massachusetts–Boston and Connecticut College.

MARILYN FRENCH is a novelist, educator, and literary scholar. Her publications include *The Women's Room* (Summit Books, 1977), which is considered one of the major novels of the feminist movement, and *Beyond Power: On Women, Men, and Morals* (Summit Books, 1986). She has held academic appointments at Harvard University, Hofstra University, and the College of the Holy Cross.

MILTON FRIEDMAN is a senior research fellow at the Stanford University Hoover Institution on War, Revolution, and Peace. He received the 1976 Nobel Prize in economic science for his work in consumption analysis and monetary history and theory and for demonstration of stabilization policy complexity. He and his wife, **ROSE FRIEDMAN,** who also writes on economic topics, have coauthored several publications, including *Tyranny of the Status Quo* (Harcourt Brace Jovanovich, 1984).

FRANCIS FUKUYAMA, a former deputy director of the U.S. State Department's policy planning staff, is a consultant for the RAND Corporation in Santa Monica, California. He is the author of *The End of History and the Last Man* (Free Press, 1992).

GEORGE GILDER is a senior fellow of the Hudson Institute in Indianapolis, Indiana, a nonprofit research organization founded in 1961 to analyze and make recommendations about public policy for business and government executives and the public at large. He is also a contributing editor for *Forbes* magazine and the author of several books, including *Microcosm: Into the Quantum Era of Economics and Technology* (Simon & Schuster, 1989).

PHILIP L. HARVEY is the author of the "Forgotten Agenda: American Social Policy" column for the *Los Angeles Times.* His publications include *Securing the Right to Employment: Social Welfare Policy and the*

Unemployment in the United States (Princeton University Press, 1989).

JOHN E. JACOB is the president and chief executive officer of the National Urban League in New York City, a voluntary, nonpartisan community service agency of civic, professional, business, labor, and religious leaders that works to eliminate institutional racism and to provide direct service to minorities in areas such as employment, housing, education, and social welfare.

JONATHAN KOZOL, a graduate of Harvard University and a former teacher, is a writer and social commentator who writes on the problems of the American education system. His publications include *Death at an Early Age: The Destruction of the Hearts and Minds of Negro Children in the Boston Public Schools* (Plume Books, 1968), which was the winner of the National Book Award in 1968, and *Savage Inequalities: Children in America's Schools* (Harper-Perennial, 1991).

MICHAEL LEVIN is a professor of philosophy at City College, City University of New York. He has published books and articles that deal with the relation between the mind and the body, feminism, and a number of other social issues.

GLENN C. LOURY is a professor of economics at Boston University in Boston, Massachusetts, and he has held academic appointments at Harvard University and the University of Michigan. He has been actively involved in public debate and analysis of the problems of racial inequality and social policy toward the poor in the United States, which is reflected in his publication *Achieving the Dream* (The Heritage Foundation, 1990). And he has been an adviser and consultant with state and federal government agencies and private business organizations in his fields of expertise.

EDWARD N. LUTTWAK holds the Arleigh Burke Chair in Strategy at the Center for Strategic and International Studies in Washington, D.C.

MYRON MAGNET is a senior fellow of the Manhattan Institute for Policy Research in New York City, a coalition of corporations, foundations, and individuals that assists scholars, government officials, and the public in obtaining a better understanding of economic processes and the effect of government programs on the economic situation.

THEODORE R. MARMOR is a professor of public management and political science in the Institution for Social and Policy Studies at Yale University in New Haven, Connecticut. His research interests focus on the American version of the welfare state, which is reflected in his many publications, including *Social Security: Beyond the Rhetoric of Crisis* (Princeton University Press, 1988), coauthored with Jerry L. Mashaw.

JERRY L. MASHAW, a lawyer and an educator, is the William Nelson Cromwell Professor at the Yale University School of Law in New Haven, Connecticut, and a consultant for the Center of Administration Justice. He is a former editor in chief of the *Tulane Law Review,* and he is the author of *Due Process in the Administrative State* (Yale University Press, 1985) and the coauthor, with David L. Harfst, of *The Struggle for Auto Safety* (Harvard University Press, 1990).

RUTH MESSINGER is New York City's Manhattan Borough President.

RICHARD D. MOHR is a professor of philosophy at the University of Illinois, Urbana. His research interests focus on ancient philosophy, particularly the teachings of Plato, and on gays in contemporary social life. His publications include *Gay Ideas: Outing and Other Controversies* (Beacon Press, 1992) and *A More Perfect Union: Why Straight Americans Must Stand Up for Gay Rights* (Beacon Press, 1994).

GRETCHEN MORGENSON is a senior editor of *Forbes* magazine.

ETHAN A. NADELMANN is an assistant professor of politics and public affairs in the Woodrow Wilson School of Public and International Affairs at Princeton University in Princeton, New Jersey. He was the founding coordinator of the Harvard Study Group on Organized Crime, and he has been a consultant to the Department of State's Bureau of International Narcotics Matters. He is also an assistant editor of the *Journal of Drug Issues* and a contributing editor of the *International Journal on Drug Policy.*

DAVID POPENOE is a professor of sociology and an associate dean for the social sciences at Rutgers–The State University in New Brunswick, New Jersey. He is the author of *Disturbing the Nest: Sweden and the Decline of Families in Modern Societies* (Aldine de Gruyter, 1988).

DENNIS PRAGER is the publisher of *Ultimate Issues,* a quarterly journal on Judaism and society. He is a former director of the Brandeis-Bardin Institute in Brandeis, California, an experiential education institution on Judaism. His publications include *Why the Jews? The Reason for Antisemitism* (Simon & Schuster, 1983), coauthored with Joseph Telushkin, and *Liberalism and the Los Angeles Riots* (Heritage Foundation, 1992).

JEFFREY REIMAN is the William Fraser McDowell Professor of Philosophy at American University in Washington, D.C. An expert on moral philosophy and applied ethics, he is the author of over 40 articles and numerous books on moral, political, and legal philosophy, including *In Defense of Political Philosophy* (Harper & Row, 1972) and *Justice and Modern Moral Philosophy* (Yale University Press, 1992). He is also a member of the American Society of Criminology.

MORGAN O. REYNOLDS, a visiting scholar for the U.S. Congress Joint Economic Committee, is a professor of economics in the Department of Economics at Texas A & M University in College Station, Texas, and a senior fellow of the National Center for Policy Analysis in Dallas, Texas. He has published over 50 articles in academic journals, and he is the author of *Power and Privilege: Labor Unions in America* (Universe Books, 1984), which won the National Book Award from Freedoms Foundation at Valley Forge in 1985, and *Making America Poorer: The Cost of Labor Law* (1987).

WILLIAM RYAN is a professor in the Department of Psychology at Boston College in Chestnut Hill, Massachusetts, and a consultant in the fields of mental health, community planning, and social problems. His publications include *Distress in the City* (UPB, 1969).

JULIAN L. SIMON is a professor of economics and business administration in the College of Business and Management at the University of Maryland at College Park. His research interests focus on population economics, and his publications include *The Economic Consequences of Immigration* (Basil Blackwell, 1989), *Population Matters: People, Resources, Environment, and Immigration* (Transaction Publishers, 1990), and *The Ultimate Resource,* 2d ed. (Princeton University Press, 1994).

JUDITH STACEY is a professor in the Department of Sociology at the University of California, Davis. She is a coeditor, with Susan Bereaud and Joan Daniels, of *And Jill Came Tumbling After: Sexism in American Education* (Dell Publishing, 1974) and the author of *Patriarchy and Socialist Revolution in China* (University of California Press, 1983).

SHELBY STEELE is an associate professor of English at San Jose State University in San Jose, California.

MURRAY WEIDENBAUM is the Mallinckrodt Distinguished University Professor and the director of the Center for the Study of American Business at Washington University in St. Louis, Missouri. His publications include *Public Policy Toward Corporate Takeovers* (Transaction Publishers, 1987), coedited with Kenneth Chilton.

INDEX